UPDATE 2025

MICROSOFT OFFICE 365 BIBLE

5 BONUS

Productivity Boost Edition

10 IN 1

Word
Excel
Power point
Outlook
Teams
Skype
Access
OneDrive
Publisher
OneNote

Zen Tasker Publishing

Table of Contents

Overview

The Digital Revolution in Office Software

Can you envision operating a computer without Microsoft's core productivity tools? For those born in the digital age (post-1990), this might be unthinkable. Microsoft's groundbreaking office suite, launched for Windows in the early 1990s, fundamentally transformed workplace computing. The distribution methods evolved dramatically - from multiple floppy disks to CD-ROMs, and finally to digital downloads secured by product keys. Each iteration brought significant improvements to these essential tools.

While Microsoft began with three cornerstone applications, their software portfolio rapidly expanded to address diverse business requirements. A pivotal transformation occurred as the suite transitioned from local installation to cloud-based solutions, enabling seamless integration across platforms. This interconnectivity represents one of the suite's most powerful features - users can effortlessly incorporate Excel data into Word documents or PowerPoint slides, creating sophisticated, data-enriched content.

Microsoft Office's innovation and functionality inspired numerous competitors, most notably Google's productivity suite. The similarities in user interface design are no coincidence - **Microsoft Office established itself as the gold standard in business software.** A particularly significant innovation was the ribbon toolbar (introduced in 2007), which revolutionized how users interact with these applications.

While this overview doesn't capture the complete history, Microsoft Office's impact on contemporary work life is profound. Today's professional landscape typically requires at least basic competency in these applications. While many users grasp fundamental operations intuitively, there's an extensive array of advanced capabilities waiting to be discovered.

The suite's capabilities are remarkable: **Excel contains over 1,000 calculation functions**, ranging from basic arithmetic to complex statistical analysis. Word transcends simple text editing with advanced document design and team collaboration features. PowerPoint enables the creation of engaging, interactive presentations, while Access offers robust database development capabilities.

A crucial factor in Microsoft Office's dominance was its innovative **keyboard shortcut system.** This represented a significant improvement over earlier programs like WordPerfect, which required complex coding for formatting. The shortage of computer mice in early computing made these intuitive shortcuts particularly valuable, offering efficient alternatives to mouse-based navigation.

The Power of Keyboard Commands

With over 100 keyboard shortcuts available across the suite, users can significantly boost their productivity. These shortcuts vary slightly between operating systems - Windows users employ the Ctrl key, while MacOS users use the Command key. Combined with additional keys (numbers, letters, or function keys), these shortcuts create powerful command combinations.

Here's a deeper look at keyboard efficiency:

The most commonly used shortcuts across all Office applications include **Ctrl+C (copy), Ctrl+V (paste), and Ctrl+Z (undo).** However, each program has its specialized shortcuts. For example, in Excel, **Ctrl+Shift+L** instantly creates a filter for your data table, while **Alt+="** automatically sums the cells above. In Word, **Ctrl+Alt+M** creates a new comment, and Shift+F5 returns to your last editing position.

Time-saving benefits of keyboard shortcuts are substantial. Research suggests that using keyboard shortcuts can save an average of 8 working days per year compared to mouse-only navigation. Professional users who master these commands can execute complex operations in milliseconds, maintaining their workflow without the need to search through menus or move their hands from the keyboard.

Microsoft has also introduced **customizable shortcuts** since Office 2010, allowing users to create their own keyboard combinations for frequently used commands. This feature particularly benefits users with specific needs or those working in specialized fields who repeatedly perform certain actions.

> **Productivity Tip:** *Modern versions of Office include a built-in shortcut discovery feature - pressing the Alt key reveals all available keyboard shortcuts for visible commands, helping users learn new shortcuts organically while working.*

1. Word:

The Art of Document Creation

Microsoft Word has established itself as the **indispensable foundation of digital document creation** in our contemporary era. From research papers to corporate documents, and from storytelling to custom labels, Word's adaptability stands unrivaled. Though it's essential for students working on dissertations, its reach extends significantly beyond academic environments. This **sophisticated tool** presents an extensive range of capabilities, effortlessly connecting professional requirements with personal needs.

In corporate settings, Word demonstrates excellence in developing **refined professional materials** - from expertly formatted CVs to compelling brochures and elegant business letters. On the personal side, it serves as a creative engine for crafting event invitations, developing comprehensive travel plans, or producing engaging family updates. This software's remarkable adaptability enables it to handle virtually any text-based creative endeavor you might conceive.

For those not yet familiar with Word's **comprehensive feature set**, there's no need for concern. This thorough chapter will walk you through unlocking its full potential, beginning with fundamental concepts and advancing to sophisticated features that can elevate your document development process. For example, Word's **integrated formatting system** ensures consistency across extensive documents, while its **collaborative tools** facilitate effective team editing.

Mastering the Initial Interface

Upon opening Microsoft Word, users encounter a **well-designed welcome screen** crafted for efficient workflow initiation. The startup interface offers several key choices:

1. Launch a fresh blank document (providing an empty canvas for your creativity)
2. Select from numerous pre-designed templates (formatted for various specific uses)
3. Open your recent documents (quickly resume ongoing projects)
4. Access pinned files (your essential documents)

The modern interface reflects years of refinement, offering powerful features while maintaining accessibility. The **streamlined command system** arranges tools intuitively, providing easy access without complexity. Let's begin our exploration of Word's capabilities!

> ***Productivity Tip:*** *Harness the power of the pinning functionality. Activating the pin icon adjacent to a document's modification timestamp ensures* ***permanent visibility*** *at the top of your document list. This feature becomes increasingly valuable as your document library expands, preventing critical files from disappearing into the depths of your "recent" documents section.*

The navigation panel located on the left serves as your **command center**, providing these fundamental options:

- **Home:** Your default landing screen, offering quick access to essential functions
- **New:** Initiate a fresh document or explore template options
- **Open:** Access files from your local storage or cloud platforms
- **Account:** Manage your Microsoft credentials and monitor software updates
- **Feedback:** Share your experience to contribute to product enhancement
- **Options:** Fine-tune Word's settings to match your workflow preferences

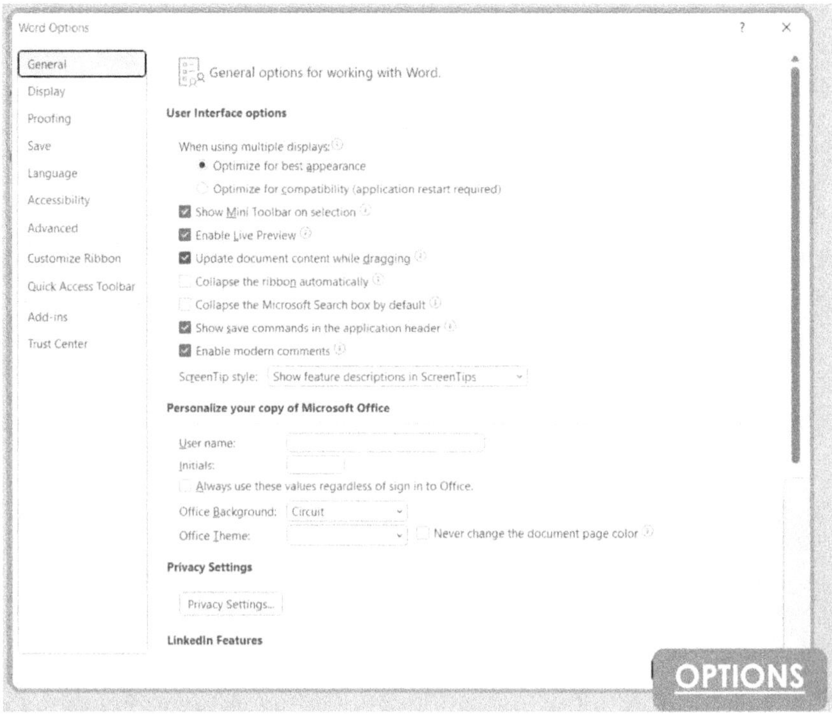

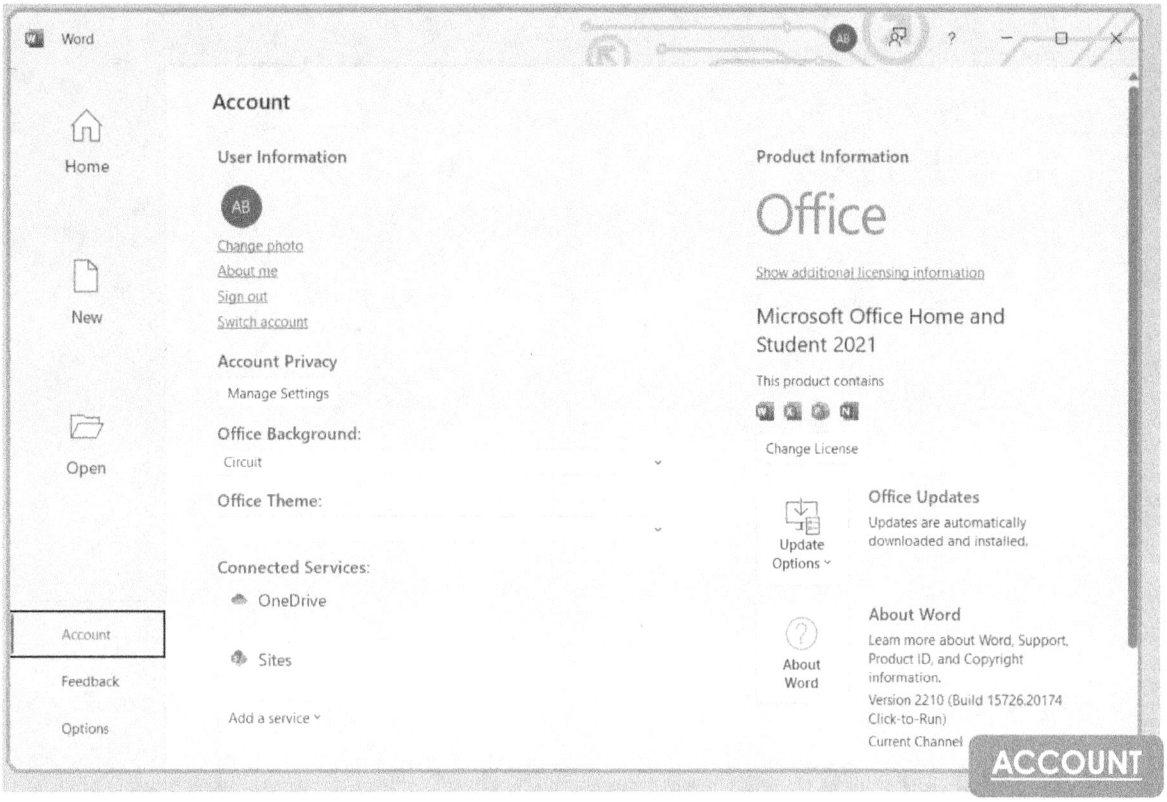

ACCOUNT

For our hands-on exploration, we'll begin by creating a new document. This action presents you with a clean workspace, crowned by the ribbon interface – Word's comprehensive control panel. Let's explore the ribbon's extensive capabilities and discover its powerful features.

Understanding the Ribbon: Your Gateway to Word's Tools

Let's break down the **essential elements** of Word's ribbon interface. Consider this an introduction, as we'll examine each component in detail throughout later sections. Remember that many functions offer keyboard shortcuts, which we'll compile at the chapter's conclusion for easy access.

When you create a new document, you'll spot a **control panel** at the top. If it's not immediately visible, move your mouse over the blue menu area to make it appear. For **constant accessibility**, click the pin icon in the upper-right corner. The arrow in the same location allows you to collapse the ribbon when needed.

File Tab

The **File tab** serves as your entry point, providing access to core functions like creating, opening, saving, exporting, and printing documents. Since we've covered these fundamental operations, let's explore more advanced features.

Moving right, you'll find the **Home tab**, which serves as your formatting control center. It's organized into five distinct sections: clipboard, font, paragraph, styles, and editing. The clipboard section enables essential operations like paste, cut, copy, and the format painter tool - a powerful feature that lets you duplicate formatting from one text selection to another.

Home Tab

The **font section** serves as your text styling command center. Here you can select from hundreds of typefaces, apply **bold** formatting for emphasis, create *italic* text for distinction, or underline key phrases. Advanced options include text highlighting for review purposes, color modification for visual impact, and size adjustments for hierarchy. The font group also includes subscript and superscript options, strikethrough formatting, and text effects like shadow and outline.

The **paragraph section** offers comprehensive layout control. Create structured bullet points and numbered lists, manage document indentation for professional formatting, and organize text with sorting capabilities. Fine-tune your document's appearance with precise line spacing controls and design clear, effective tables. The paragraph group includes alignment options (left, center, right, justify), shading tools for visual emphasis, and border controls for section definition. These features work together to ensure your document maintains consistent, professional formatting throughout.

HOME TAB

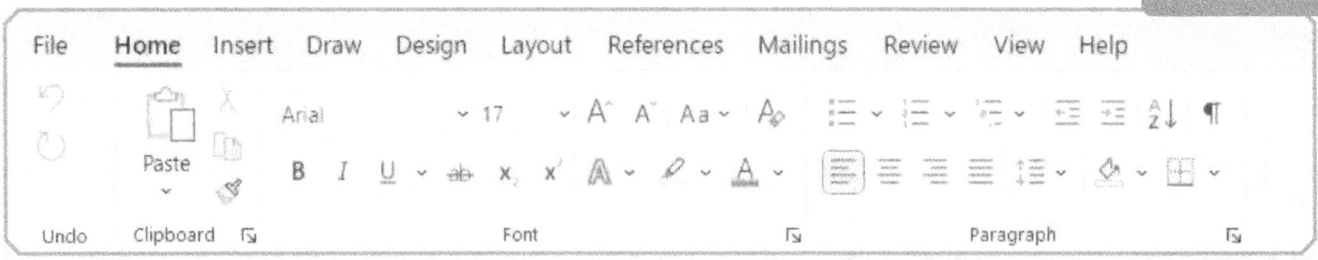

Both sections work in harmony with the **styles gallery**, which enables consistent heading formatting - a crucial element for generating automatic tables of contents and maintaining document structure. The **editing zone** rounds out these features with robust search, replace, and selection tools, allowing for efficient document management.

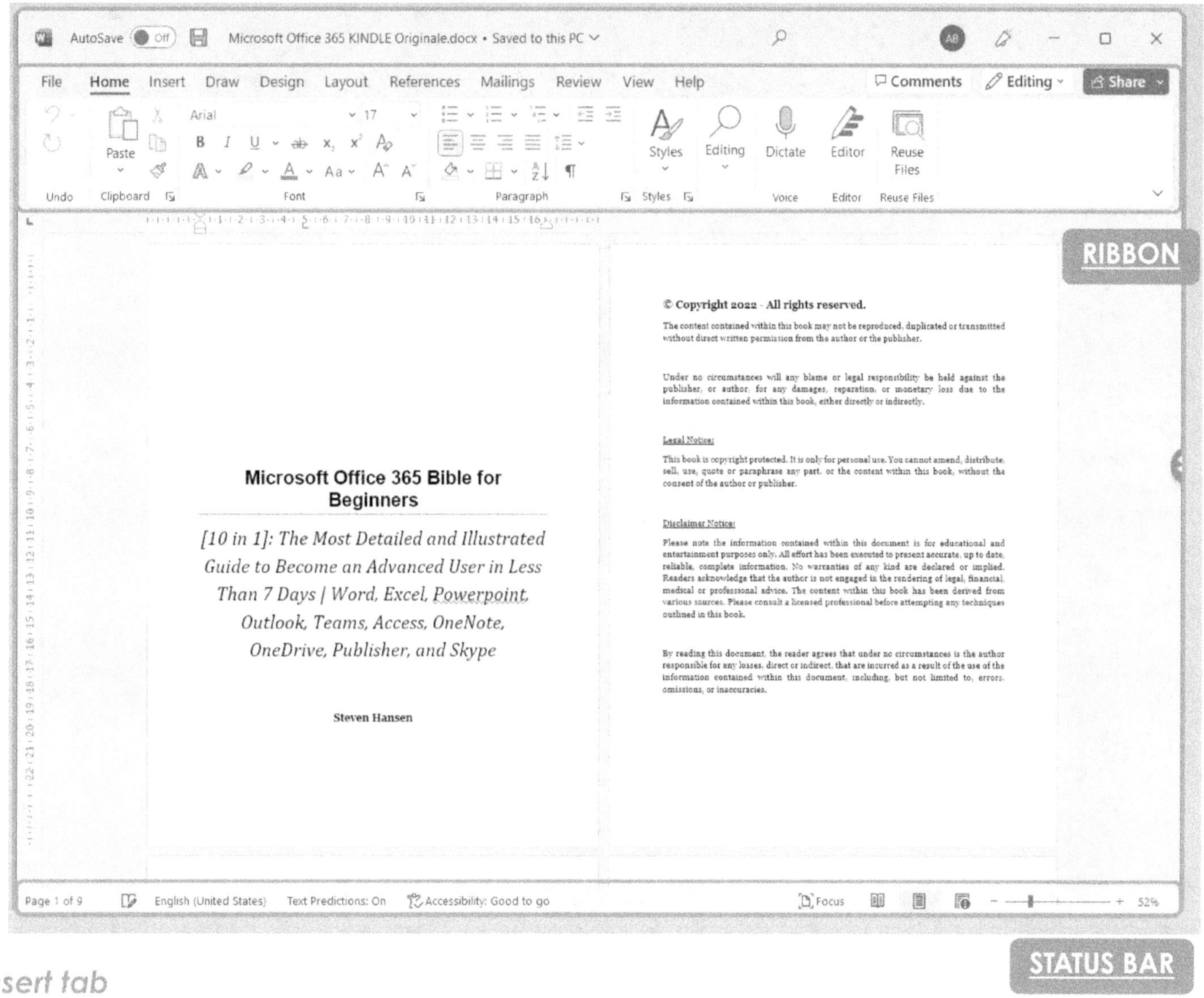

Insert tab

The **Insert tab** functions as your content enrichment center, offering tools to incorporate diverse elements like headers, footers, visuals, and shapes. It's structured into ten distinct sections: pages, tables, illustrations, add-ins, media, links, comments, header and footer, text, and symbols. You can embed videos, manage hyperlinks, and incorporate mathematical equations. Here's a streamlined process for image insertion:

1. Navigate to the Insert tab
2. Choose **'Pictures'** within Illustrations
3. Specify your image location (This Device, Stock Images, Online Pictures)
4. Pick your image and confirm with **'Insert'**

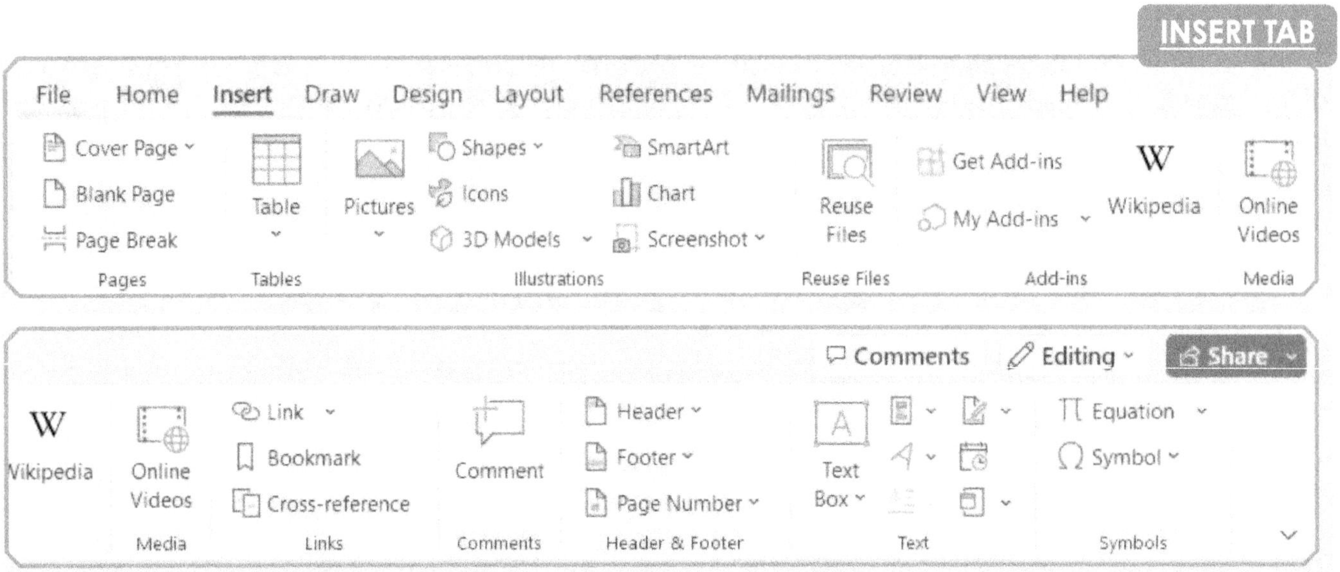

Design Tab

The **Design tab** provides ready-to-use document styles for efficient formatting. It's particularly valuable for quick professional document creation, offering options for background colors, borders, and watermarks - essential for draft documents or controlled materials. **Advanced design features** include theme effects that coordinate colors, fonts, and graphic elements across your entire document. You can also create and save custom themes to maintain consistent branding across multiple documents or an entire organization.

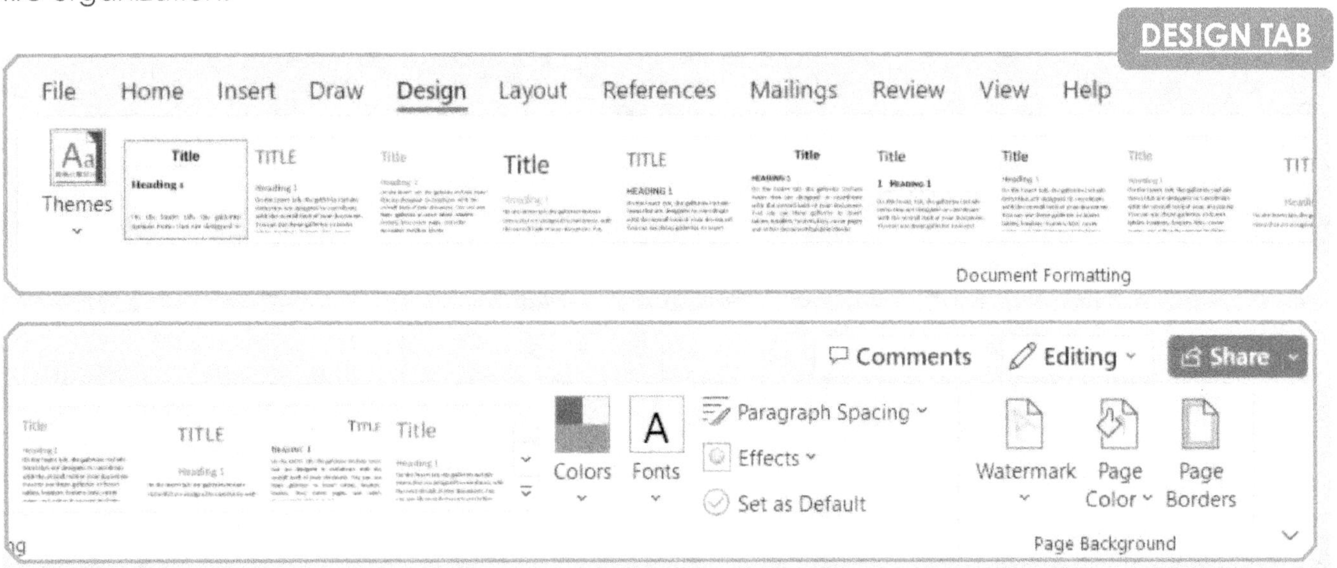

Layout Tab

The **Layout tab** governs document structure. Toggle between landscape and portrait orientations, implement columnar text layouts, and refine paragraph settings. It also manages visual element positioning and text flow control. A particularly powerful feature is the **Section Break** tool, which allows you to create different layouts within the same document - perfect for complex reports that require varying page orientations or column layouts. The margin presets can be customized and saved for future use.

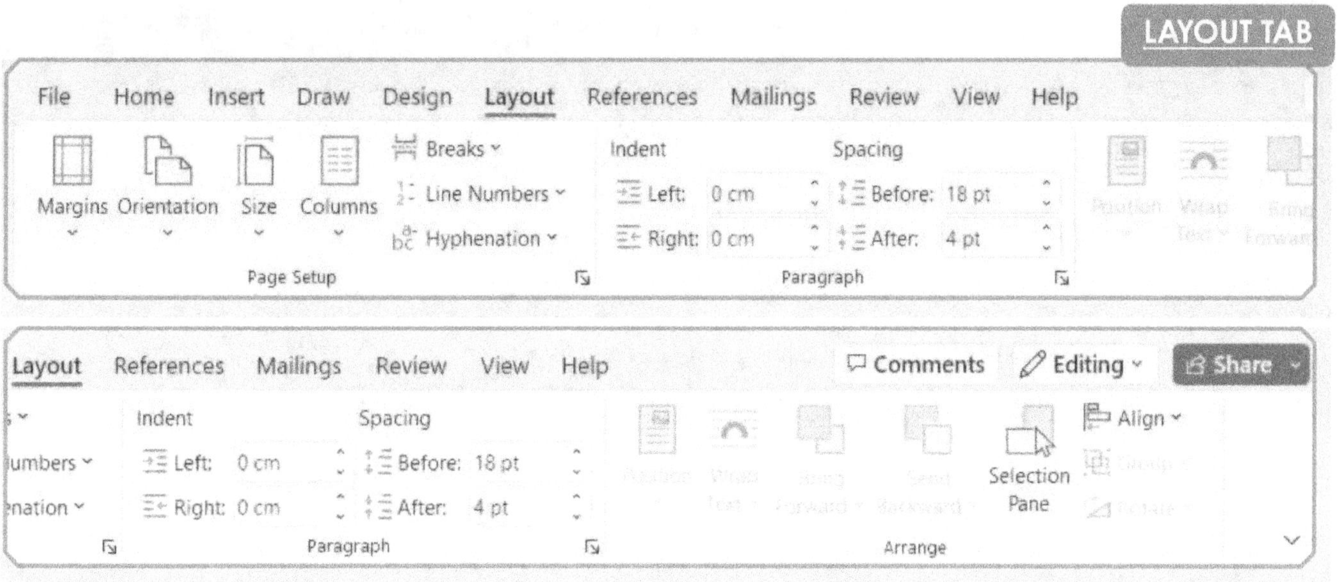

References tab

For academic writing, the **References tab** is essential. It houses tools for generating tables of contents, footnotes, citations, bibliographies, and indexes. Supporting 12 citation formats, including APA and Harvard, it significantly reduces manual formatting time. The **Cross-reference** feature allows you to link to other sections within your document, automatically updating page numbers and content as your document changes. The citation manager can also import references from external bibliography management software.

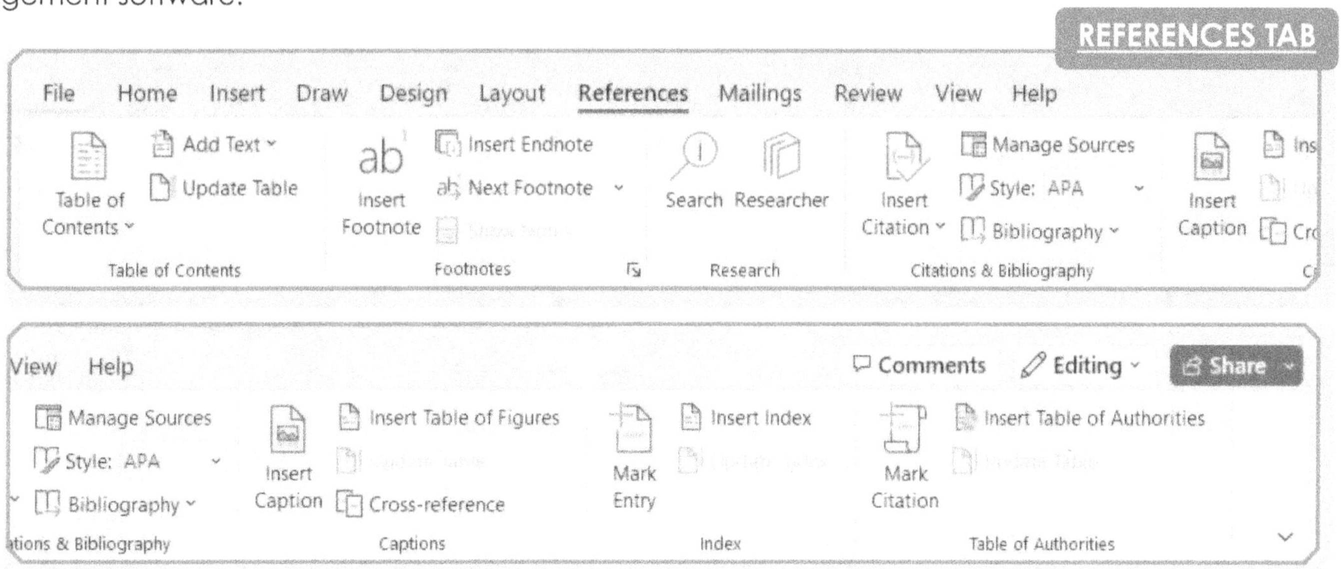

Mailing Tab

The **Mailing tab** excels in business communication, facilitating mailing list and label creation. The mail merge functionality enables efficient personalized mass mailings, perfect for everything from business correspondence to holiday cards. The **Rules** feature within mail merge allows for conditional content based on your data fields - for example, customizing salutations based on gender or including specific paragraphs based on customer categories. You can also preview your merged documents before sending.

MAILINGS TAB

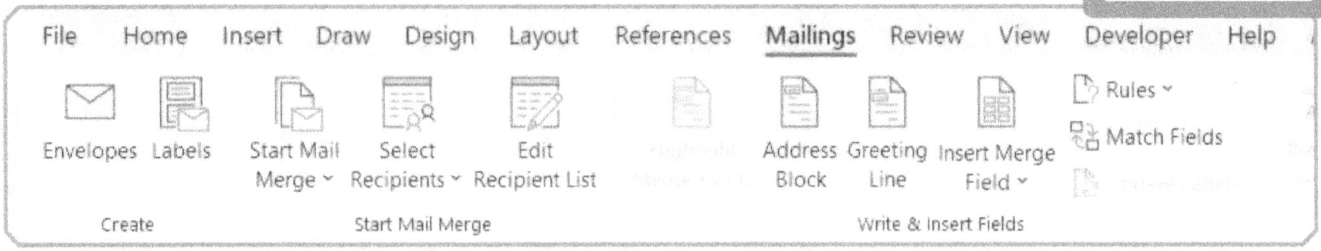

Review Tab

Post-writing, the **Review tab** offers comprehensive editing tools. Access change tracking, commenting features, translation capabilities, and document comparison tools - crucial for collaborative projects and maintaining document quality. The **Accessibility Checker** helps ensure your documents are re-adable by screen readers and accessible to all users. The **Smart Lookup** feature provides contextual information without leaving Word.

REVIEW TAB

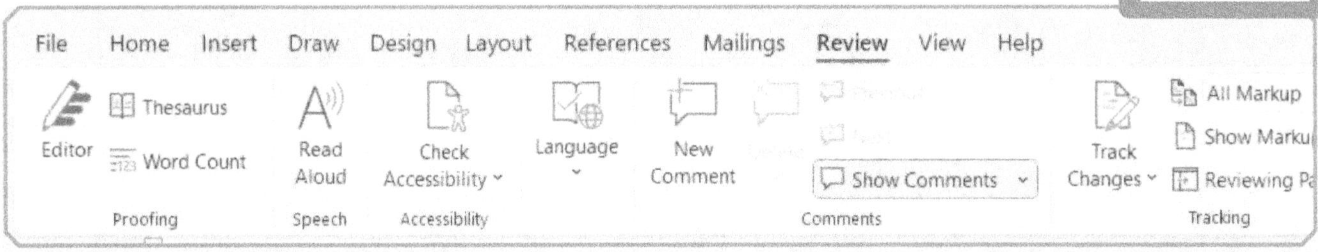

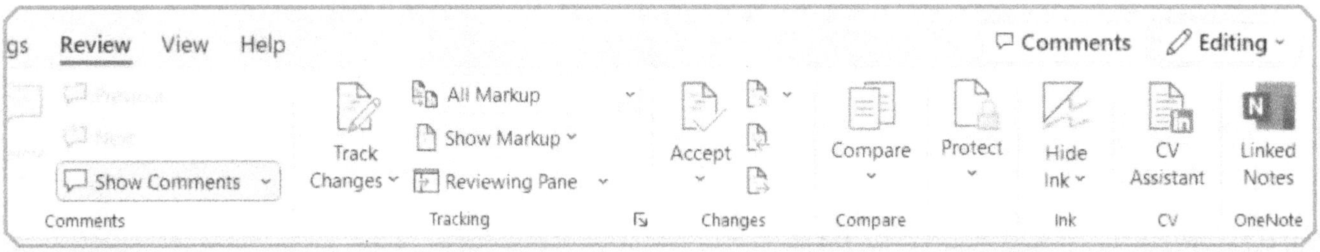

View Tab

The **View tab** enables interface customization. Modify zoom settings, toggle ruler visibility, implement split-screen viewing, and more, enhancing your working efficiency. The **Multiple Pages** view allows you to see and edit several pages simultaneously, while the **Read Mode** removes distracting toolbars for comfortable document review. The **Navigation Pane** can be customized to show headings, pages, or search results.

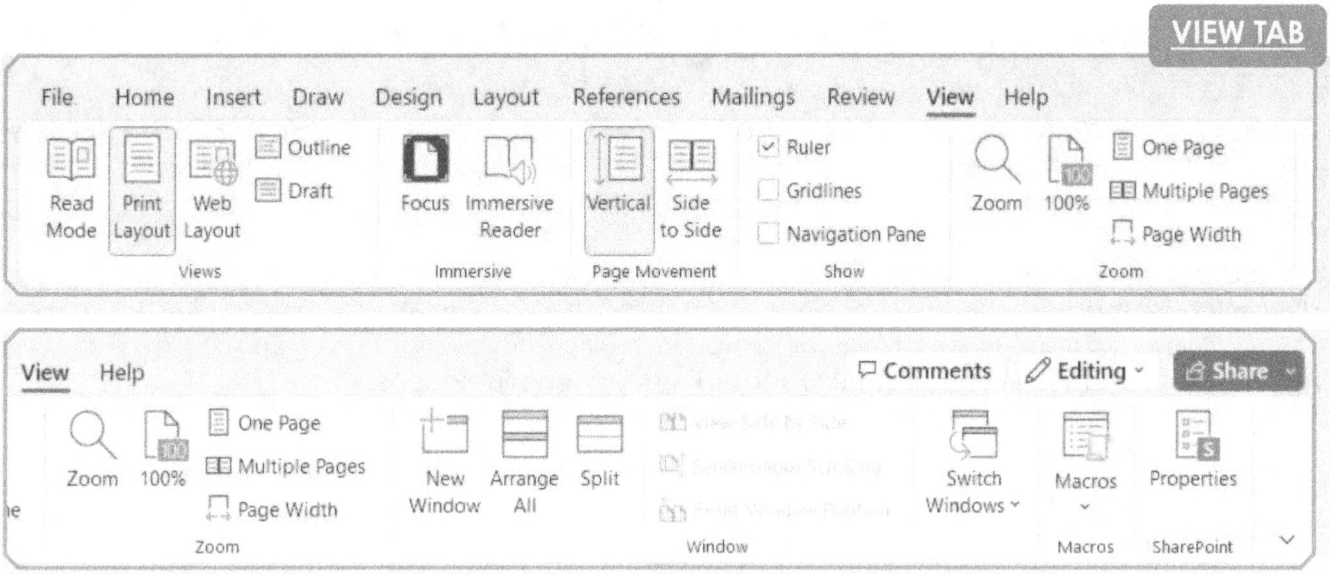

Help Tab

The **Help feature** provides comprehensive support, feedback options, and detailed feature explanations. Use this valuable resource for troubleshooting or feature exploration. Beyond basic search, it includes **Interactive Guides** for common tasks and **Smart Lookup** for contextual information. The **Tell Me** feature acts as a command search tool, helping you quickly find specific features without navigating through ribbons and menus.

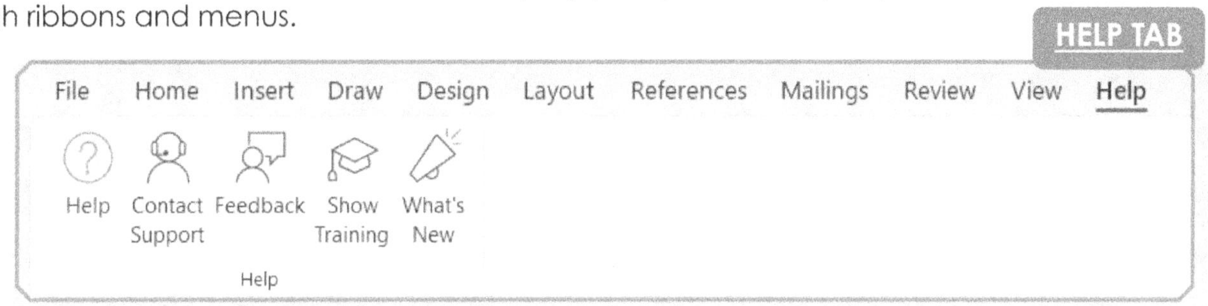

Advanced Ribbon Customization:

One often-overlooked feature of the ribbon is its **customization capability**. Users can create their own tabs, rename existing ones, and organize commands according to their workflow. This becomes particularly valuable for specialized tasks - for instance, academic writers might want quick access to citation tools, while business users might prioritize mail merge and template features.

You can access these customization options through **File > Options > Customize Ribbon.** Additionally, the Quick Access Toolbar (QAT) above the ribbon can be personalized to include your most frequently used commands, regardless of which tab they originally appear in.

Note the status bar at your document's base - it displays crucial document metrics. We'll explore its functionality next. Mastering these ribbon tools transforms you into a Word expert, capable of producing sophisticated documents efficiently.

Status Bar: Your Document's Dashboard

The **status bar**, positioned at your Word window's base, serves as your **real-time document dashboard**. At first glance, you'll notice the **page counter**, showing "page x of x" - a quick reference tool for monitoring your document's scope and current location.

The **word count** functionality offers enhanced monitoring capabilities. Beyond displaying total counts, it **dynamically updates** when text is selected, showing "x of x words" - revealing selected text count versus document total. This **smart feature** proves invaluable for content creators working with specific length requirements, providing **instant feedback** on section dimensions.

The **proofing indicator**, represented by a book icon, acts as your **quality control** monitor. A **checkmark** indicates error-free content, while an **'x'** signals needed revisions. Double-clicking activates the **proofing pane** for efficient error resolution. This sophisticated tool employs **advanced language processing** to detect contextual grammar and spelling issues.

Next to the proofing tool sits the **language selector**, displaying your active proofing language with regional specificity (example: **English (United States)**). This precision matters for handling **regional language variations**, ensuring accurate proofreading. Language preferences can be modified by double-clicking the indicator and selecting from available options.

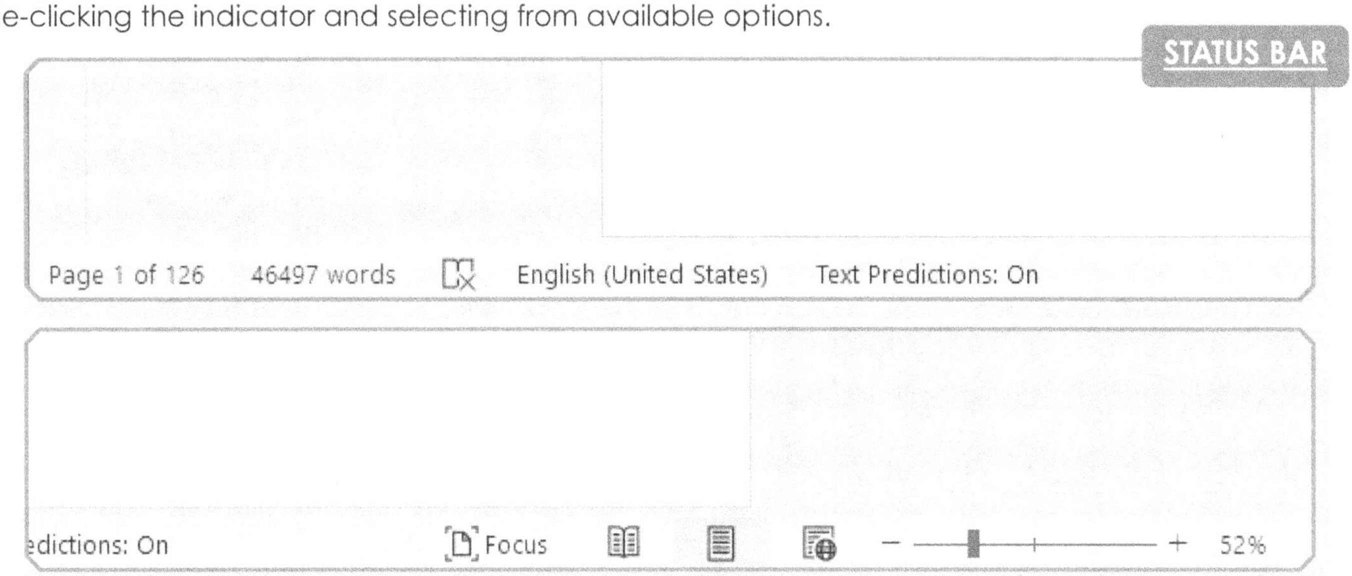

Launching Your Word Experience

Initiating a new document requires clicking the **File button** and selecting **New Document**. This action creates your digital workspace, activating Word's document framework in the background. File management offers two key options: **Save** and **Save As**. The Save function updates existing files, while Save As generates **new file instances**, enabling modifications to name, location, or format (such as **.pdf** conversion). This distinction plays a crucial role in **version management**.

To access existing content, navigate via the **File tab**. Here you'll find **recently accessed documents** and **pinned files**, utilizing Word's efficient file retrieval system. The **Open** option in the left toolbar provides full system navigation capabilities. Word's **template system** offers pre-configured document frameworks. These structured **XML-based files** include predefined formatting, styles, and content placeholders.

Leveraging templates enhances **efficiency** in document creation while maintaining **consistency** across similar document types.

Mastering Word Templates

Word intelligently tracks your document usage patterns, presenting frequently accessed templates on your home screen. For broader selection, the **"More templates"** option reveals an extensive **categorized library** of options. From professional documents to personal designs, the collection spans numerous needs. The integrated search functionality extends to online templates, expanding possibilities beyond local options. This **smart system** employs advanced algorithms to anticipate user preferences and suggest relevant choices.

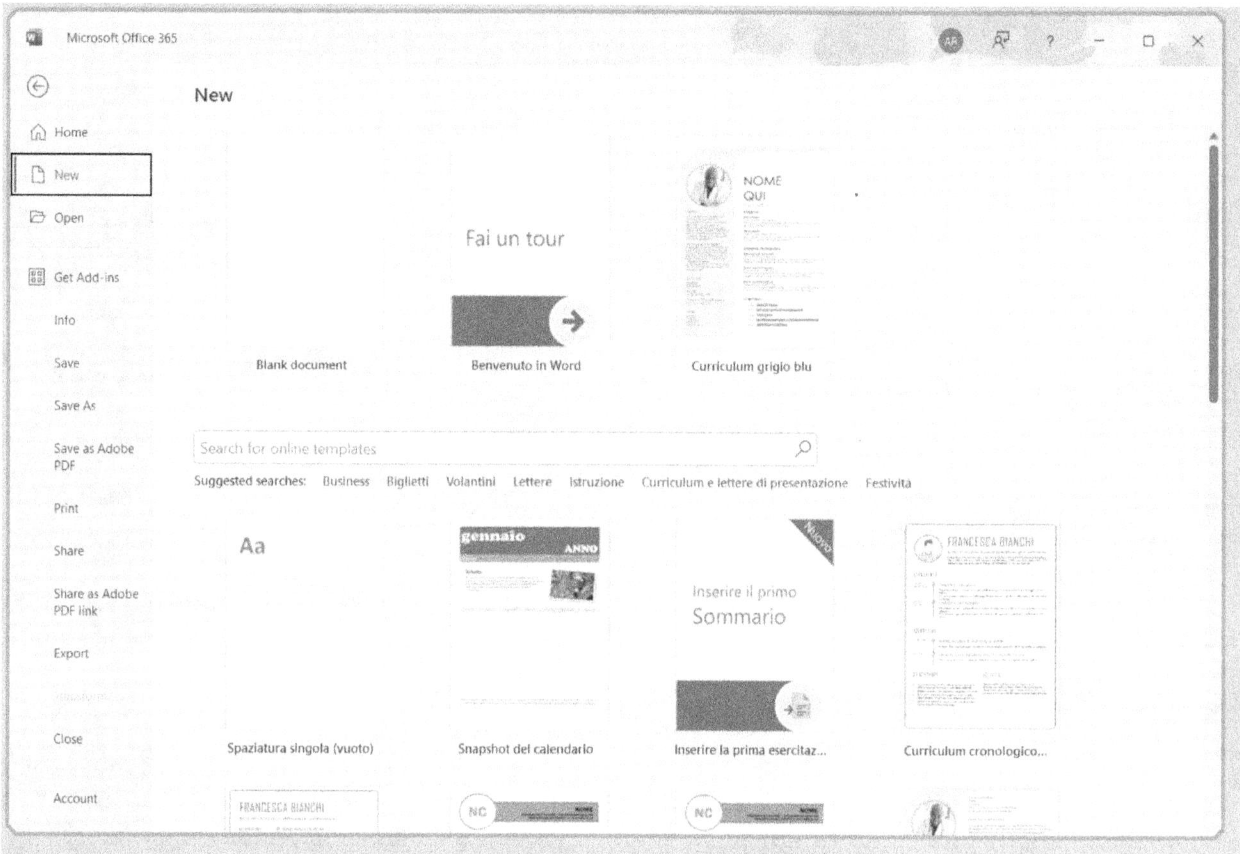

Text Formatting: Visual Document Design

The visual impact of your document, from typography to alignment, plays a crucial role in its effectiveness. Let's explore the key formatting tools that enhance your document's presentation.

Word Processing Fundamentals

When creating a new document, establishing basic text properties is fundamental. The **Home tab's font section** offers dual formatting approaches: real-time or post-writing adjustments. The comprehensive font dialog box, accessed via the font arrow, provides live previews of your selections, using advanced rendering for immediate visual feedback.

This interface includes both **standard formatting options** and sophisticated features like superscript and strikethrough. The Advanced tab enables precise control over character spacing and positioning, utilizing typography enhancement algorithms for optimal readability.

The ribbon provides quick access to common formatting tools. The **font selector** displays typefaces visually, using vector technology for crisp presentation. Size adjustments offer both preset options and custom values for precise control.

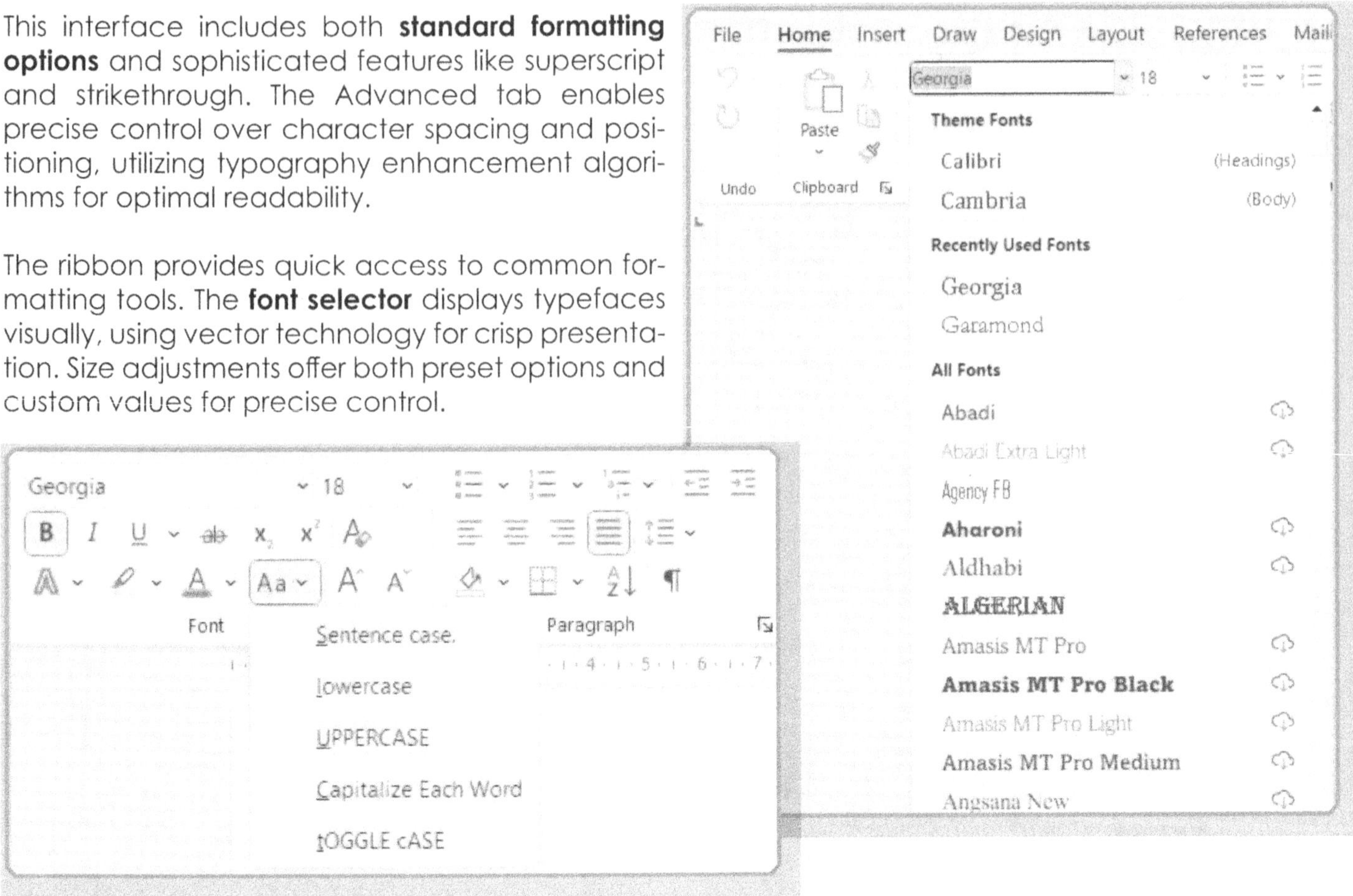

The **case transformation tool (Aa)** modifies text capitalization efficiently. Additional features include highlighting, color selection, and text positioning options.

A standout tool is the **Clear Formatting** function (marked by an **"A" with pink square**), resetting text to default settings. This feature efficiently removes formatting modifications using style sheet principles.

Productivity Tip: *The paintbrush icon in the Home tab represents the **Format Painter**, a powerful formatting replication tool. Here's the usage process:*

1. *Select your reference text with desired formatting*
2. *Click the paintbrush once for single use, twice for multiple applications*
3. *Highlight target text*
4. *Watch formatting transfer instantly*

This tool employs **style inheritance systems**, temporarily storing formatting attributes. It uses cascading style algorithms for accurate property transfer and rendering.

The Format Painter's strength lies in its ability to simultaneously transfer multiple formatting elements, including fonts, paragraph settings, and advanced properties. This functionality relies on a sophisticated attribute mapping system ensuring precise replication.

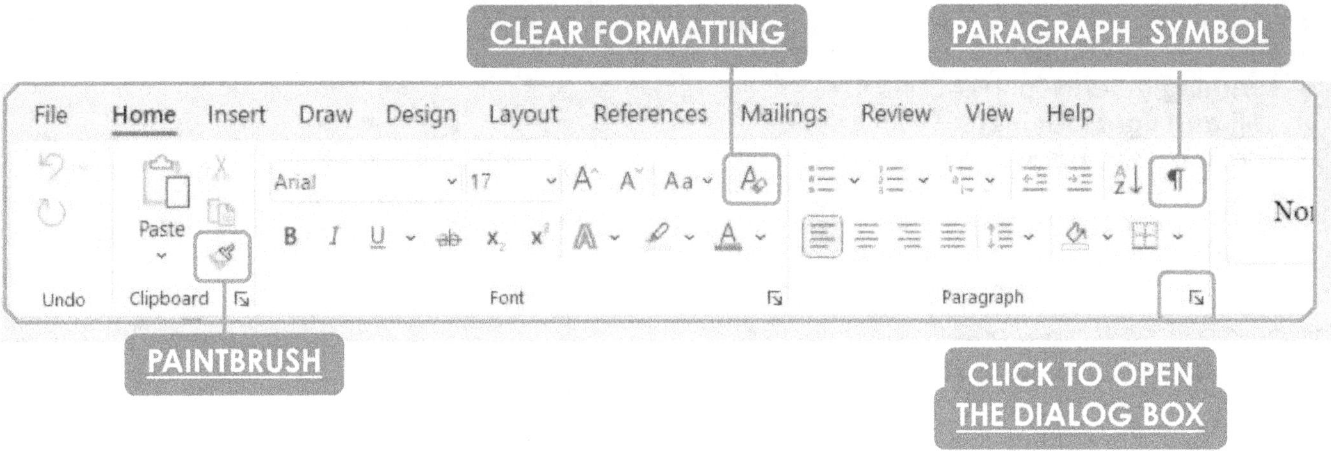

Paragraph formatting: Structure and Style

After refining your text appearance, mastering **paragraph formatting** becomes crucial. While Word's default left alignment serves basic needs, the formatting capabilities extend far beyond. The **paragraph function** provides a sophisticated dropdown menu leading to a **comprehensive dialogue box.** This advanced interface, though more complex than ribbon shortcuts, offers powerful tools with real-time preview capabilities.

Productivity Tip:

*The **paragraph symbol (¶)** in the paragraph section's top-right corner serves as a vital formatting aid. This tool reveals **non-printing characters** - spaces, paragraph breaks, and tabs - using Unicode visualization. While invisible in the final document, these markers prove essential for precise formatting control and troubleshooting.*

For professional document layout, Word offers multiple **alignment options**:

- **Right** alignment (ideal for addresses in formal letters)
- **Center** alignment (perfect for titles and headings)
- **Justified** alignment (creating clean margins on both sides using advanced text distribution algorithms).

The **indentation system** provides sophisticated paragraph control:

- **First-line indentation** for traditional paragraph starts
- **Hanging indents** for bibliographies
- **Left and right indents** for block quotes
- The **line spacing tool** (marked by directional arrows) offers both preset options (1.0, 1.5, 2.0) and custom settings, using percentage-based calculations for precise vertical spacing. Advanced options include controlling space before and after paragraphs, crucial for professional document formatting.

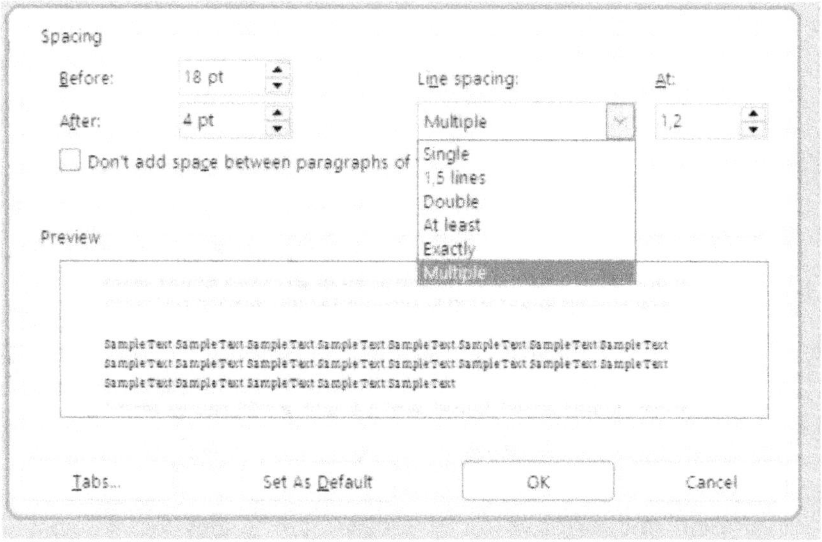

This precise control becomes particularly vital in **academic and professional writing**, where formatting standards are strict.

The **"set as default"** feature applies your chosen settings globally, utilizing Word's XML-based template system for consistent formatting across documents.

The paragraph section excels in **list creation**, offering:

- **Bullet points** for unordered lists
- **Numbered lists** for sequential information
- **Multilevel lists** using hierarchical data structures for complex organization

Productivity Tip: *Word's intelligent list system employs pattern recognition for automatic continuation. The Enter key creates new list items, while Tab manages sub-levels, automatically adjusting the list hierarchy. This smart system significantly enhances document organization efficiency.*

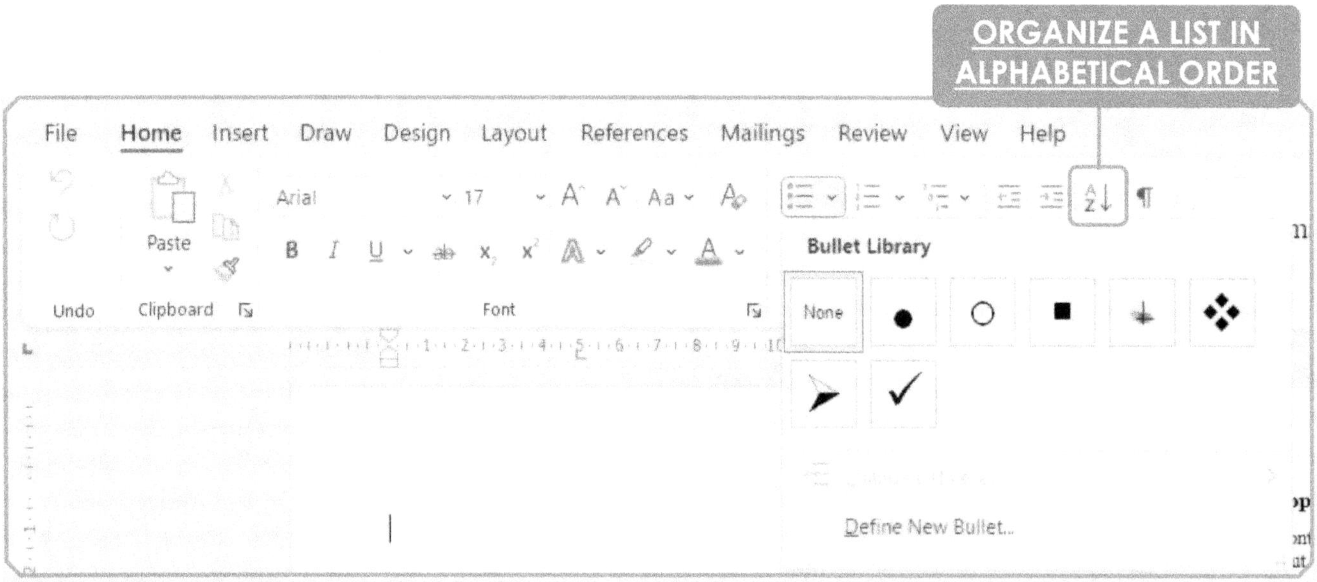

Word's paragraph formatting extends to powerful **organizational features**. The alphabetical sorting tool **(marked by 'AZ↓')** employs an advanced quicksort algorithm for efficient list reorganization. This feature proves invaluable when managing:

- Reference lists
- Glossary entries
- Directory listings
- Index items

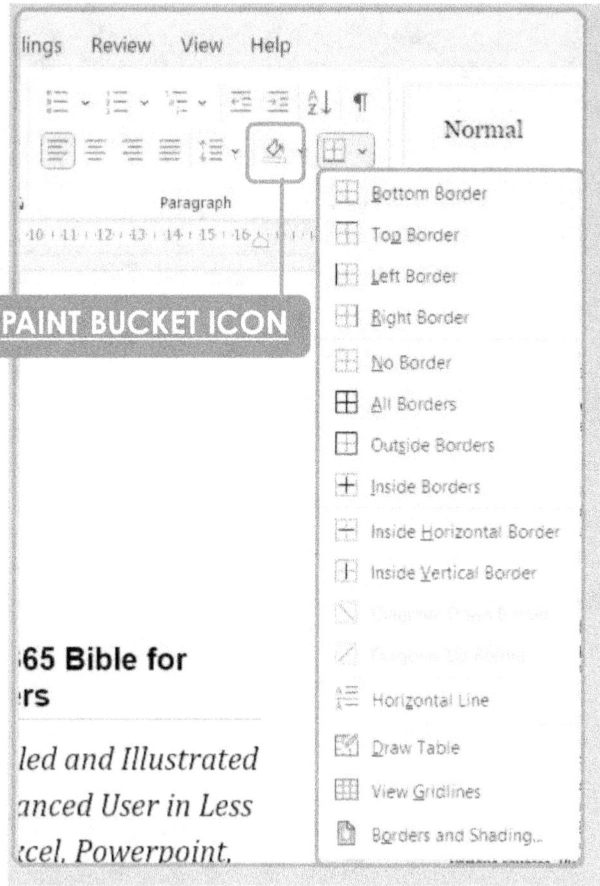

The **border function**, activated by the square button in the ribbon, utilizes sophisticated vector graphics for crisp, scalable formatting. This versatile tool enables you to:

- Frame entire text blocks
- Add specific border lines to paragraphs
- Create custom table borders
- Enhance document hierarchy through visual separation

The **shading tool (paint bucket icon)** implements intelligent color application across various document elements. Operating within Word's layered structure, it ensures precise color placement without affecting surrounding content. You can apply shading to:

- Individual paragraphs
- Table cells
- Selected text sections
- Custom page elements

Multi-Column Layout: Professional Document Design

For creating sophisticated professional layouts like newsletters, brochures, and academic journals, Word's **column feature** offers comprehensive text management capabilities. Accessed through the **layout tab,** this powerful tool employs dynamic text flow algorithms that automatically redistribute content when modifications are made, ensuring optimal readability and visual balance.

The advanced column settings provide precise control through these essential options:

1. **Width Control:** Set exact measurements for each column, ranging from precise inches to percentages of page width. This flexibility allows for both symmetric and asymmetric layouts to match your specific design needs.

2. **Gutter Spacing:** Adjust the space between columns using professional typography standards. The recommended minimum is 0.3 inches for optimal readability, though this can be adjusted based on font size and column width.

3. **Vertical Lines:** Add separator lines for enhanced visual organization. These lines can be customized in style, weight, and color to match your document's design theme.

4. **Section Control:** Define specific areas for column application using section breaks. This allows you to combine different layouts within the same document - for example, single-column introductions followed by multi-column content.

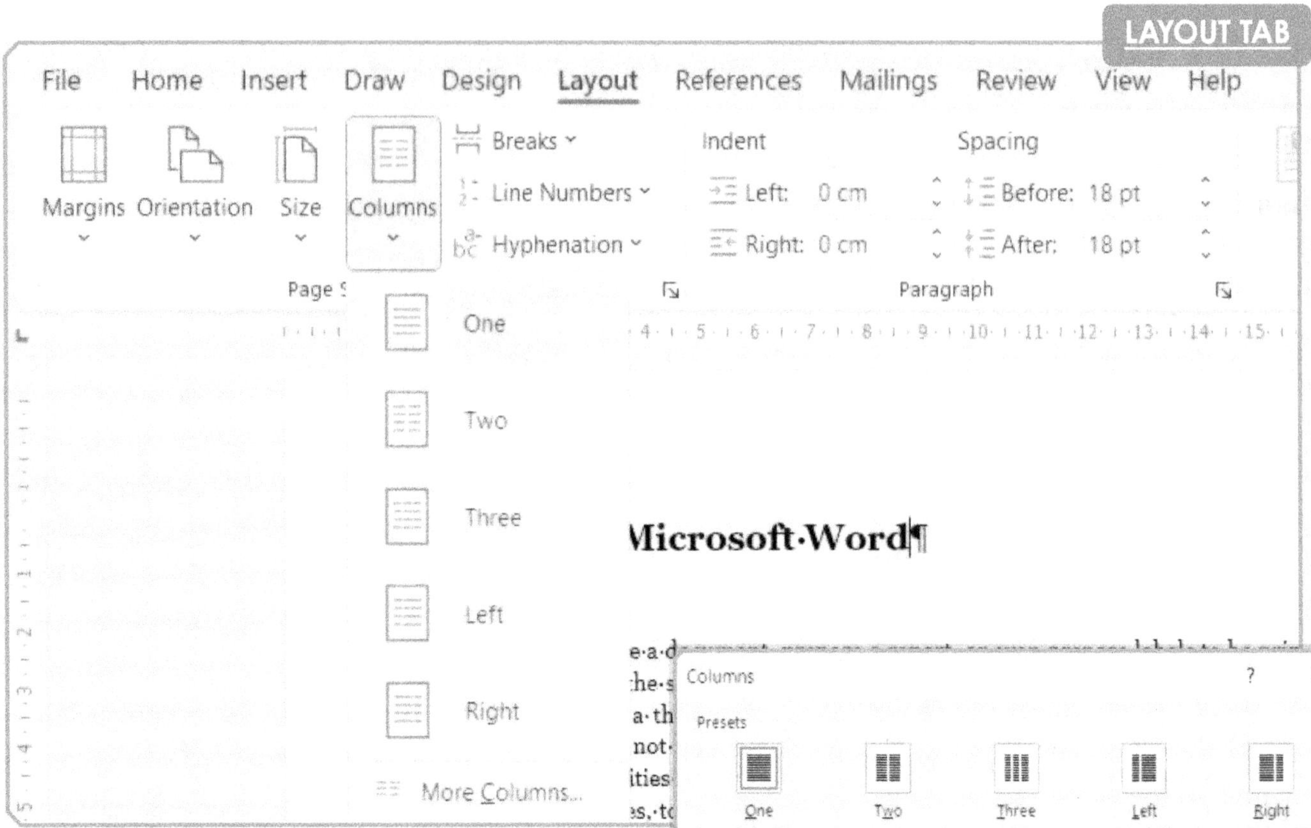

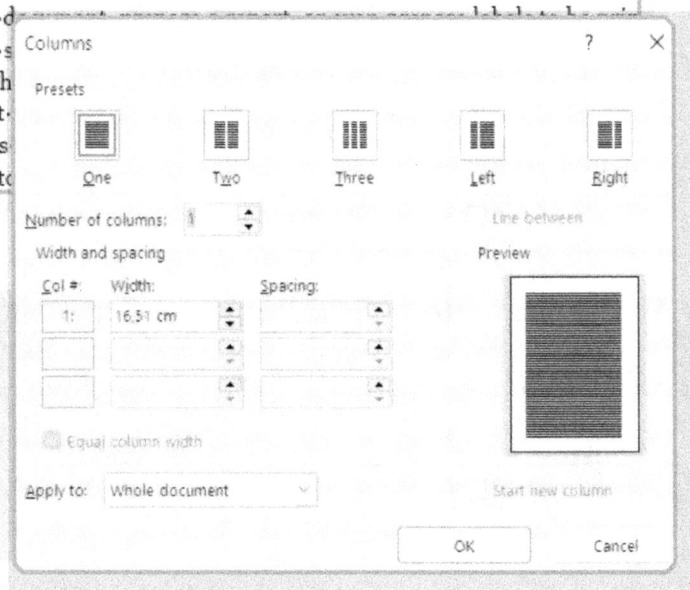

Pro Design Tip: *For optimal column layout, consider using:*

1. *Equal column widths for formal documents*
2. *Varying widths for creative layouts*
3. *Appropriate gutter spacing for readability*
4. *Column breaks for content control*

Document Visualization and Display Settings: Enhancing Your Document's Visual Impact

The management of your document's visual presentation extends beyond basic text formatting. **Microsoft Word provides comprehensive tools** for controlling every aspect of your document's appearance and layout. Understanding these tools is crucial for creating professional-looking documents that effectively communicate your message.

1. **Print layout View:** For the most accurate preview of your work, **accessing the Print Layout View through the ribbon's View tab** is essential. This viewing option implements **WYSIWYG technology** (What You See Is What You Get), ensuring that your screen display precisely matches the final printed or PDF output. This is particularly important when creating documents that will be shared across different platforms or printed professionally.

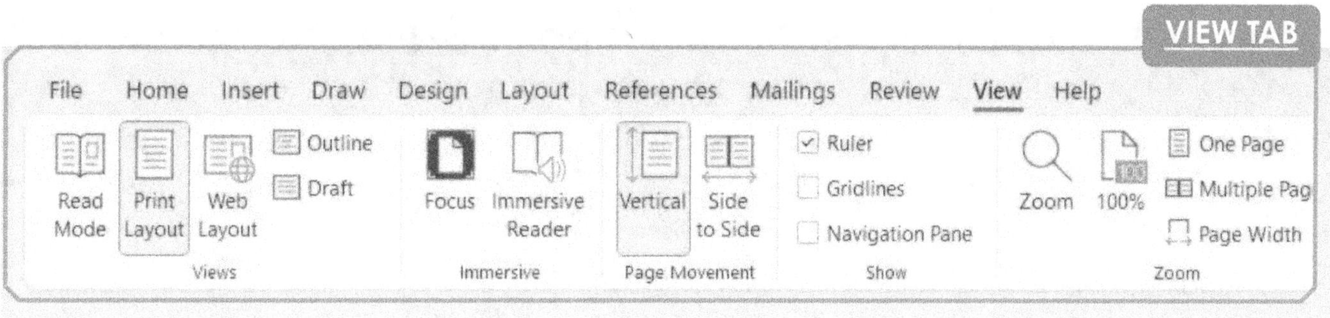

The **Print Layout View's** sophisticated technology excels at displaying several **critical document elements**:

- Precise margin and page perimeter visualization, including custom margin settings and gutter margins for binding
- Complete header and footer presentation, with support for different headers on odd and even pages
- Advanced multi-column configurations, including column breaks and balanced columns
- Seamless integration of images with surrounding text, supporting multiple wrapping styles and precise positioning
- Real-time preview of watermarks, background colors, and border effects

Word also features two additional specialized viewing modes, each designed to enhance specific aspects of the document creation process:

2. **Read Mode**: This setting transforms your document for optimal digital consumption. It employs advanced algorithms to maximize screen usage by removing unnecessary toolbars and adapting the layout for various devices. The mode typically eliminates traditional page breaks and automatically adjusts text parameters for enhanced readability.

3. **Draft View**: This streamlined option prioritizes content creation and editing. It uses a simplified rendering system that focuses on text and basic formatting while omitting certain visual elements like margins and complex graphics. This makes it **particularly efficient for rapid content development**.

Each viewing option utilizes **distinct rendering approaches**:

- Print Layout emphasizes exact visual replication, perfect for final document preparation
- Read Mode focuses on adaptive, screen-optimized presentation, ideal for digital consumption
- Draft View prioritizes performance through simplified display, best for initial content creation

Additional Features across all views:

- Zoom controls for detailed editing
- Document map navigation for quick movement between sections
- Split screen capability for comparing different parts of the document
- Ruler display options for precise measurement and alignment
- Real-time collaboration tools with change tracking

Essential Guide to Page Layout and Margins Configuration

The first crucial step in document formatting is **choosing your page orientation**. This fundamental decision between landscape and portrait modes can be made through the Layout tab, immediately transforming your document's basic structure and visual flow.

Understanding when to use each orientation is crucial:

- **Portrait:** Ideal for text-heavy documents, reports, and letters
- **Landscape:** Better suited for wide tables, charts, and presentations

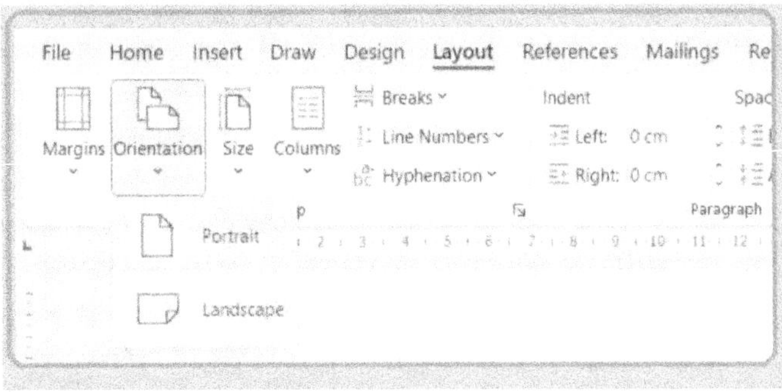

Margin configuration is a critical element that affects both readability and professional appearance. While **preset margin options** provide quick solutions, the customize margins dialog box enables precise control over every dimension of your page layout.

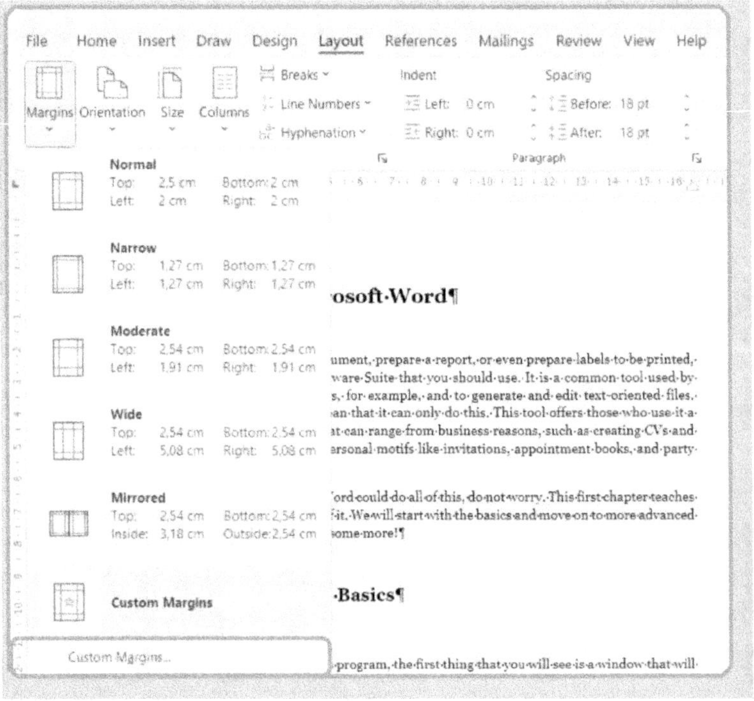

Standard margin recommendations include:

- **Professional documents:** 1-inch margins all around
- **Academic papers:** 1.5-inch left margin for binding
- **Marketing materials:** Narrower margins for maximum content space

Productivity Tip: *For visual margin adjustment, utilize the* ***ruler*** *feature.*
The ***ruler tool****, accessible through the View tab, represents one of Word's most sophisticated formatting aids. This dynamic feature provides real-time visualization of margins as you work, transforming the way users interact with document spacing. Through the ruler's intuitive interface, users can manipulate paragraph indents with precise control, while non-printing guidelines offer clear visual cues for formatting decisions.*

The system operates on a sophisticated coordinate-based framework that updates document layout instantly as changes are made. Furthermore, the ruler accommodates various measurement standards, seamlessly switching between inches, centimeters, and points to suit different regional and professional requirements.

The **margin configuration dialog** extends well beyond basic settings, offering sophisticated options for professional document preparation. A particularly powerful feature is the **book fold setting**, which automatically adjusts layouts for professional publication requirements.

Through the paper tab, users can select from **standardized paper dimensions** or create custom sizes for specialized projects. These advanced settings are supported by **complex layout algorithms** that ensure your document maintains consistent formatting regardless of the final output medium, whether it's digital display, professional printing, or mobile viewing.

INSERT TAB

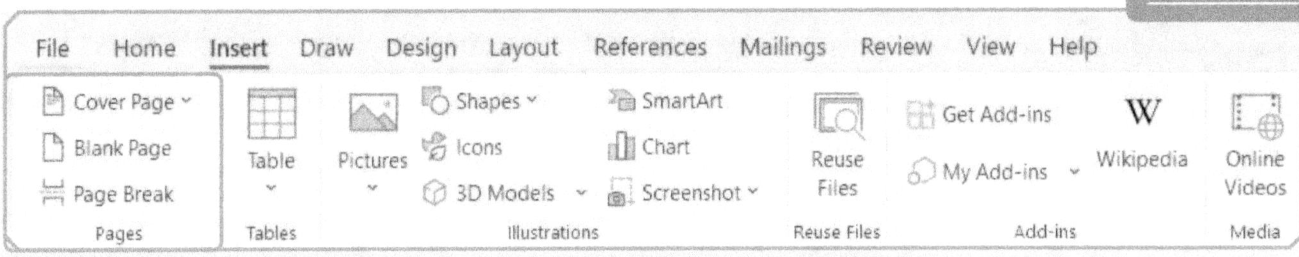

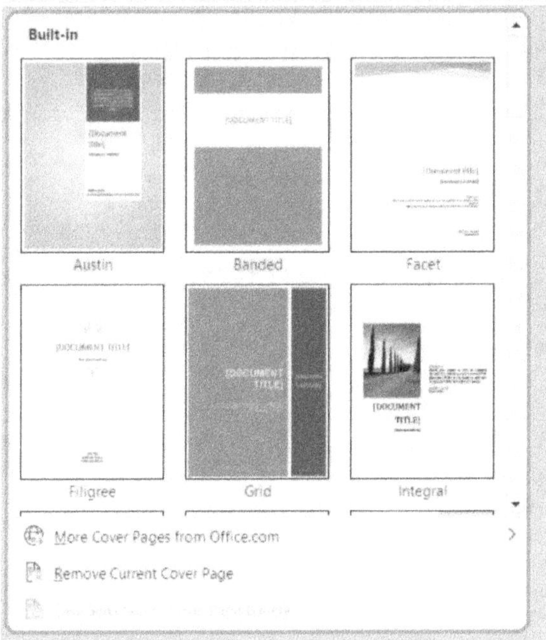

COVER PAGES OPTIONS

Rather than relying on multiple manual line returns, professional document formatting demands the use of **proper page breaks**. These can be easily accessed through the Insert tab's pages section, which provides a comprehensive suite of options including professional **cover pages** and strategically placed blank pages.

The page break feature leverages sophisticated **document object model (DOM) manipulation** to create clean, logical divisions within your document, ensuring consistent formatting and proper page numbering.

Advanced Break Types and Document Organization

The **Layout tab** in Microsoft Word provides access to a **comprehensive suite of specialized break types**, each designed for specific formatting needs and document control. Understanding these different break types is crucial for professional document management.

Column Break Functionality - Column breaks offer **precise control over multi-column layouts**. When working with multi-column text, these breaks ensure optimal text flow by forcing subsequent content to begin at the top of the next column. This feature is particularly valuable when:

- Creating newspaper-style layouts
- Formatting academic journals
- Designing newsletters with balanced column lengths
- Managing complex text distribution across multiple columns

LAYOUT TAB

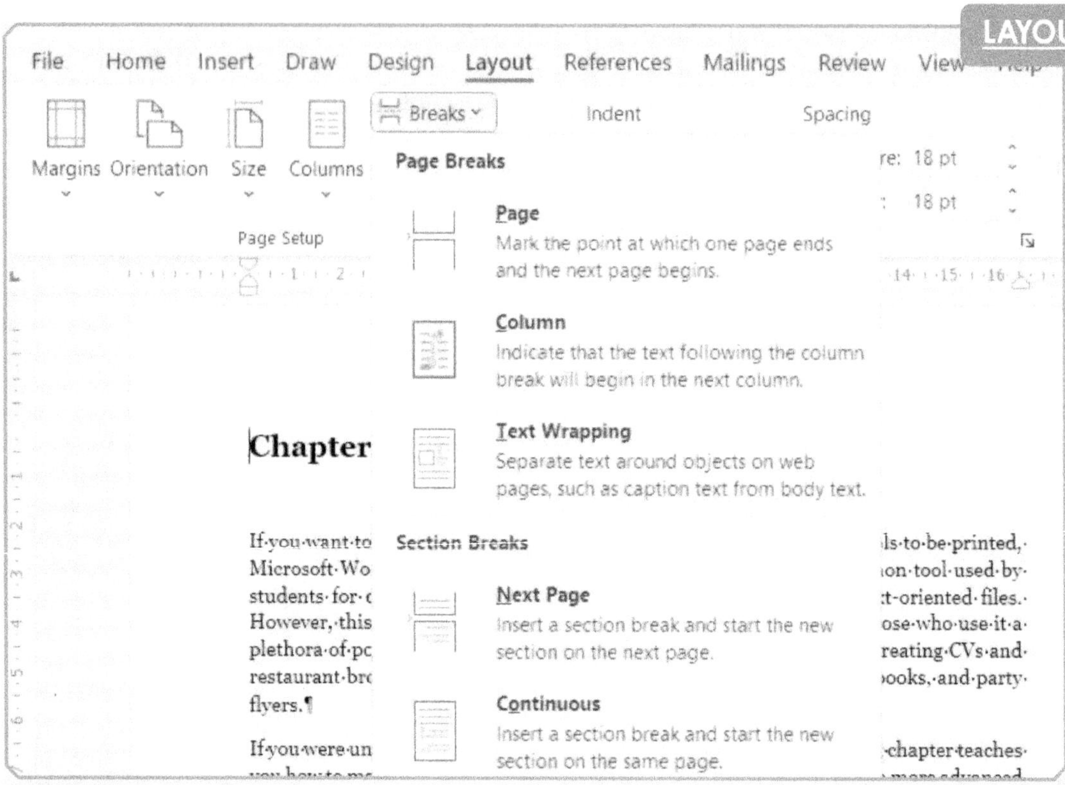

Text Wrapping Break Capabilities - Text wrapping breaks provide sophisticated control over text-image relationships. These specialized breaks help maintain proper formatting when working with inline images and complex page layouts by:

- Creating clean breaks between text and images
- Preventing awkward text wraparound
- Maintaining consistent spacing around visual elements
- Ensuring proper alignment of subsequent paragraphs
- Managing complex page layouts with multiple design elements

Section Break Advanced Features - The **section break system** represents Word's most sophisticated document division tool, offering multiple specialized options:

1. **Next Page Section Breaks**: These breaks create a complete separation by starting the new section on a fresh page. This is particularly useful for:

- Beginning new chapters
- Starting new document segments with different formatting
- Creating distinct areas within complex documents
- Maintaining separate page numbering systems

2. **Continuous Section Breaks**: These allow formatting changes while maintaining continuous text flow by:

- Enabling different column layouts on the same page
- Adjusting margin settings within a page
- Changing page orientation mid-document
- Implementing varied header and footer designs

3. **Even/Odd Page Section Breaks**: These breaks provide professional-grade control for double-sided printing by:

- Starting new sections on either even or odd pages
- Maintaining proper page layout for bound documents
- Supporting professional publishing requirements
- Enabling different headers/footers for even and odd pages

Table Organization and Implementation

The **table system** in Microsoft Word represents a fundamental tool for structured document organization. The application provides a **sophisticated yet accessible interface** for creating and managing tables, supported by advanced algorithms that protect document structure integrity..

Accessing table creation is streamlined through the **Insert tab's table menu**. This interface features an **interactive grid selector** that provides visual table dimensioning. The system's **intelligent preview mechanism** offers real-time visualization of your table structure as you explore different configurations.

For **enhanced precision**, Word offers a dedicated table insertion dialog with manual dimension controls. This system directly interfaces with the **core document architecture**, ensuring precise structural implementation within the document's foundational framework.

Word offers two **notable specialized features**: freehand table drawing and Excel spreadsheet integration. The Excel integration capability is particularly powerful, utilizing **advanced system protocols** to create and maintain dynamic connections between Word and Excel. This integration ensures continuous data synchronization and computational accuracy across both applications.

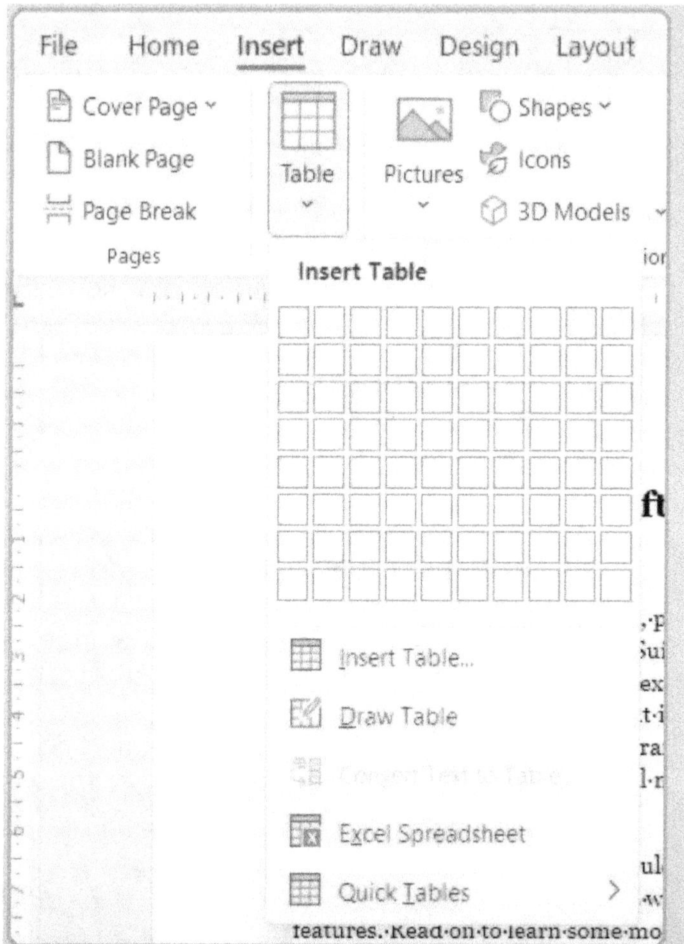

A significant enhancement is Word's **contextual interface adaptation**, which automatically presents a specialized table tools tab upon table creation. This **intelligent system** analyzes your current table interactions to present the most relevant formatting and manipulation options.

Table Design Tab provides critical functionality:

1. **Style Management:** Advanced vector-based table styling
2. **Structure Control:** Sophisticated row and column organization
3. **Cell Configuration:** Professional merging and division tools
4. **Content Organization:** Advanced sorting capabilities

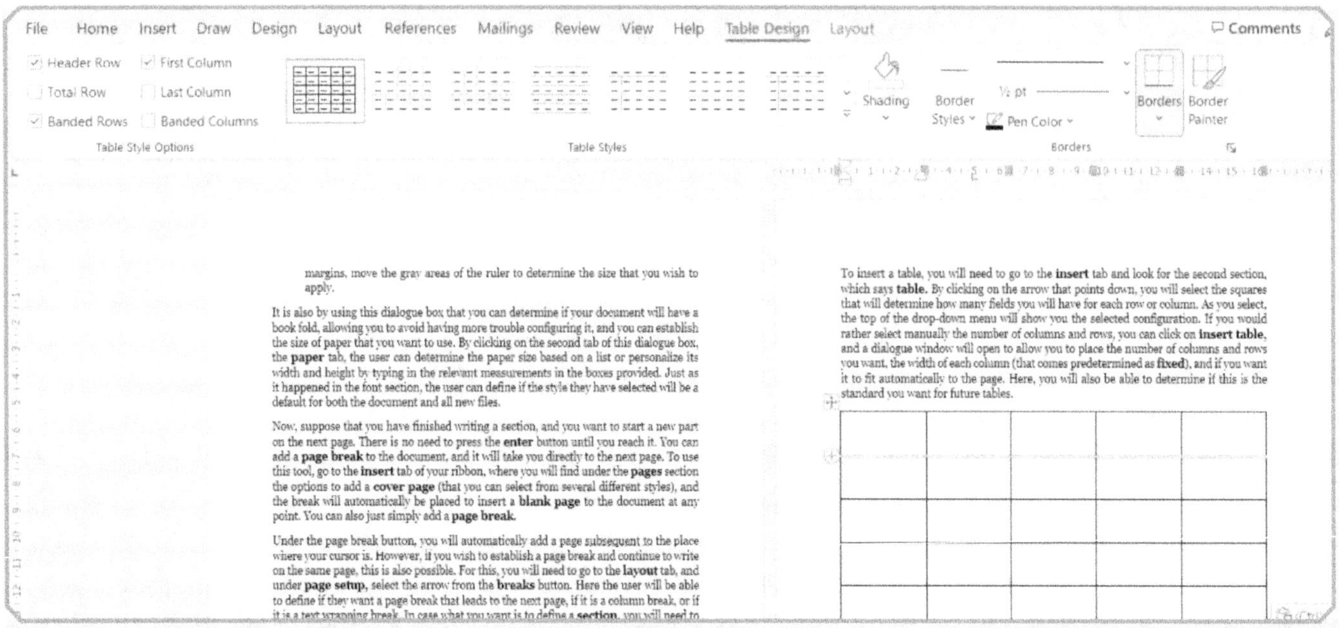

Mastering these **table capabilities** enhances document organization and data presentation options, significantly improving both visual clarity and data analysis potential. This comprehensive system supports professional document creation while maintaining flexible and intuitive operation.

Create Graphs and Formulas

Microsoft Word provides **sophisticated visualization tools** for creating compelling business reports and statistical representations. The Insert tab houses the **comprehensive chart functionality** within the illustrations section, powered by advanced algorithms that transform raw data into meaningful visual insights..

The **chart selection interface** presents users with a diverse range of visualization options, from **fundamental column charts** to **complex statistical displays**. Each selection triggers a **real-time preview system**, enabling users to make informed decisions about their data presentation.

Excel Integration Features

When implementing a chart, Word creates two key elements:

- A **visual placeholder** for the chart
- An **integrated Excel worksheet** for data management

This **dual-component system** utilizes advanced COM technology to maintain seamless communication between Word and Excel, ensuring data consistency and real-time updates.

> ***Productivity Tip:*** *To modify the underlying data, use the* ***Edit Data*** *option. For external data sources, the* ***Select Data*** *function allows you to import data from other files. This feature utilizes advanced file I/O operations and data parsing algorithms to integrate external information seamlessly.*

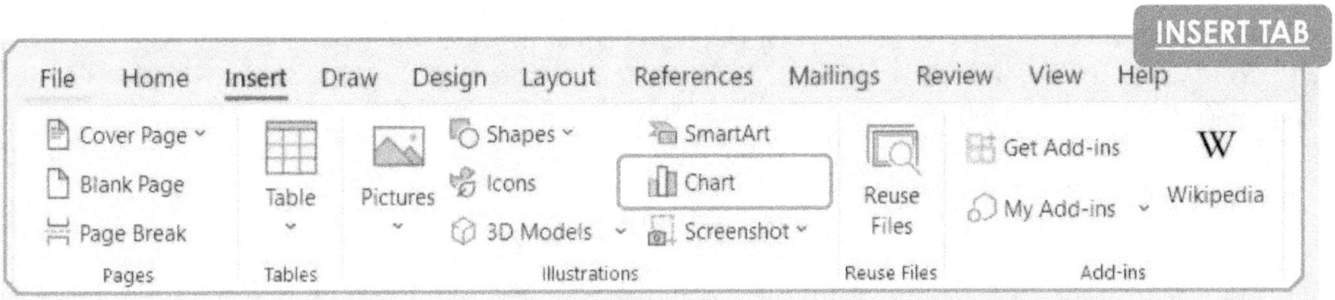

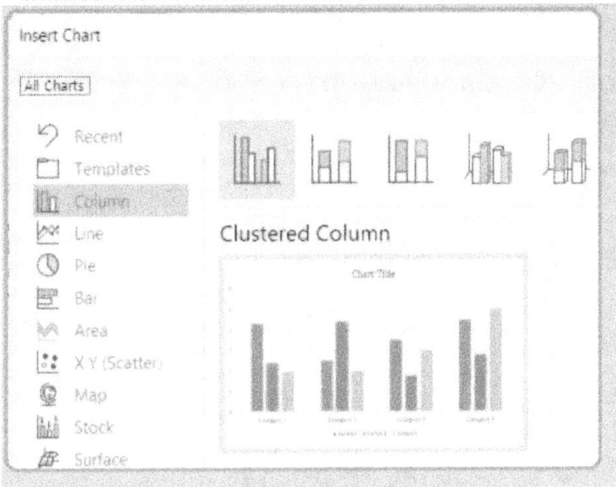

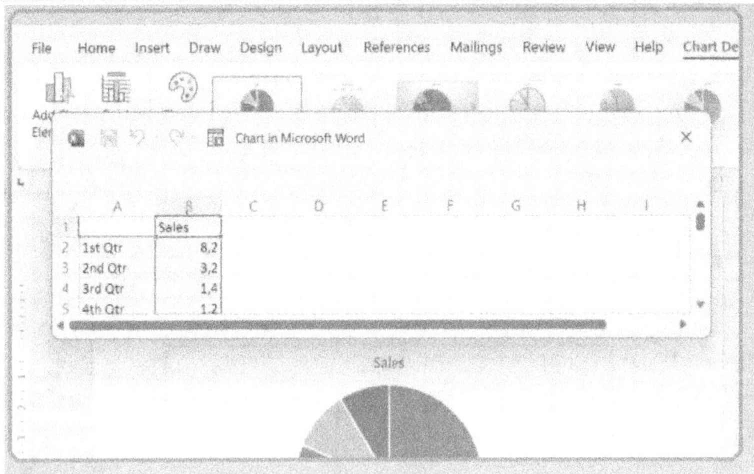

Advanced Customization Tools

The **Chart Tools contextual tab** appears automatically when you select a chart and contains three main tabs: **Design**, **Layout**, and **Format**. Located at the top of the Word ribbon, this specialized menu provides comprehensive customization options:

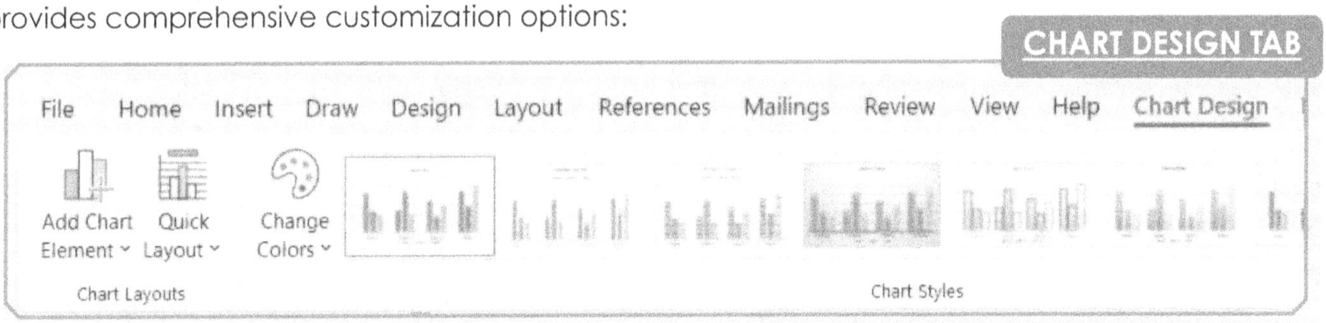

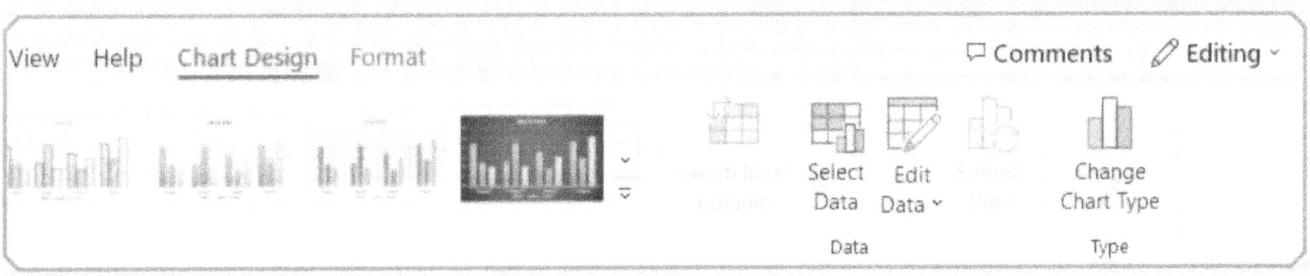

1. **Component Management** (Found in the Design Tab):

    - Access "Add Chart Element" in the top-left corner for modular chart control
    - Find "Quick Layout" in the center for instant layout configurations
    - Use "Change Chart Type" on the far left for fundamental chart modifications
    - Select "Select Data" to modify the underlying data structure

2. **Visual Enhancement** (Available in both Design and Format Tabs):

    - Browse "Chart Styles" gallery in the Design tab's center section
    - Access "Chart Colors" dropdown next to styles
    - Find advanced formatting tools in the Format tab's "Shape Styles" group
    - Locate "WordArt Styles" for title and label enhancements

Format Control and Integration -The **Format tab**, located rightmost in the Chart Tools contextual menu, provides detailed controls:

- Find "Shape Fill", "Shape Outline", and "Shape Effects" in the top ribbon section
- Access size controls in the "Size" group on the far right
- Locate position settings in the "Arrange" group
- Use "Selection Pane" on the right for layer management

Size and Position Management - Located in multiple areas for convenience:

- Right-click menu for quick access to sizing options
- "Size" dialog box in the Format tab's Size group
- Dynamic handles around the chart for manual adjustment
- Precise measurements in the Format tab's Size group

Text Integration Features - Found in the **Layout tab** under "Arrange":

- Access "Wrap Text" in the Arrange group
- Find "Position" options next to text wrapping
- Use "Align" tools for precise positioning
- Access "Bring Forward/Send Backward" for layering control

Each of these sections can be accessed through multiple pathways:

1. Direct ribbon access when chart is selected
2. Right-click context menu
3. Format pane (opened via the Format tab)
4. Quick access toolbar (if customized)

Visual Elements: Pictures, Shapes, and SmartArt

Microsoft Word's Picture Tools, Shape Tools, and SmartArt Graphics provide professional visual enhancement capabilities through the Insert tab. While each tool has distinct features, they share common formatting and layout options in the ribbon interface.

Pictures

The **Picture** command offers multiple insertion methods:

- Through the **Insert tab** in the **Images** group
- Using the **Alt + N, P** keyboard shortcut
- **Insert Online Pictures** for web resources
- Standard copy and paste operations

When you insert a picture, Word activates the **Picture Tools Format tab**, which contains the **Picture Styles** group, **Arrange** group, and **Size** group for comprehensive image control.

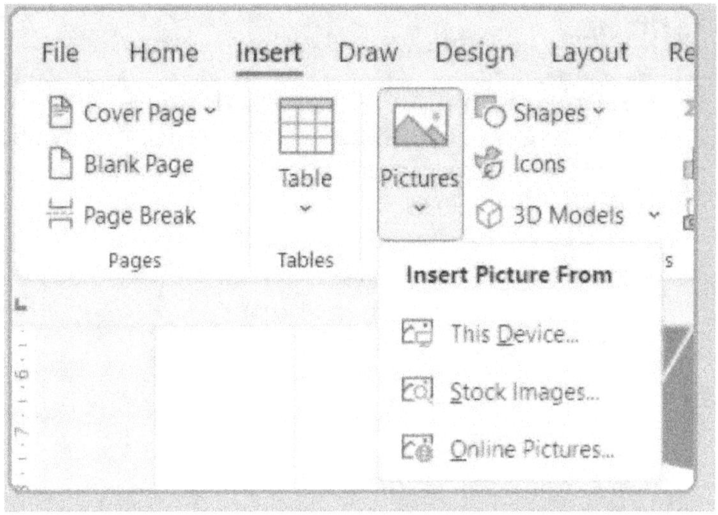

Picture Format Options - The **Corrections** button in the **Adjust** group provides image enhancement tools:

- Brightness and Contrast presets
- Sharpen/Soften image controls
- Color Saturation and Tone adjustments
- Artistic Effects gallery

Word implements **Reset Picture** functionality, allowing you to restore the original image settings at any time.

PICTURE FORMAT TAB

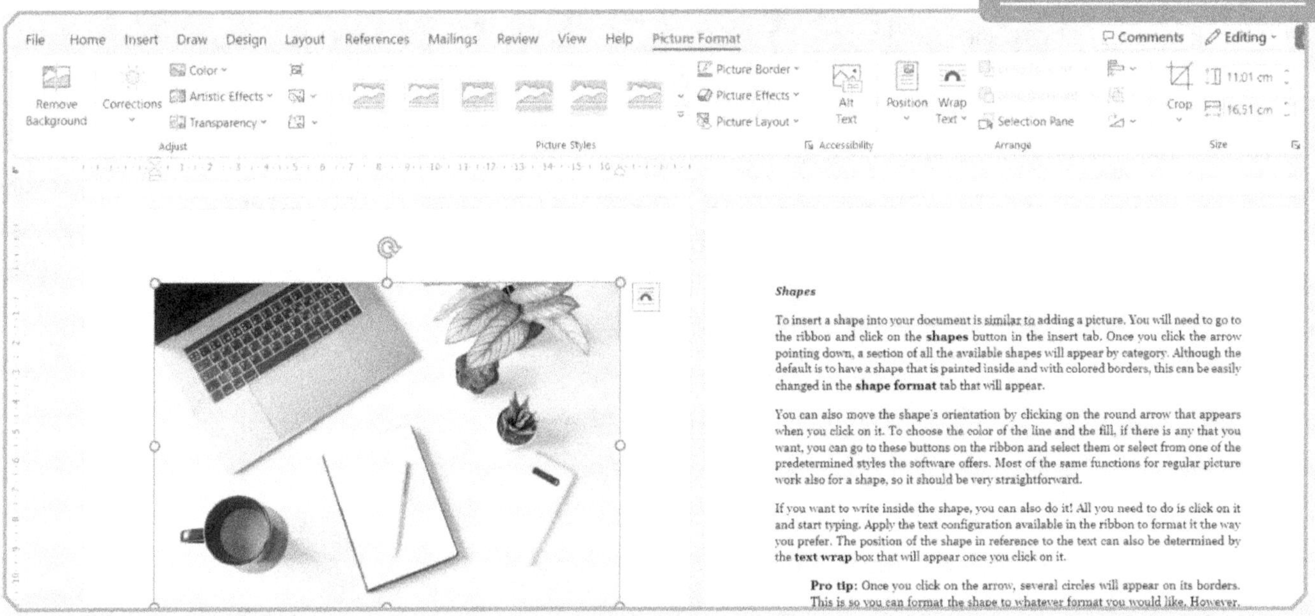

Picture Compression - The **Compress Pictures** dialog box offers advanced options:

- **Resolution** selection (web, print, or custom PPI)
- **Compression** options for all pictures or selected only
- Option to **delete cropped areas** of pictures
- **Apply to selected pictures only** checkbox

Manual Picture Manipulation -The **Picture Tools Format** tab enables:

- Drag handles for real-time resizing
- **Crop** tool in the **Size** group
- **Position** options in the **Arrange** group
- **Rotation** controls for precise angle adjustments

Productivity Tip: *Hold the Shift key while using the corner resize handles to maintain aspect ratio during picture resizing.*

Shapes

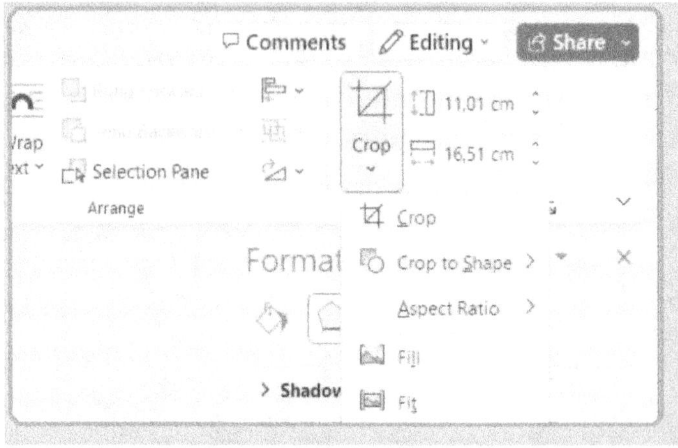

The **Shapes** command in the **Insert tab** provides access to Word's vector-based drawing tools. The **Shapes gallery** offers an extensive collection of pre-defined shapes organized in categories:

- Lines and Connectors
- Rectangles and Basic Shapes
- Stars and Banners
- Flowchart elements
- Callouts

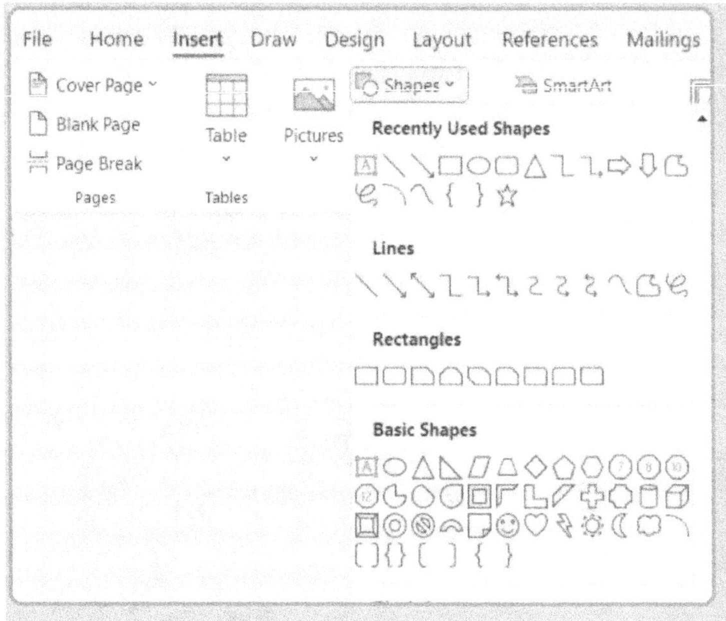

Shape Formatting - When a shape is selected, the **Shape Format tab** activates, providing:

- **Shape Styles** for pre-defined formatting options
- **Shape Fill** dropdown for color, gradient, and pattern options
- **Shape Outline** for border customization
- **Shape Effects** for 3D, shadow, and glow effects

Text Integration with Shapes - Shapes can incorporate text through several methods:

- Right-click and select **Add Text**
- Start typing when shape is selected
- Use the **Edit Text** button in the ribbon

The **Text Options** in the **Shape Format** tab provide:

- **Text Box** margins adjustment
- **Vertical alignment** options
- **Text direction** controls
- **Word wrap** within the shape

Advanced Shape Manipulation

Yellow adjustment handles appear on certain shapes, enabling:

- Customization of star points
- Arrow head size adjustment
- Rounded corner modification
- Shape proportion controls

***Productivity Tip:** While regular resize handles (white squares) change overall size, yellow handles modify specific shape characteristics without affecting the basic shape dimensions.*

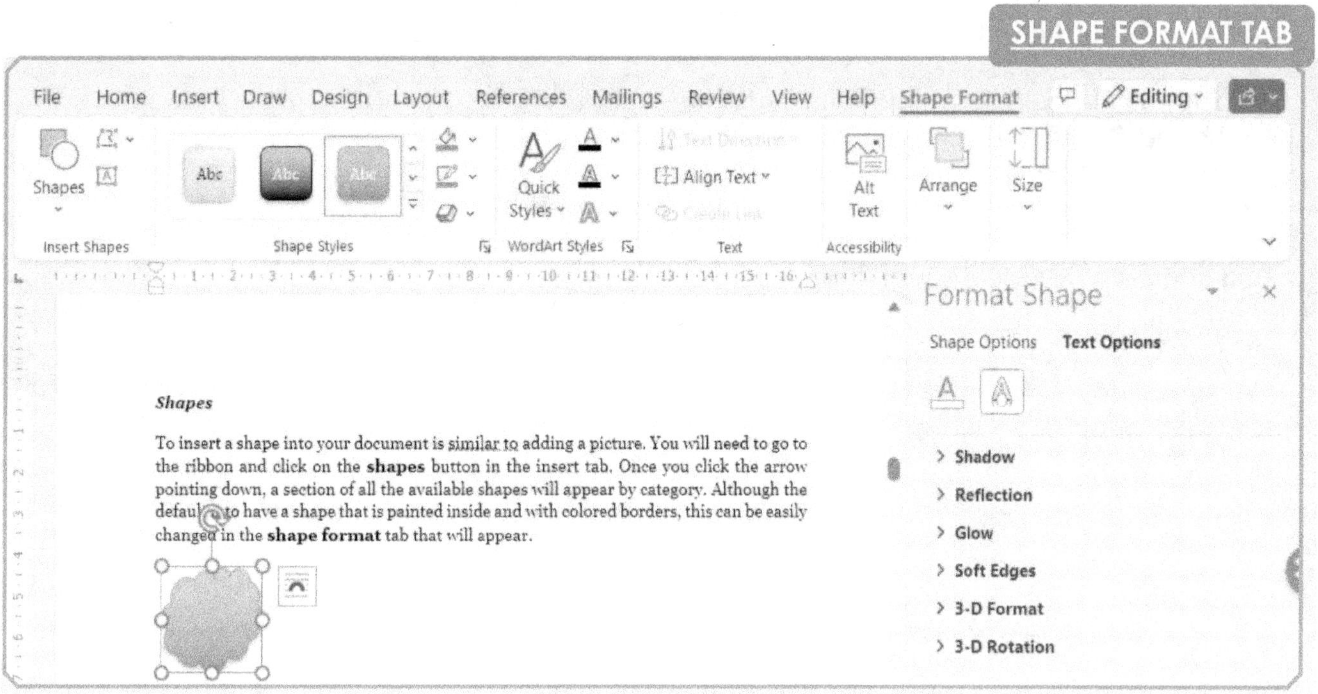

SmartArt

Microsoft Word's SmartArt feature represents a sophisticated approach to visualizing conceptual information and relationships. This powerful tool transforms simple text and ideas into professional-quality diagrams with minimal effort. Whether you're creating business presentations, educational materials, or organizational charts, SmartArt provides a comprehensive solution for visual communication.

The **SmartArt Graphics** command in the **Insert tab** provides access to Word's advanced diagram creation tools. The **SmartArt gallery** is thoughtfully organized into intuitive categories, each designed for specific visualization needs:

- Process diagrams for sequential information
- Hierarchy charts for organizational structures
- Cycle diagrams for continuous processes
- Relationship matrices for interconnected concepts
- List graphics for simplified information presentatio

Dynamic Layout Features - When working with SmartArt, Word provides two specialized tabs that offer comprehensive control over your diagrams:

1. **SmartArt Design tab:**

    - **Layouts** gallery for seamless diagram type changes
    - **Colors** options for professional color scheme selection
    - **SmartArt Styles** for rapid, consistent formatting
    - **Reset** graphic options for starting fresh

2. **SmartArt Format tab:**

- **Shapes** style modification for individual elements
- **Shape Effects** controls for visual enhancement
- **WordArt Styles** for dynamic text formatting
- **Size** and arrangement options for perfect positioning

The **Text Pane**, accessible through the Design tab, serves as the primary interface for content input and organization.

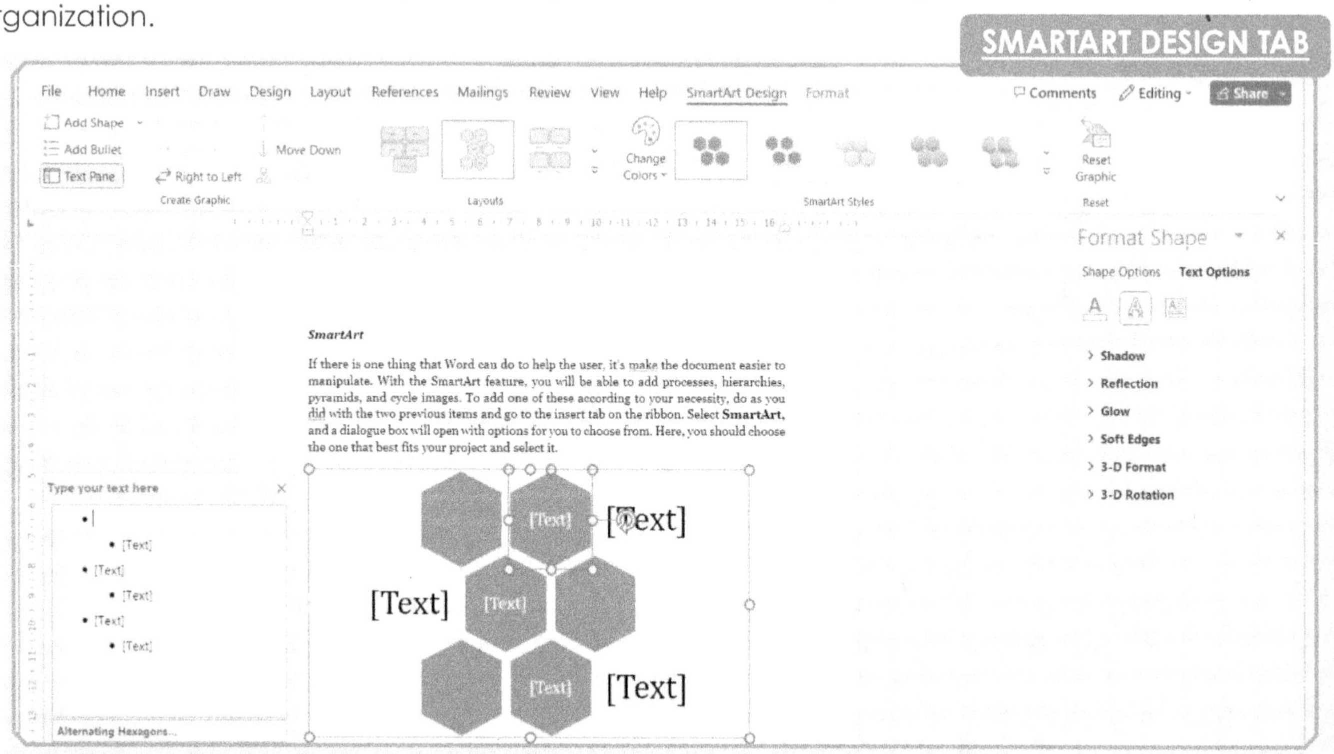

The **Add Shape** functionality represents one of SmartArt's most powerful features, providing context-sensitive options for diagram expansion:

- **Add Shape After** for sequential additions
- **Add Shape Before** for insertions
- **Add Shape Above** for hierarchical expansion
- **Add Shape Below** for subordinate elements
- **Add Assistant** for specialized hierarchy layouts

Productivity Tip: *For precise structural control, select a specific shape before utilizing the* ***Add Shape*** *commands. This ensures new elements integrate exactly where intended within your diagram's hierarchy.*

Table of Contents, Footnotes, Captions and Bibliography

Microsoft Word's document organization features provide essential tools for creating professionally structured documents. Whether you're writing a thesis, creating a business report, or developing technical documentation, these automated tools significantly reduce the time and effort required for document organization while ensuring consistency and accuracy.

Table of Contents Generation

The **Table of Contents** feature in Word represents a sophisticated approach to document navigation and structure. By leveraging the **Styles** system in the **Home tab**, Word creates dynamic, updateable content listings that automatically reflect changes in your document structure and pagination.

Working with Heading Styles - Word's heading system implements a logical hierarchical structure:

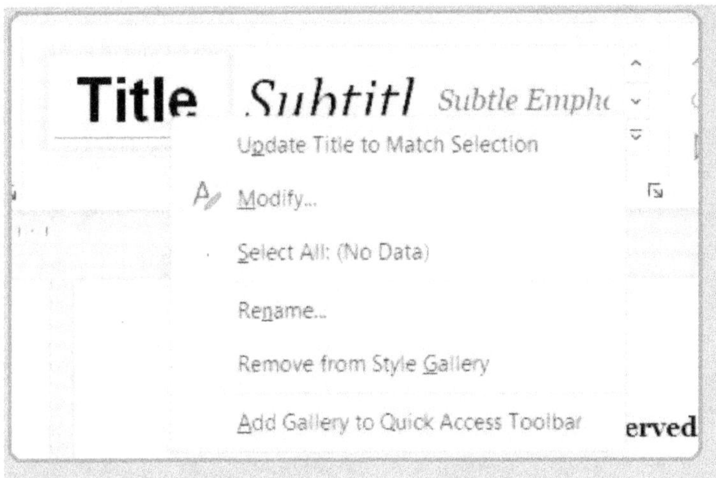

- **Heading 1** style serves as the primary organizational level, typically used for chapter titles or major sections
- **Heading 2** style creates clear subsections within primary content areas
- **Heading 3** and subsequent styles enable detailed content organization for complex documents

Style Application Process - The implementation of heading styles follows a straightforward yet powerful process:

1. Select the text requiring style formatting
2. Access the comprehensive **Styles gallery** in the **Home tab**
3. Apply the appropriate heading level with a single click
4. Use the **Style Inspector** for verification and detailed formatting information

Through the sophisticated **Modify Style** dialog, users gain access to extensive customization options:

- Direct formatting modifications for font, size, and color
- Style inheritance settings for maintaining formatting consistency
- **Update to Match Selection** feature for rapid style updates
- Detailed style behavior configurations for automatic formatting

Creating the Table of Contents - The generation process demonstrates Word's commitment to user-friendly automation:

1. Position the cursor at the intended table location
2. Navigate to the **References tab** for access to document tools
3. Select the **Table of Contents** button to view available options
4. Choose from professionally designed **built-in formats**

The **Update Table** function ensures document accuracy by automatically synchronizing page numbers, updating heading text, adjusting structural changes, and maintaining consistent formatting across all entries. This automated system continuously monitors and updates your table of contents to reflect any modifications in your document.

The **Update Table** function can be accessed in multiple ways:

- Right-click on the existing Table of Contents and select "Update Field"
- Click "Update Table" in the **References tab** when the cursor is in the Table of Contents
- Press F9 when the cursor is in the Table of Contents

The **Custom Table of Contents** dialog provides professional control through comprehensive customization tools. Users can adjust page number displays, alignment settings, tab leader styles, and formatting options for each level of the table. This flexibility enables the creation of precisely formatted tables that meet specific document requirements.

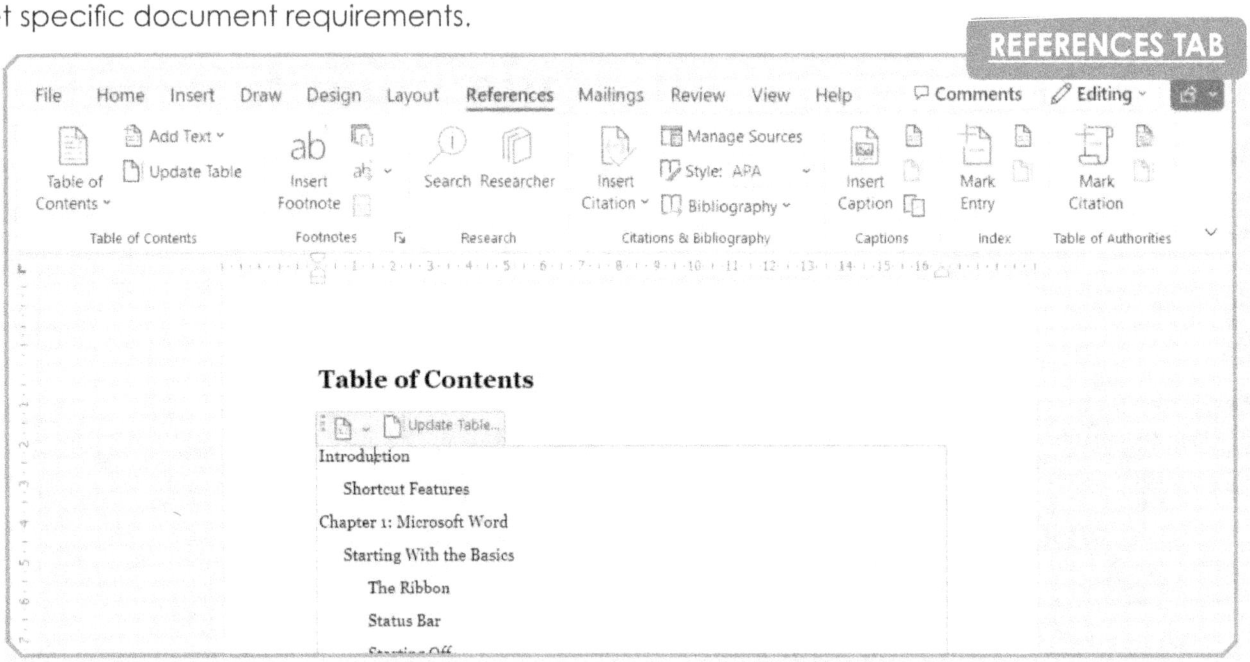

Access the **Custom Table of Contents** dialog through:

- **References tab > Table of Contents > Custom Table of Contents**
- Or click the Table of Contents button and select "Custom Table of Contents" at the bottom

Advanced Footnote Implementation in Word

The footnote system in Microsoft Word provides essential documentation capabilities for academic and professional documents. The feature employs sophisticated automatic numbering and dynamic layout management for precise reference control.

To implement footnotes in your document, follow this procedure in the **References tab**:

1. Place your cursor where you want the footnote reference
2. Find the **Footnotes** group in the ribbon
3. Select the **Insert Footnote** command (or use Alt+Ctrl+F)

Automatic Formatting Features - When you insert a footnote, Word automatically:

- Creates a superscript number in the main text
- Generates a separator line at the page bottom
- Places the cursor in the footnote area
- Applies appropriate formatting and spacing

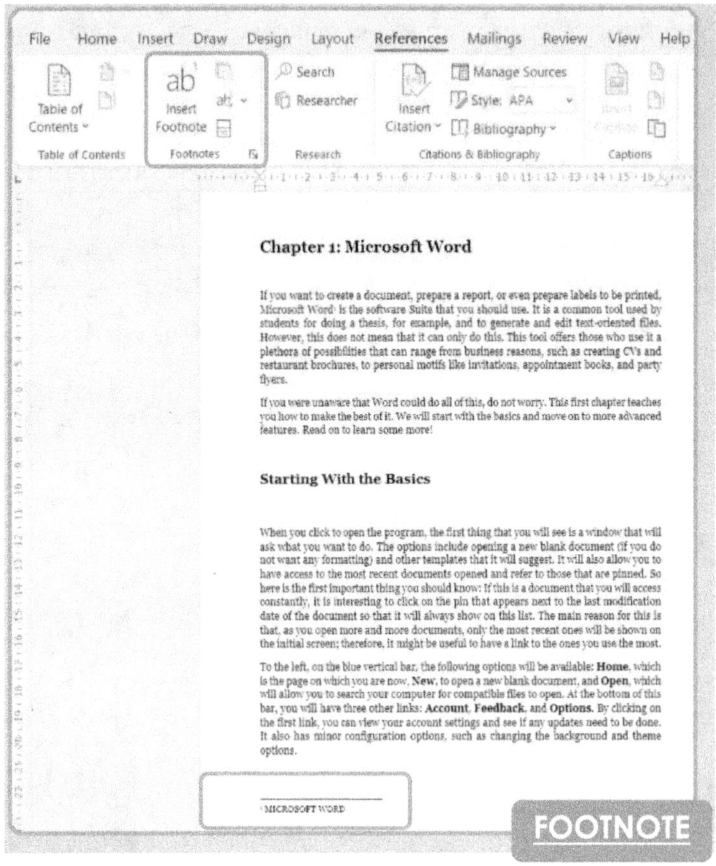

Navigation and Management - The **Next Footnote** button in the **Footnotes** group provides quick navigation between references. Additional controls include:

- **Show Notes** button for reviewing all footnotes
- **Convert** options for changing footnote types
- **Footnote Separator** for customizing the dividing line

Dynamic Update System - Word maintains automatic management of footnotes through:

- Continuous renumbering as you add or delete notes
- Automatic repositioning when text moves
- Format consistency across all footnotes
- Cross-reference updating

Caption Insertion Process

Microsoft Word's caption system provides professional labeling and organization for document elements like figures, tables, and equations. This feature integrates with Word's reference system for accurate document management.

Access caption controls through the **References tab**:

1. Select your target element (image, table, etc.)
2. Locate the **Captions** group
3. Click **Insert Caption**

Caption Configuration Options - The **Caption** dialog box offers comprehensive control:

- Enter caption text in the main field
- Select element type (Figure, Table, Equation) from the **Label** dropdown
- Configure numbering through the **Numbering** button
- Set position using the **Position** dropdown

Additional options in the **Caption** dialog include:

- Exclude label from caption checkbox
- New Label button for custom categories
- AutoCaption settings for automatic insertion
- Chapter number inclusion options

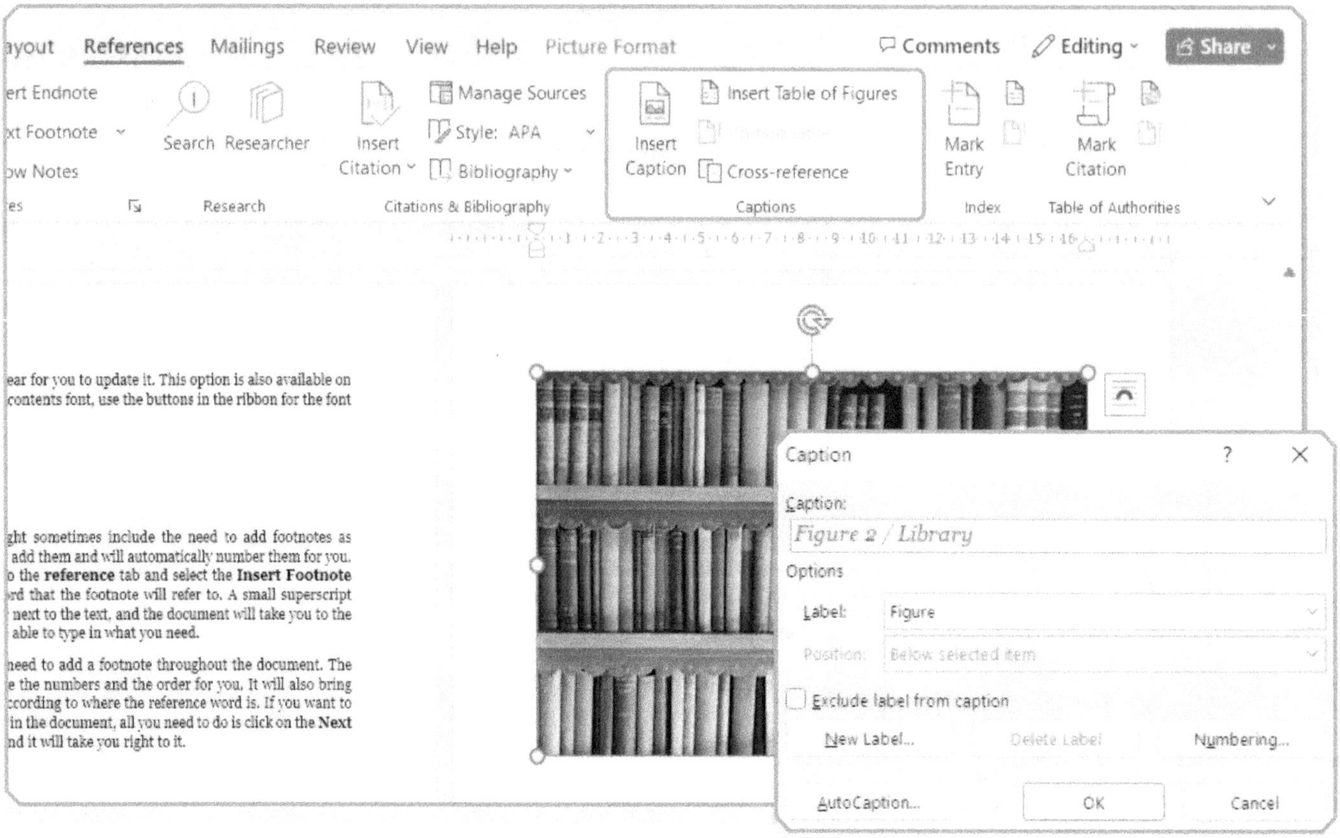

Table of Figures Creation - Generate a list of captioned items through:

- **References tab > Captions group**
- Click Insert Table of Figures
- Choose formatting in the resulting dialog

The system maintains automatic updating of caption numbers and references throughout your document, ensuring professional organization and accurate cross-referencing of visual elements.

Citations & Bibliography

Microsoft Word's bibliography system offers comprehensive citation management for academic and professional documents. This feature streamlines reference handling through automated formatting and organization.

Citation Style Selection - Access citation controls in the **References tab**:

- Click the **Style** dropdown in the **Citations & Bibliography** group
- Choose from standard formats (APA, MLA, Chicago, etc.)
- Apply the selected style throughout your document

Citation Implementation Process - To add citations to your document:

1. Position cursor at the citation point
2. Click **Insert Citation** in the **References tab**
3. Select **Add New Source**
4. Complete the **Create Source** dialog fields

Managing Source Information - The **Source Manager** provides comprehensive control:

- Access through **Manage Sources** button
- Edit existing citation information
- Create new source entries
- Organize master and current list

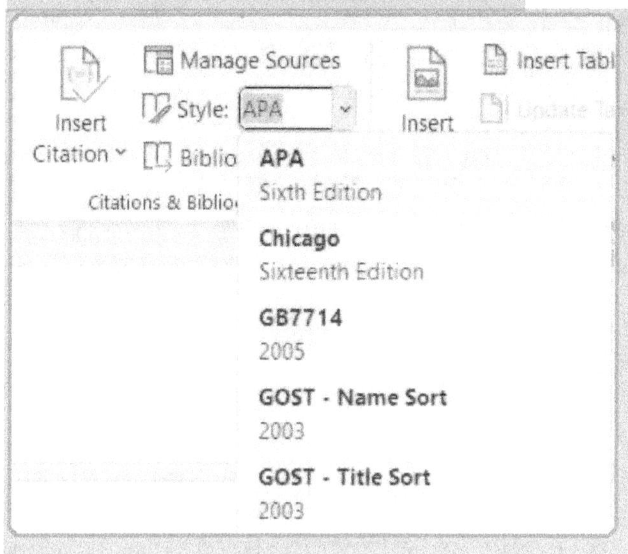

Bibliography Generation - Create your bibliography through the **References tab**:

- Place cursor at desired location
- Click **Bibliography** button
- Select from built-in formats
- Choose **Insert Bibliography** option

Spell Check and Language Tools

Proper spelling and grammar are essential for document professionalism. Word's spell check system implements advanced NLP algorithms for comprehensive error detection and correction suggestions. Language settings can be accessed through:

1. The language indicator in the **status bar**
2. The **Review tab** in the ribbon interface

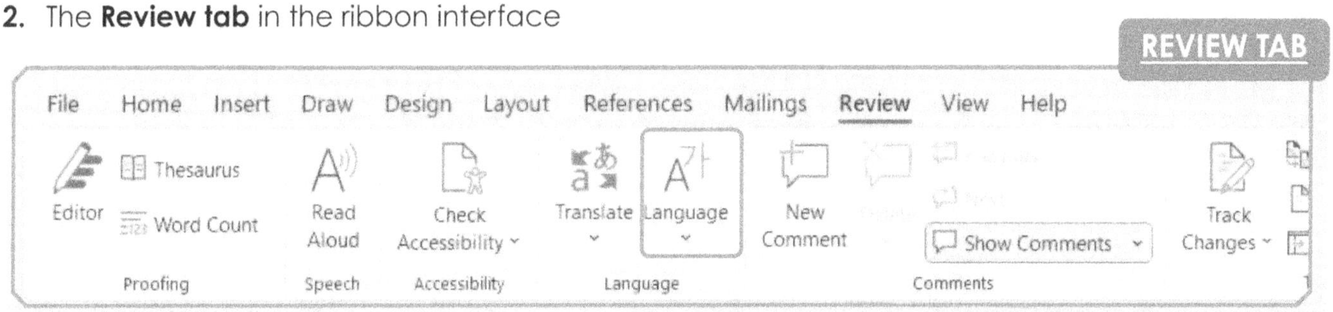

Word's intelligent language system enables:

- Comprehensive document checking
- Multi-language section support
- Real-time error detection

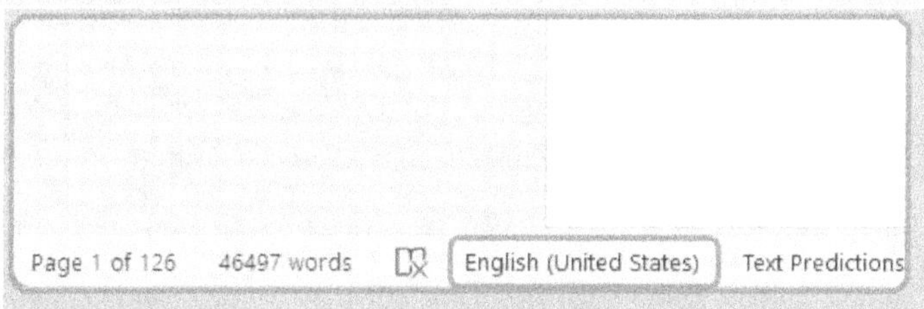

The translation capabilities integrate machine learning models to provide:

- Complete document translation options
- Partial content translation tools
- Instant translation previews

This system connects to cloud-based language models for continuous accuracy improvements. Post-translation verification ensures linguistic accuracy.

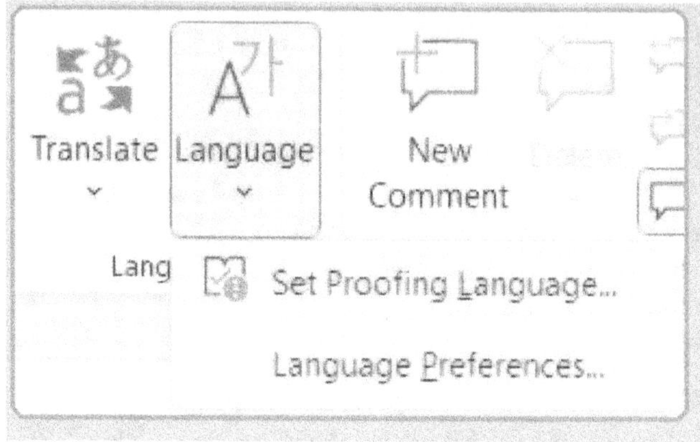

Document Review and Collaboration

These features transform the editing process from a simple text markup system into a sophisticated collaborative workflow management solution.

Track Changes System - The Track Changes feature, accessible through the Review tab, creates a complete documentation trail of all modifications. When activated:

- Text additions appear in a distinct color (typically red) with underlines
- Deletions show as strikethrough text or margin balloons
- Formatting changes display with special indicators
- Each modification includes author identification and timestamp

REVIEW TAB

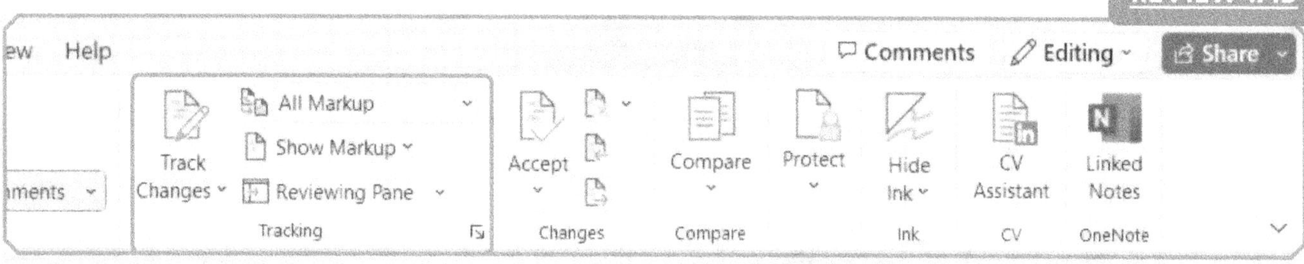

For example, when an editor corrects "recieved" to "received," the original text appears with a strikethrough while the correction appears in color, allowing all team members to see both versions.

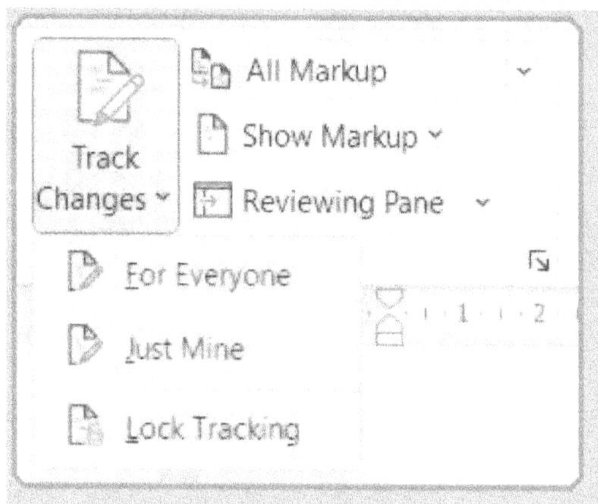

Change Management Process - Reviewers can process modifications through several methods in the Review tab:

- Accept or reject individual changes by right-clicking
- Use the Changes group buttons for bulk operations
- Navigate between changes using Previous and Next buttons
- Filter changes by reviewer or type

A practical example: When reviewing a business proposal, team members can accept all formatting changes while individually reviewing content modifications.

Comments and Feedback - The commenting system enables detailed discussion without altering the main text:

- Insert comments tied to specific text selections
- Reply to existing comments to create threaded discussions
- Mark comments as resolved when addressed
- Filter and navigate through comments efficiently

Document Comparison Features

The Compare function offers sophisticated version control capabilities:

- Analyze documents side-by-side
- Generate detailed change reports
- Merge multiple versions
- Track structural and formatting changes

For instance, when comparing contract versions, Word can identify not only text changes but also modifications to tables, headers, and formatting.

These collaboration tools make Word an indispensable platform for professional document development, whether working on legal contracts, academic papers, or business proposals.

Keyboard Shortcuts on *Word*

FUNCTION	PC SHORTCUT	MAC SHORTCUT
Start a new document	*Ctrl + N*	*Command + N*
Open a new document	*Ctrl + O*	*Command + O*
Save the document	*Ctrl + S*	*Command + S*
Cut content	*Ctrl + X*	*Command + X or F2*
Paste content	*Ctrl + V*	*Command + V or F4*
Copy content	*Ctrl + C*	*Command + C or F3*
Make font bold	*Ctrl + B*	*Command + B*
Underline selection	*Ctrl + U*	*Command + U*
Make font italic	*Ctrl + I*	*Command + I*
Undo previous action	*Ctrl + Z*	*Command + Z or F1*
Print	*Ctrl + P*	*Command + P*
Move cursor to top	*Ctrl + Alt + Page Up*	*Command + Page Up*
Move cursor down	*Ctrl + Alt + Page Down*	*Command + Page Down*
Select whole document	*Ctrl + A*	*Command + A*
Insert page break	*Ctrl + Enter*	*Command + Return*
Insert line break	*Shift + Enter*	*Shift + Return*
Insert column break	*Ctrl + Shift + Enter*	*Command + Shift + Return*
Insert copyright symbol	*Ctrl + Alt + C*	*Not available*
Insert trademark symbol	*Ctrl + Alt + T*	*Option + 2*

2. Excel:

A Powerful Data Processing Platform

Core Overview

Microsoft Excel, a cornerstone of the Office Suite, transcends its reputation as a mere spreadsheet tool. While **primarily known for data analysis and financial calculations**, it serves as a comprehensive platform for **data visualization, form creation, and even basic programming applications**. The software shares interface elements with other Office applications but possesses unique capabilities that set it apart.

Fundamental Structure and Navigation

The **foundation of Excel is its grid-based spreadsheet system**, which opens with a default worksheet. For more complex projects, users can create **multiple interconnected worksheets** through the '+' tab feature, enabling sophisticated data relationships across different sheets. This multi-sheet capability is crucial for **managing large-scale data projects** and maintaining organized datasets.

Users can optimize their workflow through several **key customization features**:

- Worksheet renaming for better organization
- Color-coding tabs for visual distinction
- Sheet protection and visibility controls
- Strategic sheet management (with particular attention to deletion, which is permanent)

> ***Productivity Tip:*** *Optimize worksheet management through* ***custom sheet properties****. Modify sheet identifiers by double-clicking the default nomenclature (e.g., "Sheet1") and inputting a descriptive title. Enhance visual organization through* ***tab color customization*** *accessed via the context menu, which also provides sheet manipulation options including relocation, protection, and visibility controls. Exercise caution with sheet deletion operations, as they represent irreversible data modifications.*

Excel implements a **cell reference system** based on column letters and row numbers. This coordinate structure is fundamental for **formula syntax** and cell referencing. Column and row dimensioning can be adjusted through dynamic resizing - position the cursor at dimensional boundaries until the resize indicator appears, then modify as needed.

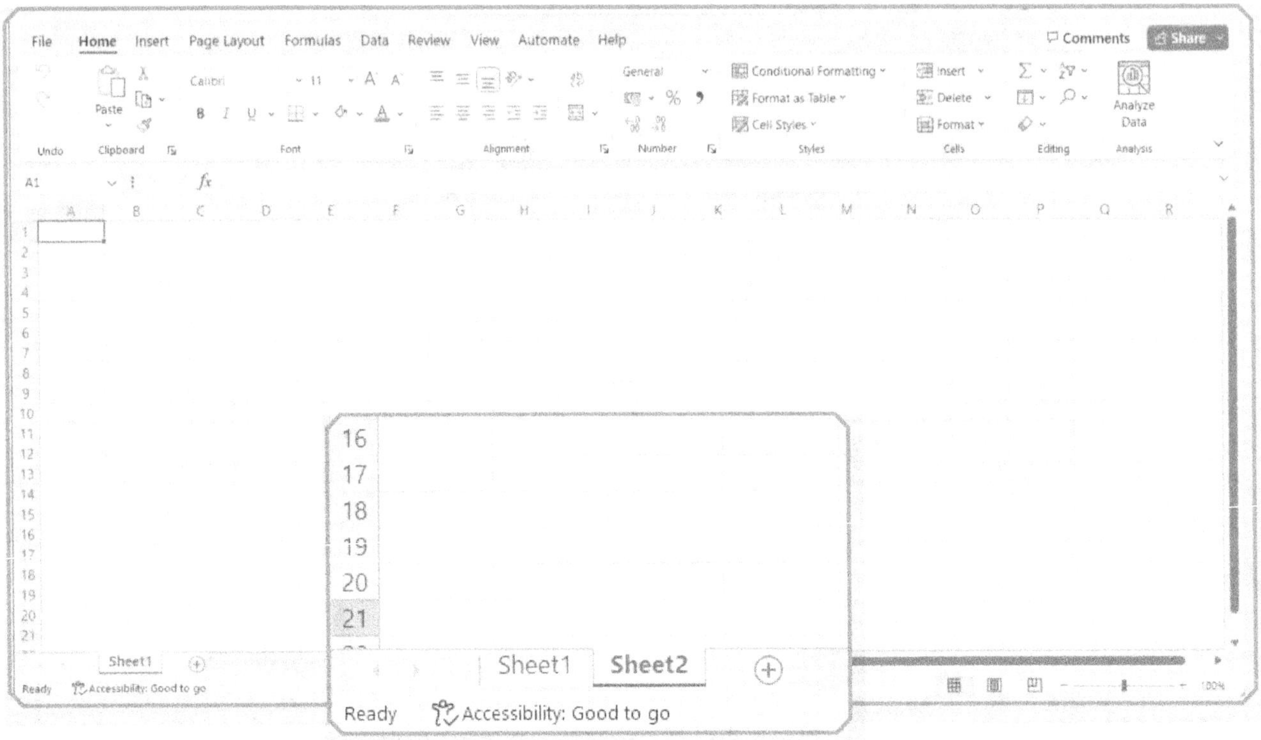

The software's **cell-based architecture** supports:

- Multiple data types (numerical, textual, temporal)
- Complex formula creation
- **Programming-style logical operations**
- Conditional processing through functions like IF statements

This comprehensive system makes Excel an indispensable tool for both basic data management and advanced analytical applications, setting it apart as a versatile computational platform in modern business environments.

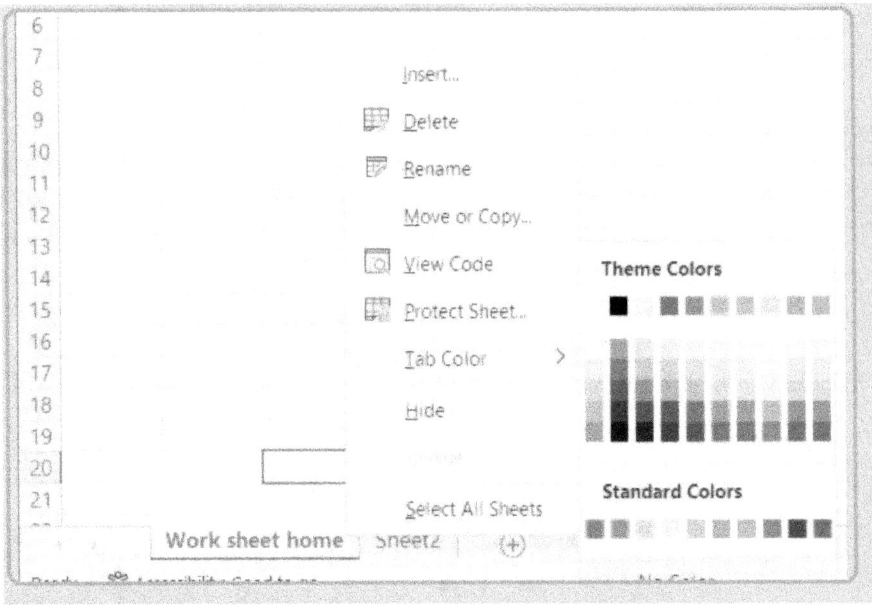

__Productivity Tip__: Utilize Excel's __AutoFit functionality__. Double-clicking column separators triggers the intelligent width optimization algorithm, which analyzes content length and adjusts accordingly, enhancing data visibility and presentation efficiency.

While Excel incorporates standard Office formatting capabilities, it features specialized **data analysis tools** and **computational functions**. These include advanced statistical operations and machine learning integrations for complex dataset analysis. The **PivotTable feature** exemplifies this through its dynamic data aggregation capabilities.

Excel's **cell-based architecture** facilitates sophisticated data organization. Each cell functions as an independent data container supporting multiple formats: numerical values, text strings, datetime objects, and formula expressions. This structural design, combined with Excel's **computation engine**, enables complex modeling and real-time analytics.

The application's **formula language** represents a comprehensive computational framework based on programming principles. It supports operations ranging from basic arithmetic to advanced financial modeling, enabling users to implement complex logical structures. The **IF function**, for example, demonstrates conditional logic implementation, facilitating dynamic data evaluation within the spreadsheet environment.

Layout and Visualization Tools

Excel's interface offers **sophisticated visualization and layout capabilities** that extend beyond basic spreadsheet functionality. Users can access **three distinct viewing modes** from the bottom-right interface: Normal, Page Layout, and Page Break Preview. The latter two modes offer specialized features for document preparation and output management.

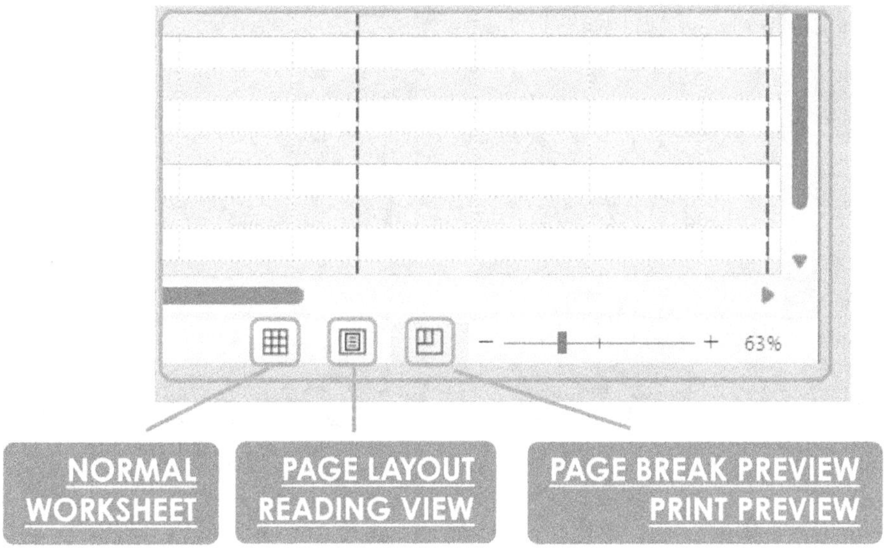

Page Layout View: Advanced Document Prepatarion

This specialized view combines **active editing capabilities** with comprehensive header and footer visibility, essential for professional document output in both PDF and printed formats. The Page Layout ribbon provides granular control over:

- Document orientation switching (portrait/landscape)
- Dynamic page break visualization
- Margin adjustment system
- **Smart layout engine** that automatically recalculates display parameters

Enhanced Header and Footer Configuration

Excel implements a **tri-sectional header/footer system** (left, center, right) that maintains structural integrity regardless of column quantity. This sophisticated architecture enables advanced document control with practical applications:

Section Alignment Management

- Access through **Page Layout > Custom Header/Footer**
- Each section can be independently formatted using the built-in text editor

> ***Productivity Tip**: The header/footer image integration process utilizes Excel's **proprietary object embedding system**. Standard clipboard operations (Ctrl+C/Ctrl+V) are not supported for header/footer image insertion. Instead, users must utilize the dedicated Picture tool within the ribbon interface. Image manipulation is handled through the **Format Picture dialog**, which implements precise scaling algorithms to maintain visual fidelity while conforming to header/footer spatial constraints.*

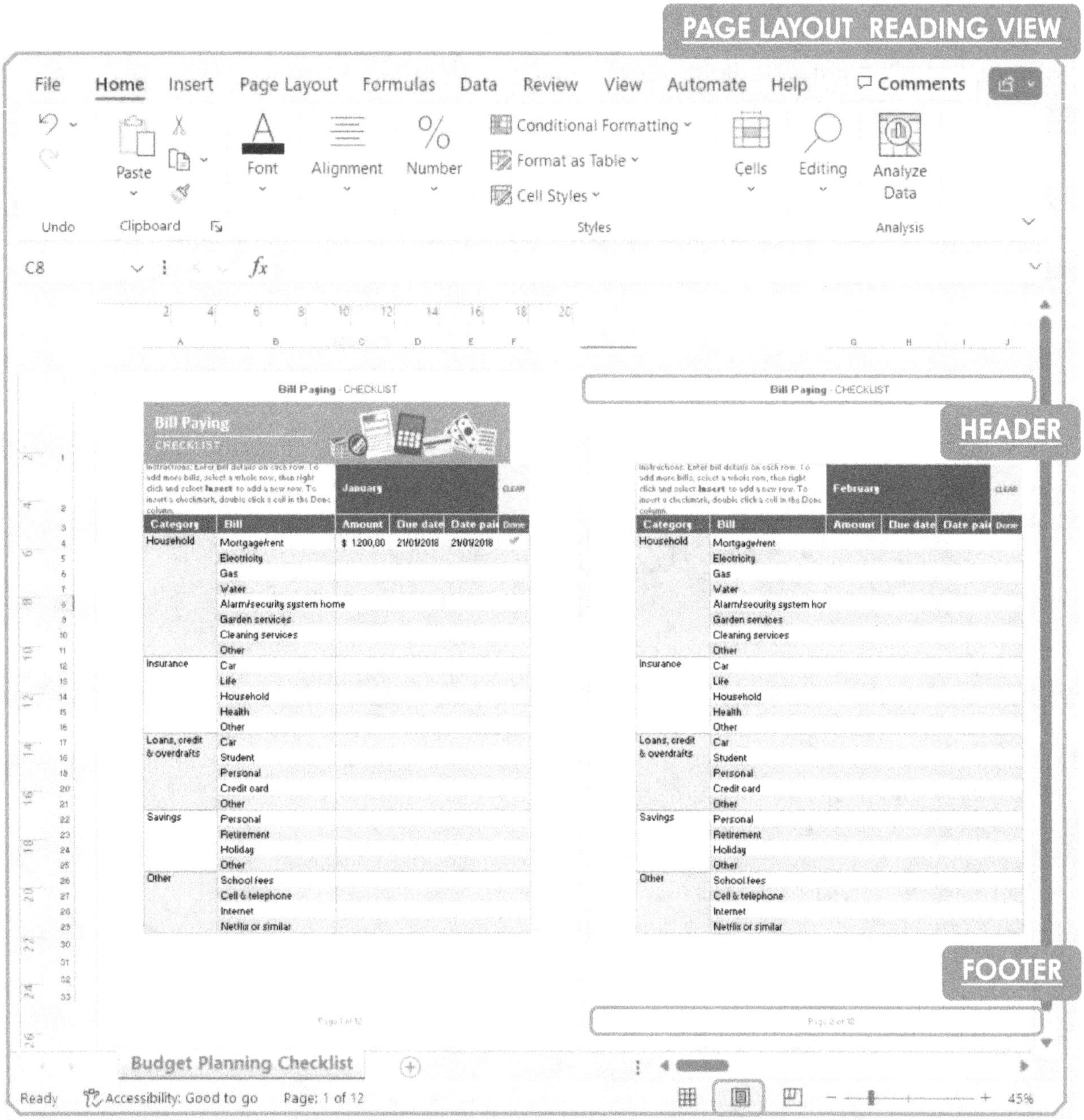

Page Break Preview: Advanced Output Management

Page Break Preview mode transforms Excel's standard grid into an intuitive print management interface. **Essential print area management tools** provide a comprehensive visual system for document output control. The interface uses a color-coded system where **blue boundary lines** clearly delineate content-rich areas that will appear in the final output. Areas outside the active content zone are displayed with **gray screening**, instantly highlighting portions of the worksheet that won't be included in the printed document. This visual distinction is crucial for ensuring that all necessary data is captured in the final output.

PAGE BREAK PREVIEW

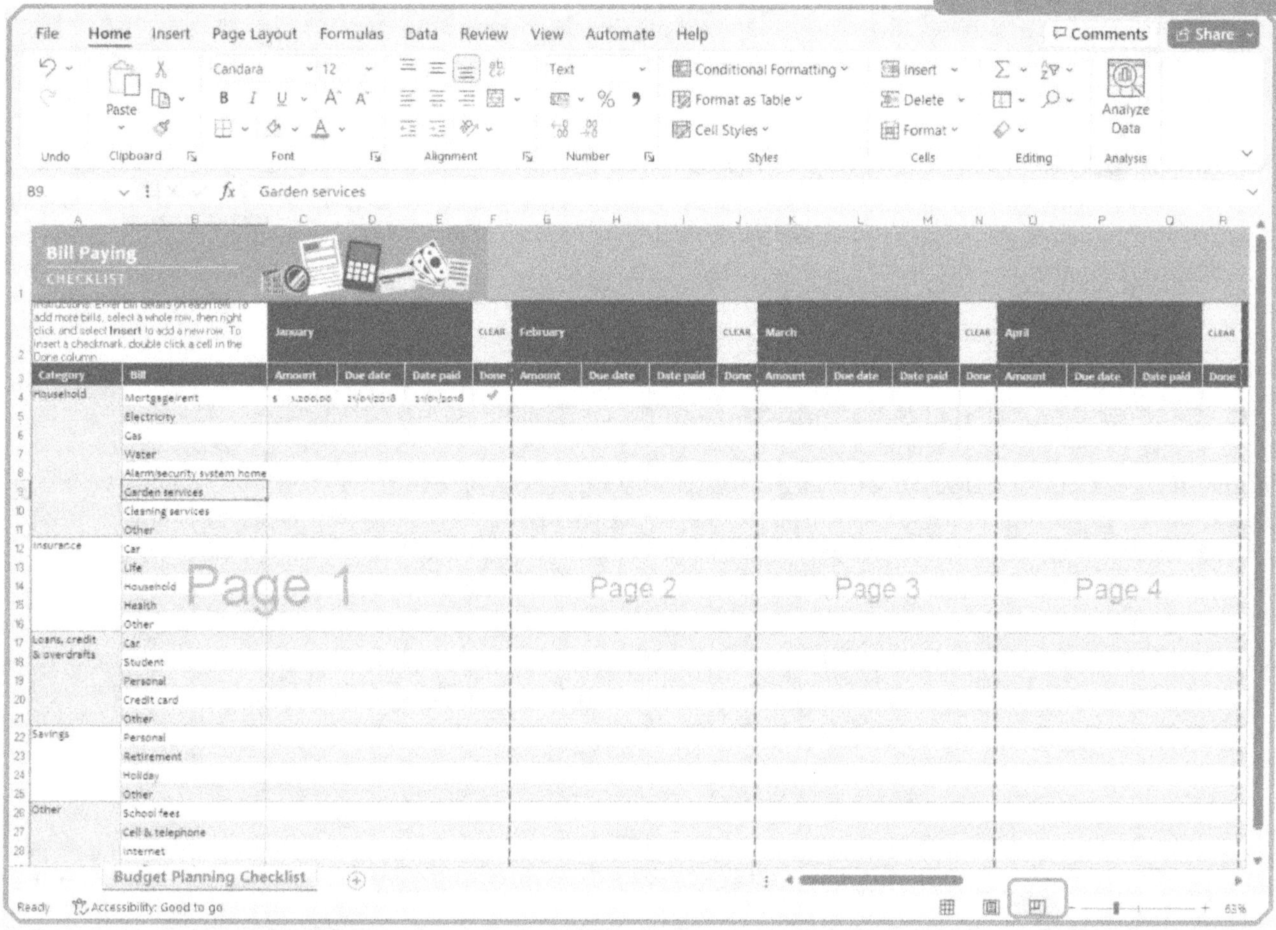

Smart Break Management

The **Smart break suggestion system** represents Excel's intelligent print optimization feature. Blue dashed lines indicate Excel's recommended page breaks, calculated based on content density and standard page dimensions. Users can interact with these suggestions by clicking and dragging the lines to create custom break points, offering granular control over how content flows across pages. This system adapts dynamically to content changes, ensuring optimal page distribution throughout the document lifecycle. Excel's output system provides multiple approaches to content organization.

Single-page content optimization automatically adjusts scaling and layout to fit designated content within a single page - ideal for summary reports or dashboards. For larger datasets, **multi-page distribution management** enables logical content segmentation across multiple pages. The **custom break point definition** feature allows users to override automatic page breaks, providing precise control over where content splits occur.

Productivity Tip: Batch Processing Excellence *For complex workbooks, Excel offers sophisticated* ***batch printing operations****. By holding the Ctrl/Command key while selecting worksheet tabs, users activate the* ***bulk processing system****. This powerful feature enables simultaneous configuration of multiple sheets, streamlining the printing process for large documents. The system provides a consolidated preview of all selected sheets, ensuring consistency across the entire workbook before printing.*

Print management - Excel's print management system includes several advanced features for output customization:

- **Print Scale Optimization:** The automatic scaling system intelligently adjusts content to fit specified page dimensions. Users can choose between **"Fit to Page"** for automatic scaling or set specific percentage values for precise control. This feature ensures readable output regardless of the original content size.

- **Margin Templates:** Excel provides a collection of predefined margin settings conforming to common document standards. These templates include options for narrow, wide, and custom margins, facilitating quick adaptation to different printing requirements. Users can also save custom margin configurations for consistent document formatting.

- **Custom Print Areas:** The ability to save frequently used print selections as named print areas streamlines the printing process for regularly used document sections. This feature is particularly valuable for reports that require consistent printing of specific data ranges.

- **Print Titles:** For multi-page documents, the print titles feature enables automatic repetition of header rows or columns on each printed page. This ensures that column headers or row labels remain visible throughout long documents, enhancing readability and professional appearance.

- **Sheet Order Management:** The sheet order management system provides control over the sequence of printed worksheets. Users can arrange sheets in any desired order, independent of their position in the workbook, ensuring logical document flow in the final output.

PRINT VIEW

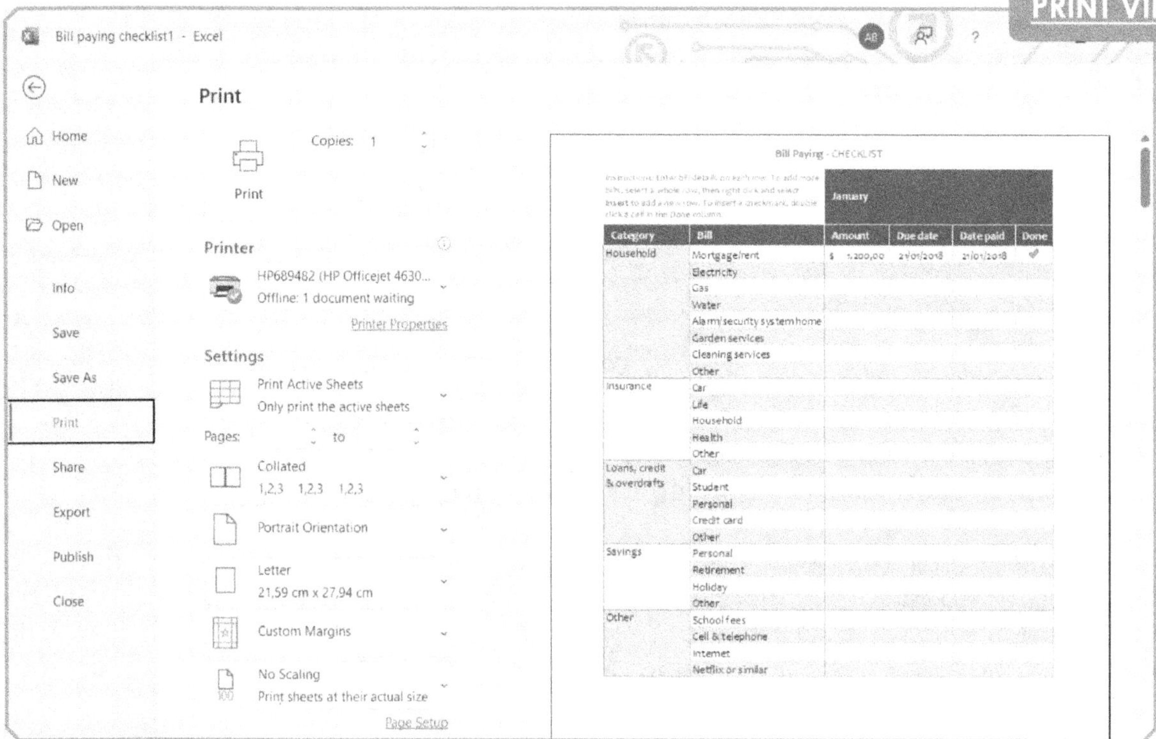

Practical Guide to Excel Printing - Here's a step-by-step process to print your Excel file effectively:

1. **Preview Setup** (Optional but Recommended)

   - Press **Page Layout View** button (bottom-right corner) to check page breaks and margins
   - Or use **File > Print** (Ctrl+P) to see the print preview directly

2. **Quick Print Settings**

   - Select your **print area** by highlighting the cells you want to print
   - Go to **File > Print** (or press Ctrl+P)
   - Choose your **printer** from the dropdown menu
   - Select number of **copies**
   - Pick a **print range**: specific sheets, selection, or entire workbook

3. **Essential Print Options**

   - **Orientation**: Choose Portrait or Landscape
   - **Scaling**: "Fit Sheet on One Page" or "Custom Scaling"
   - **Margins**: Normal, Wide, or Narrow
   - **Headers/Footers**: Add if needed through "Page Setup"

Productivity Tip: *Before printing large workbooks, always use Print Preview to verify page breaks and scaling. For frequent printing of the same area, use* ***Set Print Area*** *(Page Layout > Print Area > Set Print Area) to save your selection for future use.*

Cell Formatting: Essential Skills

Mastering cell formatting represents a critical skill in Excel proficiency. While foundational formatting principles were covered previously, we'll explore Excel's specialized formatting capabilities that enhance data presentation and analysis. **Proper formatting** not only improves visual clarity but also ensures accurate data interpretation and calculation reliability.

Number Formatting Controls

The **Home tab** contains the comprehensive **Number section**, which serves as your primary formatting command center. This section provides:

- Quick access formatting buttons for common needs - instantly apply currency, percentage, or decimal adjustments
- An expandable dialog box for detailed options - access through the small arrow in the bottom-right corner
- Custom format creation tools - develop specialized formats for unique data requirements

The Number section represents Excel's most frequently used formatting tools, designed to handle everything from basic numerical displays to complex custom formats.

Important: *Always select your target cells before applying any formatting changes to ensure consistent application. This practice prevents formatting errors and saves time in large spreadsheets.*

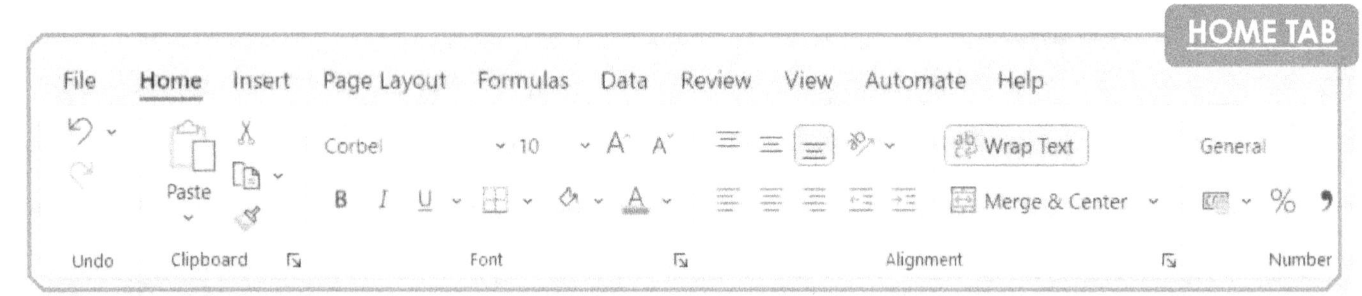

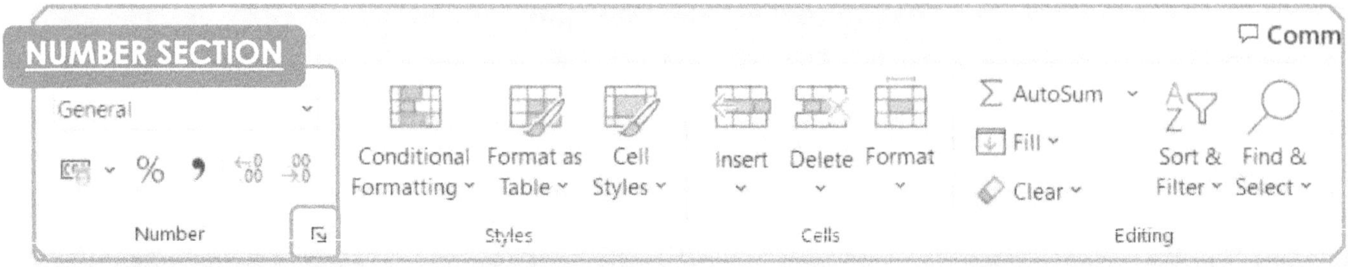

Format Cells Dialog: Data Type Configuration

The **Format Cells dialog box (accessible via Ctrl+1)** serves as the command center for all formatting operations, offering multiple data type options essential for accurate calculations:

- **Number formats** with decimal control: Specify exact decimal places and thousand separators
- **Currency** with various symbol options: Choose from multiple currency symbols and formats
- **Date and time** with regional settings: Display dates and times in locally appropriate formats
- **Percentage** with automatic scaling: Convert decimal values to percentages automatically
- **Text alignment and wrapping**: Control how text fits within cells
- **Special formats** for specific data types: Handle phone numbers, zip codes, and social security numbers
- **Custom format patterns**: Create specialized formats for unique requirements

Additional formatting controls enhance visual presentation:

- **Alignment options**: Control content positioning horizontally and vertically
- **Font selection**: Choose typefaces, sizes, and styles
- **Border customization**: Add visual separation between data
- **Background fill**: Apply colors and patterns for visual emphasis
- **Cell protection**: Control access to cell content

Data Protection - Implement data protection in shared workbooks through these steps:

1. Select the cells requiring protection (use Ctrl+A for entire worksheet)
2. Open the **Format Cells dialog box** (Ctrl+1)

3. Navigate to the **Protection tab**
4. Enable the cell locking option (checkbox)
5. Go to the **Review tab** in the ribbon
6. Click **"Protect Sheet"**
7. Set appropriate permissions (allow or restrict specific actions)
8. Create a secure password (minimum 8 characters recommended)
9. Document your protection settings for team reference

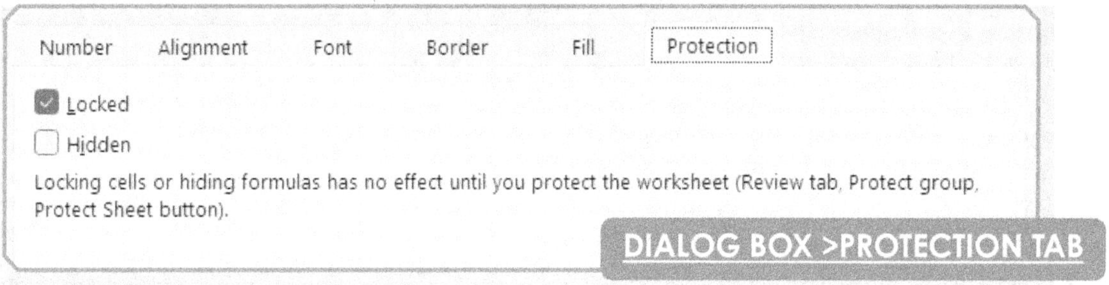

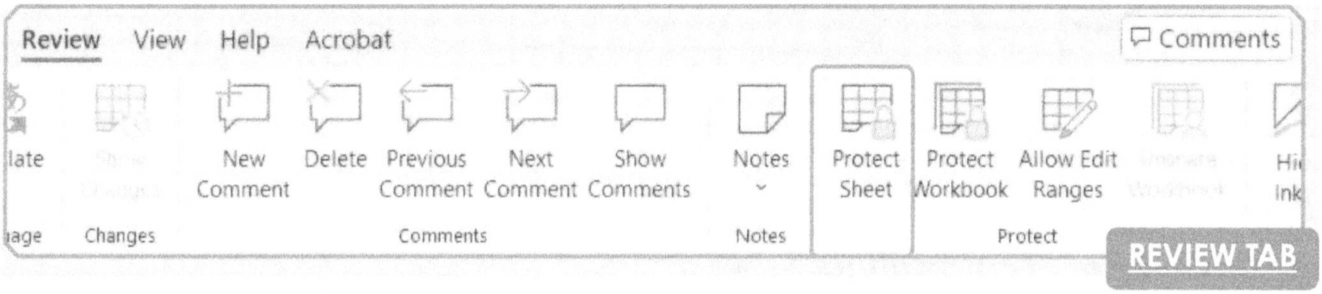

Conditional Formatting: Understanding Dinamic Rules

Conditional Formatting represents one of Excel's most powerful **data visualization tools**, enabling automatic cell formatting based on specific content or conditions. Access this feature through:

- **Home tab > Conditional Formatting**
- Quick Access Toolbar (if customized)
- Keyboard shortcut **Alt+H+L**

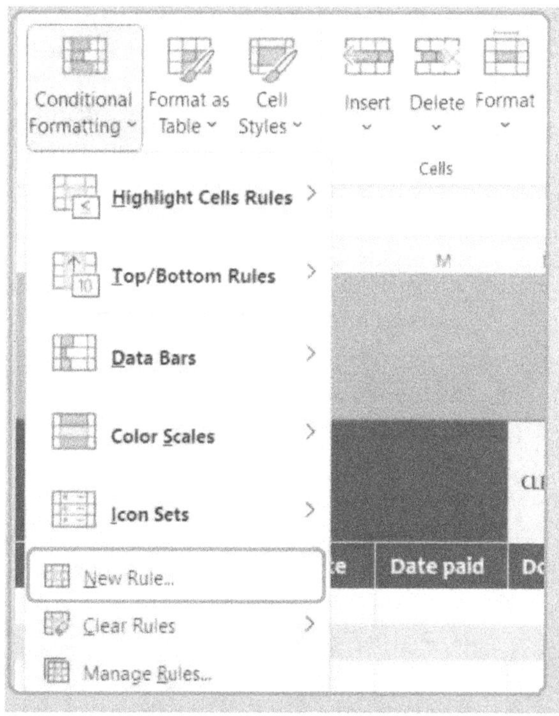

Creating New Rules - The New Rule dialog provides several rule types:

1. **Format cells that contain:**
   - Greater than/Less than values
   - Text containing specific strings
   - Dates occurring in specific periods
   - Duplicate or unique values
2. **Format cells based on their values:**
   - Numerical comparisons
   - Formula-based conditions
   - Text pattern matching

After establishing rules, click Format to determine the visual representation of qualifying cells.

> ***Productivity Tip****: Before applying any conditional formatting, ensure your target cells are pre-selected. This practice prevents accidental formatting of unintended ranges and saves time in large datasets.*

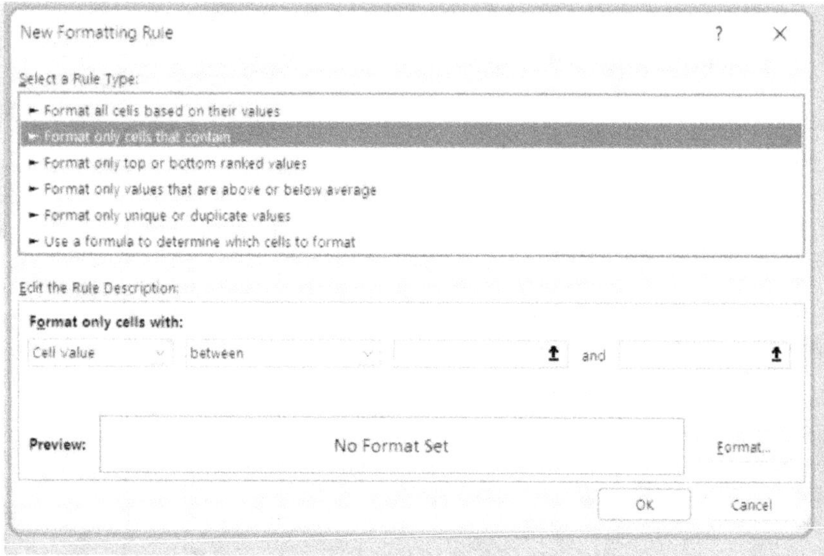

Excel provides an extensive array of **preset conditional formatting options**, including intuitive color scales, dynamic icon sets, proportional data bars, and sophisticated ranking systems. These visualization tools harness Excel's advanced data interpretation capabilities, converting numerical data into clear, meaningful visual patterns that enhance comprehension and analysis.

The **Conditional Formatting menu** serves as the central hub for rule administration. This unified control panel facilitates efficient rule management, allowing users to modify, update, or remove formatting rules with precision. This systematic approach ensures that spreadsheets maintain their organizational integrity and visual clarity throughout development and updates.

Advanced Excel Formatting: Essential Techniques

After establishing fundamental cell management skills, users can leverage Excel's advanced formatting capabilities.

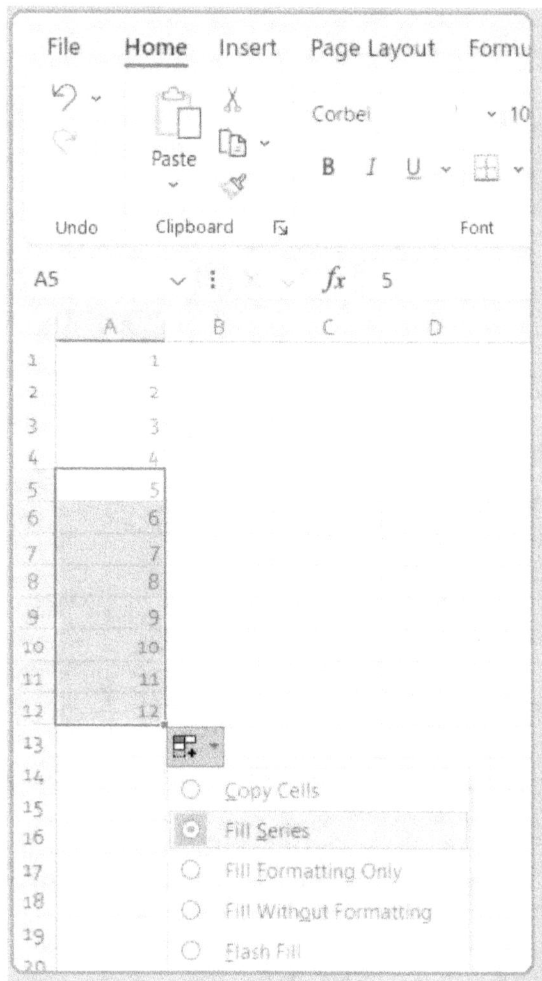

Core Formatting Tools - Here are key techniques for enhanced spreadsheet management:

1. **Format Painter Implementation -** The Format Painter tool provides efficient formatting replication across multiple cells:

    - Single click for one-time use
    - Double click for multiple applications
    - Preserves all formatting attributes

2. **Automatic Content Filling -**Excel's AutoFill feature streamlines data entry:

    - Access via the fill handle (small cross in cell corner)
    - Drag to extend content or formatting
    - Smart tag options include:
    - Series continuation
    - Pattern recognition
    - Format-only copying

3. **Content Relocation Techniques -** For precise cell content

movement:

- Select target cell(s)
- Position cursor over border until four-arrow cursor appears
- Drag to new location
- All formatting and formulas are preserved

Productivity Tip: *Exercise caution when moving cells referenced in formulas. Cell relocation can impact calculation accuracy. Always verify formula integrity after content movement.*

4. **Date Management** - Understanding Excel's sophisticated date handling system is crucial for accurate data management:

   - **Serial Number System**: Excel stores dates as sequential numbers starting from January 1, 1900 (serial number 1). For example, January 2, 1900 is 2, and so on. This enables mathematical calculations with dates.

   - **Display Formatting**: While dates are stored as numbers, proper formatting ensures they appear in a readable format. Without formatting, you might see numbers like 45321 instead of an actual date.

   - **Default Date Structure**: The standard format follows your system's regional settings (day/month/year or month/day/year). This can be customized through Excel's format menu.

   - **Format Customization**: Access comprehensive date formatting options through the Number Format dialog (Ctrl+1), including various date and time displays, custom formats, and regional standards.

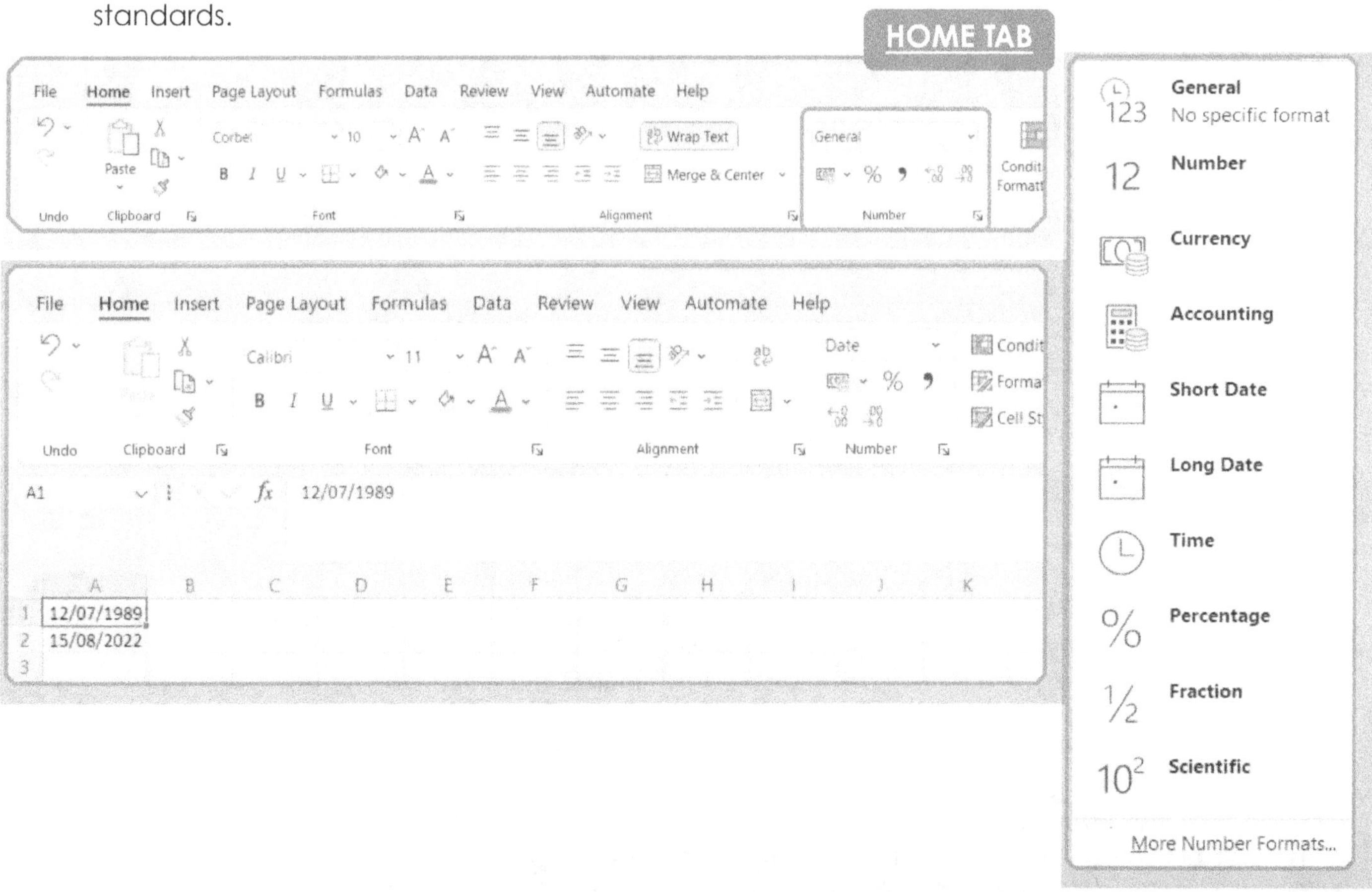

5. **Text Management and Line Breaks Controls:** Excel offers multiple sophisticated approaches for handling text across multiple lines:

   - **Manual Line Control**: Using Alt+Enter while editing in the formula bar creates deliberate line breaks exactly where you want them, providing precise control over text layout.

   - **Automated Text Flow**: The Wrap Text feature automatically manages how text flows within a cell based on column width, eliminating the need for manual breaks.

   - **Width Adaptation**: Excel can automatically adjust column widths to accommodate text content, either through double-clicking column borders or using the AutoFit feature.

Productivity Tip: *The Wrap Text function serves as a powerful text management tool:*

- ***Smart Width Adaptation***: *Automatically fits text to the current column width without losing content*
- ***Intelligent Height Adjustment***: *Rows automatically expand to show all content*
- ***Format Retention***: *Maintains all text formatting (bold, italic, etc.) while wrapping*
- ***Enhanced Readability***: *Creates clear, professional-looking cells with properly spaced text*

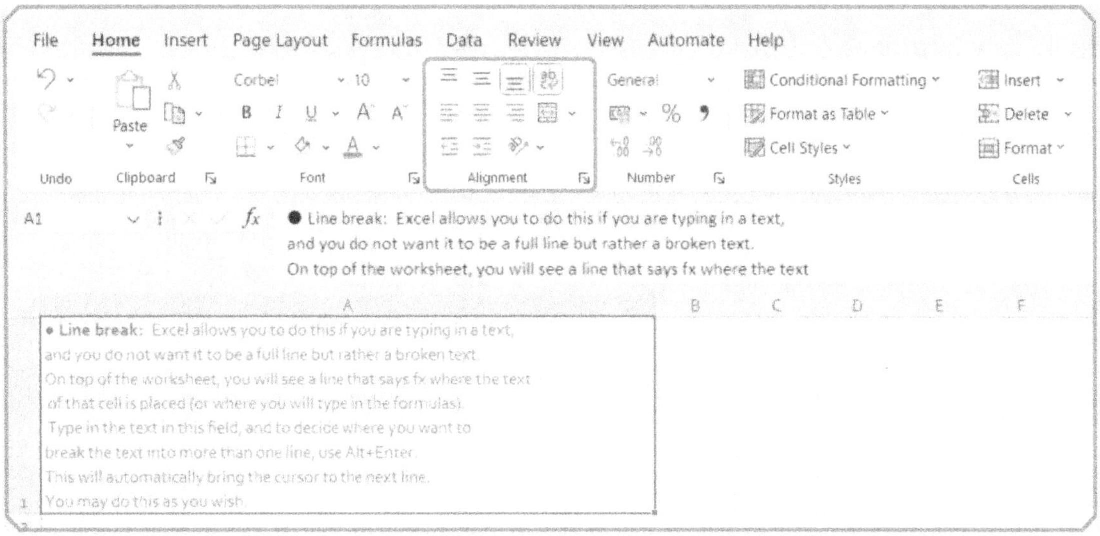

Excel's Formula System: The Engine of Calculation

At the heart of Excel's power lies its **formula system**, which can be accessed in three key ways:

1. Through direct entry in the **formula bar**
2. Via the comprehensive **Function Library** found in the Formulas tab
3. Using the **fx button**, which provides step-by-step guidance for formula creation

The foundation of formula creation revolves around **initialization symbols**. The most commonly used is the **equal sign (=)**, though you can also start formulas with plus (+) or minus (-). However, multiplication (*) and division (/) cannot be used as starting symbols. An important technical detail: When you need to display text that starts with these special characters (+, -, =), simply add an apostrophe (') before the text. This **invisible prefix** tells Excel to treat the entry as text rather than a formula. The apostrophe won't appear in printed documents, maintaining clean output.

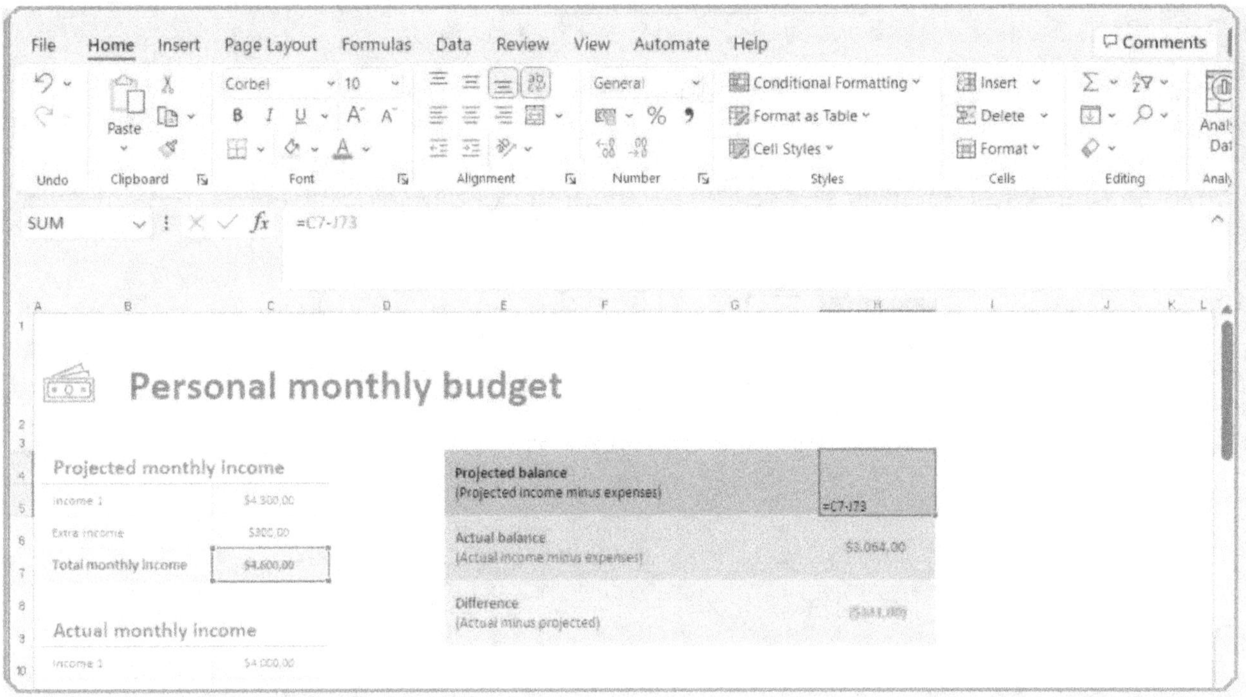

Direct Calculations are a powerful feature of Excel's formula system. You can perform immediate calculations like =5+7+9 without referencing cells, making Excel useful for quick computations. This functionality essentially turns your spreadsheet into an advanced calculator when needed.

While Excel provides an extensive **built-in function library**, the real power comes from combining these functions with custom formulas. This flexibility allows you to create **specialized solutions** for unique business challenges. For instance, you might combine mathematical functions with logical operators to create complex decision-making formulas.

The true value of Excel formulas extends beyond basic arithmetic. They enable you to create **dynamic worksheets** that automatically update when data changes.

AutoSum: Quick Calculations Made Simple

Excel's AutoSum functionality offers immediate access to five core functions: sum, average, count number, maximum, and minimum. You can find this feature conveniently placed in both the **Home and Formulas tabs**, making data analysis more efficient.

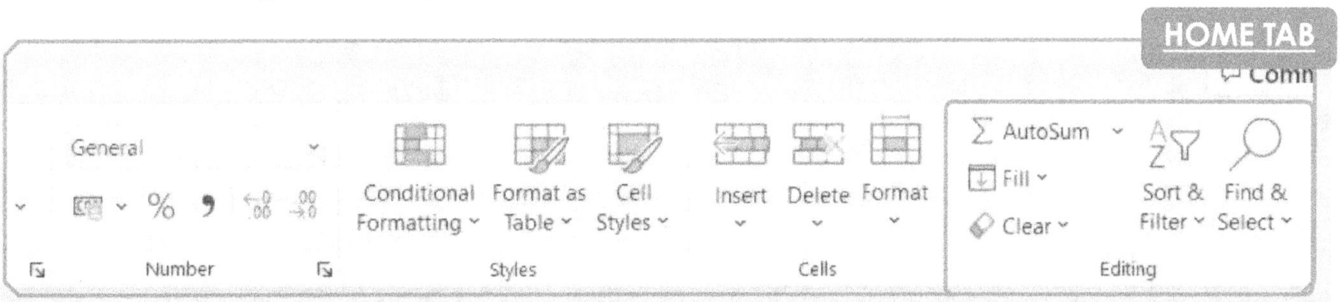

Let's examine these functions using this dataset: 6, 15, 1, 27, 9, 3, 65, 87, 41, 2, 7 (located in cells B1 through B11).

SUM Function

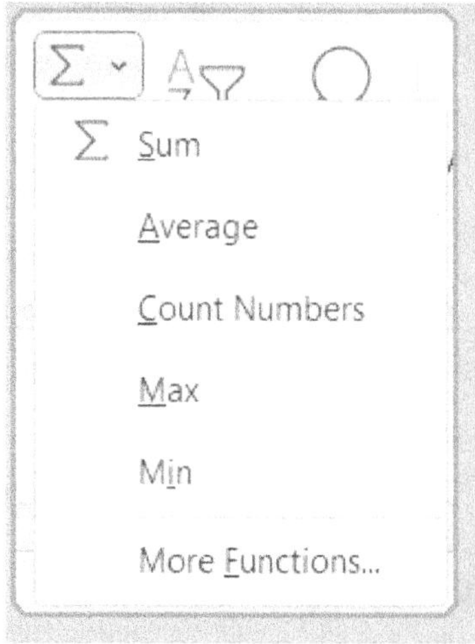

SUM: Totals all selected values. Start by choosing the cell for your result and select the AutoSum icon's Sum option. When your chosen cell is right below the numbers (cell B12), Excel automatically selects the range above (B1-B11). If automatic selection doesn't occur, you can manually select the range.

The formula bar will display: **=sum(B1:B11)**. Excel then calculates the total of all values from B1 through B11. After pressing enter, your result appears: 263. For greater flexibility, you can also sum non-adjacent ranges by holding the CTRL key while selecting multiple ranges, or use SUM with multiple arguments like =SUM(B1:B11,D1:D11). The SUM function automatically ignores text and logical values in the selected range, making it robust for mixed data.

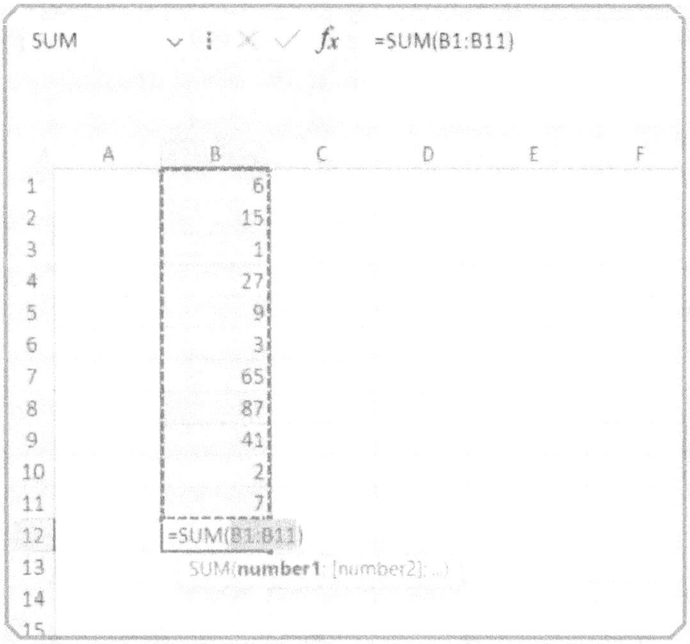

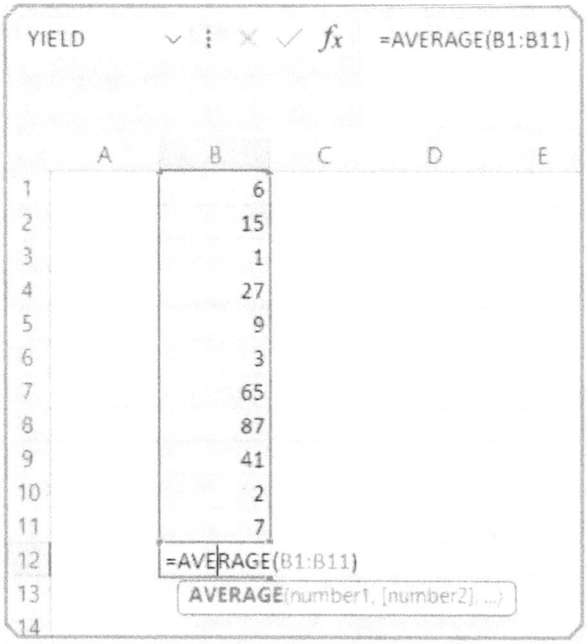

AVERAGE Function

AVERAGE: Determines the arithmetic mean. This function follows similar selection rules as the sum function. The formula displayed will be: **=average(B1:B11)**. Excel then processes the average of all numbers from cells B1 through B11. After pressing Enter, you'll see the result: 23.90909.

The AVERAGE function has some important nuances: it ignores empty cells and text values but counts zero values in its calculation. For more specific needs, you might consider AVERAGEIF to average numbers meeting certain criteria, or AVERAGEA if you want to include logical values (TRUE=1, FALSE=0) in your average. You can also combine AVERAGE with other functions - for example, =AVERAGE(B1:B11)/2 would give you half of the average value.

> ***Productivity Tip:*** *You can adjust how many decimal places appear by using the Increase Decimal and Decrease Decimal options in the Home tab's Number section. This changes only the display format, not the actual calculated value.*

COUNT NUMBER Function

Count number: This function specifically counts cells containing numbers within your selected range. Using **=count(B1:B11)** gives us 11 in this case. It's important to note that COUNT only includes cells with numerical values - it ignores text, logical values (TRUE/FALSE), and empty cells. For more comprehensive counting, you might consider:

- **COUNTA:** counts cells that aren't empty
- **COUNTBLANK:** counts empty cells
- **COUNTIF:** counts cells meeting specific criteria

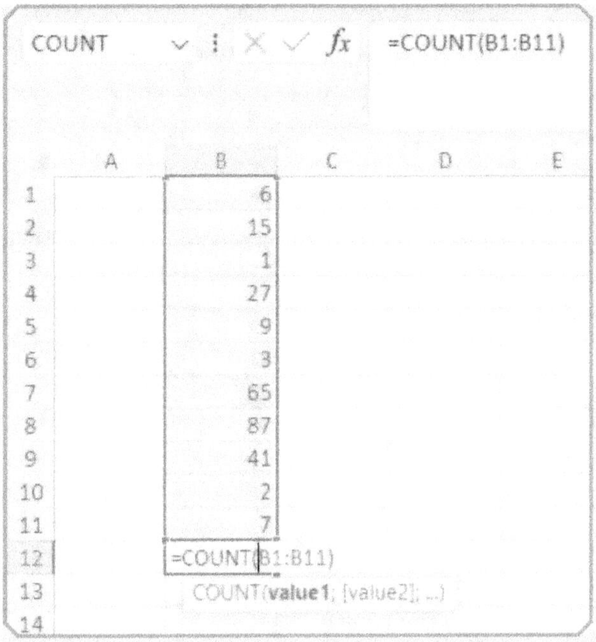

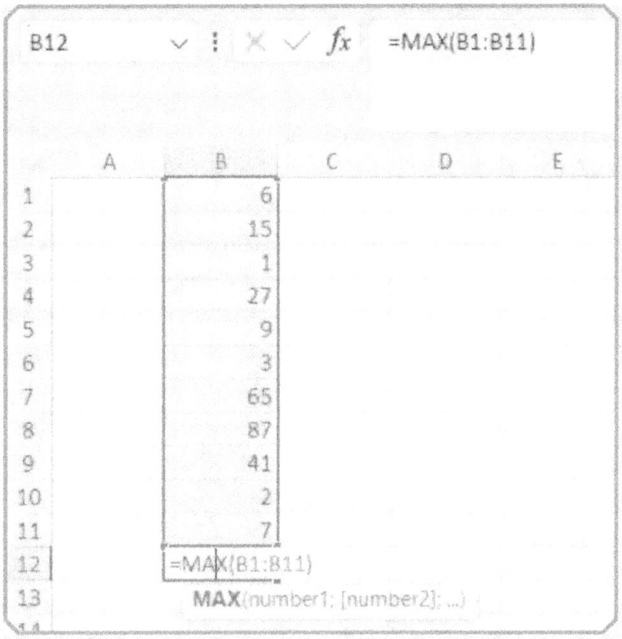

MAXIMUM Function

Maximum: Using **=max(B1:B11),** Excel finds the highest value (87) in your range. The MAX function is particularly useful for:

- Finding peak values in time series data
- Identifying top performances in datasets
- Setting upper boundaries for data validation Note that MAX ignores text values but will evaluate logical values (TRUE=1, FALSE=0).

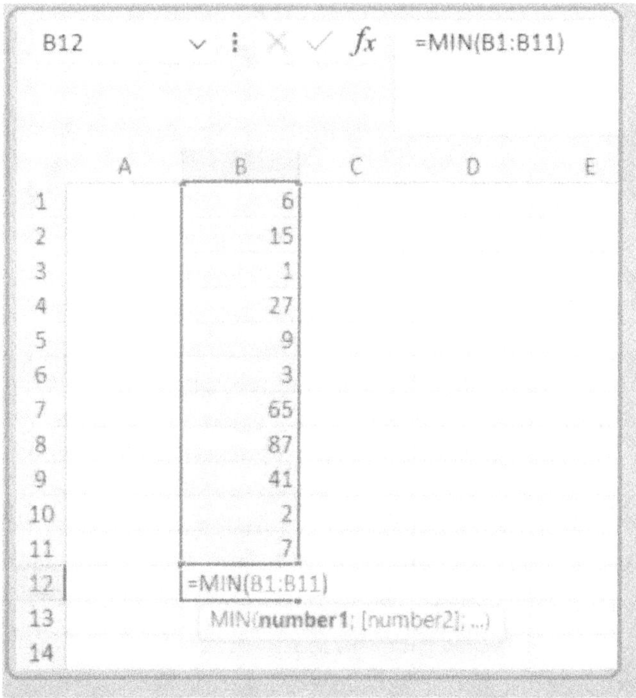

MINIMUM Function

Minimum: With =min(B1:B11), we find the lowest value (1) in the range. Like MAX, MIN ignores text but includes logical values. Common applications:

- Finding lowest prices or scores
- Establishing baseline values
- Setting lower boundaries for data validation

Pro Tips for Advanced Usage:
Excel's formulas can handle multiple data sets simultaneously. While our examples used a single range (B1:B11), you can easily expand this to include additional data by:

1. *Holding the Ctrl key (Command on Mac) while selecting non-adjacent ranges*
2. *Using commas to separate ranges in formulas: =MAX(B1:B11,D7:D13)*
3. *Avoiding spaces within formulas to prevent syntax errors*

For optimal performance:

- Use absolute references ($) when your formula needs to maintain specific cell references during copying
- Consider using named ranges for frequently accessed data sets
- Combine these functions with logical operators (IF, AND, OR) for more sophisticated analysis

Financial Formulas

Excel functions as a vital financial analysis platform, used extensively by corporations and individuals to track and evaluate financial data. The program includes a comprehensive set of financial formulas designed for various types of monetary calculations and forecasting.

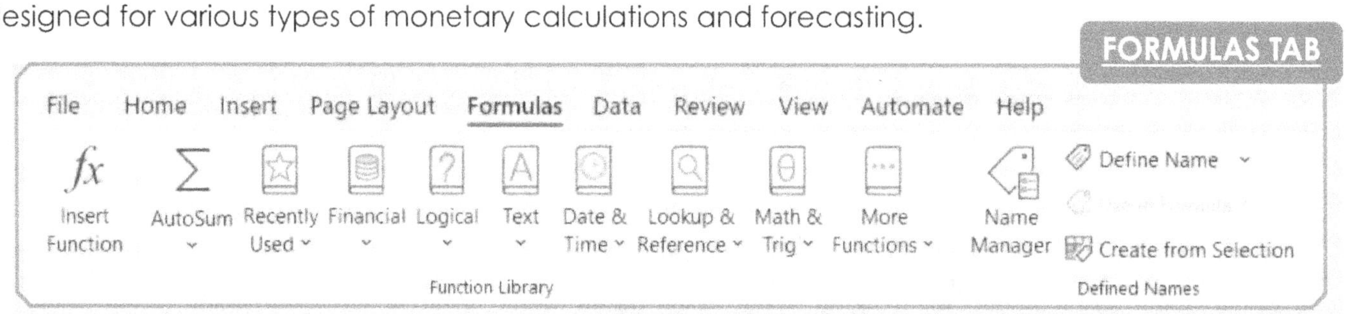

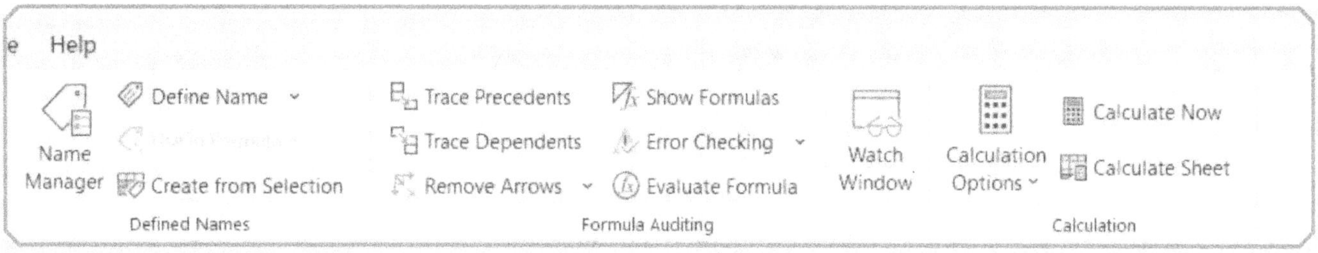

This section examines five fundamental financial formulas available in Excel. These tools are vital for activities like budget management, investment evaluation, and monetary planning.

For users requiring additional financial functions, Excel's Formulas tab features a dedicated Financial button. This opens access to numerous specialized financial formulas, enabling users to conduct detailed financial analysis specific to their requirements.

Whether you're running a business and monitoring cash movement, evaluating investment opportunities, or handling household finances, understanding these Excel financial functions can greatly improve your money management decisions. Let's explore these essential financial calculation tools that Excel provides.

YIELD Function

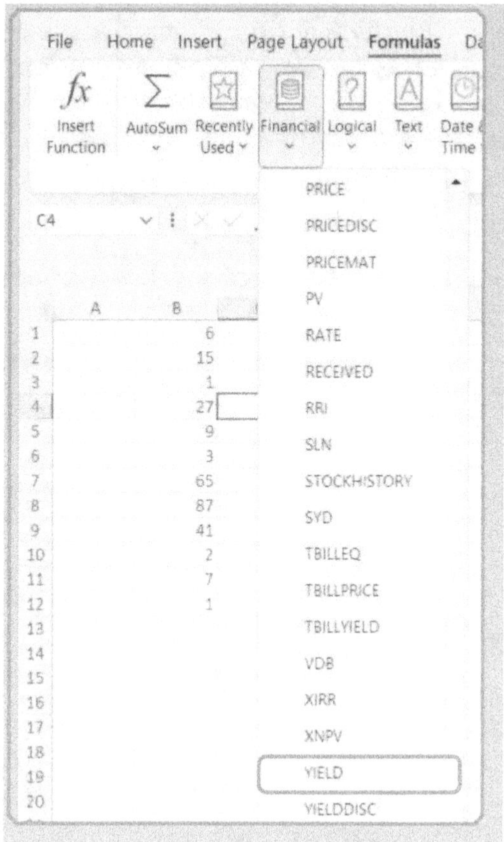

YIELD: The YIELD function within Excel determines investment returns across defined time periods, handling both regular and one-time payments. Here's a detailed component breakdown:

- **Settlement date**: Input as a serial date number (e.g., 44,566 for 05/01/2022).
- **Maturity date**: Also entered as a serial date (e.g., 45,299 for 08/01/2024).
- **Annual coupon rate**: Expressed as a decimal (e.g., 0.06 for 6%).
- **Pr (Price)**: The security's price per $100 face value (e.g., $105).
- **Redemption value**: Per $100 face value (e.g., $140).
- **Frequency**: Payment periodicity (e.g., 2 for semiannual).
- **Basis**: Day count basis (e.g., 3).

First enter the settlement date as an Excel serial number - January 5, 2022 becomes 44,566.

Next input the maturity date, also as a serial number - August 1, 2024 becomes 45,299. Then enter the yearly coupon rate as a decimal - 0.06 represents 6%.

The formula requires the security's $100 face value price, which in this example is $105.

Input the redemption value per $100 face value next - we're using $140. Then specify payment frequency, with 2 indicating twice-yearly payments.

Finally, enter the day count basis number, here we use 3. Properly entering these elements allows accurate yield calculation using Excel's YIELD function.

This calculation produces a 20% yield. The complete formula appears as:

=YIELD(44566,45299,0.06,105,140,2,3)

Alternatively, organize your data in a table format:

	K	L
14	*Settlement date:*	05/01/2022
15	*Maturity date:*	08/01/2024
16	*Rate of interest:*	6%
17	*Price per $100 FV:*	105
18	*Redemption value:*	140
19	*Payment terms*	Semi-annual

Your formula would then be: **=YIELD(L14,L15,L16,L17,L18,2,3)**

> **Productivity Tip:** *Watch for error messages like '#NUM!' or '#VALUE!' when using this formula. A '#VALUE!' error typically indicates non-numeric inputs or invalid dates. A '#NUM!' error might mean the settlement date exceeds the maturity date or invalid numeric inputs. These errors help identify where formula inputs need adjustment.*

PRICE Function

Price: Here's an alternative scenario where we flip our previous calculation: instead of finding yield,

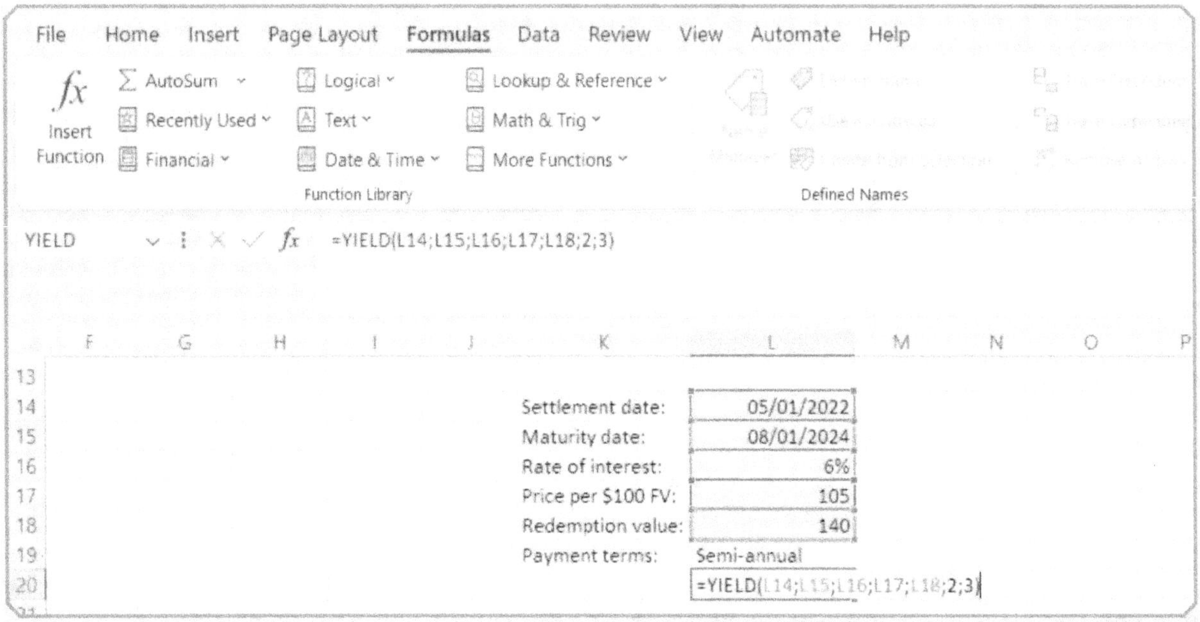

we'll determine a security's price when we know the yield rate. Excel's PRICE function handles this calculation elegantly. We'll use identical values from our last example, but we'll plug in the yield where we previously used price. Here's how the formula looks:

=PRICE(44566,45299,0.06,0.2,140,2,3)

When we run this calculation, we get $105 as our result - perfectly matching the price we used in our yield example, which confirms our calculations are working correctly. Just as before, we can set up a clear reference table to organize our inputs. Our table structure stays largely the same, but switches out the price entry for yield:

	K	L
14	*Settlement date:*	05/01/2022
15	*Maturity date:*	08/01/2024
16	*Rate of interest:*	6%
17	*Yield:*	20%
18	*Redemption value:*	140
19	*Payment terms*	Semi-annual

Using this organized table approach, our formula transforms to:

=PRICE(L14,L15,L16,L17,L18,2,3)

This structured method makes it simpler to track our inputs and adjust them as needed for different scenarios.

RATE Function

Rate: The RATE function in Excel proves invaluable when determining the interest rate for a potential loan. This formula requires several key inputs. First, you need the Nper, which represents the total number of payment periods. For a two-year loan, this would be 24 months.

Next is the Pmt, the fixed monthly payment, entered as a negative number. In our example, it's -$351. The Pv represents the principal amount of the loan, which in this case is $6,000. The Fv, or future value, is typically used for investments rather than loans, so we'll use 0. The Type specifies whether payments are made at the beginning (1) or end (0) of the period. For loans, we'll use 0. Lastly, the Guess is an initial estimate of the interest rate, expressed as a decimal. We'll use 0.1 (10%).

The complete formula looks like this:

=RATE(24,-351,6000,0,0,0.1)

This calculation yields a 3% result, representing the monthly interest rate. For better organization, you can arrange this information in an Excel table using columns K and L. Column K would list the parameters: Payment, Loan amount, Monthly payment, Number of months, and Payments per year. Column L would contain the corresponding values: Monthly, 6,000, 351, 24, and 12. Using cell references, the formula becomes:

	K	L
10	*Payment:*	Monthly
11	*Loan amount:*	6,000
12	*Monthly payment:*	351
13	*Number of months:*	24
14	*Payments per year:*	12

=RATE(L13,-L12,L11,0,0,0.1)

This structured approach enables quick adjustments to loan parameters, making it efficient to calculate interest rates across various scenarios.

NOMINAL Function

Nominal: The NOMINAL function in Excel serves as an efficient tool for determining the annual nominal interest rate in financial calculations. This straightforward formula requires just two essential inputs to produce its result. Let's break down the required inputs:

- **Effect_rate:** This represents your effective annual interest rate. In our case, we're using 16% (input as 0.16). This percentage accounts for the actual yearly interest rate when considering compounding effects.
- **Npery:** This indicates how many times interest compounds per year. Using 12 indicates monthly compounding over a year's period.

Putting these elements together, our formula appears as:

=NOMINAL(0.16, 12)

Running this calculation provides a 15% result - our annual nominal interest rate. This outcome makes sense because nominal rates (15%) are typically lower than effective rates (16%), as they don't factor in compounding effects. This calculation helps differentiate between stated interest rates (nominal) and actual rates when accounting for compounding effects (effective).

VDB Function

Variable Declining Balance (VDB): This advanced formula enables precise calculation of asset depreciation across time periods. Let's explore how to utilize it for calculating a car's daily depreciation rate.

The formula requires several crucial inputs. Start with the asset's initial cost - in this example, a car valued at $15,000. Then determine the salvage value, which represents the estimated worth after a specific period - here we're using $13,000 after one year.

For the asset's lifespan, we're setting 10 years as our timeline. Since we're calculating daily depreciation, we convert this to days (multiplying by 365). The formula uses 0 as the start period (purchase date) and 1 as the end period (measuring one day's depreciation). The decline rate factor can remain at 1 if not specified otherwise. Combining these elements, our VDB formula appears as:

=VDB(15000,13000,10*365,0,1)

Excel calculates this to $8.22 - representing the daily depreciation rate for the vehicle from its purchase date.

For better data organization, structure a table like this:

	K	L
10	*Initial cost:*	15.000
11	*Salvage:*	13.000
12	*Life:*	10 years

The formula using table references becomes:

=VDB(L10,L11,L12*365,0,1)

This structured approach allows quick modifications to variables, facilitating depreciation calculations across different scenarios and assets.

Logical Formulas

Logical formulas in Excel serve as sophisticated tools for merging multiple conditions and calculations. These functions enable users to execute complex logical operations efficiently, eliminating the need for multiple separate formulas distributed across different cells. Let's explore these powerful capabilities:

AND Function: Comprehensive Multi-Condition Testing

AND: The AND formula functions as a conditional connector, joining two or more logical tests. This function evaluates whether all specified conditions meet the true criteria. It only returns TRUE when every single condition within the function evaluates as true. If even one condition proves false, the entire function outputs FALSE. Consider these illustrative examples:

> **=AND(1>2, 2>1)** This outputs FALSE because while the second condition (2>1) is true, the first condition (1>2) is false. When any single condition fails, the entire function returns FALSE.
>
> **=AND(3>2, 2>1)** This returns TRUE because both conditions evaluate as true: 3 is indeed greater than 2, and 2 is greater than 1.

The AND function's versatility extends beyond simple two-condition tests:

=AND(A1>10, B1<20, C1=15) This more complex example returns TRUE only when all three conditions are simultaneously satisfied: A1 must exceed 10, B1 must be less than 20, and C1 must equal exactly 15.

You can construct conditions using either direct numerical comparisons or cell references:

=AND(A1>B1, C1=D1) This formula evaluates whether A1 exceeds B1's value AND if C1's value matches D1's value. This flexibility in referencing makes the AND function particularly powerful for dynamic spreadsheet analysis.

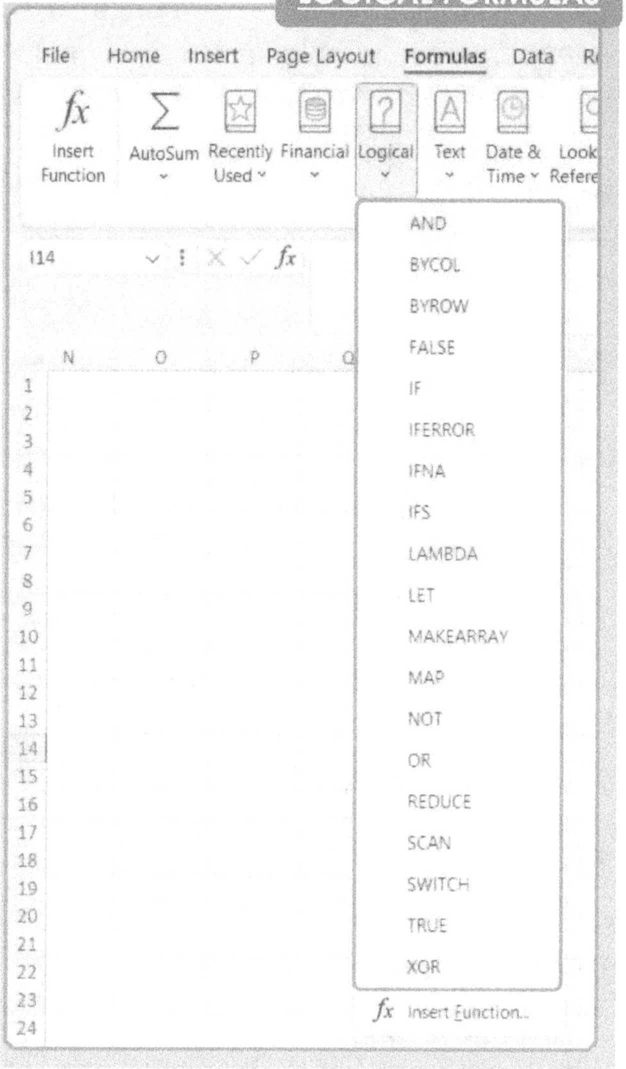

OR Function: Versatile Logical Testing

OR: represents another essential logical operator that shares similarities with AND, but operates with a fundamentally different evaluation approach. Let's delve into its detailed functionality.

OR evaluates multiple conditions and returns TRUE when at least one condition proves true, only returning FALSE when every single condition fails. This makes it particularly useful for testing multiple acceptable scenarios.

Let's examine some practical applications:

=OR(1>2, 2>1) Returns TRUE because while the first condition fails (1>2 is false), the second condition succeeds (2>1 is true). The presence of just one true condition satisfies the OR function.

=OR(1>2, 3<2) Outputs FALSE since both conditions evaluate to false - neither 1 is greater than 2, nor is 3 less than 2. OR requires at least one true condition to return TRUE.

For more complex scenarios:

=OR(A1>10, B1<20, C1=15) This formula returns TRUE if any of these conditions are met: A1 exceeds 10, or B1 falls below 20, or C1 equals exactly 15.

The function accepts both direct text comparisons and cell references:

=OR(A1="Yes", B1="Maybe", C1="Possibly") Returns TRUE if any referenced cell contains the specified text values.

Advanced usage allows combination with other logical functions:

=OR(AND(A1>0, A1<10), AND(B1>0, B1<10)) This nested formula checks if either A1 or B1 falls within the range 0-10, demonstrating OR's capability to work with complex logical structures.

IFERROR Function: Advanced Error Management

IFERROR: serves as an essential error management tool, significantly enhancing spreadsheet clarity and functionality. Let's explore its comprehensive capabilities:

IFERROR performs dual functions: it evaluates expressions while providing customized responses for error situations. When encountering an error, it returns your specified alternative value; otherwise, it displays the original calculation result. Basic structure:

=IFERROR(value, value_if_error)

Practical examples:

> **=IFERROR**(12/0, "incorrect") Outputs "incorrect" since dividing by zero generates a #DIV/0! error.
>
> **=IFERROR**(L15, "incorrect") If L15 contains an error-producing formula, returns "incorrect". Otherwise, displays L15's actual value.

The function addresses multiple error types:

- **#DIV/0!** (zero division errors)
- **#N/A** (missing value errors)
- **#NAME?** (unrecognized formula errors)
- **#NULL!** (invalid reference errors)
- **#NUM!** (invalid numeric errors)
- **#REF!** (broken reference errors)
- **#VALUE!** (incorrect argument type errors)

Common applications include:

1. Visual enhancement by replacing errors with empty cells: =IFERROR(formula,"")
2. User-friendly error messaging: =IFERROR(VLOOKUP(A1, B:C, 2, FALSE), "Not found")
3. Fallback calculations: =IFERROR(1/A1, 0)

> ***Productivity Tip**: Text error values require quotation marks, while numeric values or cell references don't. This distinction ensures proper error value formatting and function execution.*

COUNTIF Function: Counting with Criteria

COUNTIF serves as a tool for analyzing datasets by counting specific value occurrences within a defined range. Here's a comprehensive breakdown:

Basic syntax: =COUNTIF(range, criteria)

Example Analysis:

=COUNTIF(B4:B17,1)

- **Range:** B4:B17 contains the sequence: 6, 15, 1, 27, 9, 1, 3, 65, 87, 1, 41, 2, and 7
- **Criteria:** Counting occurrences of 1
- **Result:** Returns 3 (as 1 appears three times)

Essential COUNTIF Features:

1. **Versatile Value Support**
   - Handles numbers, text strings, and logical values (TRUE/FALSE)
   - Text requires quotation marks: **=COUNTIF(A1:A10, "Apple")**
   - Supports wildcards for text patterns: **=COUNTIF(A1:A10, "A*")** counts all "A" starters

2. **Advanced Criteria Options**
   - Accepts comparison operators: **=COUNTIF(B4:B17, ">10")** for numbers exceeding 10
   - Allows cell references as criteria: **=COUNTIF(B4:B17, D1)**
   - Performs case-insensitive text matching

The function excels at processing large datasets, automating what would be tedious manual counting tasks. It's particularly valuable in data analysis projects requiring precise frequency counts of specific values or conditions.

IF Function: Making Logical Decisions

The IF function stands as one of Excel's most essential and frequently used logical tools. It enables automated decision-making within spreadsheets based on specified conditions. Let's examine its functionality through clear examples.

Core IF Components: The function consists of three critical elements:

1. Logical test (evaluates true/false conditions)
2. Result for true condition
3. Result for false condition

=IF(logical_test, value_if_true, value_if_false)

Practical Examples:

Example 1: =IF(1>2, "CORRECT", "RECALCULATE")

Function Analysis:

- Excel evaluates whether 1 exceeds 2
- Finding this false, returns "RECALCULATE"

Example 2: =IF(2>1, "CORRECT", "RECALCULATE")

Function Analysis:

- Excel evaluates whether 2 exceeds 1
- Finding this true, returns "CORRECT"

Productivity Tip: *The function accepts cell references for dynamic comparisons: =IF(A1>B1, "A1 is bigger", "B1 is bigger or equal") This allows for flexible, reusable logical tests across your spreadsheet.*

Understanding Excel Cell References:

Cell references in Excel behave dynamically when copying formulas. Understanding the distinction between different reference types is crucial for effective spreadsheet manipulation. Let's explore these essential concepts in detail.

Reference Types Explained

1. **Relative References** (A1, B2) automatically adjust when copied throughout your spreadsheet. These references change relative to their new position and represent the most commonly used reference type in everyday Excel work.

2. **Absolute References** ($A$1, $B$2) remain fixed when copied to new locations. They maintain the exact same cell location regardless of where you paste the formula, making them essential for consistent calculations across your worksheet.

3. **Mixed References** ($A1 or A$1) serve as partially fixed references where either the column or row remains constant while the other changes. These prove particularly useful in complex calculation scenarios requiring selective reference locking.

Practical Example:

Consider **=SUM(A1:A7) placed in cell B1.**

Without dollar signs, copying this formula down to B2:B5 changes the references progressively. In B2, it becomes =SUM(A2:A8), in B3 it shifts to =SUM(A3:A9), and so forth. However, with dollar signs (=SUM($A$1:$A$7)), the formula remains identical in all cells, maintaining its original reference points.

Quick Implementation Guide: Start by entering your formula normally. Then select the reference you want to lock and use the F4 key to cycle through different reference options: $A$1 for fully absolute, A$1 for relative column with absolute row, $A1 for absolute column with relative row, and A1 for fully relative references.

> ***Productivity Tip**: Mastering these reference types enhances formula flexibility and power significantly. Regular practice with different scenarios will improve your Excel proficiency and enable you to create more sophisticated spreadsheet solutions.*

Text Formulas

CLEAN Function

The CLEAN function serves as an essential data cleanup tool in Excel, specifically designed to eliminate non-printable characters that often infiltrate text when copying from external sources. Let's examine its functionality and practical applications.

The basic syntax is straightforward: **=CLEAN(text)**

Consider this practical scenario: If cell A1 contains "Hello World" with unwanted hidden characters (like line breaks or control characters), applying **=CLEAN(A1)** produces "Hello World" with all those invisible, non-printable characters removed, resulting in clean, usable text.

Important technical note: The CLEAN function preserves visible spaces in your text. However, if you need to remove all spaces, including the visible ones, you can combine CLEAN with the SUBSTITUTE function: **=SUBSTITUTE(CLEAN(A1), " ", "")**

This powerful combination first removes non-printable characters (CLEAN), then eliminates all spaces (SUBSTITUTE), delivering completely stripped text.

Productivity Tip: *Before applying the CLEAN function to your working data, always test it on a duplicate dataset to ensure it produces your desired results. This precautionary step helps prevent unintended data loss or alterations.*

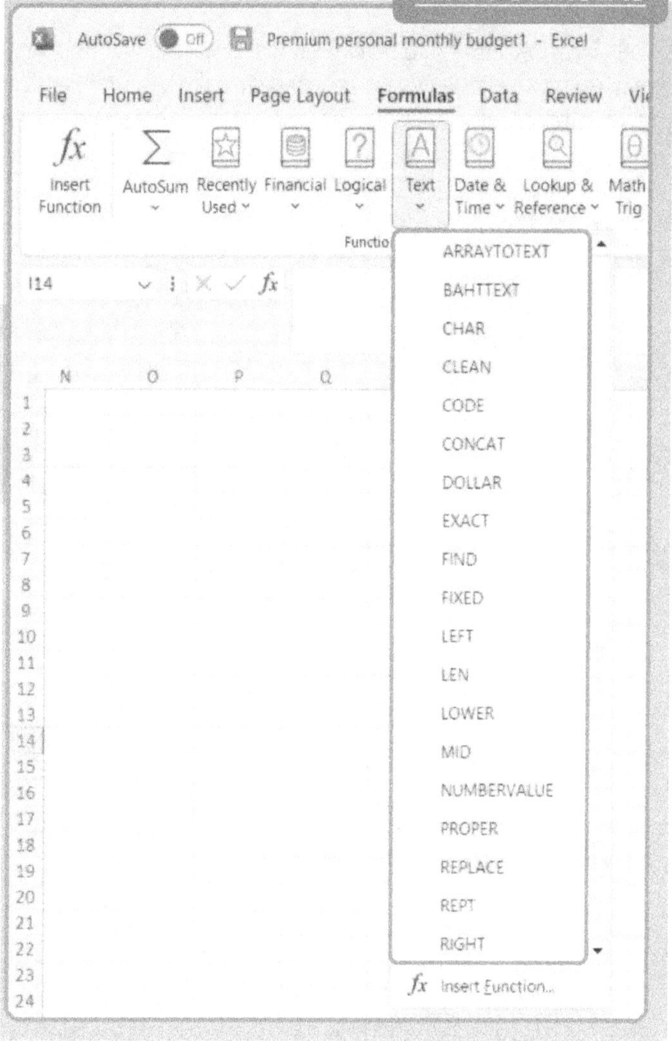

CONCATENATE Function

The CONCATENATE function in Excel serves as a powerful text combination tool, enabling users to merge text from various cells or strings into a unified output. Its versatility makes it essential for data consolidation and custom text string creation.

Basic Formula Structure:

=CONCATENATE(text1, [text2], ...)

Required and Optional Elements: text1 is mandatory and accepts text, cell references, or text-producing formulas [text2] and subsequent elements are optional additional components

Practical Applications:

- **Basic Number Joining:** With numbers in cells C4=1, C7=2, C11=3: **=CONCATENATE(C4,C7,C11)** produces "123"
- **Simple Word Combination: =CONCATENATE("CAR","DRIVE","ROAD")** creates "CARDRIVEROAD"
- **Enhanced Readability with Spacing: =CONCATENATE("CAR ", "DRIVE. ", "ROAD!")** yields "CAR DRIVE. ROAD!"
- **Mixed Reference Formatting:** With A1="Excel" and B1="fun": **=CONCATENATE("Learning ", A1, " is ", B1, "!")** produces "Learning Excel is fun!"

Productivity Tips: *Include spaces within quotation marks for word separation Utilize for custom data combinations like name formatting or email address creation Modern Excel versions support the & operator as an alternative:* ***="CAR " & "DRIVE " & "ROAD"*** *equals* ***=CONCATENATE("CAR ", "DRIVE ", "ROAD")***

REPLACE Function

The REPLACE function enables precise text modification by substituting specified characters. This powerful function proves especially valuable when dealing with large datasets that require systematic text alterations, whether for standardization, error correction, or format consistency. Here's a comprehensive breakdown:

Essential Components:

1. **"old_text"** - your starting text sequence
2. **"start_num"** - the position to begin replacement
3. **"num_chars"** - the count of characters to replace
4. **"new_text"** - your replacement content

Basic Formula Structure: =REPLACE(old_text, start_num, num_chars, new_text)

Example Implementation: =REPLACE(FALSE,5,1,3) Result: 'FALS3'

The versatility of REPLACE becomes particularly evident in real-world scenarios. Consider a dataset containing product codes where you need to update a specific character position across thousands of entries. Instead of manual editing, which would be time-consuming and error-prone, REPLACE can automatically perform these modifications with perfect consistency. For instance, you might need to change the third character of every product code from a letter to a number, or update date formats from European to American style across an entire spreadsheet.

Advanced Applications:

- Batch processing of serial numbers
- Standardizing data formats
- Correcting common typos automatically
- Modifying date formats across datasets

SEARCH Function

The SEARCH function locates specific text patterns within larger strings, offering flexible search capabilities. Unlike its counterpart FIND, SEARCH provides case-insensitive searching, making it ideal for general text analysis where letter case shouldn't affect results. The function returns a numeric position that can be used in other formulas for further text manipulation.

Core Formula Structure: =SEARCH(find_text, within_text, [start_num])

Key Components:

- **find_text:** target search pattern
- **within_text:** text to search within
- **start_num:** optional starting position (defaults to 1)

Practical Example: =SEARCH("A","THECARISDRIVINGDOWNTHEROAD",1)

Returns: 5 (first 'A' position)

One of the most powerful aspects of SEARCH is its ability to work with wildcards, making it incredibly versatile for complex text analysis. For example, you can use "?" to match any single character or "*" to match multiple characters. This becomes particularly valuable when dealing with inconsistent data formats or when searching for patterns rather than exact matches. Additionally, SEARCH can be combined with other text functions like LEFT, RIGHT, or MID to extract specific portions of text based on the search results, creating sophisticated text parsing solutions.

Enhanced Applications:

- Pattern matching in large datasets
- Text validation processes
- Automated data extraction
- Building dynamic text analysis systems
- Creating conditional formatting rules based on text content
- Combining with other functions for complex text operations

Both functions support wildcards (* and ?) for more flexible text manipulation and can be nested within other formulas for advanced operations.

FIND Function

The FIND function in Excel operates similarly to SEARCH but with a crucial distinction: it respects letter case in its search operations. This case-sensitivity makes FIND an essential tool for precise text matching and analysis where letter case carries significant meaning.

Formula Structure: =FIND(find_text, within_text, [start_num])

Core Components:

- **find_text:** your exact search target
- **within_text:** text to analyze
- **start_num:** optional search starting point (begins at 1 if not specified)

Consider these contrasting examples:

=FIND("A","THECARISDRIVINGDOWNTHEROAD",1)

Returns: 5 (uppercase 'A' found at position 5)

=FIND("a","THECARISDRIVINGDOWNTHEROAD",1)

Returns: #VALUE! (no lowercase 'a' present)

Advanced Usage:

The FIND function can be combined with other text functions for powerful text manipulation:

- Use with LEFT: **=LEFT(text,FIND("-",text)-1)** to extract text before a hyphen
- Combine with RIGHT: **=RIGHT(text,LEN(text)-FIND("@",text))** to get text after an @ symbol
- Nest within MID: **=MID(text,FIND(":",text)+1,FIND("/",text)-FIND(":",text)-1)** to extract text between specific characters

Error Handling:

- #VALUE! appears when the searched text isn't found
- Consider using IFERROR with FIND to handle missing matches gracefully
- Use nested IFs with FIND for complex conditional text processing

FIND proves particularly valuable in specialized scenarios where case precision matters, such as:

- Verifying programming variables
- Checking database identifiers
- Validating case-sensitive passwords
- Processing alphanumeric serial numbers
- Analyzing scientific nomenclature
- Working with multilingual text where case affects meaning

This precision makes FIND the preferred choice over SEARCH when exact case matching is required for data integrity and accuracy.

Date and Time Formulas

Excel's date and time formulas transcend simple manual date entry, revealing their true power when managing chronological data across structured spreadsheets. These functions enable dynamic, self-updating calculations that eliminate the need for constant manual adjustments, transforming static spreadsheets into living documents that maintain their relevance automatically.

DATE Function: Precision Date Construction

The DATE function serves as a foundational tool for creating and manipulating dates in Excel. Its structure follows a logical pattern that mirrors how we naturally think about dates:

The fundamental syntax reads: **=DATE(YEAR, MONTH, DAY)**

This function truly shines when working with segregated date components. Consider a database where date information is split across different columns for organizational purposes. If column B contains years, C holds months, and D stores days, you can unify this information with:

=DATE(B5,C5,D5)

The beauty of this approach lies in its flexibility. When applied to multiple rows, the formula intelligently adjusts its references, maintaining proper date construction throughout your dataset. The resulting dates appear in Excel's standard format, which you can then customize to match your documentation requirements.

TODAY Function: Automatic Date Management

The TODAY function exemplifies elegant simplicity in Excel's date management arsenal. With a remarkably straightforward syntax: **=TODAY()**

This powerful function maintains perpetual relevance by automatically updating whenever you open your workbook. This self-updating capability proves invaluable in numerous scenarios:

- Creating daily reports that always show the current date
- Tracking document access timestamps
- Calculating relative dates (like days elapsed or remaining)
- Generating dynamic date-based calculations

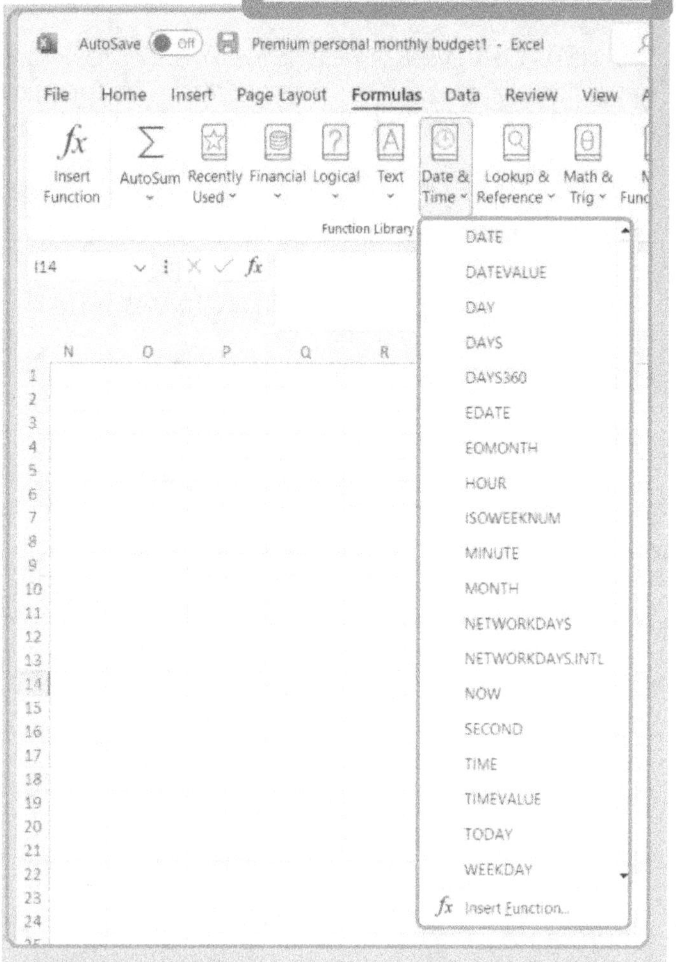

When combined with other Excel functions, TODAY becomes even more powerful. For example, you can create automated aging reports, deadline trackers, or schedule management tools that stay current without manual intervention. The function's output readily accepts formatting modifications, allowing you to present dates in whatever style best serves your needs.

TIME Function: Precise Time Management in Excel

The TIME function allows you to work with time values in Excel with the same precision and flexibility that the DATE function provides for calendar dates. Let me explain how this powerful function operates and its practical applications.

The basic structure follows a logical sequence:

=TIME(HOUR,MINUTE,SECOND)

Think of this function as creating a digital clock display within your spreadsheet. Just as a clock shows hours, minutes, and seconds in sequence, the TIME function takes these three components and combines them into a single, formatted time value.

When working with data spread across different cells, you can reference those cells directly in your formula. For example, if cell A1 contains hours, B1 contains minutes, and C1 contains seconds, you would write:

=TIME(A1,B1,C1)

One crucial aspect that often trips up new users is cell formatting. You might have entered the correct formula, but the time won't display properly unless the cell is formatted correctly. Here's why this matters: Excel stores times as decimal numbers behind the scenes, but we need to see them in a human-readable format. To achieve this, you'll need to format your cells specifically for time display through the Number section in the Home tab.

The relationship between DATE and TIME functions is worth noting. Both functions follow similar logical patterns: DATE works with year/month/day while TIME handles hour/minute/second. This parallel structure makes it easier to master both functions once you understand one of them. You can even combine them for complete datetime functionality in your spreadsheets.

NETWORKDAYS Function: Calculating Business Days with Precision

The NETWORKDAYS function in Excel serves as a sophisticated tool for determining the exact number of working days between two dates. This function goes beyond simple date subtraction by intelligently accounting for weekends and optional holidays, making it invaluable for business planning and calculations.

Let's examine its structure::

=NETWORKDAYS(START_DATE, END_DATE, [HOLIDAYS])

Key components:

- **START_DATE:** The beginning of your period
- **END_DATE:** The end of your period
- **[HOLIDAYS]:** Optional; a range of dates to exclude as holidays

Think of NETWORKDAYS as your automated calendar assistant. Just as you might manually count working days on a calendar, skipping weekends and holidays, this function performs the same task instantly and without error. Excel handles this by using its internal date system, where each date is represented by a unique serial number, ensuring accurate calculations.

For example, if you wanted to calculate working days between January 1st and January 31st, excluding company holidays on January 15th and 16th, your formula might look like this:

=NETWORKDAYS("1/1/2024", "1/31/2024", A1:A2)

where A1:A2 contains your holiday dates.

This function proves particularly valuable in several business scenarios:

- Project timeline planning, accounting for realistic work periods
- Payroll calculations, ensuring accurate working day counts
- Delivery date estimations, considering only business days
- Contract duration calculations, excluding non-working periods
- Employee leave tracking, focusing on actual working days affected

Understanding NETWORKDAYS transforms time-based calculations from tedious manual processes into efficient, automated operations, significantly improving accuracy and saving valuable time in business planning and administration.

YEAR Function: A Deep Dive into Date Component Extraction

The YEAR function in Excel represents a powerful yet elegantly simple tool for isolating the year component from dates. Think of it as a specialized lens that focuses solely on the year portion of any date value, filtering out other components like months and days.

The basic structure follows a clean, straightforward syntax:

=YEAR(SERIAL_NUMBER)

When we work with dates in Excel, they're stored internally as serial numbers - whole numbers representing days since January 1, 1900. The YEAR function understands both these serial numbers and regular date formats, making it remarkably versatile. For instance, whether you input "1/15/2024" or its serial number equivalent, YEAR will extract 2024.

Consider this practical example: imagine you have a dataset of sales transactions spanning multiple years. Rather than manually separating this data by year, the YEAR function allows you to instantly extract just the year component. This extracted value becomes a powerful tool for grouping, filtering, and analyzing your data.

The function's applications extend far beyond simple extraction. When combined with other Excel functions, YEAR becomes part of more sophisticated date-based calculations. For example, you might use it to:

- Calculate age from birthdate: **=YEAR(TODAY())-YEAR(birthdate)**
- Group financial data by fiscal year
- Track year-over-year growth trends
- Analyze historical patterns across multiple years
- Create dynamic reports that automatically update based on the current year

Understanding YEAR's functionality opens doors to more efficient data management and analysis, transforming complex date-based calculations into straightforward operations that anyone can perform with confidence.

Reference Formulas

Reference formulas in Excel, particularly VLOOKUP and its related functions, form the backbone of efficient data management in professional settings. While these formulas might initially appear complex, they actually represent intuitive tools designed to streamline data handling and analysis.

Think of reference formulas as Excel's smart search engine - they automatically locate and retrieve information across your spreadsheets, eliminating the need for manual searching and data entry. This automation not only saves time but also significantly reduces the risk of human error in data handling.

HLOOKUP Function: Horizontal Data Search Master

Formula Structure:

=HLOOKUP(lookup_value, table_array, row_index_num, [range_lookup])

LOOKUP & REFERENCE FORMULAS

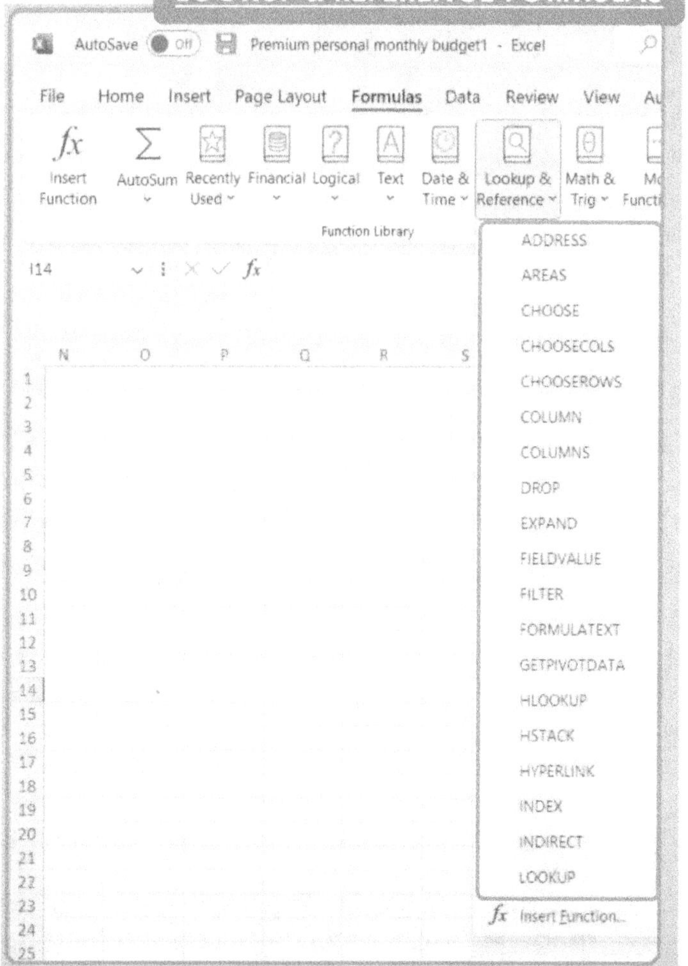

Essential Components:

1. lookup_value: Your search term (e.g., "March")
2. table_array: Your data range (e.g., A1:L10)
3. row_index_num: Target row number (e.g., 3)
4. range_lookup: Match type (TRUE for approximate, FALSE for exact)

How HLOOKUP Works:

- First, the function scans the top row of your specified table range horizontally, searching for your lookup value
- Once it finds a match in the top row, it moves down that same column to the row number you specified
- It then returns the value found at that intersection
- If range_lookup is FALSE, it needs an exact match; if TRUE, it can find the closest match (useful for numerical ranges)

Real-World Application Example: Consider a spreadsheet with months spanning columns A through L in row 1, with corresponding data in rows below. To find March's value in row 3:

=HLOOKUP("March",A1:L10,3,FALSE)

This function excels in scenarios like:

- Monthly performance tracking
- Seasonal data analysis
- Cross-departmental comparisons
- Product specification lookups
- Time-series data retrieval

Understanding HLOOKUP's horizontal search methodology opens new possibilities for data organization and retrieval, particularly when dealing with time-based or category-based information arranged in columns.

VLOOKUP Function: Vertical Data Search Expert

The VLOOKUP function stands as one of Excel's most potent data retrieval tools, operating as a vertical search mechanism to locate and extract information from tables. Unlike its counterpart HLOOKUP, VLOOKUP performs its search down columns rather than across rows.

Formula Structure:

=VLOOKUP(lookup_value, table_array, column_index_num, range_lookup)

Let's dissect each component through a practical example: Consider a spreadsheet listing months in column A (A1:A12). Your VLOOKUP needs:

1. **lookup_value:** Your target search value (e.g., "March")
2. **table_array:** Your data range (e.g., A1:L12)
3. **column_index_num:** The column containing your desired data (e.g., 5 for column E)
4. **range_lookup:** Match precision (TRUE for approximate, FALSE for exact)

Example Formula: **=VLOOKUP("March",A1:L12,5,FALSE)**

This returns 3, identifying March's position.

How VLOOKUP Works:

5. The function starts searching in the leftmost column of your table array
6. Upon finding a match, it moves right to the specified column
7. It retrieves the value from the same row where the match was found
8. The range_lookup parameter determines match precision

Practical Applications:

- Student grade tracking across subjects
- Employee information retrieval
- Inventory management
- Sales data analysis
- Customer information lookup

Key Distinction: *The fundamental difference between VLOOKUP and HLOOKUP lies in their search orientation: VLOOKUP searches vertically (down columns), while HLOOKUP searches horizontally (across rows). Choose between them based on your data's structure and organization.*

MATCH Function: Precision Position Finding

The MATCH function operates as a specialized search tool in Excel, focusing on locating the exact position of items within your data range. Think of it as a data detective that returns the location rather than the actual value.

Core Structure: =MATCH(lookup_value, table_array, match_type)

Essential Components:

1. **lookup_value:** Your target search item
2. **table_array:** Your search range
3. **match_type:** Search behavior modifier

    - 1: Less than or equal (ascending data)
    - 0: Exact match (any order)
    - -1: Greater than or equal (descending data)

The match_type parameter critically influences how MATCH behaves. With match_type 1 or -1, your data must be properly sorted, while 0 allows for exact matches in any order.

Key Applications:

- Finding relative positions in datasets
- Creating dynamic references
- Building flexible lookup formulas
- Index-based searching
- Range position identification

TRANSPOSE Function: Layout Transformation Tool

The TRANSPOSE function in Excel acts as a powerful data restructuring tool, excelling at converting information between row and column layouts. It stands out for its ability to seamlessly reorganize data presentation.

Key Features of TRANSPOSE:

- **Column-to-Row Conversion:** Transforms vertical data sequences into horizontal arrangements
- **Row-to-Column Transformation:** Shifts horizontal data structures into vertical alignments

Implementation Steps:

1. Identify and select your source data range
2. Determine the target area for transformed data
3. Input the formula and confirm with Enter

The formula structure is: **=TRANSPOSE(array)**

TRANSPOSE's value lies in its straightforward yet powerful functionality. This single function eliminates the need for complex manual data reorganization, streamlining what would otherwise be a time-consuming process.

Practical Uses:

- **Data Analysis Enhancement:** New data orientations often reveal hidden patterns and trends
- **Report Structure Optimization:** Adapt data presentation to meet various reporting requirements
- **System Migration Support:** Facilitate data restructuring when moving between different platforms

> ***Productivity Tip:*** *TRANSPOSE proves especially valuable when handling extensive datasets or in situations requiring frequent switches between horizontal and vertical data orientations. Its efficiency becomes particularly apparent when dealing with large-scale data reorganization tasks.*

FORMULATEXT Function: Formula Visibility Master

The FORMULATEXT function serves as Excel's transparency tool, expertly revealing the underlying formulas within cells. This function proves invaluable when navigating through complex spreadsheets or understanding unfamiliar workbooks.

Core Capabilities:

- **Formula Display:** Shows the complete formula contained in any referenced cell
- **Diagnostic Support:** Facilitates formula verification and error detection

Usage Instructions:

1. Find an empty cell for formula display
2. Apply the FORMULATEXT function, referencing your target cell
3. Execute with Enter to reveal the formula

The basic syntax is: **=FORMULATEXT(reference)**

Key Advantages:

- **Clarity Enhancement:** Instantly reveals hidden calculation methods
- **Educational Value**: Serves as an excellent tool for formula structure learning
- **Verification Support:** Enables thorough spreadsheet logic examination

***Productivity Tips:** FORMULATEXT excels as an analytical tool when reviewing spreadsheets from colleagues or third parties. It effectively functions as a formula decoder, bringing hidden calculations into clear view.*

This powerful function transforms the process of understanding spreadsheet mechanics from guesswork into precise analysis, making it an essential tool for Excel users across all expertise levels.

Data Validation, Transforming Text, and Filtering

Excel provides robust tools for data organization and validation, particularly valuable in collaborative environments. The chapter's next section delves into data validation, text transformation, and filtering capabilities. These features ensure data integrity, standardize information, and enhance searchability in shared workbooks. Filtering proves especially useful, enabling users to efficiently navigate large datasets and locate specific information.

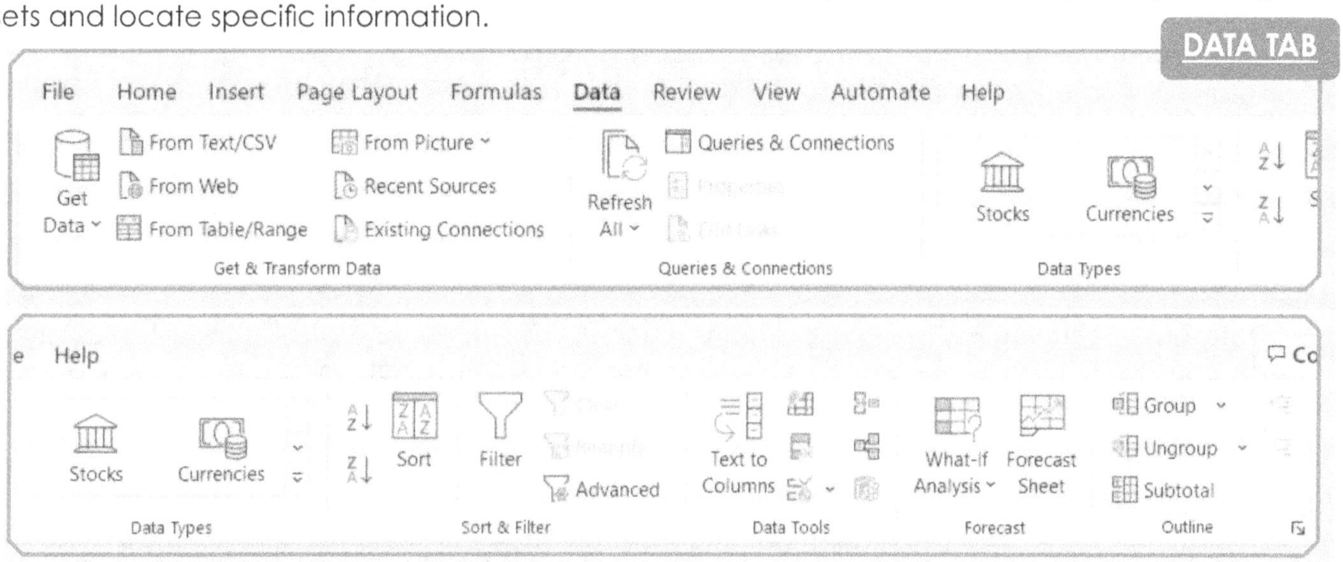

Data Validation Fundamentals

Data validation represents a powerful Excel feature that enables control over the type of data users can enter into specific cells. This tool supports various validation types, including whole numbers, decimals, lists, dates, times, text length restrictions, and custom entries.

For instance, creating a **drop-down list** with predetermined options requires:

1. Selecting "List" from validation options
2. Defining a source range containing desired values
3. Ensuring source data accessibility within Excel

Once implemented, users can only select from the predefined options in the drop-down menu, effectively restricting input to validated values.

Data validation also supports **custom messaging features**, such as error alerts for incorrect entries or input instructions when cells are selected. These elements help guide users and maintain data integrity throughout the spreadsheet.

To implement data validation, access the **Data Validation** button located in the Data tab of the Excel ribbon. This functionality proves particularly valuable when creating user-friendly forms and ensuring data consistency across shared spreadsheets.

Text to Columns: Data Transformation Tool

When importing data from external sources into Excel, you may often encounter formatting challenges, particularly when copying from PDFs. Excel typically fails to recognize original column structures, causing all information to merge into a single line. The "Text to Columns" feature offers a powerful solution to this common problem.

Location and Access: Find this tool in the Data tab of the Excel ribbon, specifically under the "Data Tools" section.

Detailed Implementation Process:

1. **Initial Data Selection** Click and drag to highlight target column(s). Before proceeding, ensure adequate empty columns exist to the right of your selection. It's crucial to create a backup of your original data before starting the transformation process.

2. **Launch the Feature** Navigate to the Data tab and locate the "Text to Columns" button. Upon clicking, you'll observe the appearance of the wizard interface that will guide you through the process.

3. **Data Type Selection** For Delimited options, choose this when your data is separated by specific characters. This works ideally with CSV files or tab-separated data and is commonly used with exported database information. For Fixed Width options, select this when your data has consistent spacing, perfect for formatted reports and mainframe data exports.

4. **Delimiter Configuration** Standard delimiters include tabs (most common in copied data), commas (standard in CSV files), and spaces (used in text-based reports). Custom delimiters might include semicolons (common in European CSV files), pipes, or multiple character separators.

5. **Preview and Adjustment** Review the split preview in the wizard window and adjust delimiter selections as needed. You can observe the impact of your changes in real-time through the preview pane.

6. **Destination Management** Choose your target location for split data. You can overwrite the original selection, select a new destination range, or create a new worksheet for the transformed data.

7. **Advanced Format Options** Specify column data formats, set date recognition patterns, configure number formatting, and handle text qualifiers according to your needs.

8. **Completion and Verification** Execute the transformation and verify your results carefully. Check for any anomalies in the transformed data compared to your source.

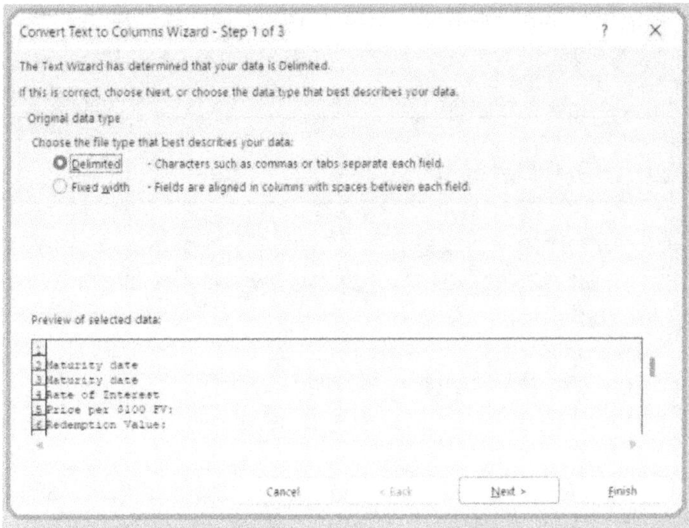

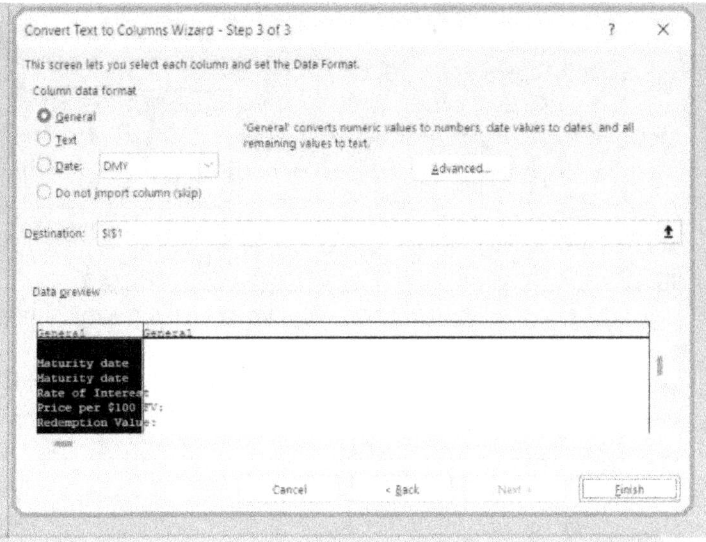

ProductivityTips: *Creating macros for repeated transformations can save significant time. Always validate your results against the source data to ensure accuracy. For complex or large datasets, consider using Power Query, which offers more advanced transformation capabilities and can handle larger volumes of data efficiently.*
This robust feature significantly enhances data preparation workflows, making Excel a more powerful tool for handling diverse data sources. Understanding and mastering Text to Columns can dramatically improve your data processing efficiency.

Sort and Filter: Data Organization Essentials

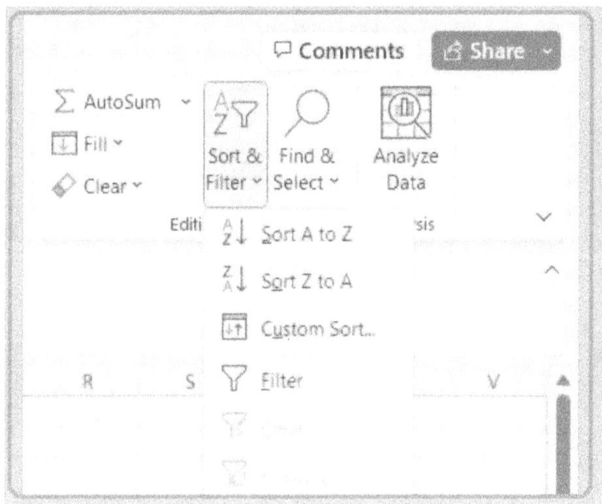

Filtering in Excel represents a fundamental tool for effective data organization and analysis. This feature enables rapid navigation through extensive datasets, allowing users to isolate and examine specific information with precision.

Accessing Filter Functions: The "Sort & Filter" functionality resides in the Home tab, serving as your primary access point. Upon activation, this tool adds dropdown arrows to each column header, unlocking various filtering capabilities.

Primary Filter Types

1. **Value Filters:** Enable users to select specific data entries while hiding others
2. **Color Filters:** Organize data based on cell or font color selections
3. **Number Filters:** Include mathematical comparisons like greater than, less than, or between values
4. **Text Filters:** Enable specific text searches and pattern matching
5. **Date Filters:** Sort information by various time periods and ranges

Advanced Functionality: Moving beyond basic filtering, Excel offers sophisticated options for complex data management. Users can implement multiple filtering criteria simultaneously, creating highly specific data views that serve particular analytical needs.

Essential Best Practices:

- *Create clear, descriptive column headers*
- *Maintain regular filter clearance to ensure data visibility*
- *Implement strategic color coding for enhanced visual organization*

Dynamic Integration: Excel's filtering system maintains dynamic connections with your data, automatically incorporating new changes as they occur. This real-time updating capability makes filters particularly valuable for ongoing data analysis and report creation.

Mastering these filtering capabilities significantly enhances data management efficiency, enabling users to identify patterns, detect irregularities, and extract valuable insights from their spreadsheets effectively.

Pivot Tables: Dynamic Data Analysis Made Simple

Pivot Tables represent an essential Excel tool that, despite their power, remain remarkably approachable for new users. These dynamic tools transform complex datasets into clear, comprehensible visualizations, especially valuable when handling thousands of data points.

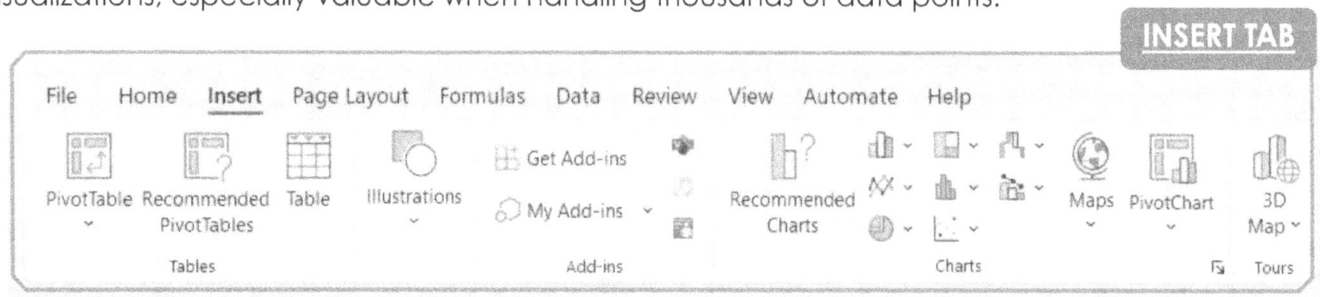

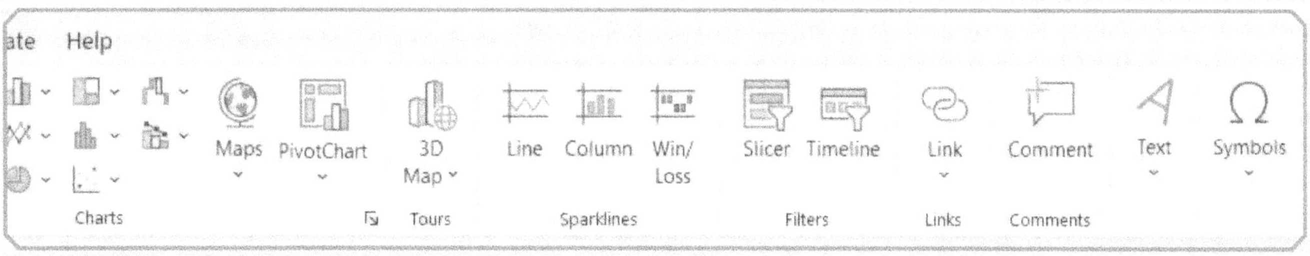

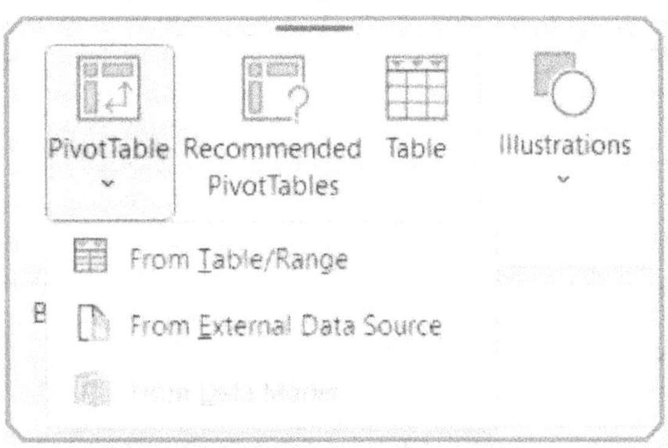

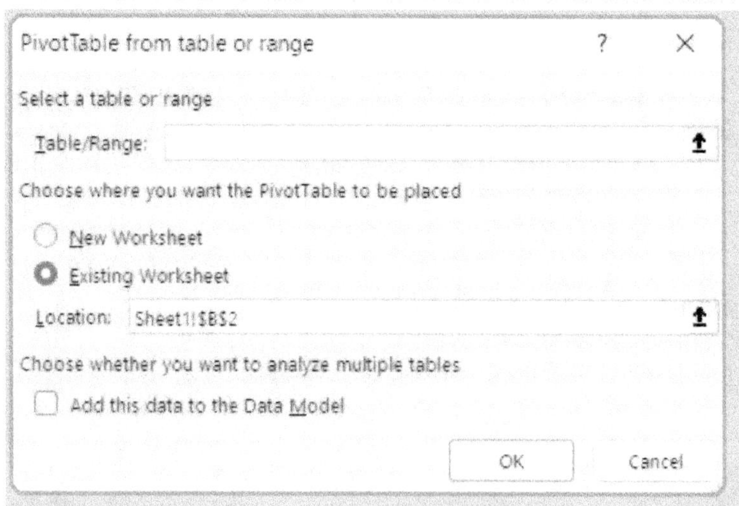

Basic Creation Process:

1. Start by accessing the Insert tab and locating the **Pivot Table button.**
2. Select **"PivotTable from table/range"** from the dropdown options. A dialog box appears, and your cursor automatically moves to the table/range selection area.
3. Make a crucial decision: place the new pivot table either in your current worksheet or a new one (new worksheet recommended for better organization).
4. Complete the process by clicking "OK" to generate your pivot table with the selected data.

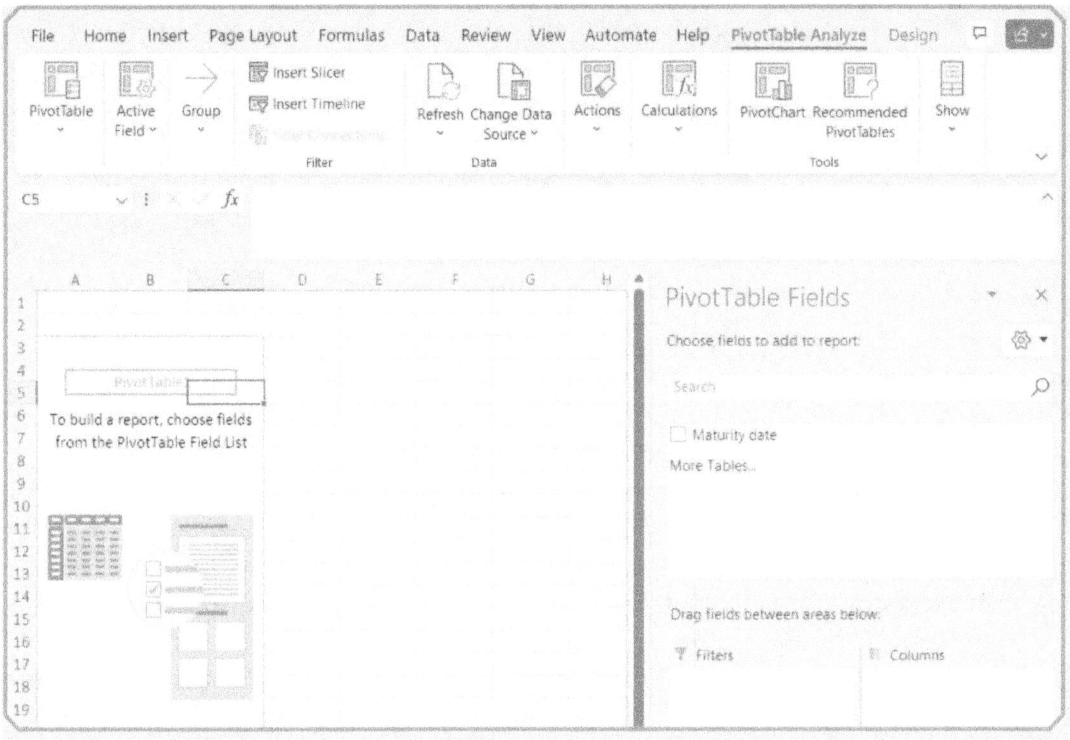

Advanced Calculation Features: The true power of Pivot Tables lies in their advanced calculation capabilities. To access these enhanced features:

1. Locate the black arrow on the right side of the values field
2. Select **"Value Field Settings"** to open additional options
3. Choose from various calculation methods:

- Sum totals
- Calculate averages
- Count occurrences
- Find products
- Create custom calculations

Customization and Enhancement: Pivot Tables offer extensive formatting options that transform them into professional-looking spreadsheets. Users can apply custom calculations such as percentages or running totals, enhancing data presentation and analysis capabilities. This flexibility allows Pivot Tables to evolve from simple data summaries into comprehensive analytical tools, providing deeper insights and more meaningful data representation.

Productivity Tip: Keyboard Shortcut *Alt + N + V creates a new Pivot Table instantly from your selected data range.*

Keyboard Shortcuts on *Excel*

FUNCTION	PC SHORTCUT	MAC SHORTCUT
Undo action	*Ctrl + Z*	*Command + Z*
Center align cell contents	*Alt + H, A, C*	*Command + E*
Edit cell	*F2*	*F2*
Lock formula	*F4*	*F4*
Add line or column	*Ctrl + +*	*Command + +*
Delete line or column	*Ctrl + -*	*Command + -*
Hide selected row	*Ctrl + 9*	*Command + (*
Hide selected column	*Ctrl + 0*	*Command +)*
Go to formula tab	*Alt + M*	*Command + Shift + U*
Move cells in worksheet	*Arrow keys*	*Arrow keys*
Move to beginning of sheet	*Ctrl + home*	*Command + home*
Zoom in	*Ctrl + Alt + =*	*Not available*
Zoom out	*Ctrl + Alt + -*	*Not available*
Extend selection	*Ctrl + Shift + Down arrow*	*Shift + Command + down arrow*
Fill selected range with current entry	*Ctrl + Enter*	*Command + return*
Repeat last command	*Ctrl + Y*	*Command + Y*
Display function arguments	*Ctrl + A*	*Command + A*
Refresh data	*Ctrl + F5*	*Command + F5*

3. PowerPoint:

Professional Presentation Creation

Creating presentations has become a fundamental skill in today's professional landscape. Among the various presentation software options available, Microsoft PowerPoint continues to dominate as the industry standard. Its comprehensive feature set serves both business professionals and personal users effectively. This chapter delves into PowerPoint's essential capabilities and real-world applications. Note that PowerPoint integrates many formatting and insertion tools found in Excel and Word - for detailed information about these shared features, consult the previous chapters. PowerPoint's sustained leadership in presentation software stems from its versatile toolkit and adaptability, making it an indispensable skill in contemporary workplaces.

Starting Your PowerPoint Journey

Opening a new PowerPoint file reveals a clean initial slide with dedicated spaces for title and subtitle content. This serves as your presentation's foundation, ready for customization with multimedia elements and text. The user interface presents a straightforward layout: a main slide workspace in the center, complemented by a navigation panel on the left displaying slide thumbnails.

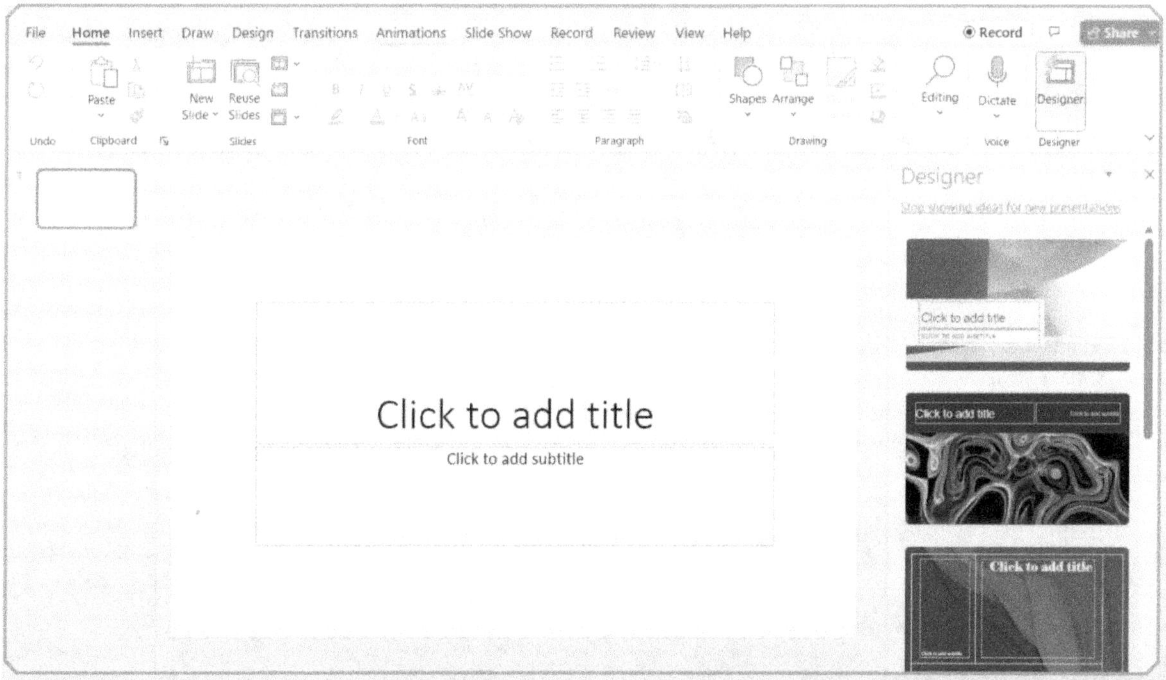

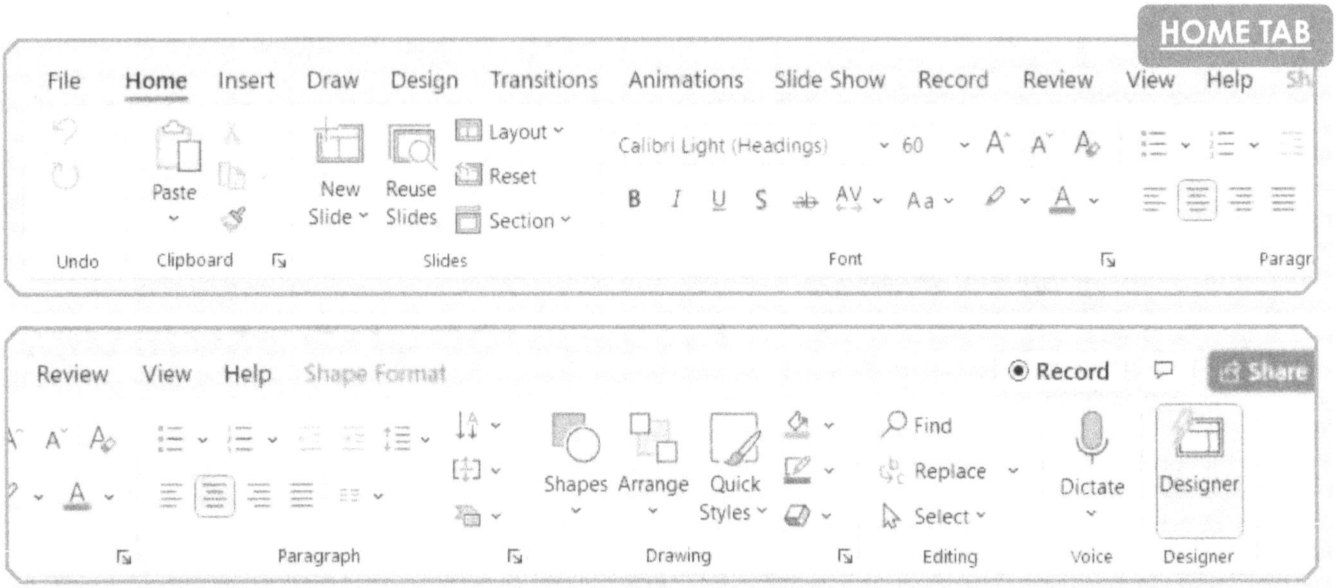

Adding Content Through New Slides

PowerPoint provides several methods for slide creation:

1. Navigate to the Home tab and use the "New Slide" button in the Slides group
2. Access the Insert tab and select the "New Slide" option
3. Use the contextual menu in the thumbnail panel to create a "New Slide"

Each new slide incorporates a default content layout. Enhance your text using the comprehensive formatting tools available in the Home tab.

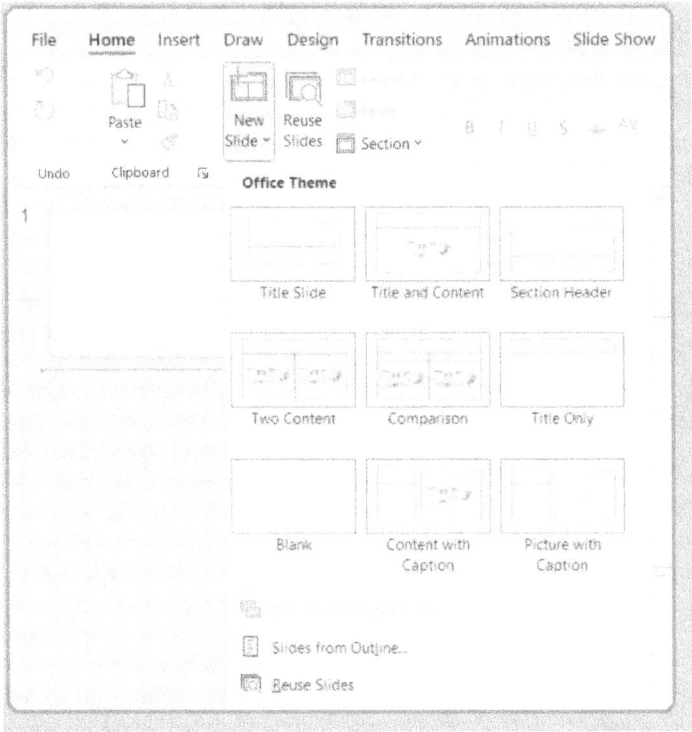

Mastering Slide Layouts

Modifying slide layouts follows two straightforward paths:

1. Select the "Layout" option from the Home tab's Slides section
2. Access the contextual menu and select "Layout"

Templates offer predefined layout options, while blank presentations provide flexible content containers for custom formatting.

Productivity Tip: *For precise slide placement within your presentation, click between existing slides in the thumbnail panel - watch for the red insertion line, then use the contextual menu to add your new slide exactly where needed.*

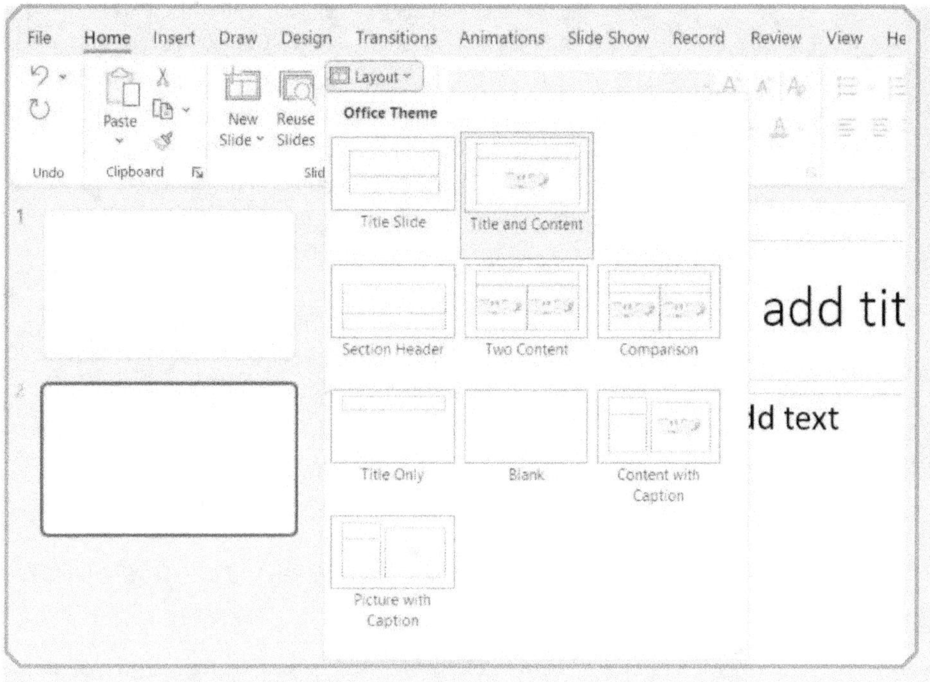

PowerPoint's adaptability enables the creation of customized presentations that precisely match your requirements, regardless of context. Its user-friendly interface combined with sophisticated tools makes it the premier choice for developing compelling visual presentations.

PowerPoint Slide Management

PowerPoint's design emphasizes efficient slide organization through its thumbnail panel, strategically positioned on the left side of the interface. This panel delivers a clear overview of your presentation's organization and progression, enabling users to maintain control over complex presentations effortlessly.

Thumbnail Navigation System:

The vertically-scrolling thumbnail panel enables complete presentation visibility, regardless of length. Each thumbnail displays a miniature slide preview, facilitating quick slide identification and access. This visual approach to navigation makes it simple to track changes and maintain presentation flow, even in documents with numerous slides. Key navigation features:

1. Vertical scrolling for quick access
2. Live preview of slide content
3. Direct click selection
4. Multi-slide selection capability

Slide Organization Process

The drag-and-drop system for reorganizing slides represents one of PowerPoint's most intuitive features. As you move slides, PowerPoint provides visual feedback through a horizontal line indicator, ensuring precise placement. This visual guidance system helps prevent errors and makes reorganization efficient, even in large presentations.

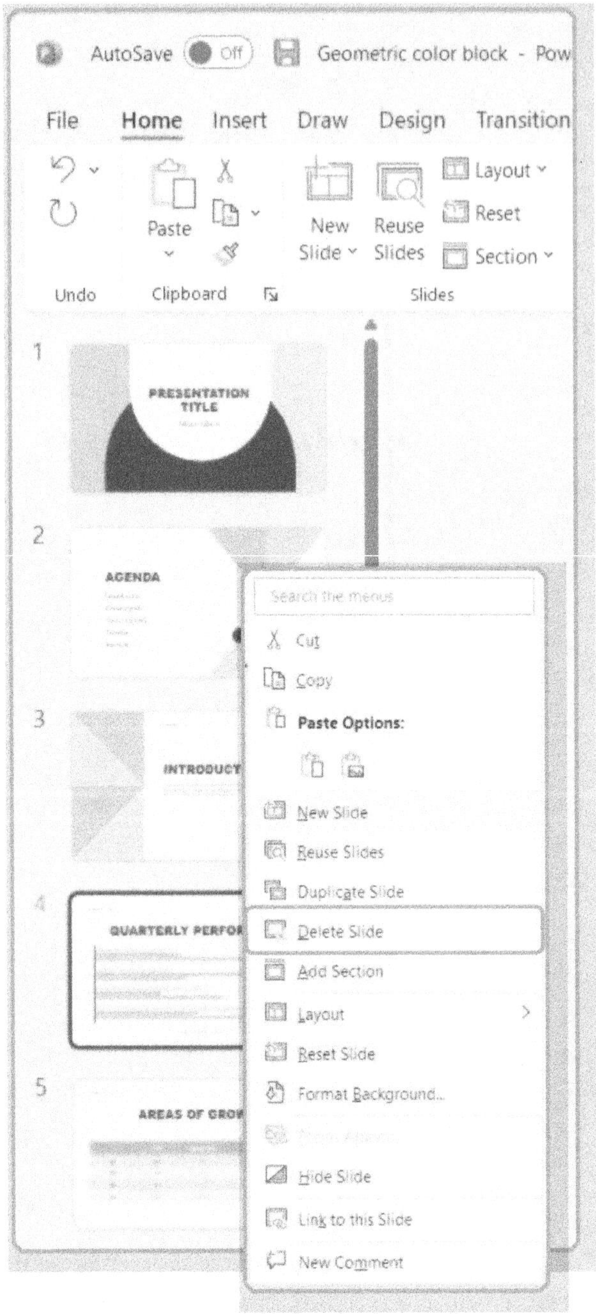

To rearrange your presentation:

1. Click and hold your target slide
2. Drag it to the intended location
3. Watch for the horizontal placement indicator
4. Release to confirm the new position

Slide Removal Options

PowerPoint's deletion system accommodates various user preferences and work styles. Each method achieves the same result but offers different advantages depending on your working style and specific needs. The multiple deletion options ensure that users can work efficiently regardless of their preferred interaction method.

PowerPoint provides multiple deletion methods to accommodate different work styles:

1. Context menu deletion via right-click
2. Keyboard deletion using Delete key
3. Ribbon deletion through Home tab
4. Multiple slide deletion with selection

Deletion Recovery

PowerPoint's recovery system protects against accidental deletions through multiple safeguards. The software maintains a robust undo history, allowing users to reverse multiple actions if needed. This protection extends to all deletion methods, ensuring consistent recovery options regardless of how the deletion occurred. Recovery methods:

1. Immediate Undo (Ctrl+Z/Command+Z)
2. Quick Access Toolbar Undo button
3. Multiple step undo capability
4. Redo function for reversed decisions

Slide Layout Elements

PowerPoint templates incorporate essential design elements like dotted lines and placeholders on slides. These components serve key purposes:

1. They establish designated areas for all types of content (text, images, and other elements)
2. These layout indicators remain invisible during presentations and slideshow mode
3. Users can modify content areas by selecting and dragging the placeholder boundaries

Creating Custom Text Areas

To incorporate additional text spaces, follow these steps:

1. Navigate to the Insert tab located in the ribbon
2. Select the "Text Box" option within the Text section
3. Create your text area by clicking and dragging across the slide
4. Begin entering your content directly into the new text box

INSERT TAB

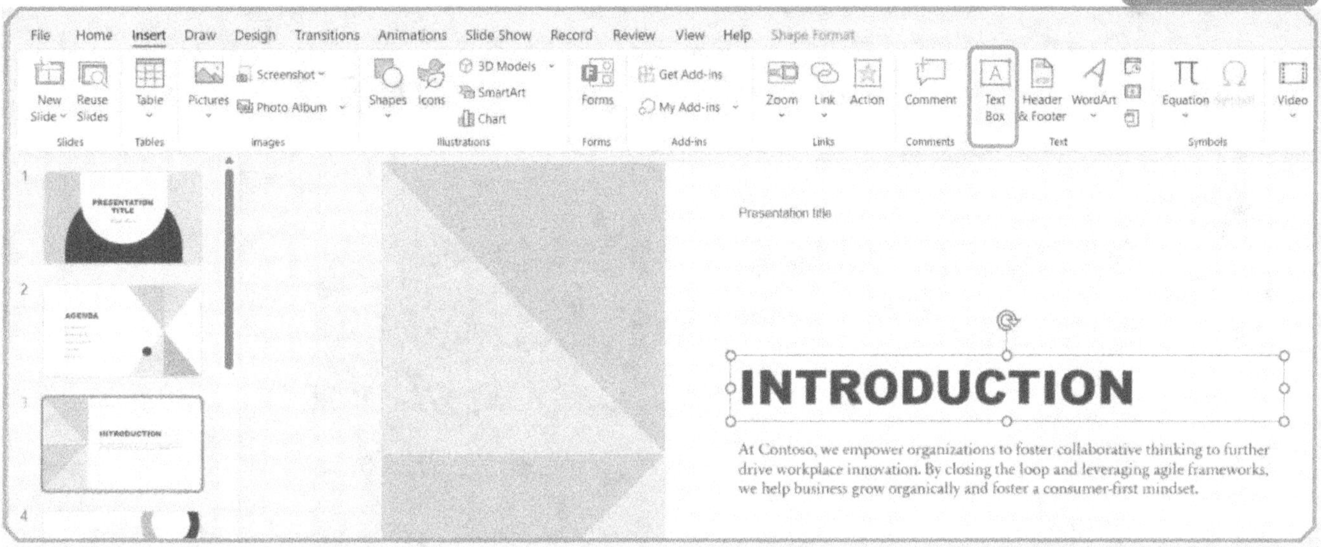

Productivity Tips:

1. ***Slide Sorter View*** *Access through the View tab for a broader overview when reorganizing multiple slides. This tool is essential for efficiently managing your presentation structure.*

2. ***Sections Feature*** *Find Add Section in the Home tab to group related slides together. This organization method is particularly valuable for longer presentations.*

3. ***Duplicate Slide Function*** *Right-click a slide and select "Duplicate Slide" to create variations without starting from scratch. This saves time while maintaining consistency.*

4. ***Hide Slide Feature*** *Right-click and select "Hide Slide" to keep slides in your presentation file without showing them during the presentation. Perfect for backup content.*

Themes and Templates: Design Tools

PowerPoint provides built-in design solutions for users who don't have access to corporate presentation templates. The software includes two key features: themes and templates, each serving distinct purposes. Themes create visual harmony through consistent color palettes and typography, while templates deliver ready-to-use layouts complete with placeholder content.

Themes excel at refreshing presentations or maintaining design consistency, whereas templates prove invaluable when building presentations from the ground up and seeking structural guidance. Understanding these differences helps users make informed choices about which tool best suits their specific needs.

From crafting business pitches to developing educational materials, PowerPoint's design tools can transform your presentation's appearance and polish. As you delve into these features, you'll learn how to craft compelling presentations that engage your audience effectively.

Themes

Enhance your PowerPoint presentations visually by implementing a theme. Themes automatically configure several design elements: Fonts, Colors, Styles and Visual effects.

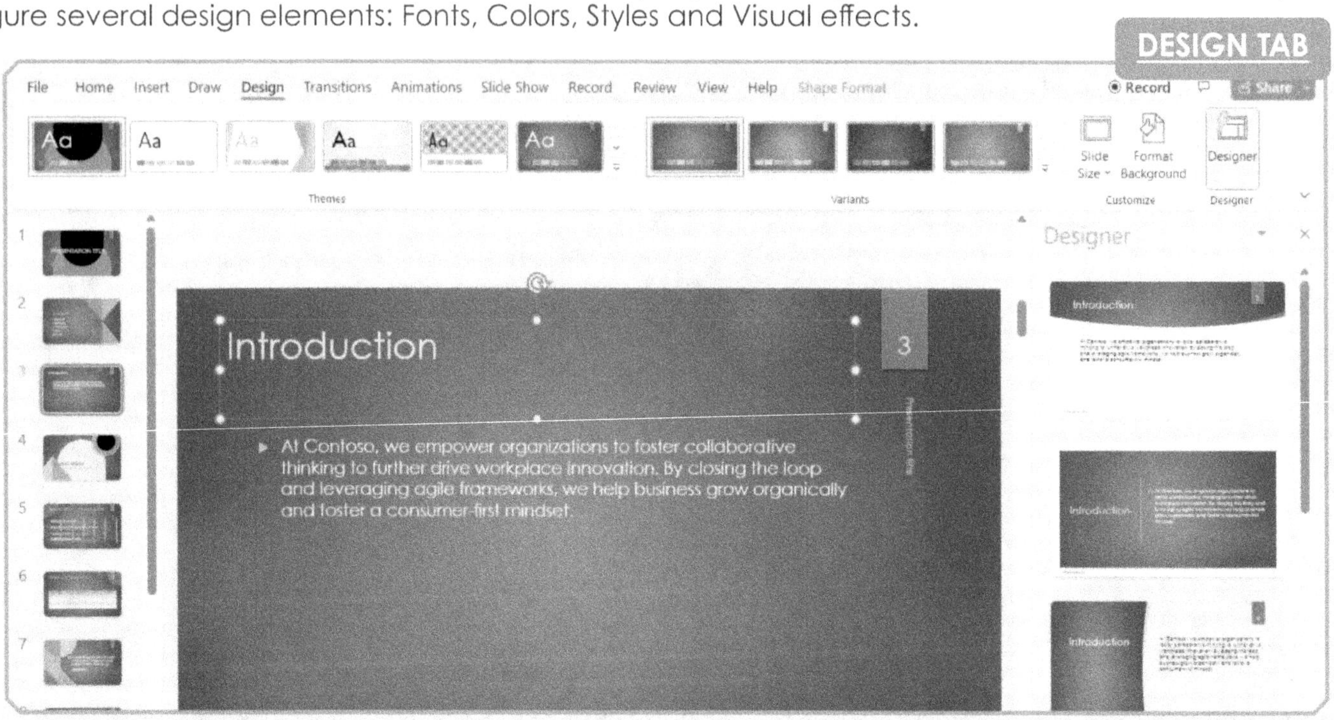

Locating Themes

1. Navigate to the **Design tab** in the ribbon
2. Find the themes section
3. Explore various presentation styles and their modifications

PowerPoint includes default themes, but you can access more

4. Select the down arrow located on the theme box's right side
5. Choose "Browse for Themes" to explore online selections

As you continue to build and expand your presentation, you'll notice that theme formatting automatically stays consistent throughout all new slides. This uniform application of design elements ensures your presentation maintains a polished and coherent appearance from start to finish, creating a professional and visually cohesive document.

Modifying Slide Layouts

To adjust a slide's arrangement:

1. Select the "New Slide" option
2. View theme-matched layout options
3. Select the arrangement that accommodates your content

Templates

Access PowerPoint templates through the File tab, where you'll discover an array of design options including both built-in and online template sources. These templates emphasize design aesthetics and layout options rather than content-specific structures. The number of available slide layouts varies significantly between templates - some offer an extensive collection of over 20 different layouts, while others provide a more focused selection.

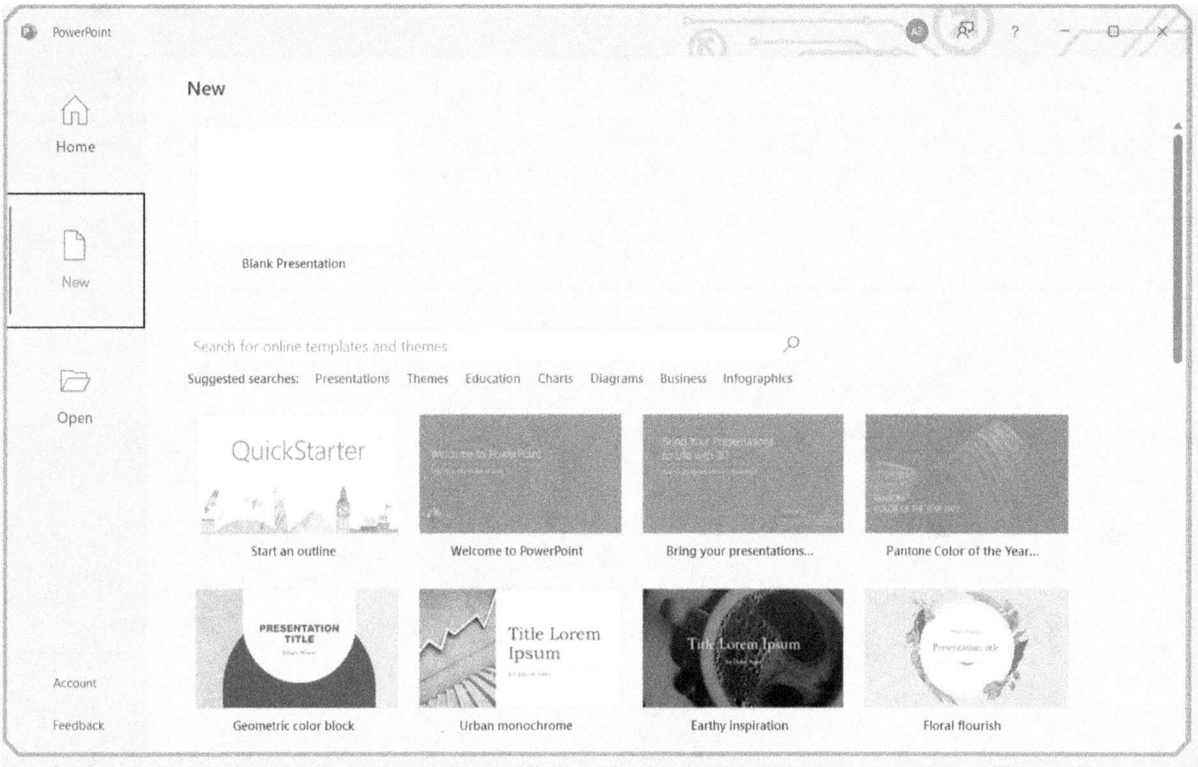

Most templates include predefined presentation structures, but they remain highly flexible. Users can easily modify and adapt these templates to match their unique presentation needs and personal preferences.

Creating a Master Presentation

When you need to establish a standardized template for company-wide use, personal business, or educational purposes, PowerPoint's master slide functionality provides the perfect solution. The master slide feature is the underlying mechanism that enables templates and styles to automatically format your new slides.

Your organization's custom template can incorporate essential elements including: Company logo, Specific fonts, Color schemes, Chart styles, and Image placeholders.

PowerPoint Master Views

PowerPoint offers three distinct master views for comprehensive presentation design control.

1. The **Slide Master** serves as the primary template, controlling the overall look of your presentation including themes, fonts, and backgrounds.

2. The **Handout Master** allows you to customize the format of printed handouts, including header and footer placement, company branding, and layout of multiple slides per page.

3. The **Notes Master** helps you format the appearance of your presentation notes, controlling elements like header design, footer content, and the layout of speaker notes that accompany each slide. Each master view can be accessed through the View tab, providing different levels of control over your presentation's final appearance and distribution formats.

To access these views:

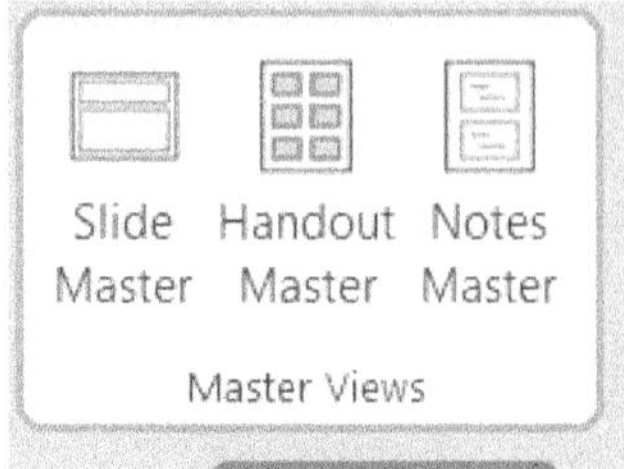

1. Go to the View tab
2. Look in the Master Views section
3. Select between Slide Master, Handout Master, or Notes Master based on your needs

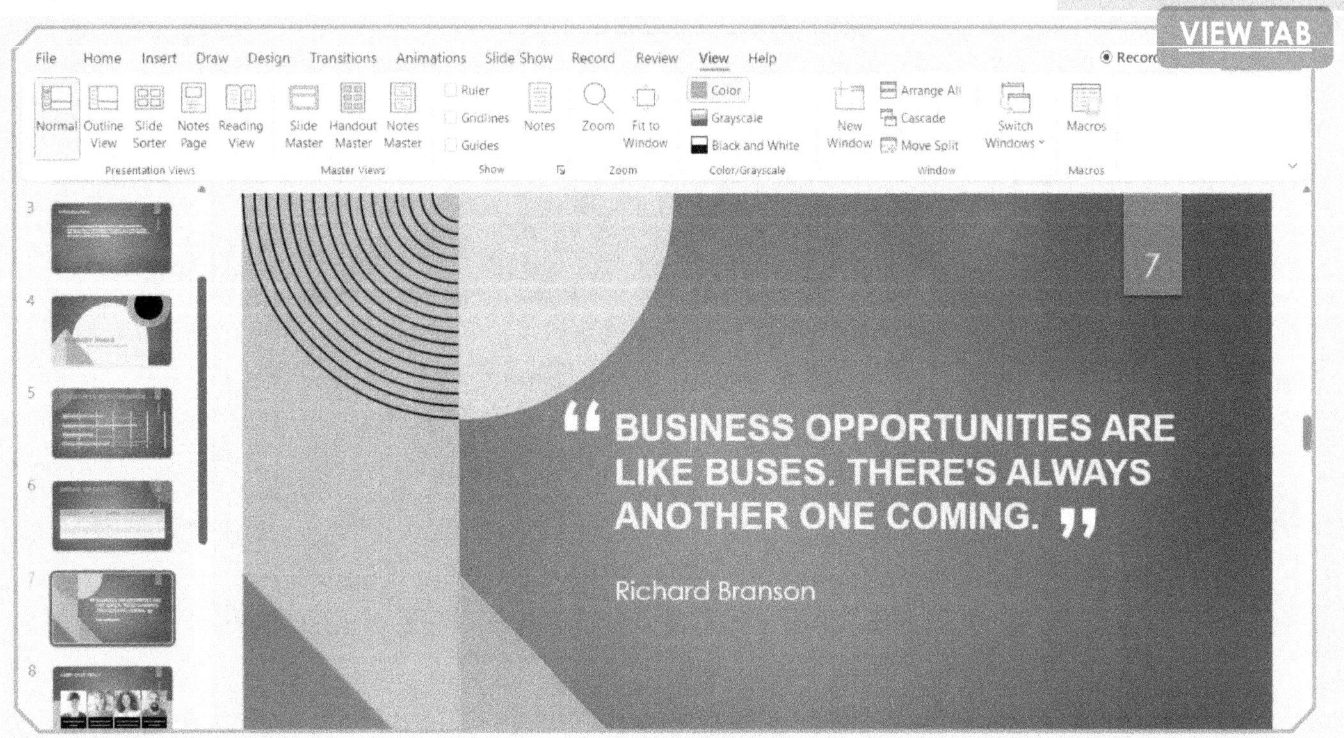

Slide Master View

In this view, you can:

- Design the **opening slide**
- Prepare different **layouts** for subsequent slides
- Add **page numbers** and **dates**
- Incorporate specific **themes** from the PowerPoint library

While working in master view, remember that all available ribbon options specifically relate to master slide editing. To exit this mode and return to standard presentation editing, locate the Close Master View button in the Slide Master tab.

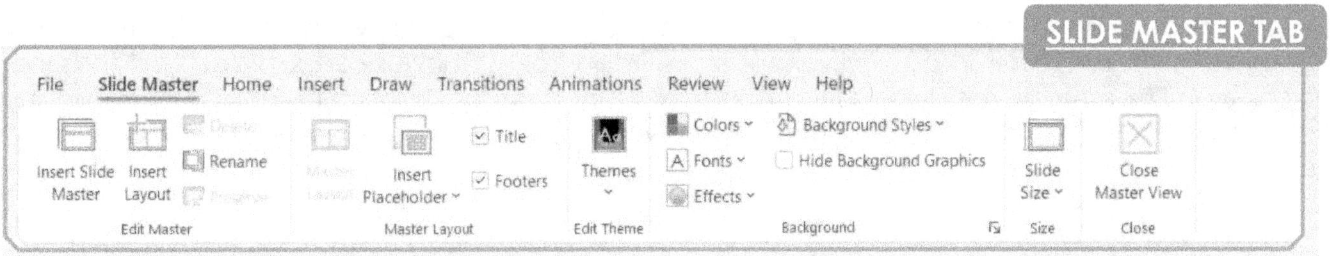

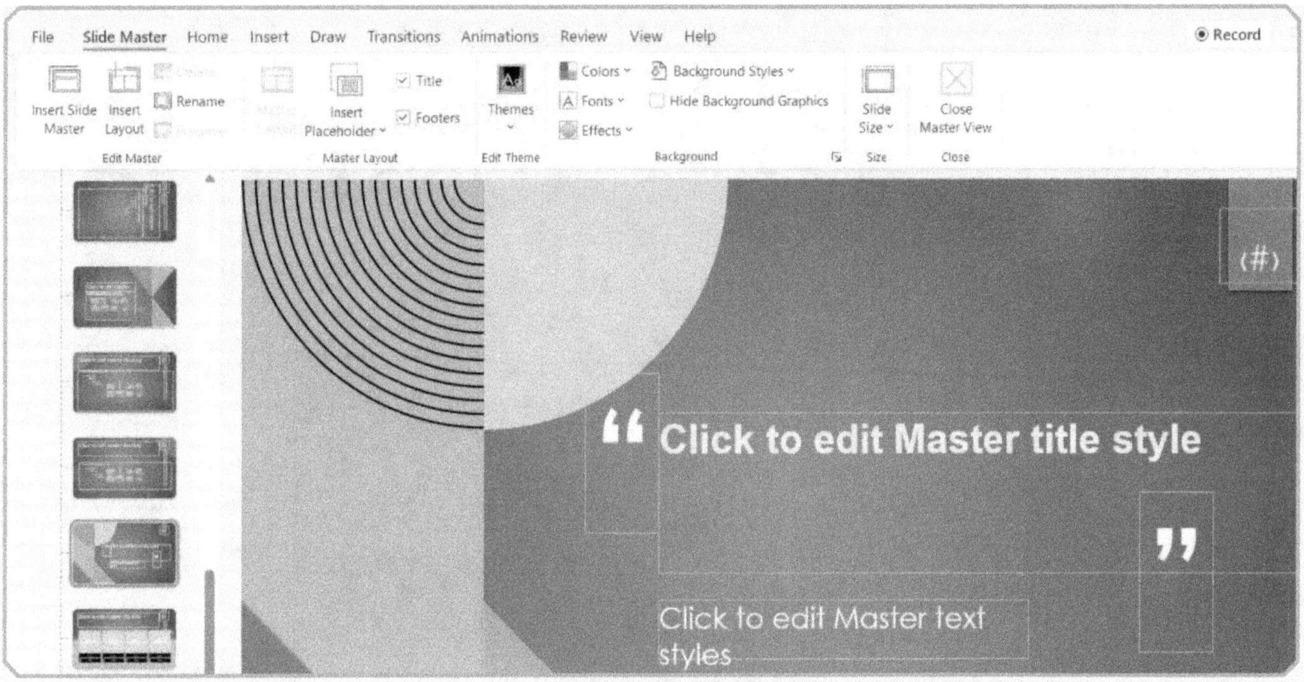

Productivity Tip: *Any new content added to your presentation will automatically conform to your master template settings, including layouts, typography, and overall visual design. You have the flexibility to either build a master template from the ground up or customize an existing template to match your needs.*

Multimedia Elements: Pictures, Videos and Charts

PowerPoint equips users with diverse visual enhancement tools including pictures, icons, and videos for effective point illustration. Modern PowerPoint versions integrate media insertion options directly into slide layouts. Users can easily access tables, graphs, shapes, 3D objects, pictures (both local and online), and icons. These capabilities enable the creation of engaging and dynamic presentations.

Pictures Addition Methods

PowerPoint provides multiple streamlined approaches for incorporating visual content into your presentations. The most efficient methods include:

- Using **copy and paste** functions
- Utilizing **keyboard shortcuts**
- Accessing options in the **ribbon interface**

Each method offers unique advantages depending on your workflow preferences and specific needs.

PowerPoint demonstrates remarkable versatility in image sourcing, allowing you to seamlessly import files from both your local storage and various online repositories. This flexible approach extends to both shapes and SmartArt elements, ensuring consistent functionality across different visual components. When first inserted, visual elements appear within your slide's designated work area, ready for customization.

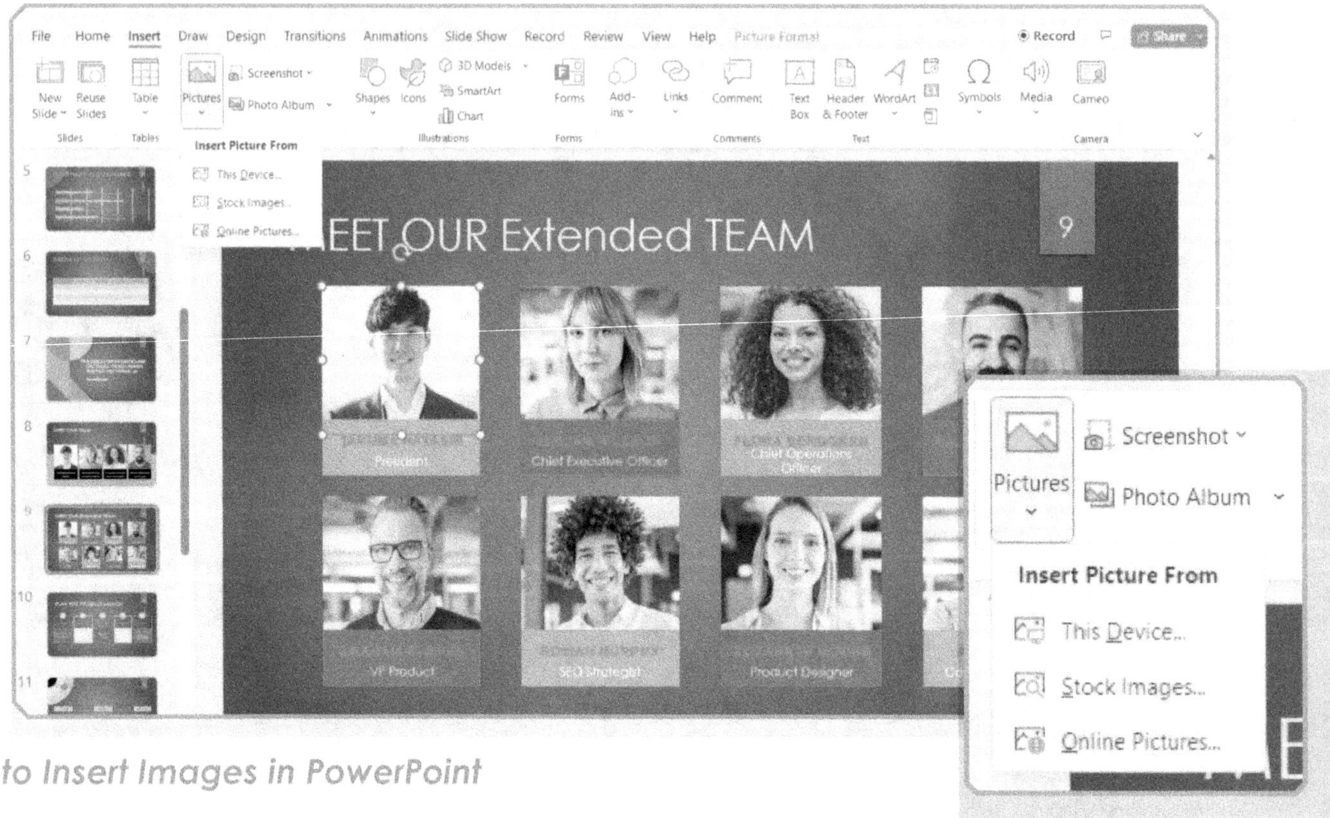

How to Insert Images in PowerPoint

1. **Using the Ribbon (Most Common Method)**
   - Click the "Insert" tab
   - Select "Pictures" in the Images group
   - Choose between:
   - "This Device" for local images
   - "Online Pictures" for web images
   - Select your image and click "Insert"

2. **Quick Keyboard Methods**
   - Press CTRL + V to paste a copied image
   - Use ALT + N, P for local pictures
   - Use ALT + N, O for online pictures

3. **Drag and Drop Method**
   - Open your image folder
   - Drag the image directly onto your slide
   - Release to place it

4. **Right-Click Method**
   - Right-click on any empty slide area
   - Select "Insert"
   - Choose "Picture"
   - Select your image source

Size and Position Control

For precise image manipulation

1. Utilize the expandable work area for maximum control
2. Employ click-and-drag functionality for intuitive positioning
3. Master the Shift key technique while resizing to preserve original image proportions

Photo Album Tool

PowerPoint's sophisticated **Photo Album** tool revolutionizes multiple image management. This powerful feature enables elegant presentation of numerous images on a single slide with controlled display timing. To harness this capability:

1. Access the **Insert tab** in your ribbon
2. Navigate to the Images section
3. Locate and select the **Photo Album button**

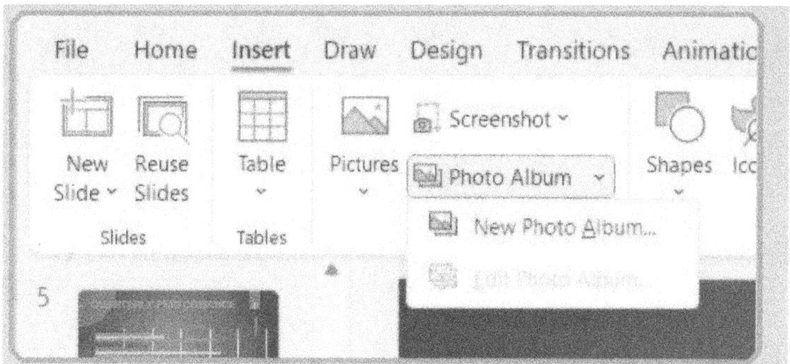

The Photo Album dialog box offers comprehensive control over your image presentation:

1. Import images directly from your computer
2. Fine-tune image fit settings for optimal display
3. Enhance with descriptive captions
4. Select from various album layouts and shapes

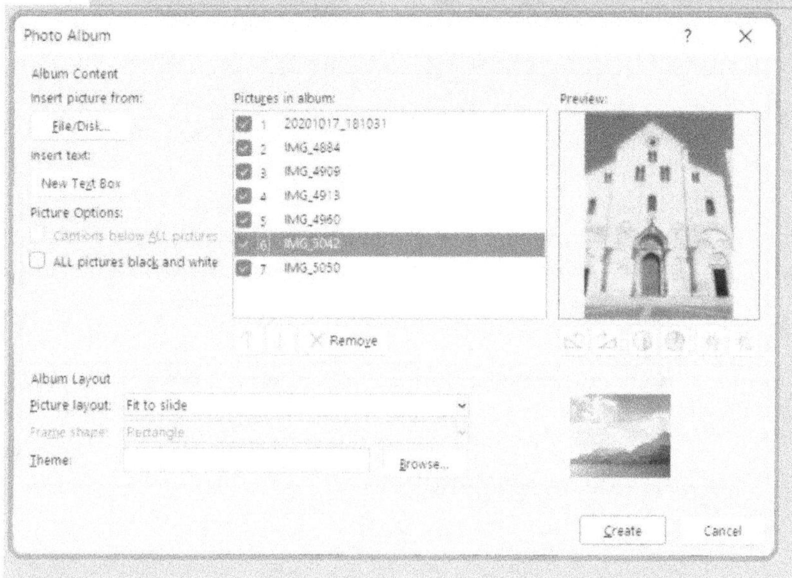

Begin your album creation by selecting images through the File/Disk option in the dialog box. PowerPoint's flexible architecture accommodates varying numbers of images, adapting to your presentation's scope and requirements. During presentations, navigate through your album effortlessly by clicking directly on the album or using the Enter key.

Videos and Sound in Power Point

PowerPoint presentations have evolved far beyond simple text and images. Whether you're delivering a business proposal, teaching a class, or sharing your creative work, the ability to incorporate videos and sound can transform your presentation from ordinary to extraordinary. This guide will walk you through the essential steps to enhance your slides with compelling multimedia elements.

In today's digital presentation landscape, integrating multimedia components like videos and audio can dramatically enhance your PowerPoint presentations' effectiveness. These dynamic elements not only capture your audience's attention but also serve as powerful tools for communicating complex ideas. Here's a detailed exploration of incorporating these features into your slides.

Incorporating Video Content

Videos can transform your slides by demonstrating concepts that might be challenging to convey through static content alone. PowerPoint provides two main approaches for video integration:

1. **Online Videos:** These digital resources stream directly from the internet without requiring downloads, offering significant storage savings on your device. Keep in mind that a reliable internet connection is essential during your presentation to ensure smooth playback of these videos.

2. **Local Videos:** These files are saved directly on your computer's hard drive, giving you the advantage of offline playback capabilities. This option proves especially valuable when working with custom-created content or confidential material that needs to remain secure and readily accessible without internet dependency.

Inserting Videos

1. Launch your PowerPoint presentation
2. Select the Insert tab in the ribbon menu
3. Look for the Insert Video dropdown option in the Media area
4. Select your preferred video source

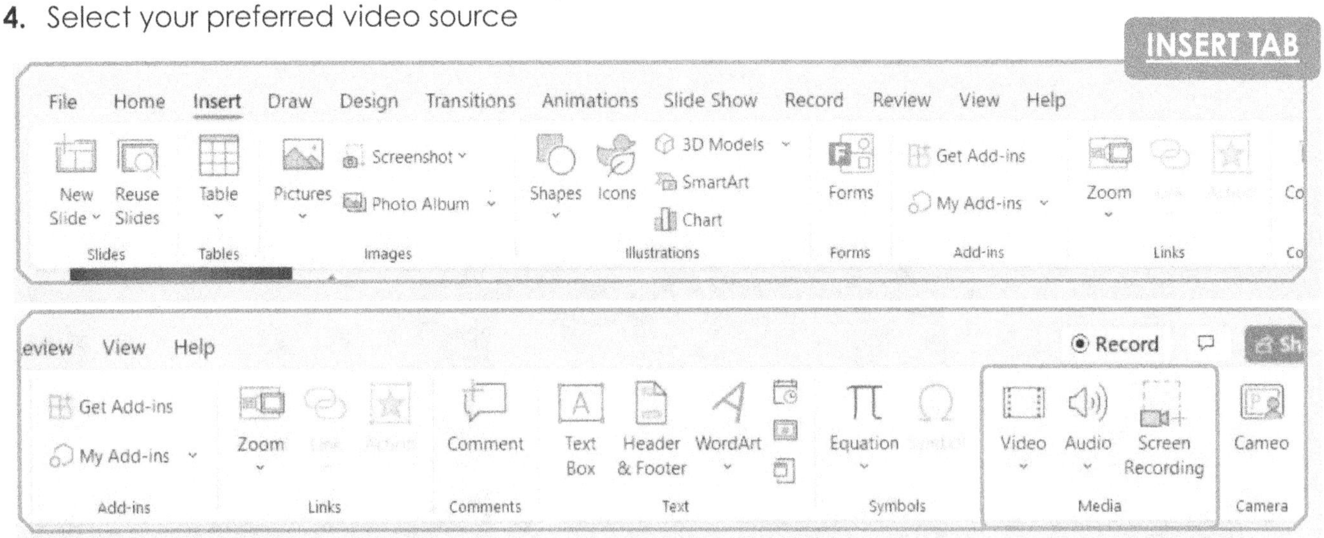

- **For Online Videos**
  - Choose "Online Video" option
  - Review available platform options: YouTube, Vimeo, SlideShare, Stream, Flip

- Locate your desired video on a supported platform
- Copy the video's web address
- Transfer the URL into PowerPoint's dialog window
- Complete insertion by clicking "Insert"

- **For Local Videos**
  - Select "This Device" option
  - Navigate through your computer's file system
  - Choose your video file
  - Finalize by clicking "Insert"

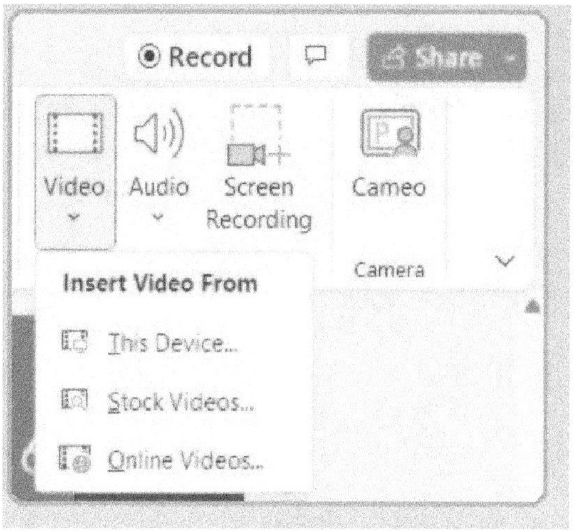

Video Playback

After inserting your video into PowerPoint, you can access powerful customization options by clicking on the video to reveal the Video Tools contextual tabs. These controls allow you to:.

1. **Adjust Video Properties**
   - Trim the video to show only essential segments
   - Select a poster frame (a static image that displays before playback)
   - Configure playback settings like auto-play and looping options

2. **Enhance Visual Presentation**
   - Apply visual styles and effects to match your presentation theme
   - Fine-tune the size of your video
   - Position the video precisely on your slide for optimal layout

Adding Sound

Transform your PowerPoint presentations from simple slideshows into engaging multimedia experiences by incorporating audio elements. Whether you're looking to add background music, sound effects, or voiceovers, audio can significantly enhance your message's impact and keep your audience engaged throughout the presentation.

Types of Audio in PowerPoint:

1. **Pre-recorded Audio Files** Professional presentations often benefit from carefully selected pre-recorded audio. You can incorporate various audio elements including background music to set the mood, strategic sound effects to emphasize key points, or high-quality narrations recorded with professional equipment. These pre-recorded files ensure consistent audio quality across all presentations.

2. **Live Recordings** For a more personal touch, PowerPoint enables you to record your voice directly within the application. This feature is particularly valuable when creating educational content or adding last-minute explanations to your slides. The built-in recording capability means you don't need external software to add your voice to presentations.

Steps to Insert Audio: Adding audio to your presentation is a straightforward process that begins at the Insert tab. Within the Media section, you'll find all the audio-related tools you need. Here's how to proceed with both pre-recorded and live audio:

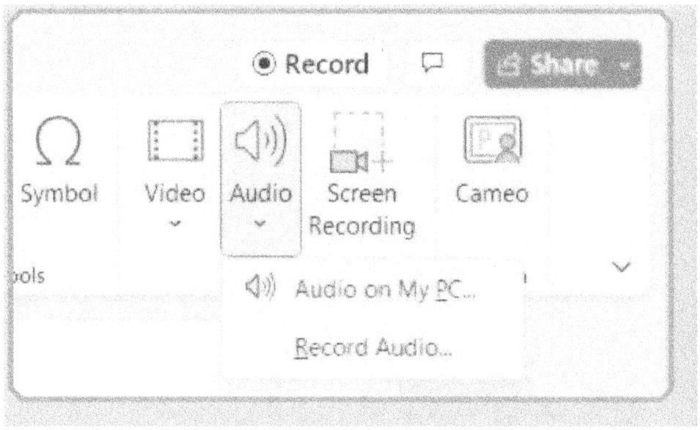

For Pre-recorded Audio:

- Start by clicking **"Audio on My PC"**
- Use the file browser to locate and select your desired audio file
- Finalize the insertion with the "Insert" button

For Recording Audio:

- Choose the **"Record Audio"** option
- Ensure your microphone is properly connected and functioning
- Begin recording by clicking the red record button
- Stop when you've finished your recording
- Give your recording a descriptive name
- Complete the process by clicking "OK"

Audio Playback Options

Once your audio is in place, PowerPoint offers extensive options for fine-tuning how it plays during your presentation. By clicking the audio icon, you'll reveal a sophisticated set of Audio Tools that allow you to:

- Perfect the timing with precise audio trimming
- Fine-tune volume levels for optimal listening
- Set smart playback options including automatic play, icon visibility, and continuous playback across slides
- Add professional polish with smooth fade-in and fade-out effects

These customization options ensure your audio enhances rather than distracts from your presentation's message, creating a seamless and professional multimedia experience.

Creating Charts and Graphs

Adding data visualizations to your presentations is crucial for effectively communicating complex information. PowerPoint offers robust tools for creating and customizing charts, seamlessly integrating with Excel for data management. Let's explore the comprehensive process:

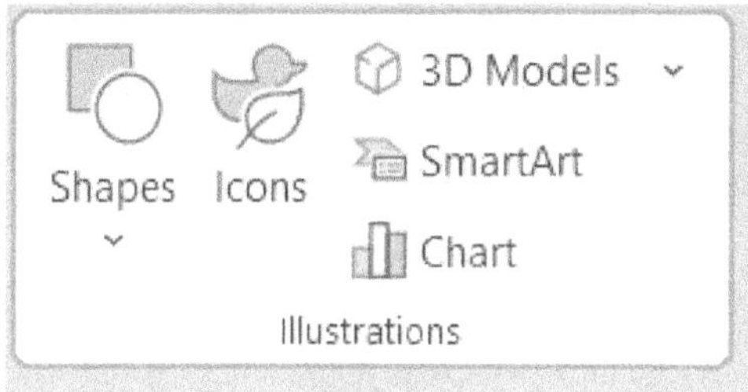

1. **Initial Chart Setup:** Start by selecting your desired slide, then access the Insert tab on the ribbon. In the Charts section, click the Chart icon to explore various visualization options including bar charts, line graphs, pie charts, and scatter plots. Choose the style that best represents your data.

2. **Data Management:** When you select a chart type, PowerPoint automatically opens an Excel spreadsheet window. This integrated approach allows you to:

   - Enter your numerical data directly
   - Watch your chart update in real-time
   - Organize your information systematically

3. **Visual Enhancement:** After entering your data and closing Excel, your chart appears ready for customization. PowerPoint provides extensive formatting tools to:

   - Adjust colors and styles
   - Modify chart elements
   - Fine-tune the visual presentation

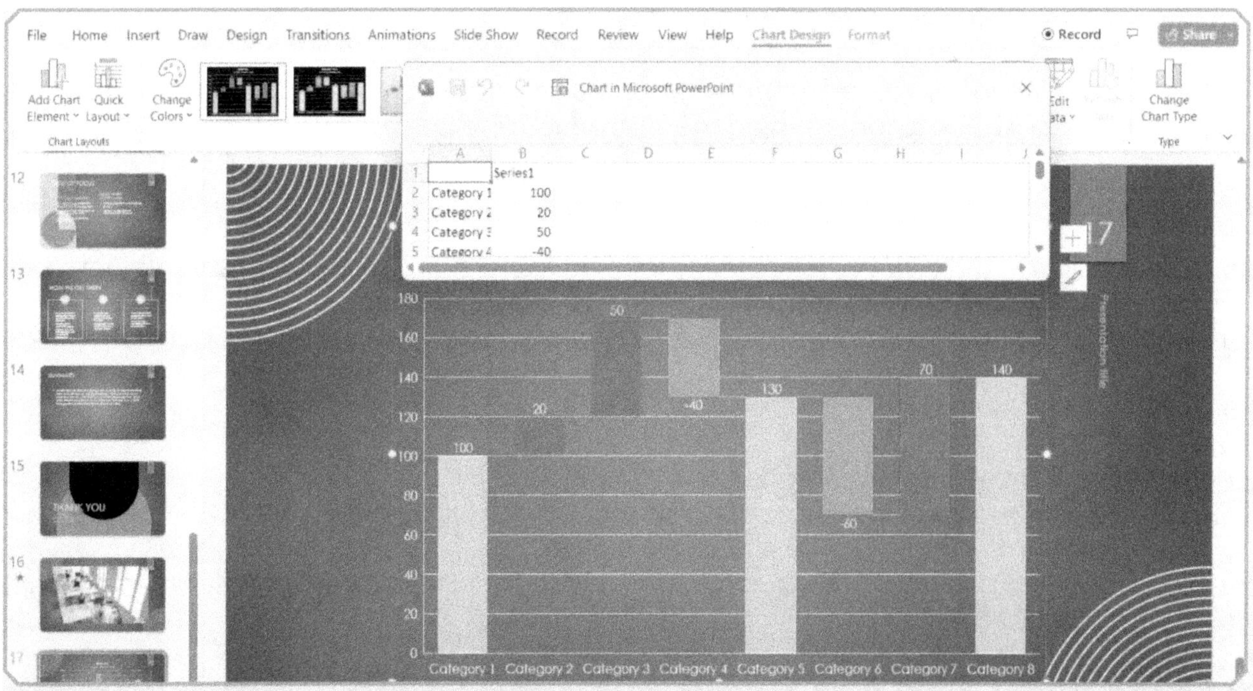

Working with Excel Charts: For situations where your data visualization already exists in Excel, PowerPoint offers flexible integration options:

1. **Basic Import Process**: Navigate to your Excel file, select and copy your chart, then paste it into your PowerPoint slide. This streamlined process ensures accurate data transfer.

2. **Advanced Paste Options:** PowerPoint provides three distinct paste methods:

   - **Picture:** Creates a static image of your chart
   - **Linked Chart:** Maintains dynamic connection to Excel
   - **Embed Chart:** Incorporates complete chart data within PowerPoint

Charts and graphs serve as powerful tools for transforming complex data into digestible visual insights. Whether creating new visualizations or importing existing Excel charts, these elements enhance your presentation's persuasive power. The key lies in selecting the right chart type and customizing it effectively to support your message and engage your audience.

Enhancing Presentations with Animation and Transitions

PowerPoint's dynamic features can transform static presentations into engaging visual experiences. Understanding how to effectively use both transitions between slides and animations within slides can help you create presentations that not only capture attention but also improve information retention and comprehension.

Understanding PowerPoint Motion Effects

PowerPoint offers two distinct types of motion effects that serve different purposes in your presentation:

1. **Transitions** create smooth visual movements as you progress from one slide to the next, helping to maintain presentation flow and visual continuity.

2. **Animations** bring individual elements within a slide to life, allowing you to control the timing and appearance of specific content pieces for maximum impact.

Slide Transitions

PowerPoint transitions are essential elements that add professional polish and smooth flow between slides in your presentations. When used effectively, transitions can enhance your message, maintain audience engagement, and create a cohesive visual experience.

Accessing Transitions

1. Launch your PowerPoint presentation
2. Click on the **Transitions tab** in the ribbon. This section contains all functionality related to transitions

Before you implement any transition, identify which slide should receive the transition effect. There are two methods to select a slide:

1. Click directly on the slide in the main work area
2. Choose the slide's thumbnail from the panel on the left side

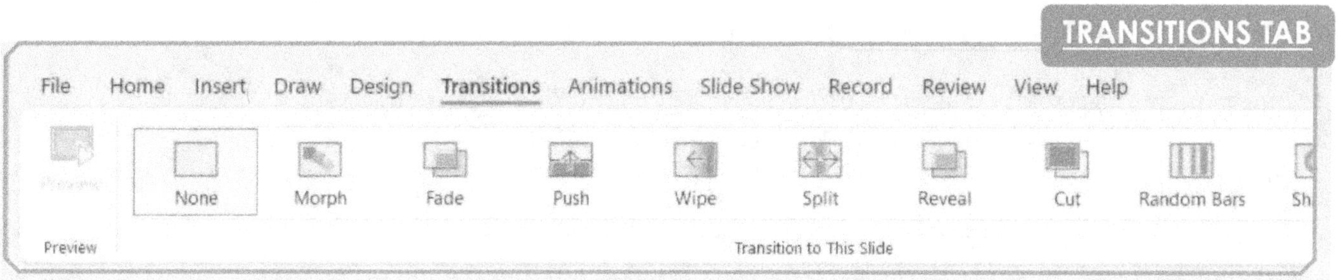

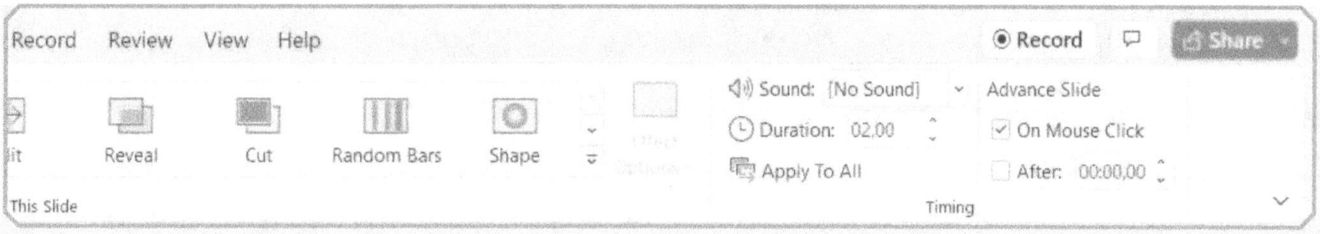

Important: *The transition you select will determine how the slide appears when entering, not when leaving.*

Choosing a Transition

1. Within the **Transitions tab**, you will find a collection of transition effects
2. Select any effect to implement it on your chosen slide
3. Click the More arrow to reveal additional transition choices

Previewing Transitions

1. PowerPoint will automatically display a preview once you select a transition
2. To watch the transition again, select the Preview button located on the far left of the Transitions tab
3. This feature helps you confirm that the transition appears exactly as you want it

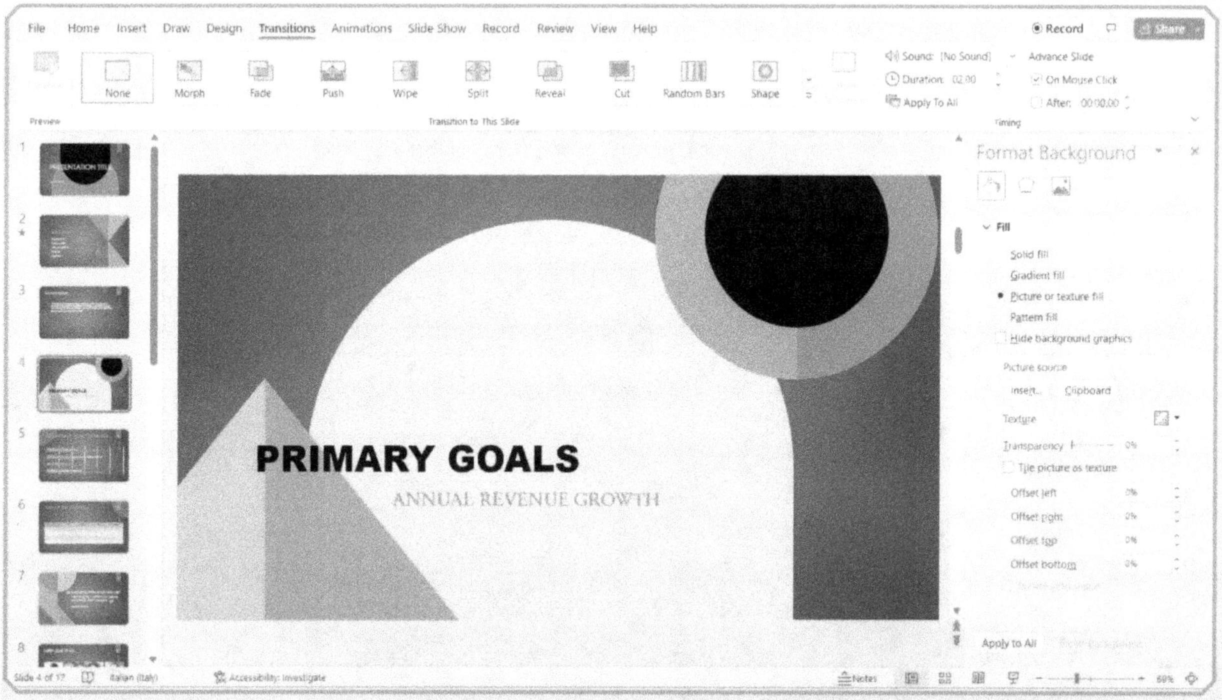

Fine_tuning Your Transitions - Several transitions offer additional customization options:

1. Search for the Effect Options button adjacent to the transitions gallery
2. Select it to view different variations of your chosen transition
3. Try different options to perfect your transition's visual appearance

Remove Unwanted Transitions

- Choose the slide or slides you want to modify
- Within the **Transitions tab,** select **"None"** from the available transition options

Custom Animations

Adding animations to specific elements within your PowerPoint slides provides a **sophisticated control** compared to slide transitions. This powerful feature enables you to **strategically reveal** information, maintaining audience engagement by controlling the flow of content presentation. Through careful timing, you can **guide your audience's attention** exactly where you want it, when you want it.

Setting Up Your First Animation

The process of implementing animations follows a **structured approach** similar to transitions, but with enhanced precision:

1. Navigate to the **Animations tab** located in the PowerPoint ribbon interface

2. Carefully select the **target element** you intend to animate (this could be text, images, shapes, or any other slide object)

3. Browse through and select your preferred animation style from the **extensive animation gallery**

4. Fine-tune the animation behavior by adjusting the **essential parameters** such as duration and trigger events (you can choose between manual triggers like mouse clicks or automatic timing)

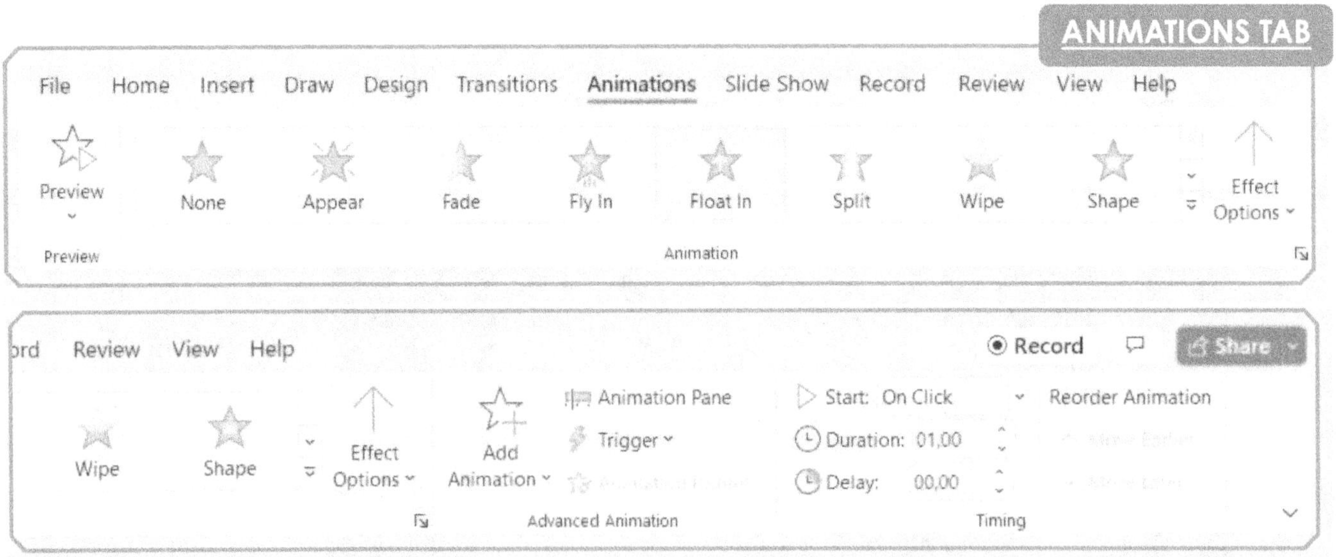

Mastering the Animation Pane

The Animation Pane serves as your **command center** for managing complex animation sequences. This essential tool, which you can access directly from the Animations tab, appears as a dedicated panel on the right side of your workspace. Through this interface, you gain **comprehensive control** over your animations:

- Monitor and manage all animations present on your current slide through a clear visual **timeline**
- Reorganize your animation sequence by dragging and dropping elements into your preferred **order**
- Configure animation trigger settings, choosing between **automatic playback** or **manual activation**
- Precisely adjust the timing and duration of each **animated element**
- Observe your complete animation sequence through an integrated **preview function**

For quick visualization of your animation effects, you can utilize the conveniently located Preview button positioned on the left side of the Animations ribbon. This allows you to **immediately assess** how your animations will appear during the actual presentation delivery.

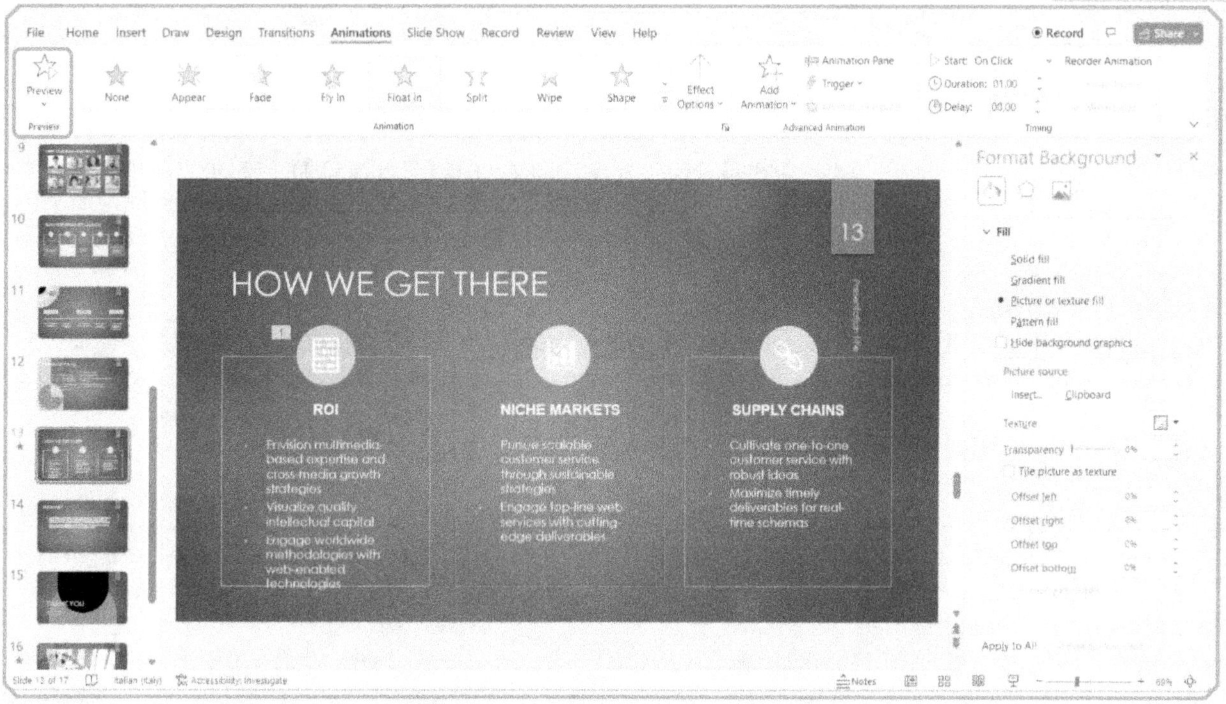

Through this sophisticated level of animation control, you can craft presentations that effectively guide your audience through **complex information**. By thoughtfully revealing content at **strategic moments**, you maintain audience focus while emphasizing key messages for maximum impact.

This **methodical approach** to content presentation helps ensure your message resonates with viewers and maintains their engagement throughout your entire presentation. The careful orchestration of animations can transform a **static presentation** into an engaging **narrative journey** that unfolds at precisely the right pace for your audience to absorb and retain the information you're sharing.

Enhancing Your Presentations with Notes and Comments

Understanding **Supplementary Information Tools** PowerPoint offers two powerful methods for adding extra information to your presentations: **speaker notes** and **collaborative comments**. These features serve distinct purposes and enhance both presentation delivery and team collaboration. Let's explore how each tool can elevate your presentation development process.

Mastering Speaker Notes

Speaker notes function as your personal presentation companion, providing private guidance during your delivery. These confidential reminders serve as your behind-the-scenes support system:

1. Locate the dedicated notes section by finding the **"Click to add notes"** panel positioned below your active slide
2. Input your key talking points, reminders, and additional context that you'll need during the presentation
3. Rest assured that these notes remain exclusively visible to you during presentation mode
4. Use this space to document essential details such as statistical references, anecdotes, or transitional phrases

Understanding Comments for Collaboration

Comments represent your toolkit for **collaborative enhancement**, enabling team members to provide feedback and suggestions. This feature proves invaluable when sharing your presentation with colleagues or stakeholders. The process of adding comments follows a straightforward approach:

1. Access the **Review tab** within the PowerPoint ribbon interface
2. Locate and select the **"Add Comment" button** to initiate your feedback
3. Input your observations, suggestions, or questions directly into the comment field

Managing Comment Visibility - To interact with existing comments effectively:

1. Utilize the **"Show Comments"** function to reveal all feedback
2. Review comments in context with their associated slides **Important Note**: Comments maintain their invisibility during the actual presentation delivery, ensuring a clean and professional appearance for your audience.

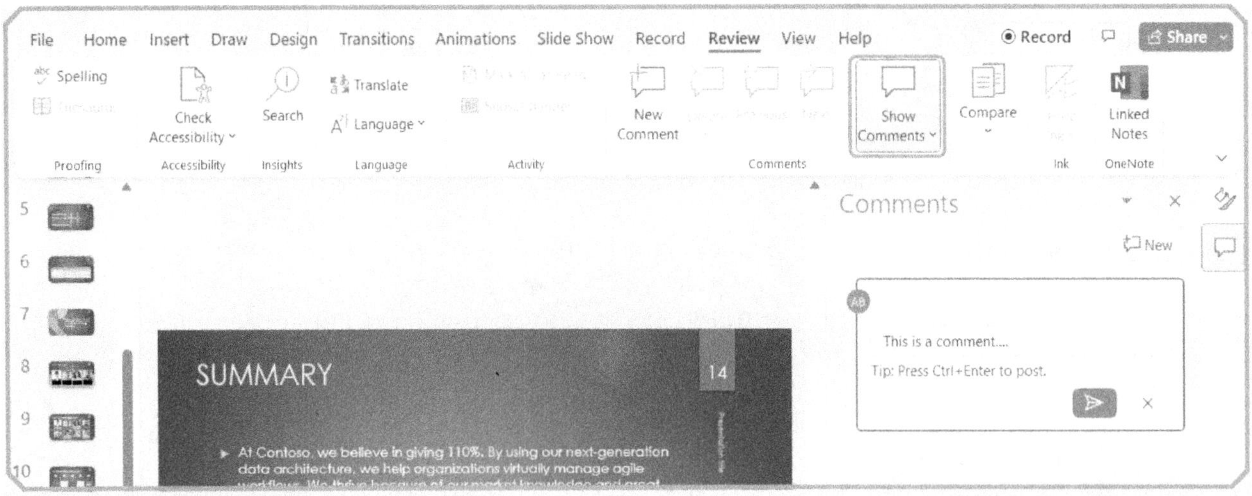

Presentation and Print

Navigating PowerPoint Views

PowerPoint's viewing options help you perfect your presentation at every stage. These essential views, accessible from the bottom right corner of your screen, each serve a distinct purpose in your presentation journey.

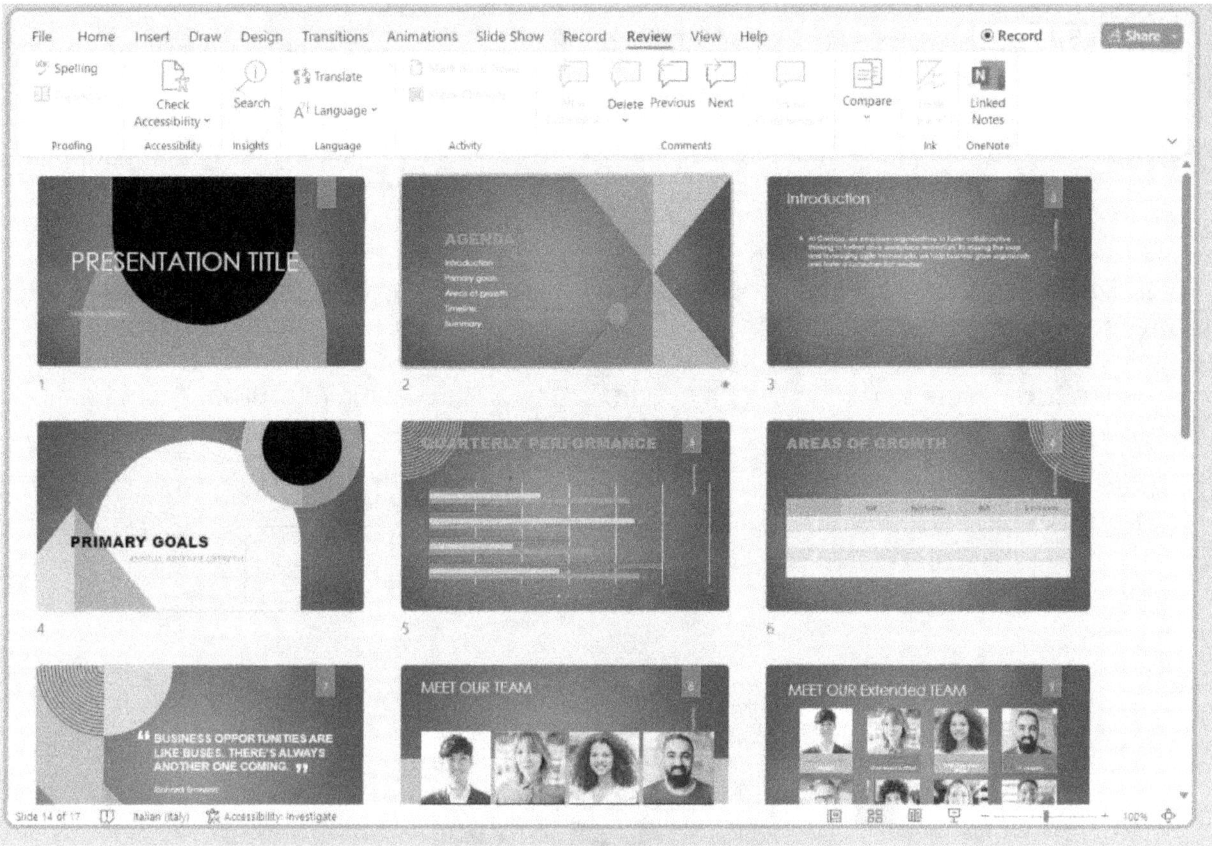

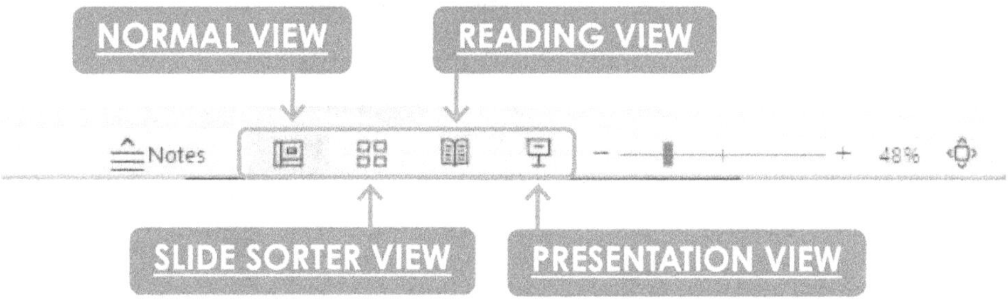

1. **Normal View - Your Creation Space:** The default view serves as your primary workspace where you'll spend most of your development time. Here, you have full access to all editing tools and features, making it ideal for detailed work on individual slides. Think of this as your creative studio, where every element can be precisely crafted and positioned.

2. **Slide Sorter - Your Organization Center:** This view transforms your presentation into an array of thumbnails, offering a comprehensive overview of your entire slide deck. While you can't edit content here, you can easily rearrange slides through drag-and-drop actions, helping you perfect your presentation's flow and structure.

3. **Reading View - Your Audience Preview:** Experience your presentation exactly as your audience will see it. This simulation helps you identify potential visual issues and ensures your content flows smoothly, serving as your presentation's dress rehearsal before the actual delivery.

4. **Presentation View -Your Performance Dashboard:** During live presentations, this sophisticated view becomes your command center, displaying:

    - Your current slide in a compact format
    - A preview of the upcoming slide
    - Your speaker notes for seamless delivery This view proves invaluable when presenting from your own device, providing all essential information while maintaining a professional appearance.

Each view serves as a specialized tool, working together to help you create and deliver more polished, professional presentations.

Printing

PowerPoint's comprehensive printing capabilities allow you to transform your digital presentation into various physical formats, each serving a distinct purpose in your professional communication toolkit. Let's explore how to access and utilize these printing options effectively. The journey to customized printing begins in the File tab, where selecting the print function reveals PowerPoint's full range of printing capabilities. This central hub gives you complete control over how your presentation translates to paper.

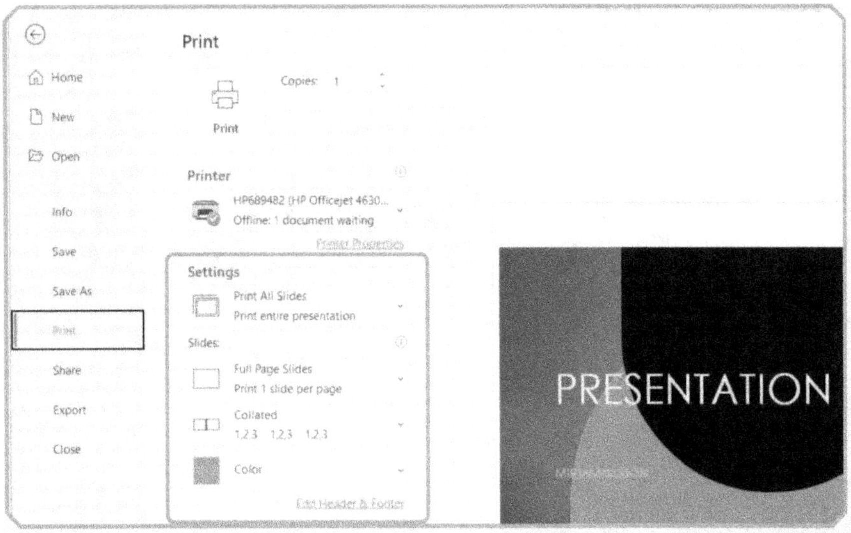

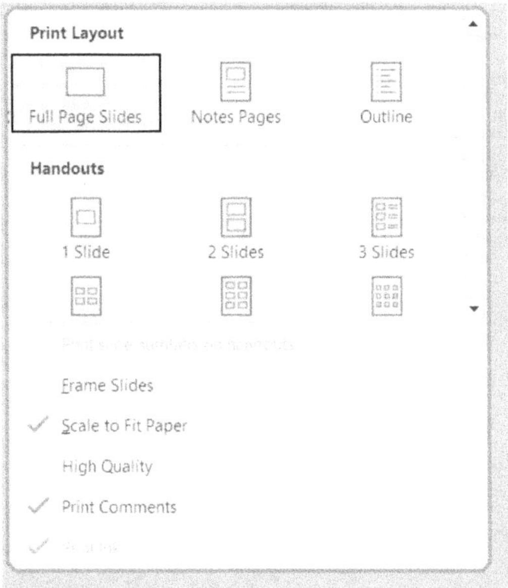

Understanding Print Formats

The **single-slide format** represents the most professional printing option, producing one slide per page with maximum visual clarity. This format proves particularly valuable for client presentations or educational materials where detail and readability are paramount. Think of it as creating a professional portfolio of your presentation.

The **notes pages format** creates a specialized layout with your slide at the top and dedicated space below for handwritten annotations. This format serves as an excellent tool for speakers who prefer to augment their printed slides with additional notes during preparation or delivery. Consider it your personal presentation companion, combining visual aids with space for your insights. For those seeking a concise overview, the **outline format** distills your presentation to its essential structure by printing only headings and titles. This streamlined approach helps you focus on the presentation's core message and organization.

Optimizing Resources

When efficiency matters, PowerPoint's **multiple slides per page** option allows you to print up to nine slides on a single sheet. This approach not only conserves paper but also creates convenient handouts that give your audience a comprehensive view of your presentation. The print settings panel offers additional customization through orientation options and single or double-sided printing capabilities. Through thoughtful use of these printing options, you can create physical materials that enhance your presentation's impact while meeting your specific communication objectives.

Creating Dynamic Recorded Presentations in PowerPoint

PowerPoint's recording capabilities transform static presentations into engaging multimedia content, opening up new possibilities for effective communication across distance and time. Understanding how to harness these recording features can significantly enhance your ability to reach and engage with audiences, whether they're students, colleagues, or clients.

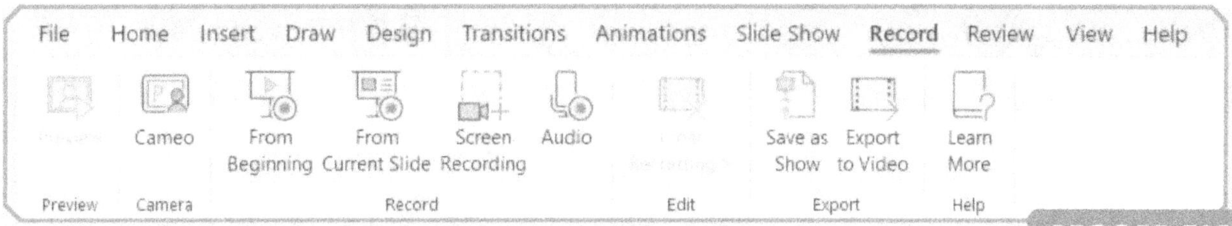

RECORD TAB

Accessing the Recording Environment

The recording journey begins in the **Record tab**, thoughtfully positioned in PowerPoint's ribbon interface. This centralized location provides access to all recording-related tools and options. You can initiate your recording from any point in your presentation, offering flexibility in how you structure your content creation process. Think of it as your personal broadcasting studio, where you have complete control over how your message is captured and delivered.

Enhancing Your Recording - Once you've completed your initial recording, PowerPoint provides sophisticated tools for audio enhancement. You can layer your presentation with:

- **Professional narration**
- **Background music**
- **Sound effects**

Finalizing Your Production - After perfecting your recorded presentation, PowerPoint offers robust export capabilities. The video export function supports multiple formats, ensuring your content remains accessible regardless of your audience's technical environment.

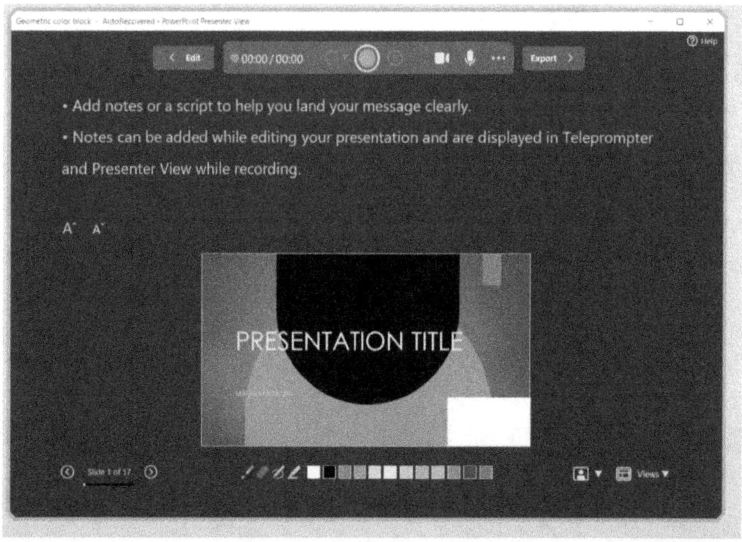

Keyboard Shortcuts on *Power Point*

Function	PC Shortcut	Mac Shortcut
Start a presentation from the beginning	*F5*	*Command + Shift + Return*
Show presenter view	*Alt + F5*	*Option + Return*
Close presenter view	*Esc*	*Esc*
Move slide during presentation	*Arrows or enter*	*Arrows or return*
Go to last slide	*End*	*End*
Go to first slide	*Home*	*Home*
Go to next slide	*Page down*	*Not available*
Go to previous slide	*Page up*	*Not available*
Hide pointer and navigation	*Ctrl + H*	*Not available*
View computer taskbar	*Ctrl + T*	*Not available*
Add new slide	*Ctrl + M*	*Command + Shift + N*
Open Zoom dialogue box	*Alt + W, Q*	*Command + (+) or (-)*
Open recording feature	*Alt + C*	*Not available*
Expand or collapse the ribbon	*Ctrl + F1*	*Command + F1*
Select all objects in a slide	*Ctrl + A*	*Command + A*
Copy animation painter	*Alt + Shift + C*	*Not available*
Insert a text box	*Alt + N, X*	*Not available*
Insert WordArt	*Alt + N, W*	*Not available*
Group a selected group	*Ctrl + G*	*Command + Option + G*
Expand all groups	*Alt + Shift + 9*	*Not available*

4. Access:

The Comprehensive Database Solution for Business Management

Microsoft Access, often overlooked by many who perceive it as too complex, emerges as one of the most dynamic and powerful tools within the Microsoft Office suite for database creation and information management. While users can create databases from scratch, the software includes numerous pre-built templates to accelerate project initiation. This comprehensive application demonstrates particular usefulness for small and medium-sized enterprises that don't have custom-developed software for their operational requirements. Access delivers an economical, expandable, and dependable platform for organizing and examining essential business information.

Essential Components and Navigation Framework

Access's interface employs a ribbon-based structure, matching other Microsoft Office programs, especially Excel. This architectural decision substantially eases the transition for individuals who already know the Office environment. The Excel similarities prove particularly advantageous for those skilled in pivot table usage, as these competencies translate directly to Access's data handling features. The intuitive design philosophy extends to database creation wizards, making complex operations more approachable for novice users.

Essential Ribbon Components of Access Interface

1. **Create**: Contains instruments for constructing new database components like tables, queries, forms, and reports, with intelligent design suggestions.

2. **External Data**: Features methods for importing, exporting, and connecting data across different platforms, including cloud services.

3. **Database Tools**: Houses tools for database upkeep, examination, enhancement, and performance optimization.

While Access concentrates primarily on data handling and investigation, it also addresses document presentation. The Home tab within the ribbon incorporates text formatting capabilities similar to those in Word and Excel. This functionality enables users to generate refined, business-grade reports and forms that align with other corporate documentation, complete with advanced charting and visualization options.

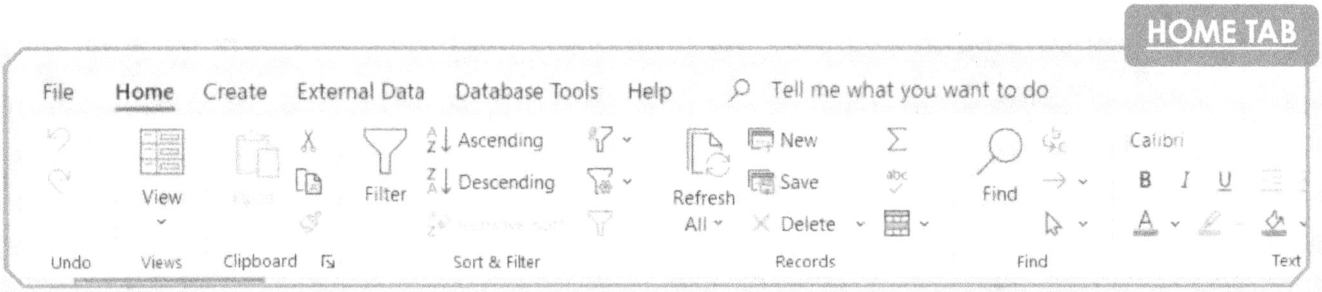

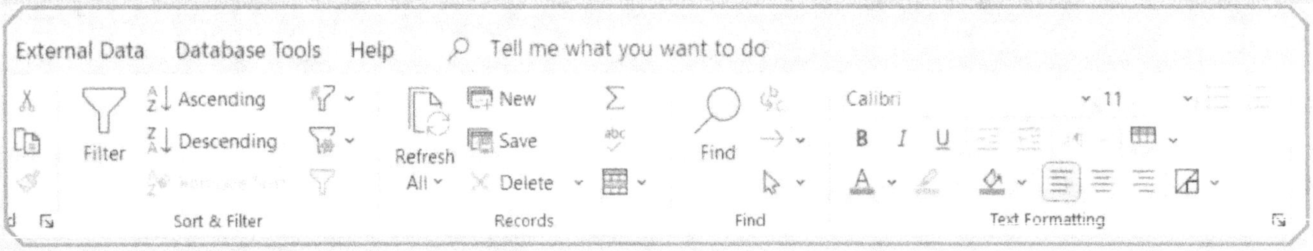

Professional-Grade Capabilities

For users with more expertise, Access presents sophisticated capabilities such as:

- **Macros and VBA** (Visual Basic for Applications) for process automation and customized functions, including error handling and debugging tools
- **Relational database architecture** to manage intricate data frameworks effectively, supporting complex relationships and referential integrity
- **SQL view** for direct query composition and database manipulation, with support for advanced JOIN operations and subqueries
- **SharePoint integration** to enhance teamwork and data distribution, including version control and change tracking
- **Web database development** for remote access to database applications, with responsive design capabilities
- **Advanced security features** including data encryption and user-level access control
- **Automated backup and recovery systems** to protect critical data
- **Custom event handling and triggered procedures** for real-time data validation

Database Creation in Access:

Launching a new database in Access mirrors the workflow of other Microsoft Office applications, accessible via startup screen or File tab. Users can choose between starting with a clean slate or selecting from Microsoft's pre-built templates.

Unlike other Office programs, Access requires database naming at creation, establishing proper organization from the start. For those seeking complete control, creating a database from scratch presents users with an empty table framework featuring unmarked columns and rows, allowing for maximum customization of the database structure.

Smart Data Entry System: Access employs intelligent row management where new rows become available only after existing ones contain data. For instance, completing data entry in the first row automatically generates a new row below it.

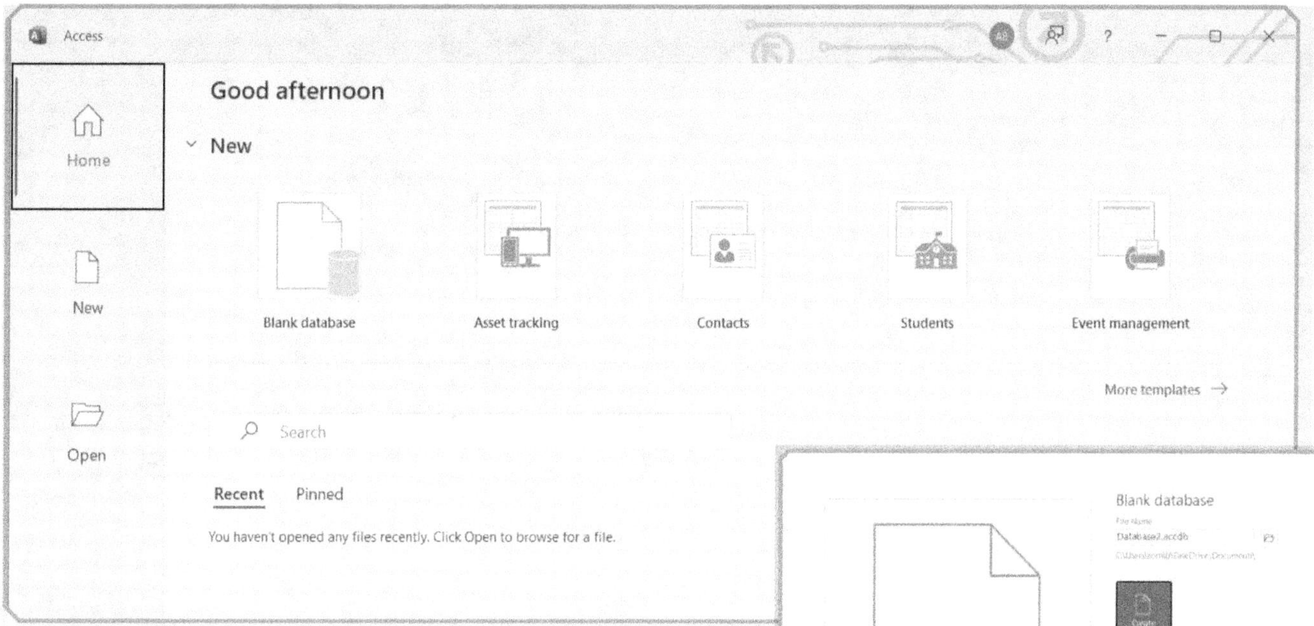

This smart design promotes systematic data entry while maintaining database structural integrity from the outset, guiding users toward creating well-organized databases and preventing common data entry errors.

Field Configuration and Management

Access's default database template arrives with standard field names that need customization for specific project requirements. The renaming process is straightforward:

1. **Quick Edit**: Double-click the target column header
2. **Direct Input**: Enter your desired field name in the editable space

This customization flexibility extends to both empty and populated fields, allowing:

1. **Content Modification**: Double-click any cell
2. **Immediate Updates**: Edit the highlighted content as needed

Intelligent Database Growth

Access implements a methodical approach to database expansion. The system requires naming existing columns before allowing new ones, promoting organized growth. Once current fields are labeled, Access automatically enables additional column creation.

Best Practices for Field Naming

- Use **descriptive yet concise** names that clearly indicate the data type
- Replace spaces with underscores for better functionality
- Maintain consistency in naming conventions
- Consider future querying needs when selecting names
- Keep names short but meaningful
- Avoid special characters or reserved words

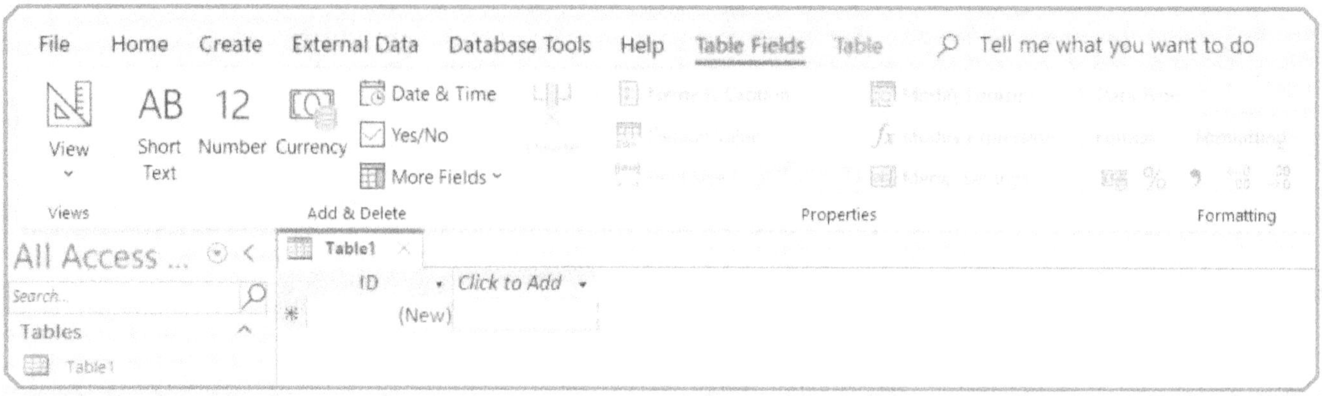

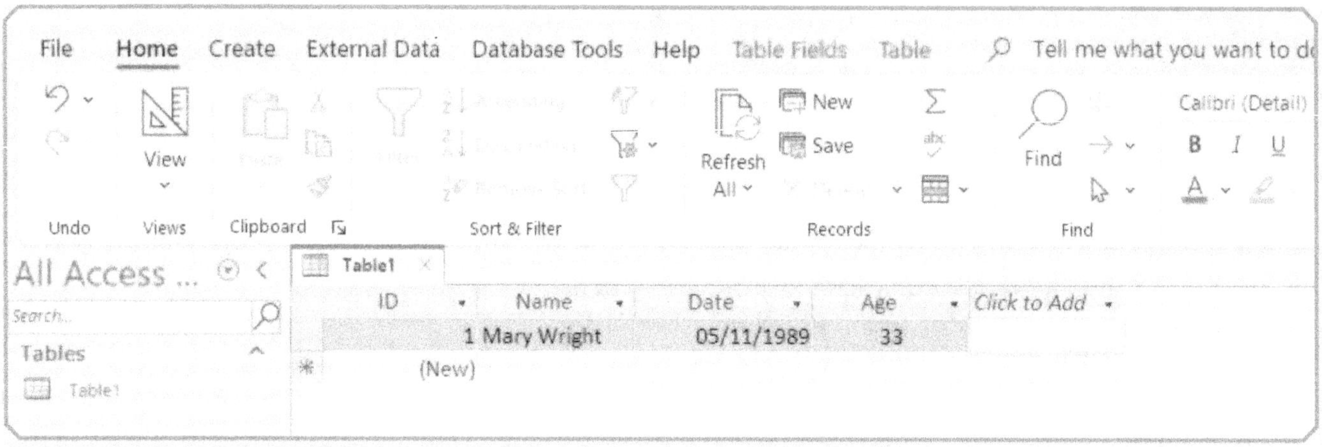

Additional Considerations:

- Field names directly impact database performance
- Well-structured names facilitate easier data validation
- Clear naming enhances report generation efficiency
- Consistent naming supports seamless data integration
- Proper field configuration simplifies database maintenance
- Names should reflect business terminology when possible

Data Management: Filtering and Sorting

Once your table contains data, Access provides robust features for information manipulation and analysis:

Advanced Filtering System - Access offers comprehensive filtering tools that enable users to:

- Isolate specific data segments
- Apply multiple filter criteria simultaneously
- Create custom filter conditions
- Save frequently used filters These capabilities ensure precise data analysis and targeted information retrieval.

Versatile Sorting Functions - The platform supports multiple sorting methods:

- **Text-based**: Alphabetical ordering for text fields
- **Numeric**: Sequential ordering for numbers

- **Temporal**: Chronological ordering for dates
- **Directional**: Both ascending and descending options
- **Multi-level**: Sorting by multiple fields simultaneously

The sorting and filtering interface mirrors Excel's design, reducing the learning curve for users familiar with Microsoft Office tools. This intentional similarity enables seamless transition between applications.

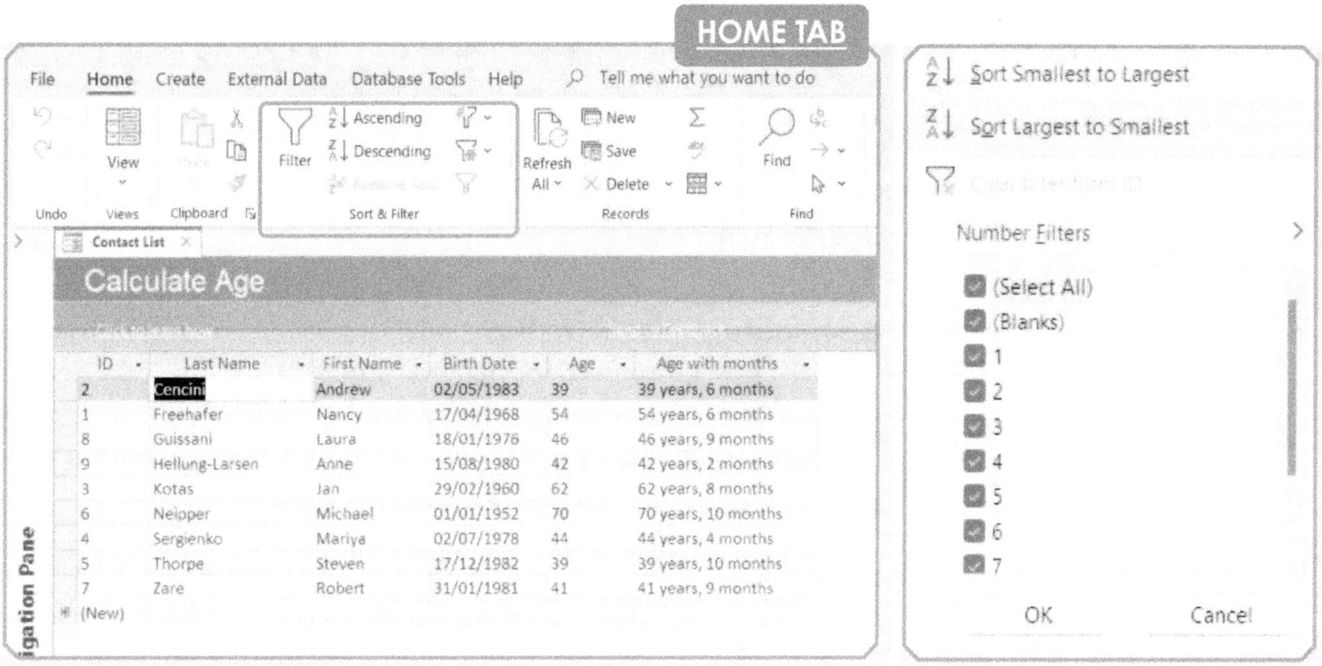

Enhanced Visualization Tools - Beyond basic organization, Access provides:

- **Dynamic Reports**: Automated data grouping and summarization
- **Custom Views**: Tailored data presentations
- **Interactive Dashboards**: Real-time data visualization
- **Cross-tab Analysis**: Multi-dimensional data examination

Productivity Tips:

- *Combine multiple filters for deeper analysis*
- *Create saved filter sets for routine queries*
- *Utilize advanced sorting for complex data relationships*
- *Leverage reporting tools for comprehensive data insights*
- *Regular experimentation with different view combinations often reveals hidden patterns and trends*

These features collectively transform raw data into actionable business intelligence, supporting informed decision-making processes.

Advanced Access Features

Beyond its core database functionality, Access provides a rich set of enhanced features that extend its data management capabilities. For example, in a customer management system, these features enable customized data entry forms and automated email notifications.

Interface Design Tools - The Create tab offers essential elements including:

- Media integration (like company logos in forms)
- Dialogue boxes (such as custom order confirmation windows)
- Checkboxes (for order status tracking)
- Customizable forms (tailored for specific departments)

Application Parts and Blank Form buttons enable the development of tailored data input interfaces. For instance, a sales team could use a simplified order entry form, while inventory managers access a more detailed stock management interface.

Data Entry Solutions - These features facilitate controlled data input, allowing users to contribute information without requiring access to the entire database. For example:

- Sales representatives can enter new orders without accessing financial data
- Customer service can update contact information without viewing sensitive pricing details
- Warehouse staff can update inventory levels without accessing customer records

Integrated Office Features - Access incorporates familiar Microsoft Office tools including:

- Spell check functionality (essential for maintaining clean customer records)
- Equation editor support (useful for calculating discounts or commissions)
- Find and replace capabilities (helpful for updating product codes or categories)

These tools maintain consistency across the Microsoft Suite, leveraging users' existing knowledge of Office applications. This means someone familiar with Excel's find and replace function can easily use the same feature in Access to update product names across multiple tables.

Adding New Tables

Tables are the foundation of **Microsoft Access**, functioning as the essential mechanism for **data organization** and **storage**. Mastering table management is essential for harnessing the full capabilities of this sophisticated database application.

When creating a new table, Access automatically assigns a tab titled "Table 2" (or subsequent numbers) at your workspace's top. This automatic naming system can become problematic as your database expands.

Table Management

Setting Up Table Properties - For enhanced database organization, renaming tables to match their function or contents is recommended. Follow these steps:

1. Find the Navigation Pane positioned on your workspace's left side.
2. Right-click the table requiring modification.
3. A menu will display, presenting several choices:

   - **Rename:** Modify the table's designation for better recognition.
   - **Delete:** Eliminate the table completely (exercise caution).
   - **Properties:** Access and adjust the table's characteristics.

CREATE TAB

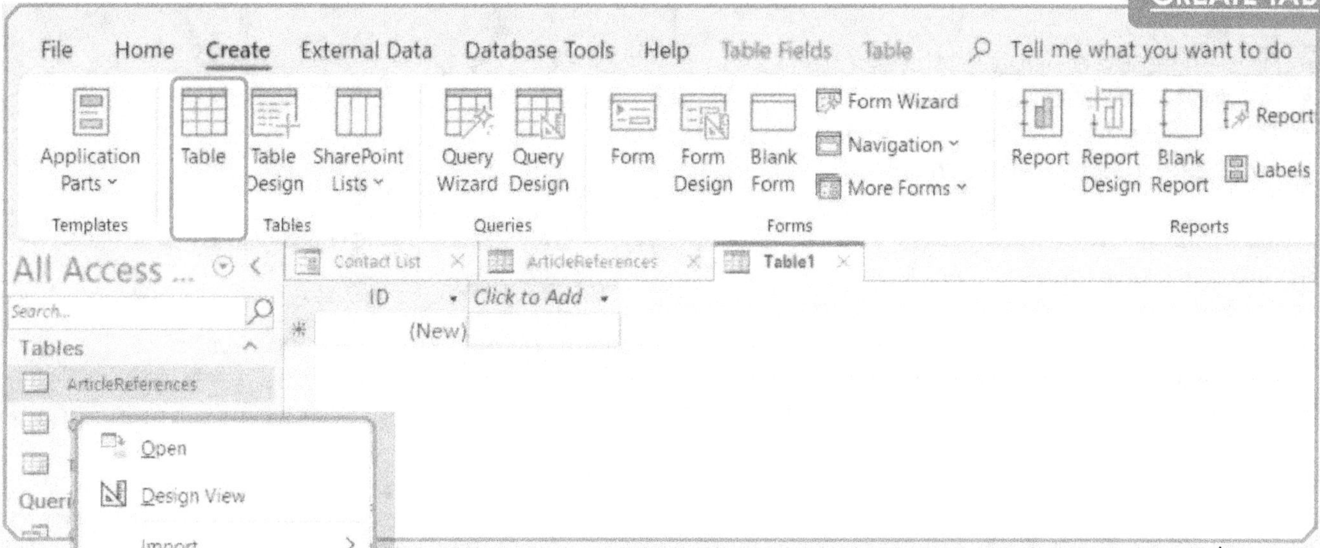

Data Entry Fundamentals - For newly created tables, follow the identical data entry methodology as your original table:

- Input data systematically through rows and columns.
- Access creates additional rows automatically as current ones are filled.
- Treat each table as an independent document with potential future connections to other database tables.

External Data Integration - Access delivers powerful capabilities for incorporating external data, facilitating efficient comprehensive database creation.

1. Select the **External Data tab** in the ribbon.
2. Select the **New Data Source** button to initiate importing.

EXTERNAL DATA TAB

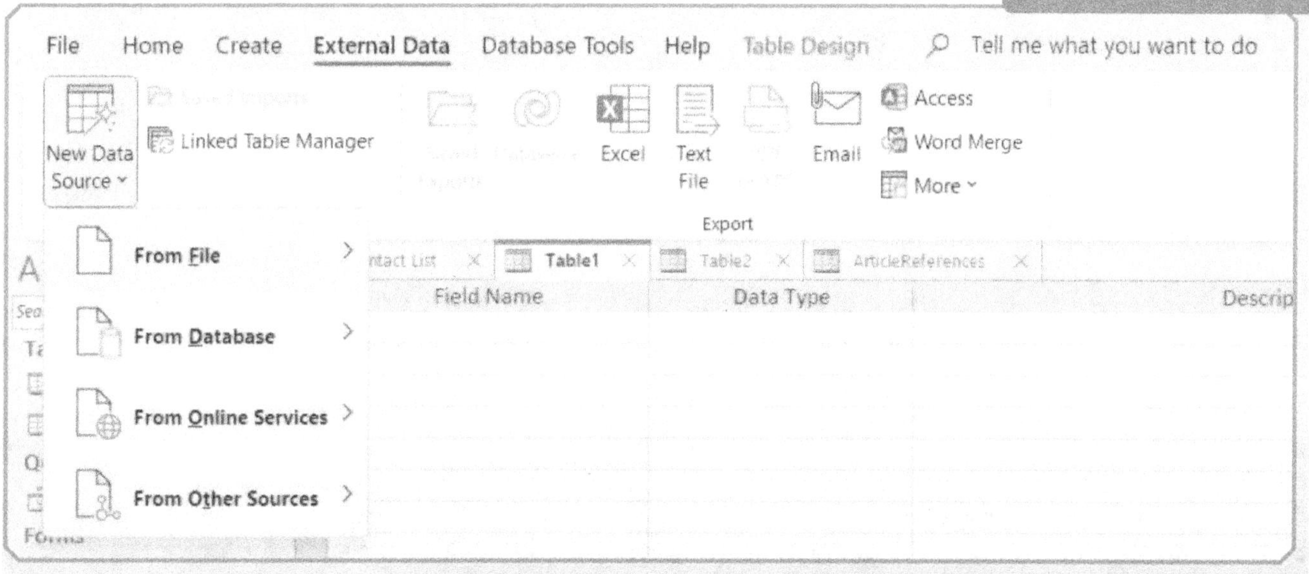

Access enables importing from various sources:

- Files on your computer's storage
- Internet-based resources
- Alternative databases
- Supplementary data sources

Data Integration Techniques - After selecting your data source, Access offers three main integration approaches:

1. **Import to a New Table:** Establishes a fresh table containing imported data.
2. **Append to an Existing Table:** Incorporates new information into a previously created table.
3. **Link to Excel:** Creates an active connection between your Access database and Excel worksheet.

Excel Linking Feature - Selecting the Excel link option ensures that modifications to the original Excel file automatically update in your Access database. This functionality maintains data consistency across platforms. If updates aren't immediate, manually refresh by selecting the Refresh button in the ribbon's Home tab. Managing multiple tables becomes crucial as your database expands. Access provides tools for effective workspace organization.

Table View Management - When tables aren't in active use, temporarily hide them:

- Select the X button on the table's tab for closure.
- This doesn't eliminate the table; it merely removes it from current view.

Restoring Hidden Tables - To display a hidden table:

- Find the table name in the left-side Navigation Pane.
- Select the table name to restore it to your workspace.

> ***Productivity Tip:*** *Leverage keyboard shortcuts to streamline your table management in Access. Press F11 to toggle the Navigation Pane visibility, creating more workspace when needed. Use CTRL+F6 to quickly switch between open tables, and CTRL+W to close the active table. These shortcuts can significantly speed up your workflow, especially when working with multiple tables in complex databases.*

Field Formatting Essentials

One of the standout capabilities in **Microsoft Access** is its sophisticated field formatting system. Compared to alternative database platforms requiring complex setup procedures, Access provides a comprehensive suite of tools to expedite field configuration.

Basic Field Format Selection - Establishing data types for table columns can be accomplished through simple point-and-click actions. The essential data type categories include:

1. **Short Text:** Accommodates brief combinations of letters and numbers
2. **Number:** Designated for pure numerical entries
3. **Currency:** Handles monetary values, incorporating appropriate currency indicators
4. **Date and Time:** Manages chronological information with customizable display formats
5. **Yes/No:** Handles binary choices, typically represented through checkbox interfaces

These fundamental options are accessible through the quick access toolbar, enabling swift table configuration.

For scenarios requiring more specialized configurations, Access offers an expanded selection of field types. The **More Fields option,** marked by a downward arrow icon, reveals an extensive catalog of specialized field configurations.

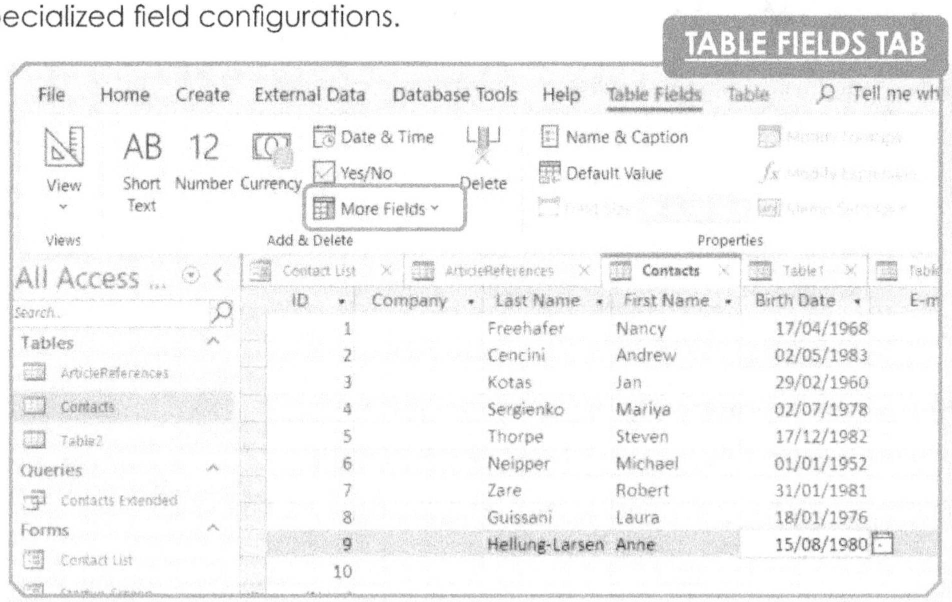

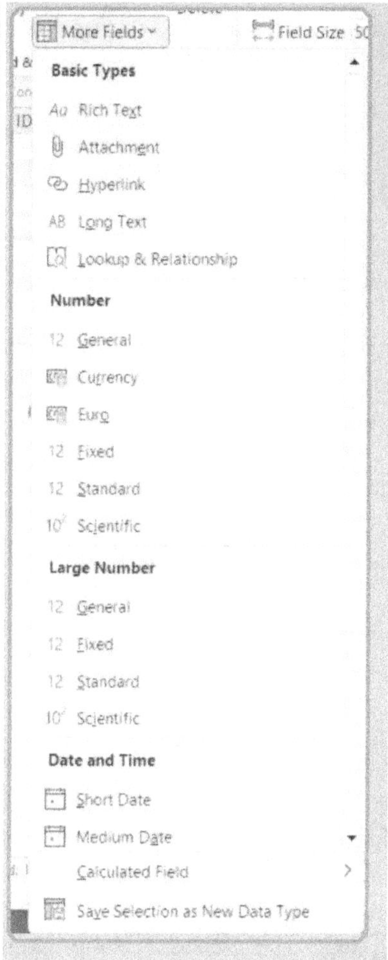

Advanced Field Options

- **Address Fields:** Creates an integrated set of fields designed for complete location data entry
- **Payment Type:** Implements a validated selection menu featuring standard payment options
- **Status Bar:** Enables visual progress tracking, particularly valuable for project oversight

These examples represent just a subset of the available field types. A thorough exploration of the complete options catalog allows for precise customization of your database architecture.

Field Implementation Strategy

When incorporating additional fields through quick formatting tools, it's crucial to understand that Access preserves existing data while expanding the table structure. For optimal table organization, consider these guidelines:

1. **Terminal Addition:** Position your cursor in the final column before creating new fields, ensuring systematic table expansion
2. **Intermediate Insertion:** For mid-table field additions, place your cursor in the column immediately preceding your intended insertion location

Field Calculation Implementation

One of **Microsoft Access's** most potent yet underutilized capabilities is its **calculated fields** feature. This functionality integrates Excel-like computation power into your Access database, enabling real-time data computation and analysis. Here's the process for implementing a calculated field:

1. **Choose the Target Column**: Select the column header where the calculated field will reside.

2. **Navigate to Table Fields**: The ribbon automatically displays this tab after column selection.

3. **Access Extended Options**: Select the "More Fields" button within the ribbon.

4. **Select Calculation Option**: Locate and choose "Add Calculated Field" at the menu's bottom.

Calculation Setup - After selecting "Add Calculated Field," a configuration window appears for formula creation:

1. **Field Identification**: Select the relevant fields for your calculation from your table's columns.

2. **Formula Development**: Utilize the text field to construct your mathematical expression.

Practical Application

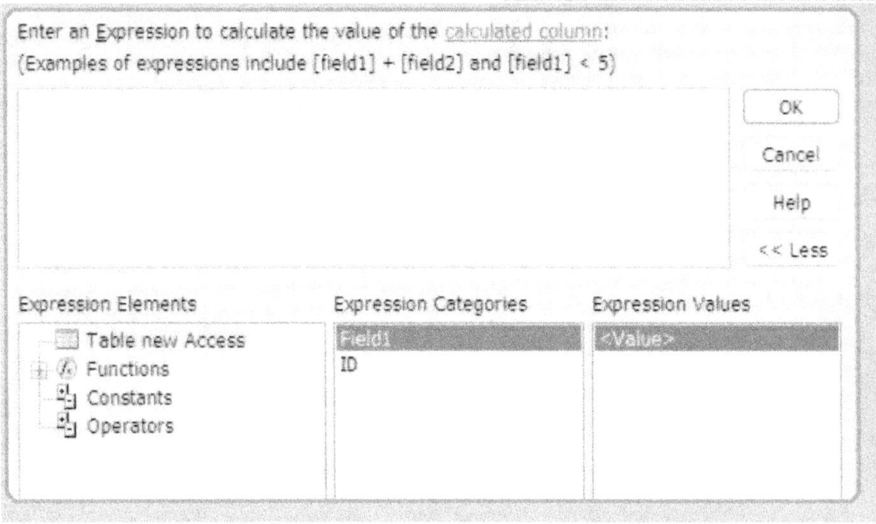

Consider this representative calculated field example:

([Field 1] + [Field 2] + [Field 3]) / 3

This expression computes a running average across three designated fields. The system automatically updates these calculations when source data changes.

Data Type Optimization

When implementing calculated fields, careful consideration of data type compatibility is essential:

- **Numerical Operations**: Verify all fields utilize number formats (Integer, Double, etc.) for precise mathematical processing.
- **Chronological Calculations**: Employ Date/Time fields for temporal computations.
- **String Operations**: Utilize Text fields for character-based manipulations.

Combining mismatched data types may result in calculation errors or unexpected outcomes. While

Access provides automatic type conversion, explicit type management ensures optimal reliability and performance.

Advanced Table Structure Management

Microsoft Access provides a sophisticated yet intuitive approach to database organization through its enhanced drag-and-drop capabilities. This functionality enables seamless column reorganization within your table structure:

1. **Column Selection**: Identify and click the column header intended for relocation.
2. **Movement Indicator**: A dynamic black line appears, marking the selected column's position.
3. **Position Adjustment**: Manipulate the column to its desired location, guided by the visual marker. This streamlined approach facilitates rapid table restructuring to accommodate specific organizational requirements.

> ***Productivity Tip**: Similar to Excel's functionality, Access enables precise control over column dimensions and row heights, enhancing data visibility and presentation effectiveness.*

Extended Field Controls - Access incorporates comprehensive field management tools, accessible via the column header context menu. Key functionalities include:

1. **Content Duplication**: Replicate column structure or data.
2. **Visibility Control**: Toggle field display status.
3. **Column Integration**: Insert new fields at specified positions.
4. **Position Locking**: Secure essential columns for enhanced navigation.

Column Freezing Functionality

The freeze feature proves invaluable when navigating extensive databases requiring horizontal scrolling. Access offers superior control compared to Excel's basic freezing mechanism:

- **Selective Immobilization**: Lock specific columns independently.
- **Sequential Organization**: Frozen columns maintain their freezing sequence.
- **Quick Release**: Instantly restore normal viewing mode.

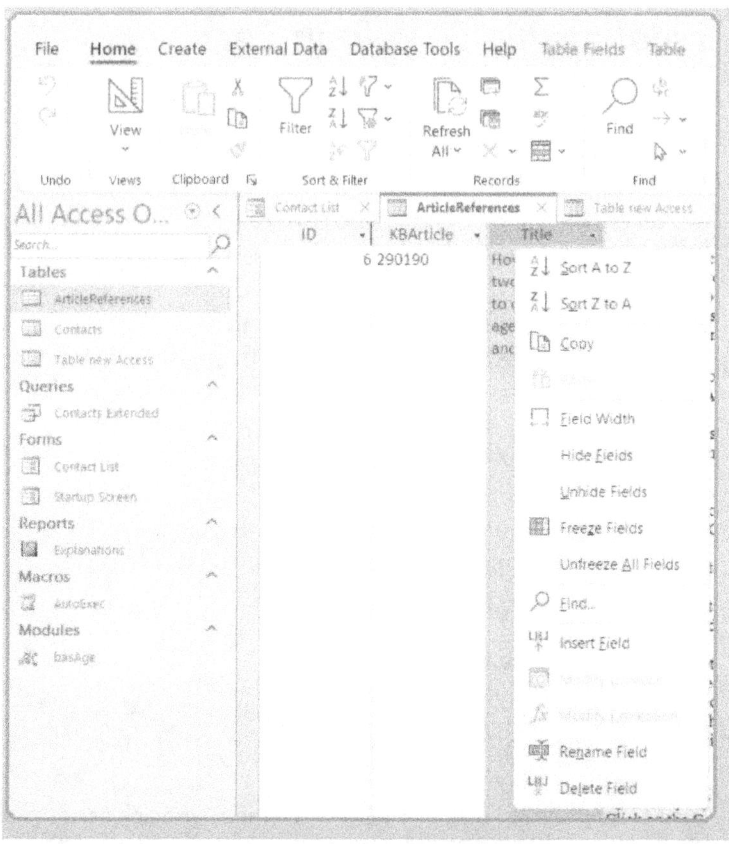

Implementation Example

Academic Records System Consider managing a comprehensive 9th-grade academic database:

- Individual rows represent student entries.
- Columns contain subject-specific grades.
- The system encompasses 20+ grade categories.

To maintain data context during navigation:

1. **Access Student Identifier**: Right-click the name column header.
2. **Activate Freezing**: Select the freeze option.
3. **Navigation Enhancement**: The identifier remains visible during horizontal scrolling.

Additional columns, such as student ID or class designation, can be frozen similarly, positioning automatically to the right of previously frozen fields.

Layout Restoration Process - To return to the default view:

1. **Access Frozen Column**: Right-click any locked column.
2. **Release Lock**: Choose the universal unfreeze option.

> ***Note:*** *The unfreeze operation releases all locked columns simultaneously. Original column arrangement must be manually reconstructed using the previously outlined drag-and-drop methodology.*

Database Connectivity and Information Retrieval: Relations and Queries

Relations and **queries** represent core functionalities in **Microsoft Access**, distinguishing it from simpler spreadsheet applications. These tools enable efficient data access, establish interconnections between database components, and support comprehensive reporting capabilities. Let's examine their implementation.

Relationship Development

To demonstrate relationship importance in Access, let's examine an academic database scenario. Consider managing both academic performance and student details. A crucial linking element must exist between these data sets to create a connection. This could be implemented through a unique student identifier or personal identifiers, though a dedicated identification system typically proves most efficient.

When constructing the personal information table, incorporate essential elements like contact details, educational assignments, and other relevant data. The critical factor is maintaining unique student identification to support efficient data management.

1. **Database Structure:**

    - **Primary Table:** Academic performance records
    - **Secondary Table:** Student biographical data

2. **Linking Field Requirements:**

    - **Primary Option:** Unique student identifier (recommended)
    - **Alternative Option:** Name-based identification

Note: Implementing unique identifiers represents optimal database practice.

DATABASE TOOLS TAB

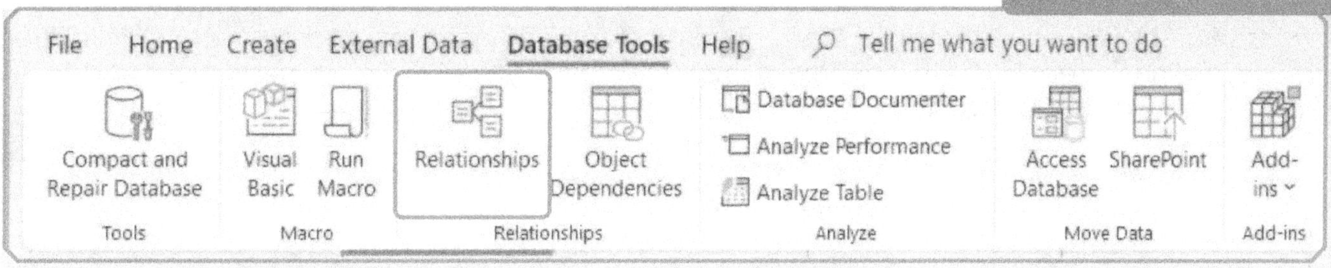

3. **Connection Implementation Process:**

    - Access the database tools section
    - Select relationship configuration
    - Display relevant tables in workspace
    - Identify primary key indicators
    - Connect corresponding fields between tables
    - Specify relationship parameters

4. **Relationship Finalization:**

    - Close relationship configuration interface
    - Preserve relationship configuration
    - Access relationship through database navigation panel

RELATIONSHIPS DESIGN TAB

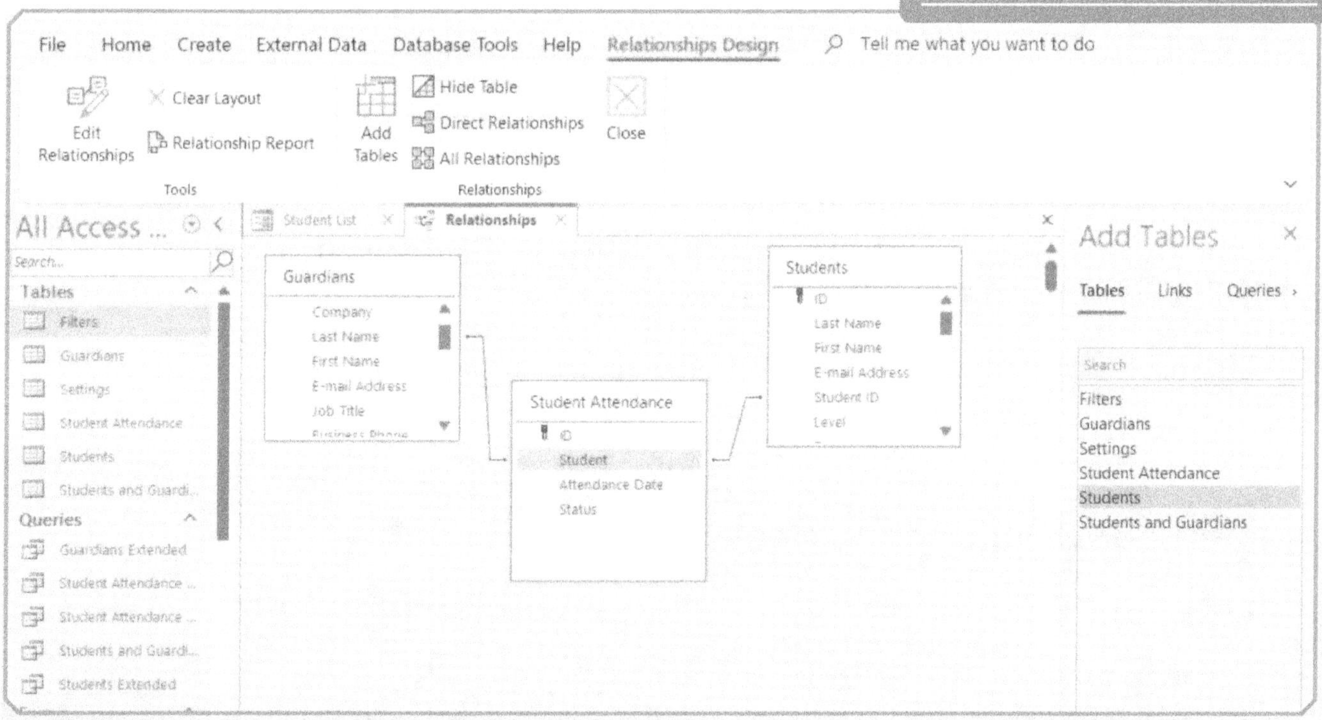

After setting up the relationship, you have the option to name and save it. Upon saving, Access will display the relationship in the left-hand pane of the database view, making it easily accessible for future use or modifications.

Queries: Data Analysis and Filtration

Queries serve as powerful analytical tools in **Microsoft Access**, enabling comprehensive data filtering and examination. From basic to advanced implementations, they facilitate customized data visualization. Here's a detailed examination of query creation:

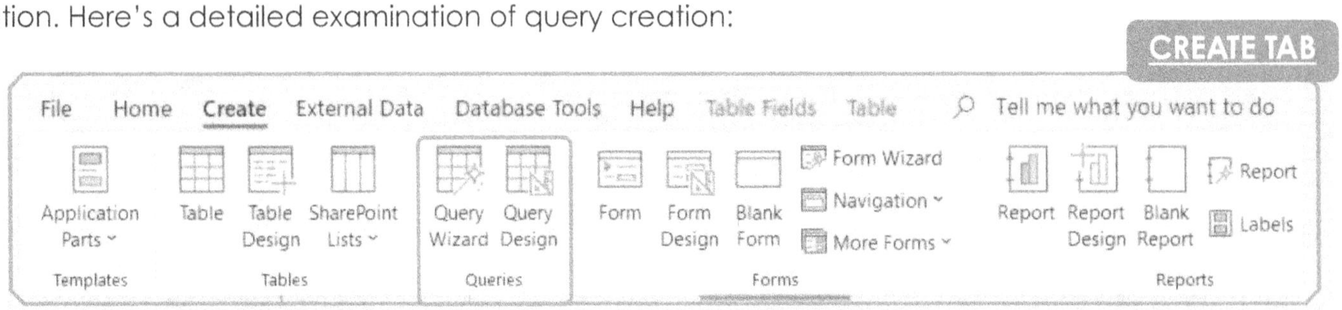

Query Implementation

1. **Access Creation Tools**: Navigate to the ribbon's create section
2. **Select Query Method**:
    - Guided creation through wizard interface
    - Manual development via query design

Custom Query Development Process

1. **Initiate Query**: Activate new query function
2. **Configure Workspace**:
    - Import relevant tables through double-click or drag-and-drop
    - Review established table connections (e.g., student identification links)
3. **Field Selection:**
    - Double-click desired data fields from table displays
    - Selected fields populate lower workspace grid
4. **Criteria Configuration:**
    - Identify target information column
    - Establish filtering conditions (e.g., "=>80%")
5. **Query Preservation**: Save and label configuration

Practical Implementation - Academic Performance Analysis Required Fields:

- Student Identification
- Student Name
- Mathematics Performance

Filter Parameters: Mathematics column: "<80%" criteria specification. This configuration identifies students scoring below 80% in mathematics, facilitating targeted academic support.

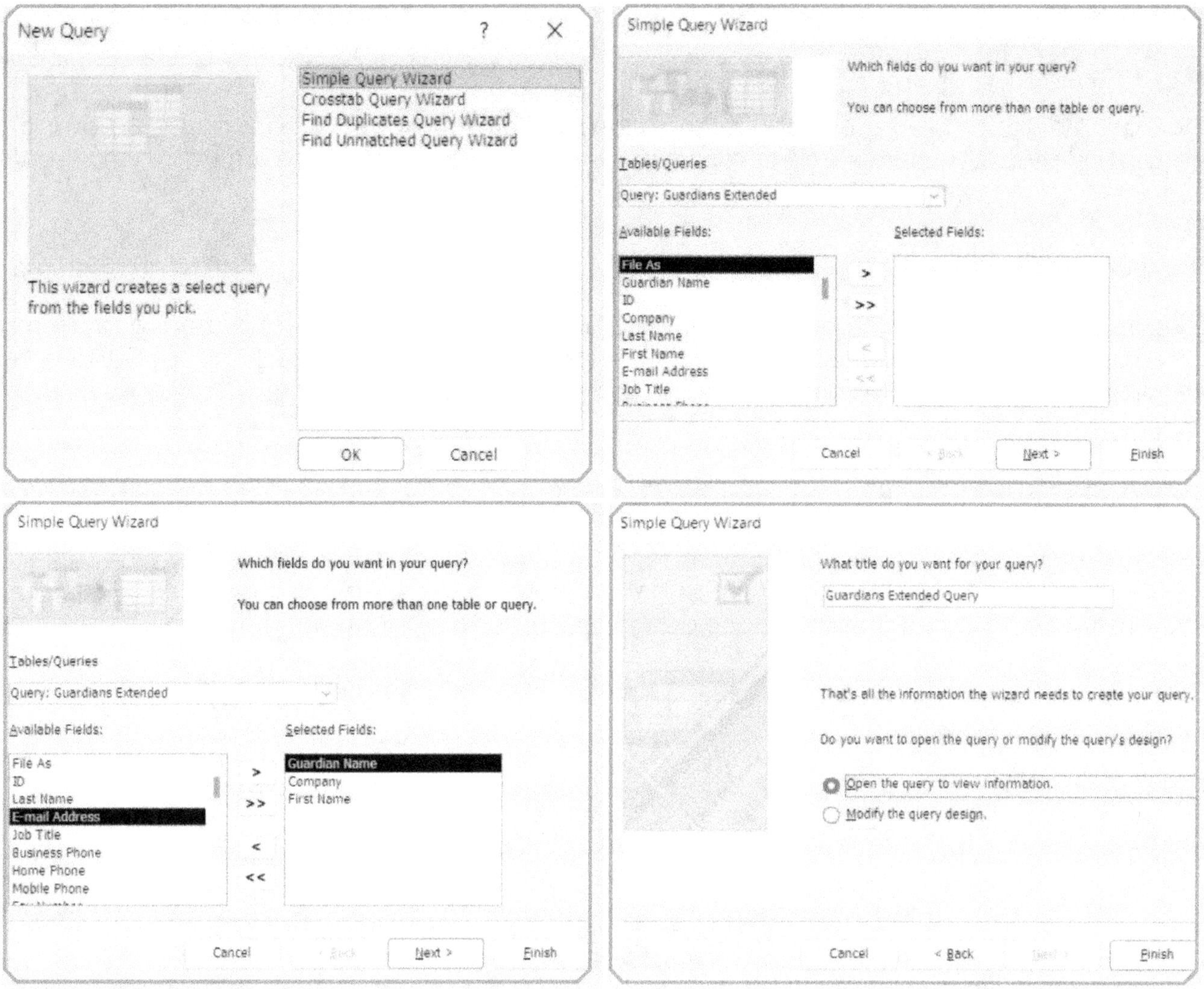

Query Classifications:

1. **Selection Queries**: Extract specific data points
2. **Filtration Queries**: Apply specific data constraints
3. **Computational Queries**: Execute mathematical analysis
4. **Matrix Queries**: Generate cross-tabulated summaries
5. **Modification Queries**: Implement data changes (updates, deletions, additions)

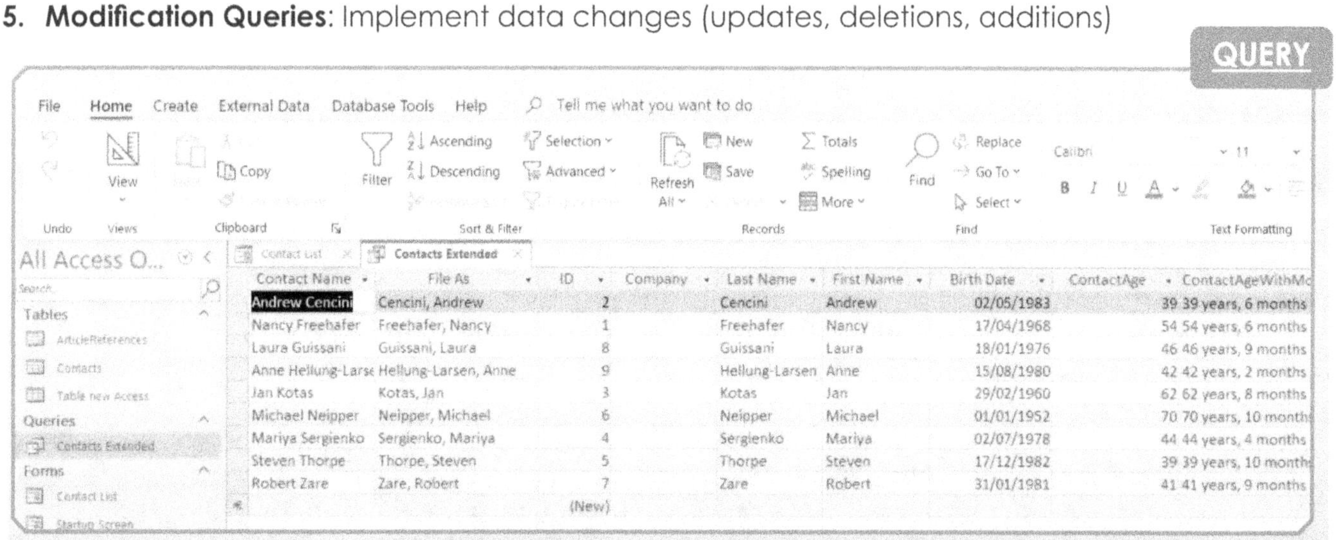

Report Generation

The creation of reports represents the culmination of **Microsoft Access's** capabilities. Following database and relationship establishment, report generation enables effective information presentation. This process builds upon previously configured elements.

Report Functionality

Access reports feature adaptable formatting options. Users can implement pre-designed templates or develop custom styles aligned with specific requirements. For example, an academic progress report can integrate personal information and academic performance metrics in an organized, visually effective layout.

Implementation Process

Navigate to the create tab and select the report function to initiate development. This action launches a dedicated window displaying report design tools. For users seeking guidance, Access provides an automated wizard that streamlines the design process and suggests optimal reporting approaches.

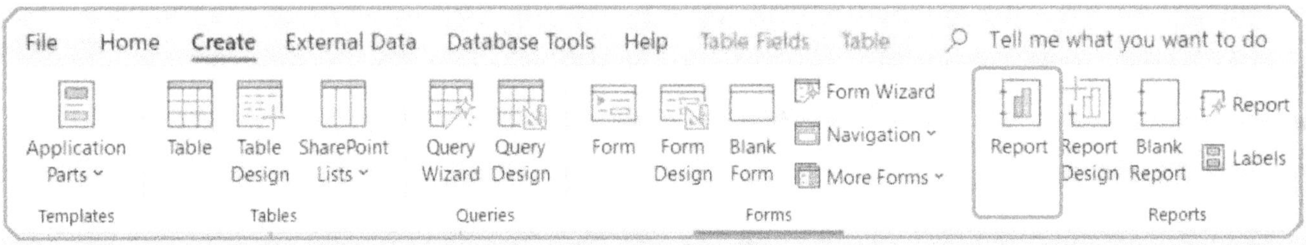

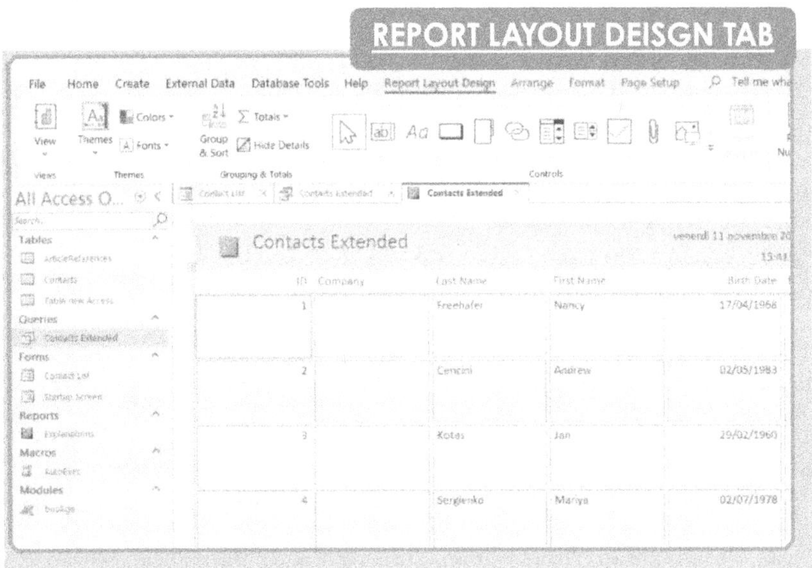

Design Customization

Report content selection follows specific informational requirements. The platform supports the integration of various elements:

- Corporate identifiers
- Document headers
- Page identifiers
- Visual elements

These components enhance both aesthetic appeal and functional effectiveness.

Finalization Steps

After configuring content and design elements, conclude by closing the development interface. Save the configuration with an appropriate identifier. The completed report appears in the navigation panel for convenient access.

***Productivity Tip**: Utilize the preview functionality to validate report appearance before finalization. This enables necessary adjustments and ensures the output aligns with intended specifications.*

Keyboard Shortcuts on Access

Function	PC Shortcut	Mac Shortcut
Go to home tab	*Ctrl + H*	*Command + H*
Open existing database	*Ctrl + O*	*Command + O*
Switch views of database	*F5*	*Not available*
Switch from edit to view mode	*F2*	*Not available*
Move to other datasheet view	*Tab key or Shift + Tab*	*Tab key*
Exit Access	*Alt + F4*	*Not available*
Go to create tab	*Alt + C*	*Not available*
Go to table tab	*Alt + J, T*	*Not available*
Go to database tools tab	*Alt+Y, 2*	*Not available*
Go to external data tab	*Alt + X*	*Not available*
Show or hide property sheet	*F4*	*Not available*
Move to beginning of entry	*Home*	*Home*
Move to end of entry	*End*	*End*
Move between lines	*Arrow keys*	*Arrow keys*
Move to next field	*Tab key*	*Tab key*
Move to previous field	*Shift + Tab*	*Not available*
Select a column	*Shift + arrow key*	*Shift + arrow key*
Remove the selected column	*Spacebar or (-) sign*	*Not available*

5. Outlook:

Electronic Mail Management System

Electronic mail has evolved into a **central method** of communication in contemporary society. To support this evolution, Microsoft has incorporated a **specialized mail program** in its collection: Microsoft Outlook. In contrast to other Microsoft tools, Outlook necessitates users to **configure their accounts** prior to operation.

Initial Configuration Process

Although multiple configuration options exist for an Outlook account, we'll examine the **standard procedure** for individual email users who have accounts with services such as Gmail, Yahoo, or Hotmail. The configuration steps vary slightly based on whether you're launching Outlook for the **initial time** or not. For those using it for the **first time**, an introductory screen containing directions will be displayed. For **returning users**, manual navigation to account settings will be necessary.

Follow these steps to set up your account:

1. Select the **File tab** in the ribbon and choose **Account Settings**
2. Navigate to the **Email tab** in the opened dialog box
3. Select the **New button** (identified by a small envelope symbol)
4. Input your **email address** in the subsequent window
5. Select **Connect**
6. Provide the following information:

    - Your name
    - Email address
    - Password

7. Click **Next** (password re-entry might be necessary)
8. Select **Finish** to conclude the setup

Upon completion of configuration, your **Inbox** will be displayed, enabling message management. The **Home tab** within the ribbon grants access to primary message functions. Outlook's ribbon maintains simplicity, featuring just **four primary tabs** alongside the Help and File tabs:

- **Home**: Contains basic email functions
- **Send/Receive**: Manages email synchronization
- **Folder**: Organizes email storage
- **View**: Customizes display settings

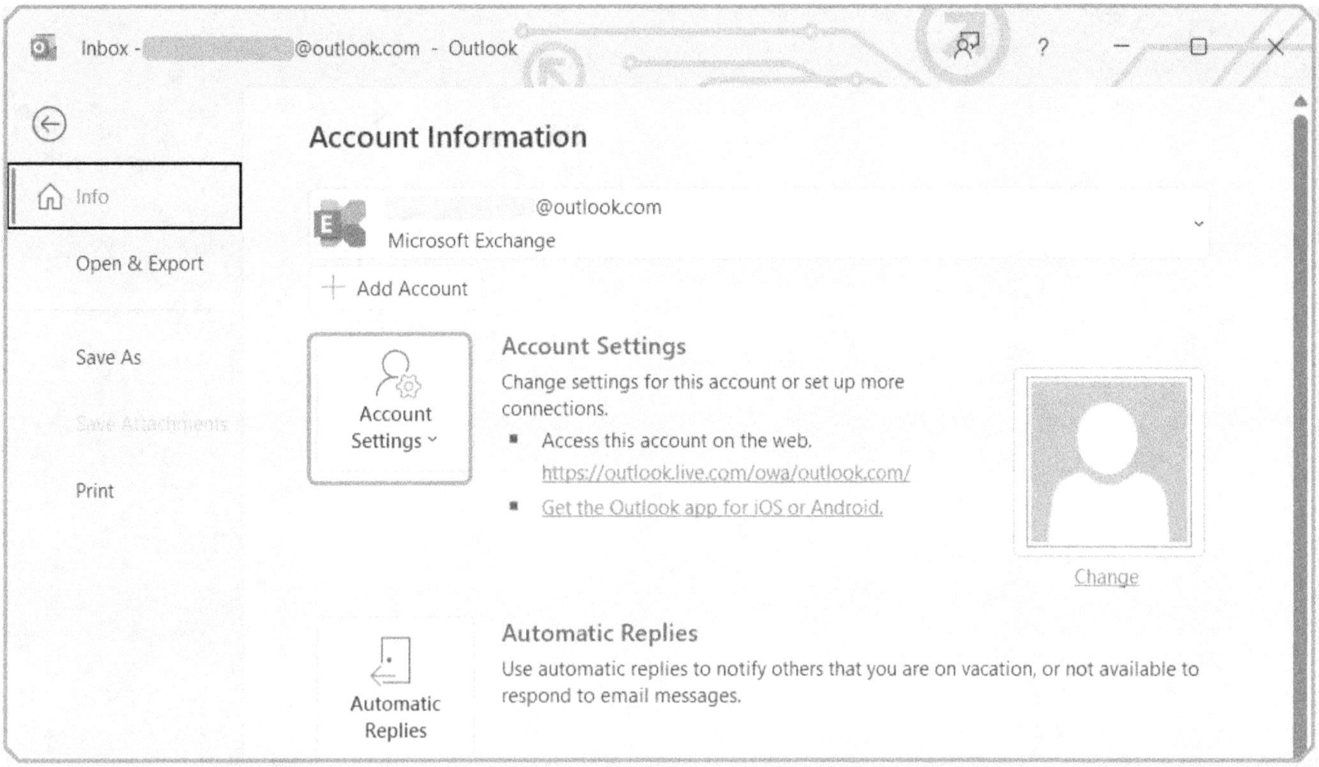

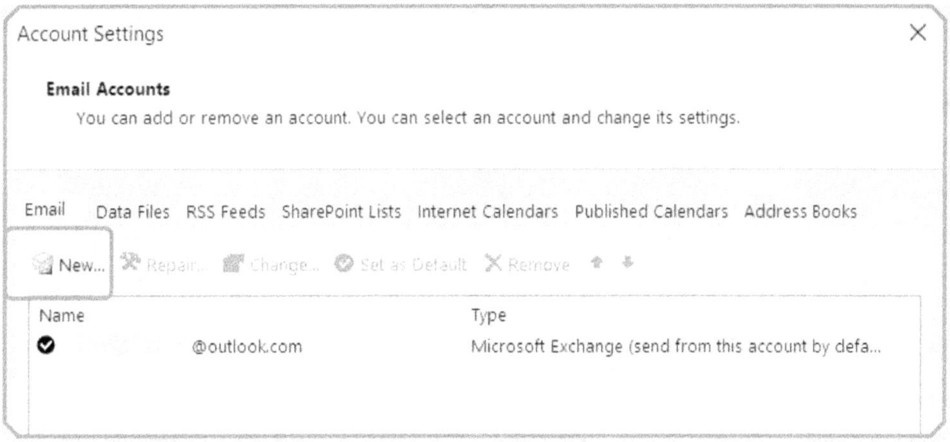

Customizing Your Digital Sign-off

Creating a **signature** represents one of the initial tasks many users seek to accomplish in Outlook. Begin this process by launching a **new message**. Actual email composition isn't necessary; this action simply provides access to signature configuration options.

To create and customize your signature:

1. Within the new message interface, locate the **"Signature" option** under the **"Include" section**
2. Select this button and choose **"Signatures"**

3. Click **"New"** and assign a title
4. In the **"Edit signature"** box, enter your desired text
5. Customize your signature using available options:

- Font style and size
- Text color
- Alignment
- Special formatting

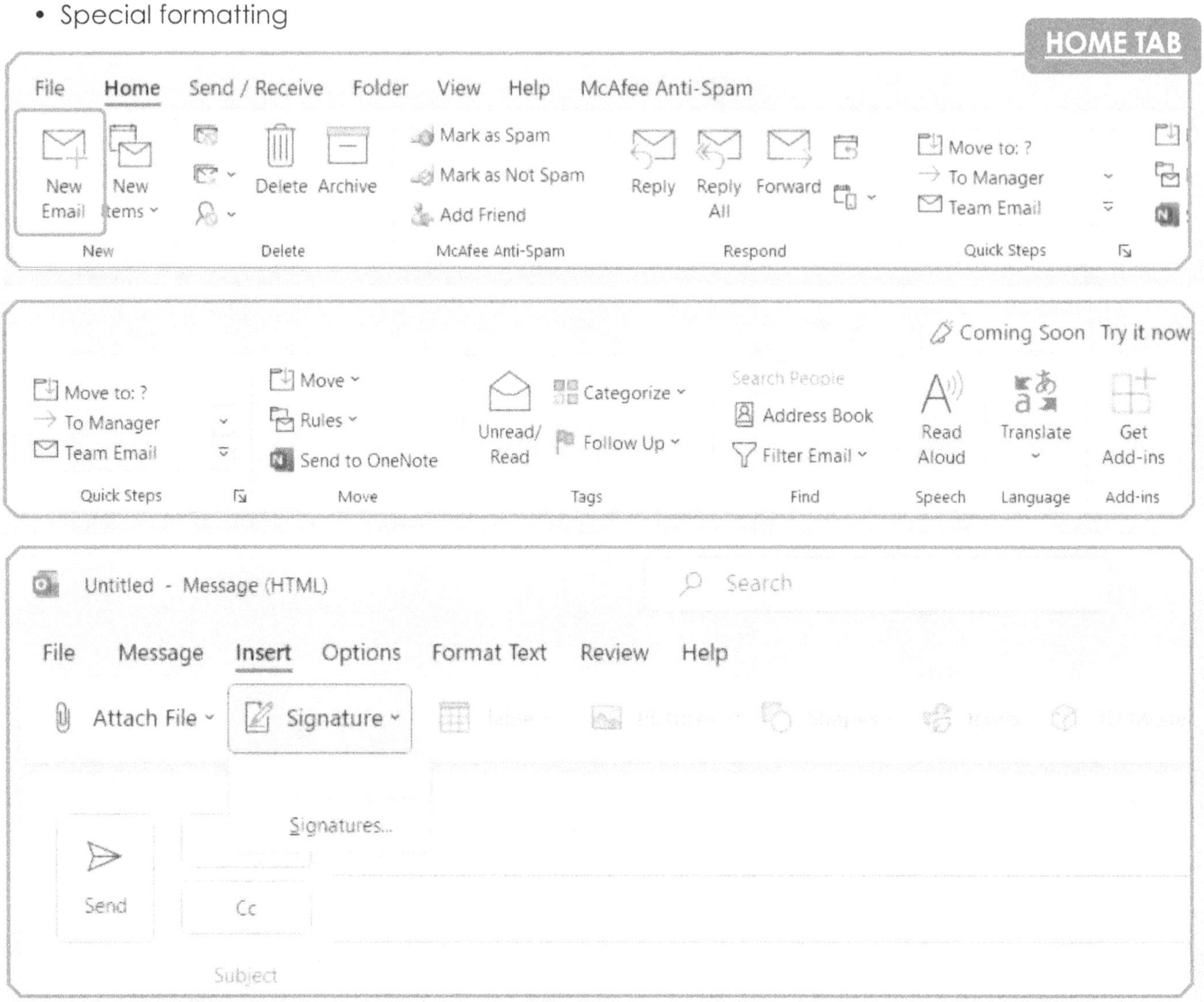

Following signature creation, you can determine its automatic implementation settings. The right-side menu labeled **"Choose default signature,"** allows assignment of various signatures to different email accounts (for users with multiple accounts). You can establish **default signatures** independently for:

- New messages
- Replies
- Forwards

Should automatic signatures not appeal to you, these settings may remain empty for manual signature insertion. In this scenario, configure your signature without setting default preferences. During message composition, you can return to the **signature button** and select the appropriate signature for each specific email.

EDIT SIGNATURE

Emails Composition

To initiate a new electronic correspondence, select the **"New Email" command**. This action reveals a composition window for your message content. Although message formatting tools are available through the ribbon interface, be aware that formatting display may vary across different email clients and recipient settings.

Recipient Fields and Management

The **"To"** and **"Cc"** (carbon copy) fields appear by default, while the **"Bcc"** (blind carbon copy) requires manual activation. Here are two methods to access the Bcc field:

1. **Primary Method:**
    - Click either **"To"** or **"Cc"** buttons
    - Locate the Bcc option in the dialog box
    - Input the desired address
    - Select **"OK"** to confirm

2. **Alternative Method through Options Tab:**
    - Navigate to the **Options tab**
    - Find the **"Show Fields"** section
    - Select buttons for:
    - **"Bcc"** field
    - **"From"** field

Message Tracking Features

The Options tab provides **notification settings** for your emails. Available tracking options:

- **Delivery receipts**: Confirm when messages are received
- **Read receipts**: Verify when messages are opened

These settings can be Applied to individual messages, set as default for all outgoing correspondence and configured to send automatic notifications upon message delivery or reading

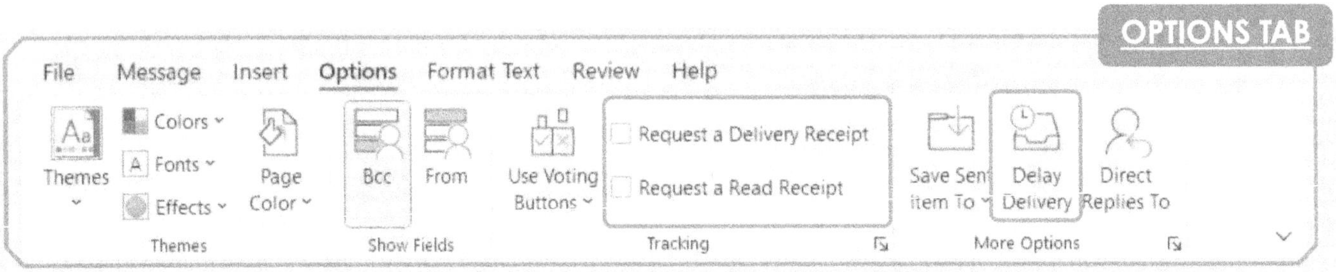

Scheduled Message Delivery

Outlook incorporates a **message timing feature** that enables future email scheduling, such as next-day delivery. Here's how to schedule your messages:

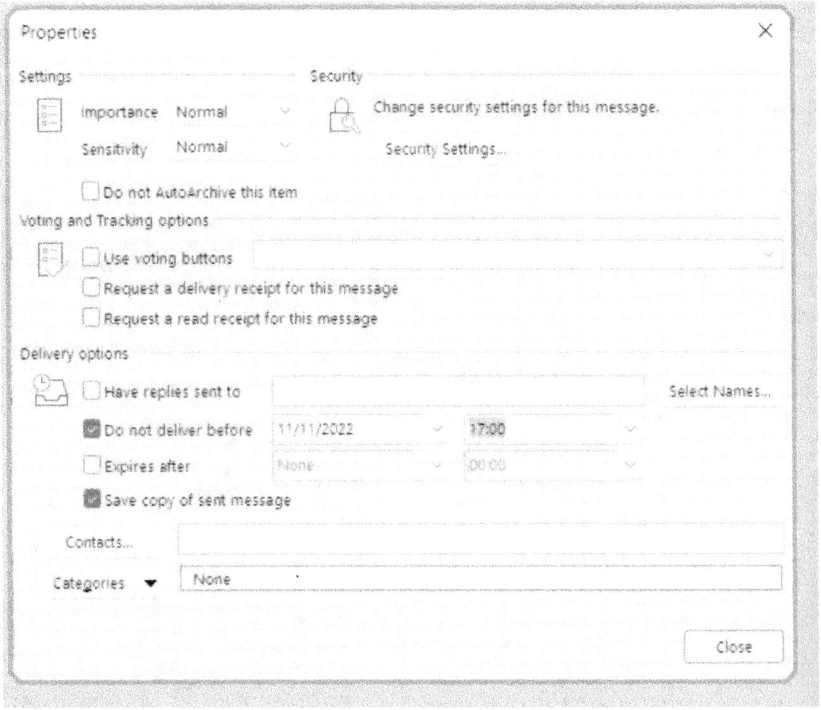

1. Access scheduling options:

    - Navigate to the **Options tab**
    - Locate the **"More Options"** section
    - Select **"Delay Delivery"**

2. In the preferences dialog box, you can configure:

    - **Delivery timing**: Set specific date and time
    - **Reply recipients**: Designate who receives responses
    - **Message expiration**: Establish when the message becomes invalid

Message Priority Management

Outlook provides various **message prioritization tools**:

1. **Priority Level Options:**

    - **High Priority**: Marked with exclamation mark icon
    - **Low Priority**: Indicated by blue downward arrow
    - **Standard Priority**: Default setting

2. **Follow-up Flagging System** - Click the **red flag icon** to access:
    - Predetermined reminder intervals
    - Custom follow-up date options
    - Specific reminder scheduling
    - Personal tracking preferences

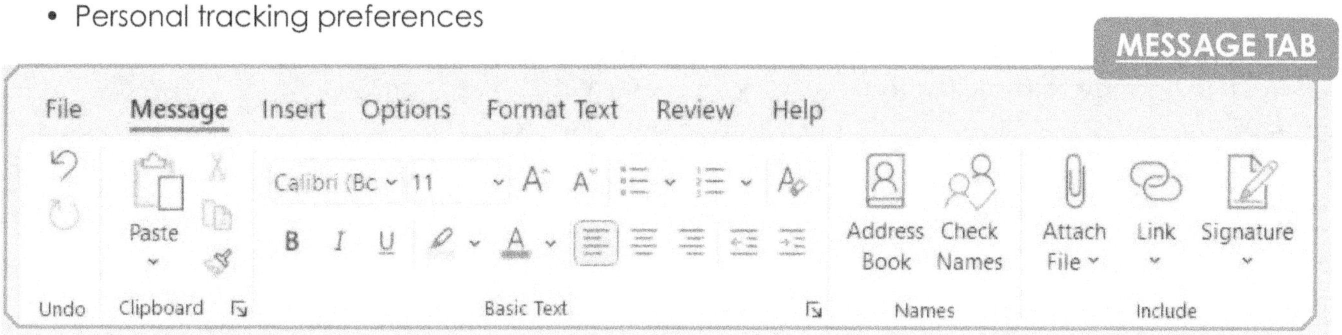

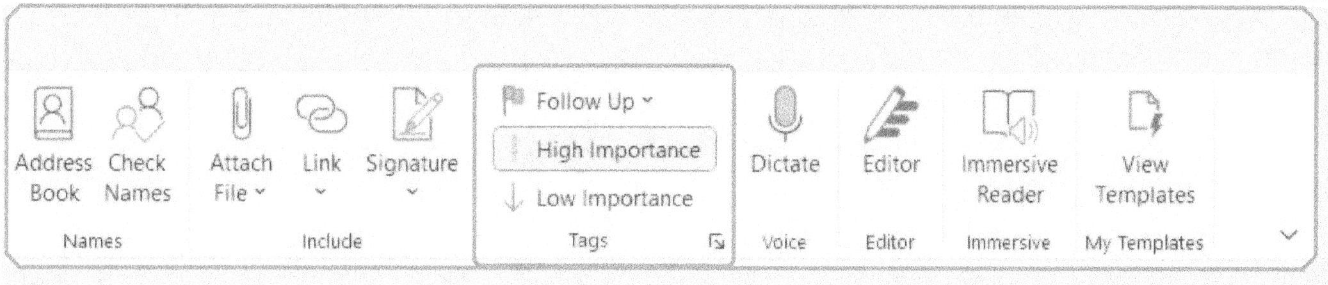

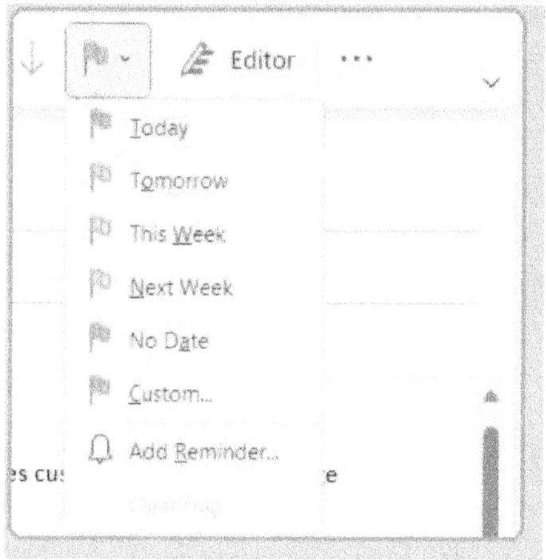

The **flagging system** allows you to:

- Mark messages for future attention
- Set customized reminder timeframes
- Select from standard reminder options
- Create personalized follow-up schedules

Electronic Survey Creation

In today's fast-paced business environment, efficient decision-making tools are essential. Outlook provides an integrated **polling mechanism** that enhances collective decision-making processes. This sophisticated yet user-friendly functionality proves especially valuable when gathering multiple opinions or approvals from recipients, transforming simple emails into powerful collaborative tools.

Creating a Poll

The poll creation process has been thoughtfully designed to be both intuitive and flexible. To initiate a survey, follow these steps:

1. Begin by composing your email
2. Access the **Options tab**
3. Locate the **Tracking section**
4. Select the **"Use Voting Buttons"** option

Available Voting Options

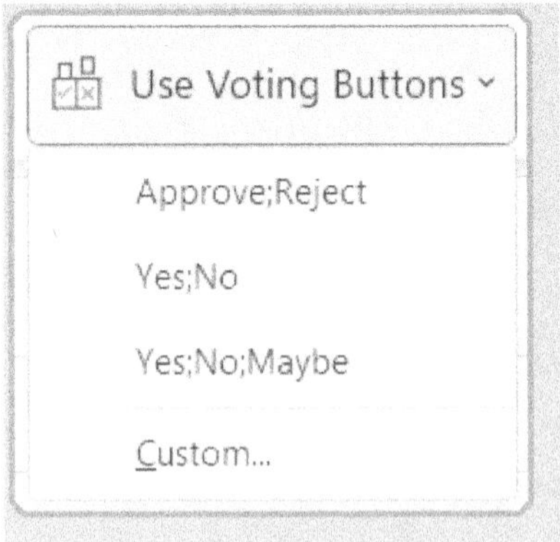

Outlook provides carefully considered default options that address common scenarios while maintaining flexibility for unique situations. Pre-configured choices include:

- **Accept/Reject** format - ideal for straightforward decisions
- **Yes/No/Maybe** format - perfect for gathering preliminary feedback
- **Custom** voting options - for specialized situations

Customization Process

When standard options don't quite fit your needs, Outlook's customization features allow for precise tailoring of your poll:

1. Select **"Custom"** from the dropdown menu
2. In the dialog box:
    - Enter your specific voting choices
    - Separate options using semicolons
    - Confirm your customized poll settings

This comprehensive polling system transforms simple email communications into powerful decision-making tools, enabling teams to move forward with clarity and confidence in their collective choices.

Adding Attachments

Modern email communication frequently requires the incorporation of visual elements and supplementary files. Outlook provides versatile methods for including **digital content** in your correspondence, though display results may vary across different email platforms. The system's flexibility allows for both simple and sophisticated content integration, ensuring your messages can effectively convey both information and visual elements.

Image Integration Options - Visual elements can be incorporated in two primary ways:

- Direct embedding within message content
- Traditional file attachment method

The **inline image process** works as follows:

1. Access the ribbon's image tools
2. Select your desired insertion method
3. Position the image within your text
4. Adjust formatting as needed

File Attachment Procedures - Multiple methods exist for attaching files to your message:

1. **Traditional Method:**
    - Find the **"attach file"** button in Home or Insert tab
    - Choose files from your recent list, computer, or cloud

2. **Alternative Approaches:**

   - **Drag-and-drop**: Select files and drag into the message
   - **Copy-paste**: Copy files and paste directly into message

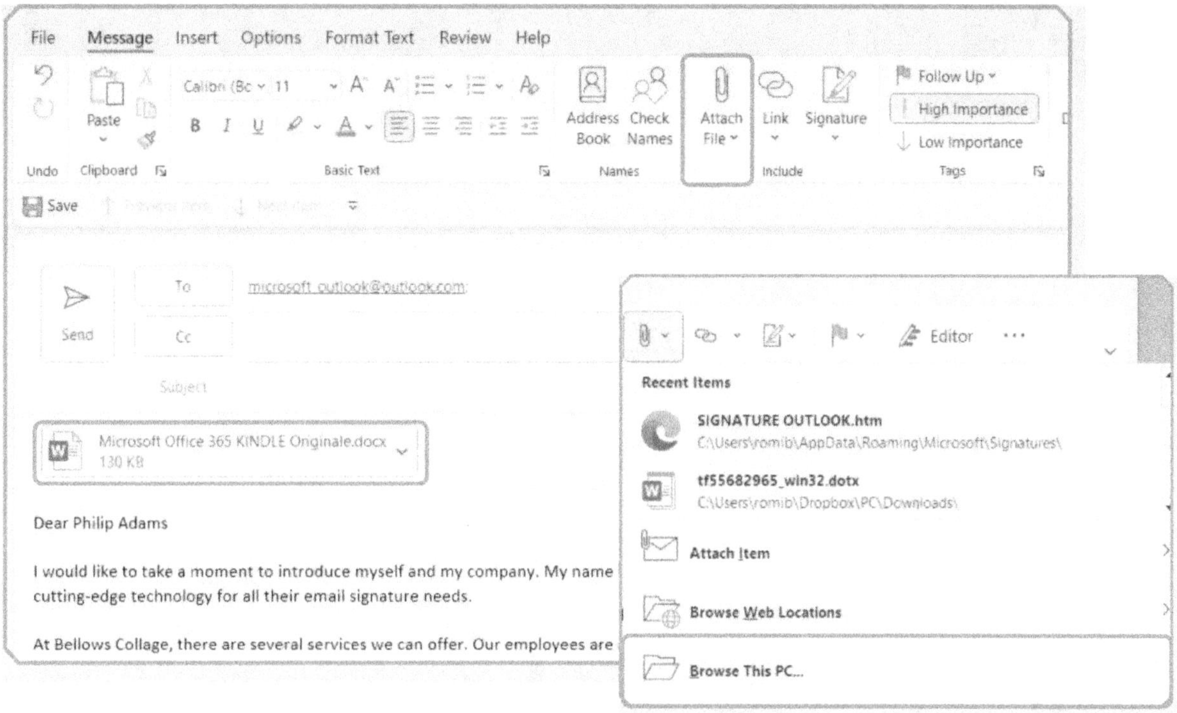

Professional Tips: *Managing attachments in Outlook is straightforward. To remove an attachment, select it and press delete - always double-check before sending. For the best recipient experience, consider file formats and total message size. Testing important messages across different email clients ensures they appear as intended and maintain professional standards.*

Email Auto-Response Systems

Among email's most essential capabilities is the option to configure an **automated response**, typically referred to as an **out of office reply**. This tool lets others know when you're temporarily unable to check or answer emails, such as during **holiday breaks** or times of restricted email access.

To configure an auto-response, click the **File** menu and choose **"Automatic Replies (Out of Office)"** located in the **Account Information** area. Within this window, select the checkbox for **"Send automatic replies"**. If you'd like to restrict the auto-response to specific dates, choose **"Only send during this time range"** and input your desired timeframe.

After that, write your message in the text field provided. You may add your **email signature** if you wish. Keep in mind that while auto-replies are active, you'll maintain regular access to incoming messages.

To enable the auto-response system, simply press **"OK"** once you've composed your message.

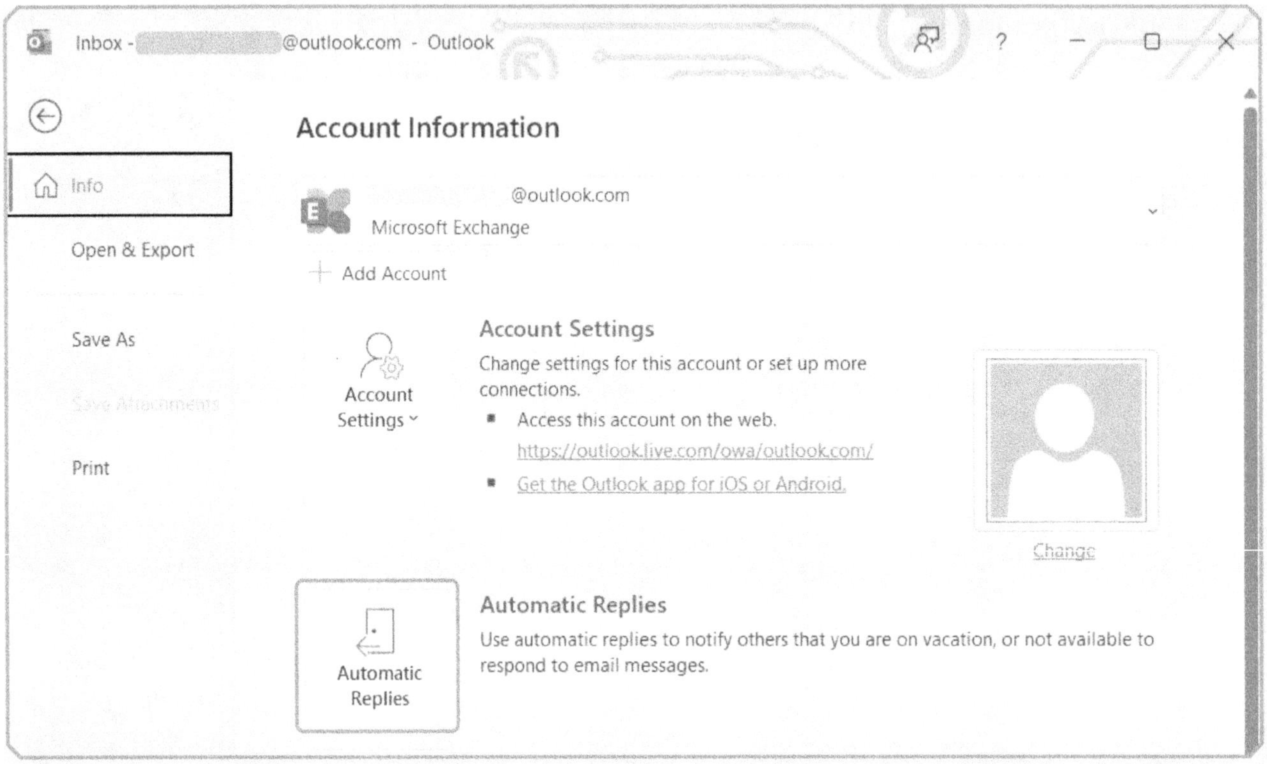

Productivity Tip:

To disable your auto-response messages, you can choose between two methods :

1. *Select the **"Turn off"** option on the yellow notification bar that shows up when you launch Outlook.*
2. *Access the **File** menu and select **"Turn off"** within the automatic replies area.*

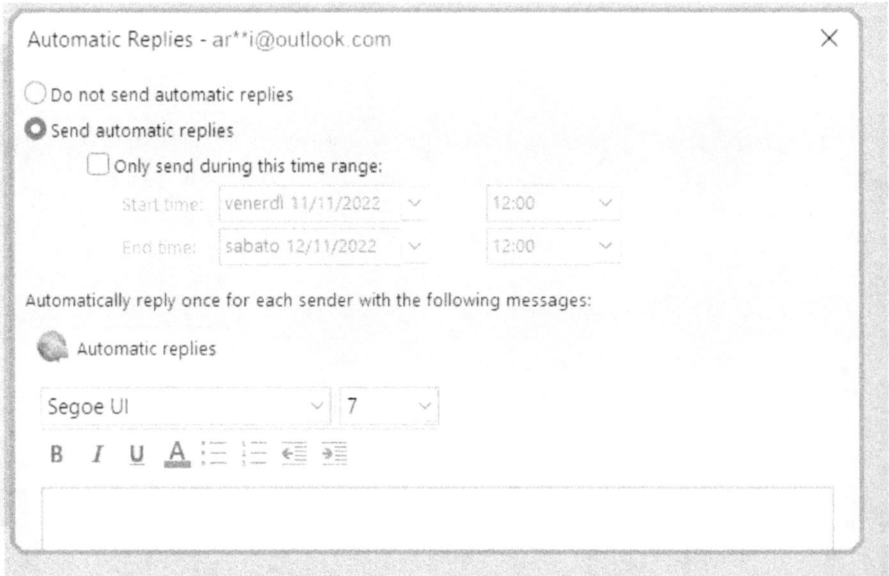

This functionality allows those who contact you to understand your current **availability status**, which helps set appropriate response expectations and sustains **professional communication** standards during your absence.

Inbox Management

The **inbox** functions as your main email collection point, except when you've configured **automatic message sorting**. You can either maintain all emails in your inbox or sort them into **folders** for enhanced efficiency.

Steps for folder creation:

1. Find the **inbox icon** along the left sidebar
2. Perform a **right-click** operation
3. Choose **"Create new folder"** from the dropdown options
4. Assign a relevant folder name Following creation, messages can be effortlessly **moved** into these folders using drag and drop functionality.

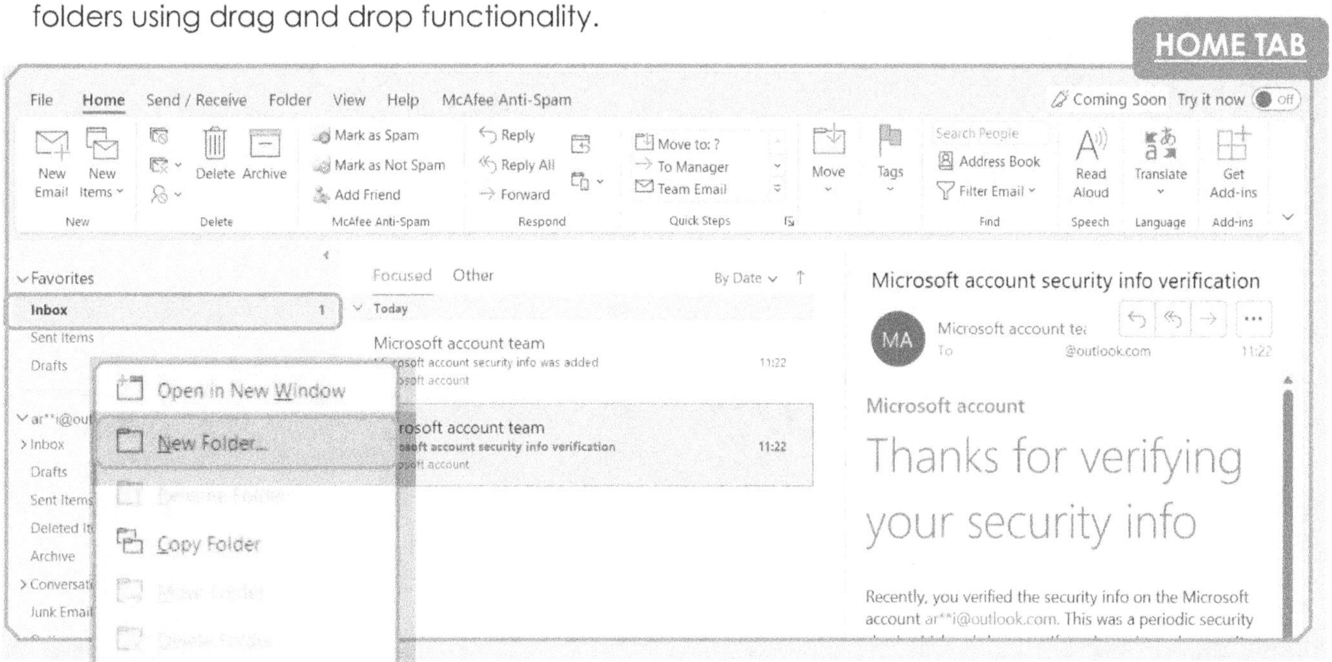

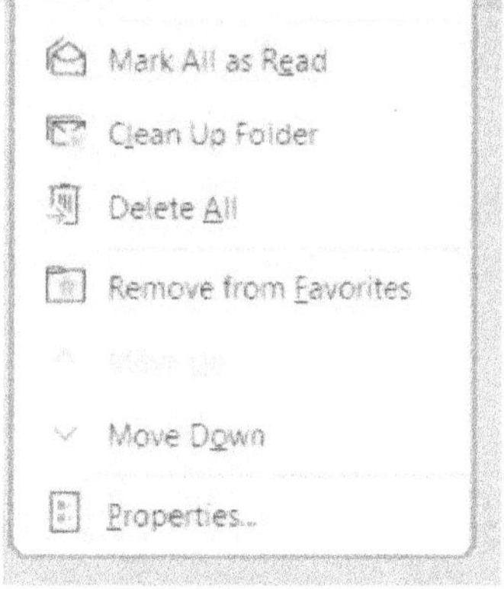

To locate particular messages within your email system, utilize the **blue search field** positioned at the window's top edge. Type your search term, and Outlook will examine both inbox and folder contents for matching messages.

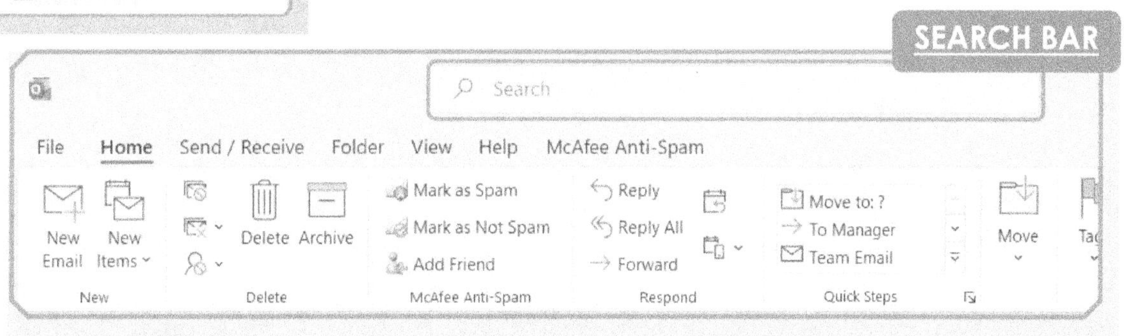

Productivity Tip: *Your search coverage varies based on your position within Outlook. When viewing the* ***inbox****, searches span your complete mailbox. When positioned within a specific* ***folder****, searches are restricted to that folder's messages only.*

You can create ***nested folders*** *by right-clicking on an existing folder and selecting "Create new folder." This hierarchical organization is particularly useful for managing multiple projects or clients, allowing you to create subfolders within main categories.*

Creating Contacts

Establishing contacts in Outlook is a simple task that enhances email efficiency. Outlook provides a dedicated area for creating detailed **digital business cards** for your contacts.

To locate this feature:

1. Look at the **left taskbar's** bottom section
2. Select the **people icon** (showing two figures)
3. This reveals the Outlook **contacts section**

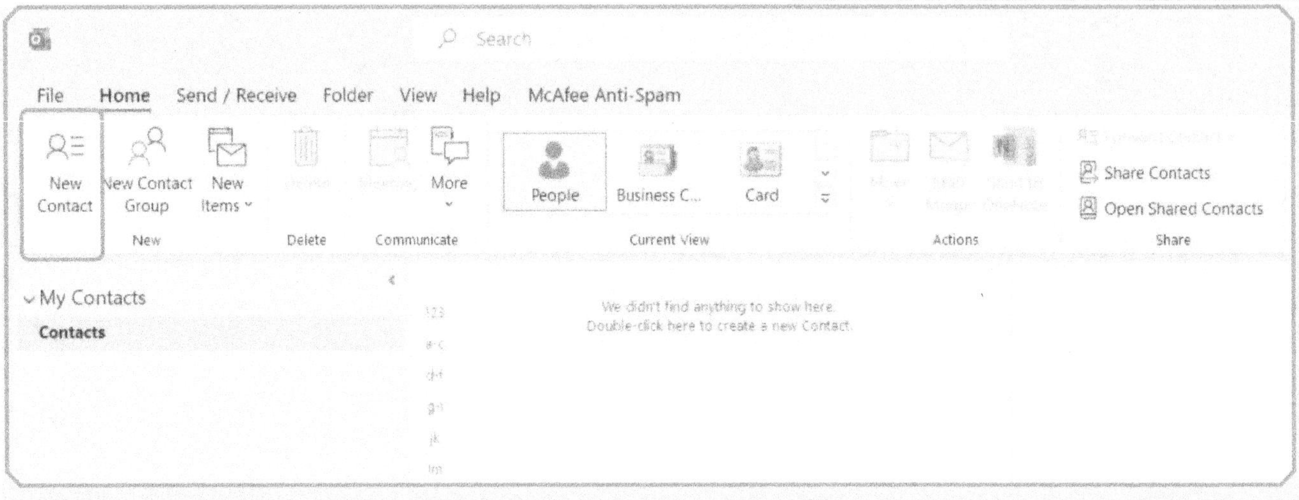

In this area, you can establish either **individual** or **group contacts. To create a single contact:**

1. Click the **"New Contact"** option positioned on the **Home tab's** left side
2. Enter the requested details in the popup window
3. The entry will appear in your **contacts list**

Productivity Tip: *After adding someone to your address book, simply entering their name in any recipient field while composing emails will trigger Outlook to automatically retrieve their complete address, making email composition more efficient and precise.*

Additional verification steps:

1. Begin typing the contact's given name in your message
2. Select **"Check Name"**
3. Outlook searches your contacts and completes the information automatically

Productivity Tip: *You can also organize your contacts into categories using color-coding. This helps you quickly identify different groups like colleagues, clients, or vendors at a glance.*

This functionality both accelerates your email composition process and helps maintain precise recipient information.

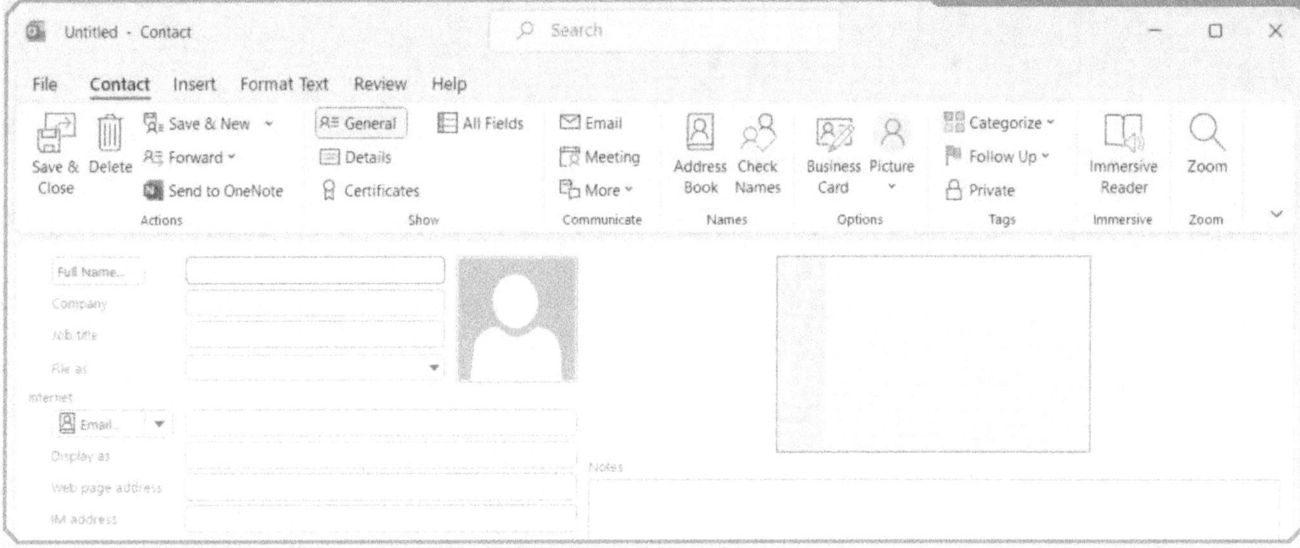

Calendar Management in Outlook

Outlook's **calendar feature** serves as a robust scheduling tool for managing appointments and meetings. It offers a streamlined method for extending event invitations and coordinating **group gatherings**.

To open the calendar:

1. Select the **calendar icon** at the task panel's bottom
2. A **calendar layout** will be displayed
3. Utilize the **"Arrange"** option in the Home tab to modify your view (**daily**, **weekly**, or **monthly**)

Event Creation - To schedule an event quickly :

1. **Double-click** your chosen date
2. **Complete the event details** in the new window :

- **Title:** Displays in your calendar view
- **Duration:** Set start and end times (or mark as **all-day**)
- Enable **"Time zones"** for international team coordination

Productivity Tip: *Microsoft Teams users can automatically generate a meeting link by selecting the* **"Teams Meeting"** *button. All invited participants will receive the necessary connection details.*

For recurring appointments:

1. Click the **"Recurring"** option
2. Define the **repetition pattern**

By using the recurring feature, you can establish regular event patterns, such as ongoing training sessions. The ribbon's tools provide additional options for setting **reminders**, indicating **meeting priority**, and customizing your **calendar display**.

CALENDAR

SCHEDULING EVENTS

Productivity Tip: *You can overlay multiple calendars (like personal and work) using different colors to easily distinguish between different types of commitments while viewing them simultaneously.*

Task and Follow-up Management

Outlook's **task management system**, marked by a **flag icon**, enables comprehensive tracking of action items and follow-ups. This feature integrates seamlessly with other Microsoft tools for enhanced productivity.

To flag emails for follow-up:

1. Navigate to the **"Tags"** area in the Home tab
2. Select the **flag button**
3. Choose your preferred **reminder timing**

Accessing your tasks

1. Click the **clipboard icon** with checkmark at the inbox pane's bottom
2. View your complete **to-do list** with pending items

Task removal options:

1. **Right-click** the flagged message
2. Select either **"Mark task as complete"** or **"Delete task"**

> ***Productivity Tip:*** *You can customize task categories with different colors and labels to organize them by project, priority, or department.*

OneNote Integration Features

From OneNote to Outlook:

1. Create a task in OneNote by typing text
2. Right-click the text and select **"Create Outlook Task"**
3. Choose the due date and priority level
4. The task automatically appears in your Outlook tasks list

From Outlook to OneNote:

1. Select any item (email, task, or calendar event)
2. Click **"Send to OneNote"** in the Home tab
3. Choose your destination notebook and section
4. Add additional notes or context if needed

> ***Productivity Tip:*** *You can also drag and drop Outlook items directly into an open OneNote window to quickly save important information.*

This comprehensive integration between Outlook's task system and OneNote creates a robust framework for managing both professional and personal commitments. The ability to flag emails, configure reminders, and synchronize tasks across platforms provides an efficient system for productivity management. For detailed OneNote functionality, consult **Chapter 9** of your guide.

Keyboard Shortcuts on *Outlook*

Function	PC Shortcut	Mac Shortcut
Close a window	*Esc*	*Command + W*
Create new message	*Ctrl + Shift + M*	*Command + N (in mail window)*
Send a message	*Alt + S*	*Command + Return*
Insert a file	*Alt + N, A, F*	*Command + E*
Search for an item	*F3*	*Option + Command + F*
Reply to a message	*Alt +H, R, P*	*Command + R*
Forward a message	*Alt + H, F, W*	*Command + J*
Reply all	*Alt + H, R, A*	*Shift + Command + R*
Check for new messages	*Ctrl +M or F9*	*not available*
Mail view	*Ctrl +1*	*Command + 1*
Calendar view	*Ctrl + 2*	*Command + 2*
Contacts view	*Ctrl + 3*	*Command + 3*
Tasks view	*Ctrl + 4*	*Command + 4*
Notes view	*Ctrl + 5*	*Command + 5*
Shortcuts	*Ctrl + 7*	*Command + 7*
Next open message	*Ctrl + .*	*Command + ~*
Previous open message	*Ctrl + ,*	*Shift + Command + ~*
Create appointment	*Ctrl + Shift + A*	*Command + N*
Create contact	*Ctrl + Shift + C*	*Command + N*
Create note	*Ctrl + Shift + N*	*Command + N*

6. Skype:

Communication Platform Evolution

Originally launched in 2003 and acquired by Microsoft in 2011, Skype replaced the **Microsoft Live Messenger** service. This comprehensive communication tool enables **video conferencing**, **instant messaging**, **voice calls**, **file sharing**, and **audio transmission**. Its **cross-platform compatibility** supports installation across **computers**, **mobile devices**, **tablets**, and **gaming systems**.

Initial Setup Process

Beginning with Skype starts by obtaining the application for your specific device. This can be accomplished through your device's native app marketplace or via direct download from Skype's website. Post-installation, account authentication is required.

For those with an existing **Microsoft account** (such as an @outlook.com address), immediate access is available. Alternatively, you may register using your personal email address. New users can create an account through Skype's registration system, which guides you through a simple setup process.

Productivity Tip: *Enhance your Skype accessibility* :

- *Enable* **"Start Skype as soon as the computer logs on"** *for immediate availability after startup*
- *Activate* **"Remember me"** *to eliminate repeated login requirements*
- *Set up* **"Automatic sign-in"** *for seamless access to your communications*

Configuring Audio and Camera Settings

It's essential to check that your microphone, sound, and camera are properly configured before you start using Skype. When you first sign in, Skype provides an integrated sound testing capability. Even if you skip this initial setup, you can always access these settings later.

To adjust your account preferences:

1. Look for your profile image at the top of the contact list and click it
2. This will trigger a menu to drop down
3. Look for and click on **Settings**
4. Within the Settings window, locate and select the **Audio and Video** section

This menu contains everything you need to fine-tune your sound and video preferences. Going through this setup ensures that your microphone, speakers, and webcam function correctly, preparing you for effective Skype conversations.

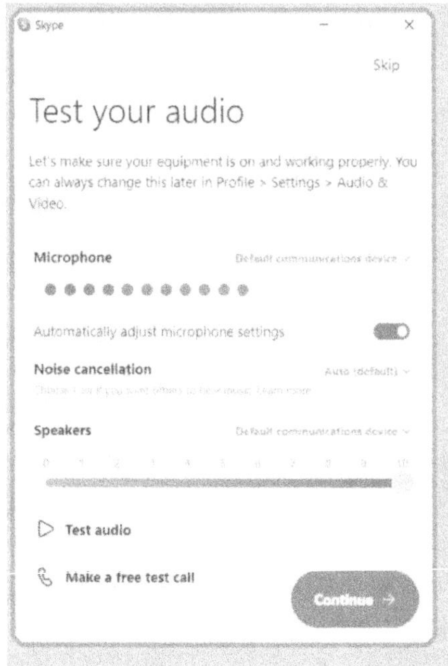

Additional Audio Settings

You can select your preferred microphone and speakers from dropdown menus if you have multiple devices connected. Skype also provides a volume slider to adjust your microphone sensitivity and speaker output.

The **Test Audio** button lets you verify your microphone is picking up sound correctly, while the **Test Speakers** function plays a sample sound to confirm your audio output works.

Making Your Skype Profile Your Own

The Settings menu lets you add your personal touch to your Skype profile. Follow these steps to customize your account:

1. Find and select **Account and Profile** in the settings menu
2. You'll have options to update:

   - The name that appears to others
   - A photo that represents you
   - Your date of birth

The same section provides additional customization features:

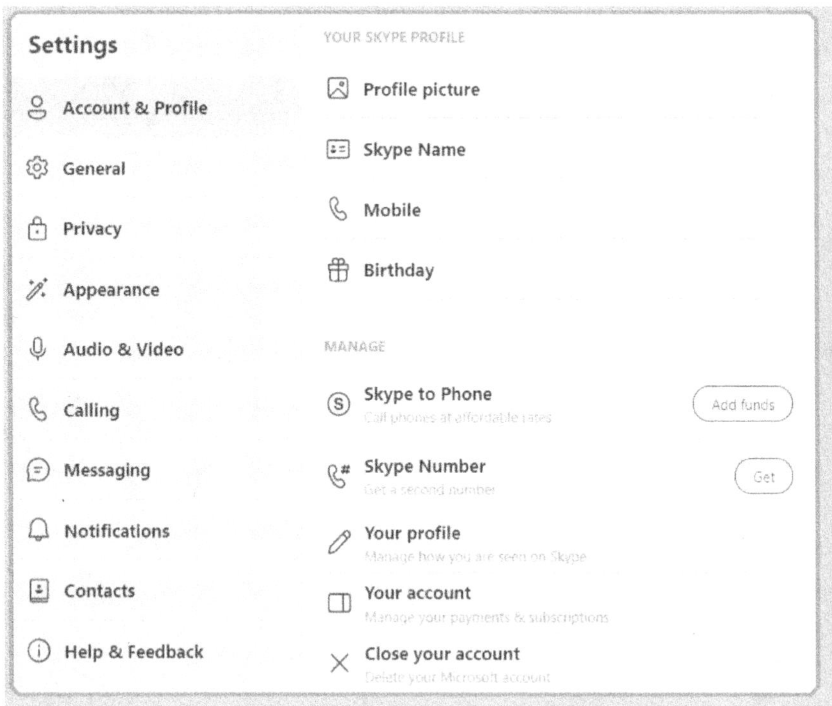

- Control whether Skype starts automatically when you log into your device
- Manage who can contact you and see your information
- Change how your chat interface looks
- Choose how and when you receive notifications

Taking time to adjust these settings can make your Skype experience more comfortable and efficient. These customizations help create a more personalized environment that matches your communication style and preferences.

Key Profile Features - You can personalize your Skype experience with these essential settings:

- Set your status message and time zone for better availability tracking
- Choose your language and connect your Microsoft account
- Set up backup contacts and emergency information for account security
- Select your preferred theme and customize message formatting
- Control your privacy with file sharing and read receipt settings

Remember that all these settings can be changed anytime to match your needs.

Personalizing Message Settings

The Settings section in Skype provides extensive options to customize how you interact with messages. You have the ability to modify various default behaviors to match both your preferences and security requirements. For enhanced protection of your device, you might prefer to disable the automatic downloading of files that others send you.

When it comes to message formatting, Skype allows you to configure how copied and pasted text appears in your conversations, with options to automatically format it as quotes. These customization choices, along with numerous other options, are available in the Messaging section within Skype's settings menu.

Adding Contacts

The real value of Skype comes from its connectivity features. To make the most of this platform, you'll need to establish your network of contacts. Here's a comprehensive look at the process:

1. **Looking for Contacts**

    - Select the search function, which you'll find marked with a magnifying glass icon
    - Type in either the name or email address of the person you want to connect with
    - The platform will display a list of possible matches automatically

2. **Evaluating Search Results -** Each person shown in the results will display:

    - Their chosen display name
    - A profile picture (when they've added one)
    - Their geographical location
    - The number of connections you share with them In a dedicated "Group Chats" area, you'll see any previous group conversations involving this contact. For new users, this section typically starts empty.

3. **Reaching Out to New Users**

    - When your search doesn't find the person you're looking for, check for an "Invite to Skype" option at the bottom
    - Select this option to initiate an email invitation
    - Input the email address of the person you'd like to invite
    - The platform will send them a custom invitation to become part of Skype's network

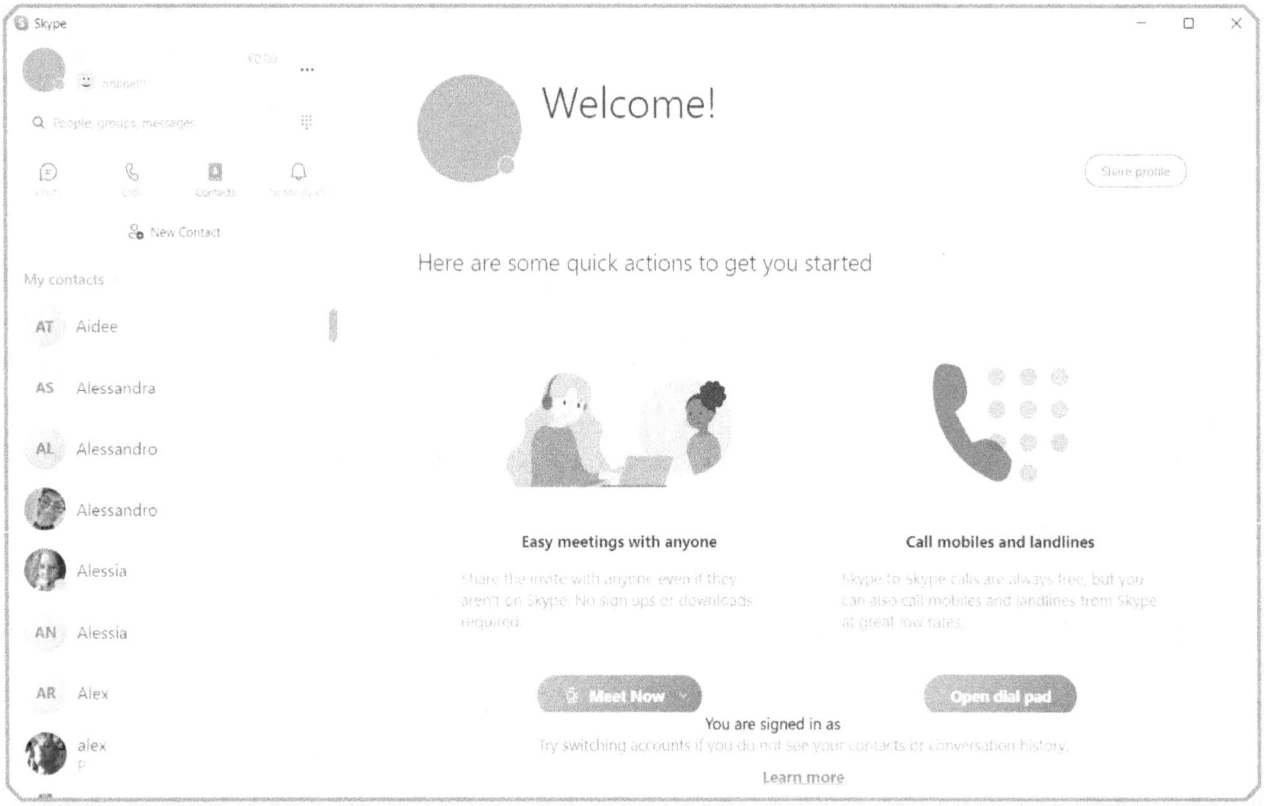

All these features work together to help you create and maintain your network of connections on Skype, while ensuring your messaging experience remains exactly as you prefer it.

Managing Your Online Presence in Skype

Skype offers a robust status system to help you manage your availability:

1. **Status Colors and Their Meaning**

    - **Green (Active)**: Shows you're connected and ready to communicate
    - **Yellow (Away)**: Indicates you're signed in but might not be actively using your device
    - **Red (Do Not Disturb)**: Signals you're online but prefer not to be interrupted
    - **White (Invisible)**: Makes you appear offline while maintaining full access to Skype

2. **How to Update Your Status**

    - Find your profile image or initials in the upper-left area of your Skype window
    - Select this icon to open a dropdown menu
    - Your active status appears as the first item below your name
    - Click on your current status to view all available options
    - Choose your preferred status from the displayed list

3. **Understanding Status Behaviors**

    - Choosing "Invisible" lets you observe others' online status while appearing offline yourself
    - When you message someone while invisible, your status automatically changes to online for that specific contact

- Selecting "Do Not Disturb" silences notifications, perfect for meetings or concentrated work periods

4. **Automatic Status Adjustments**

   - Your status may shift to "Away" automatically when you haven't used Skype for a while

   - These automatic changes can be modified through Skype's preference settings

This status system helps maintain clear communication about your availability while using Skype, ensuring others know when you're available for interaction.

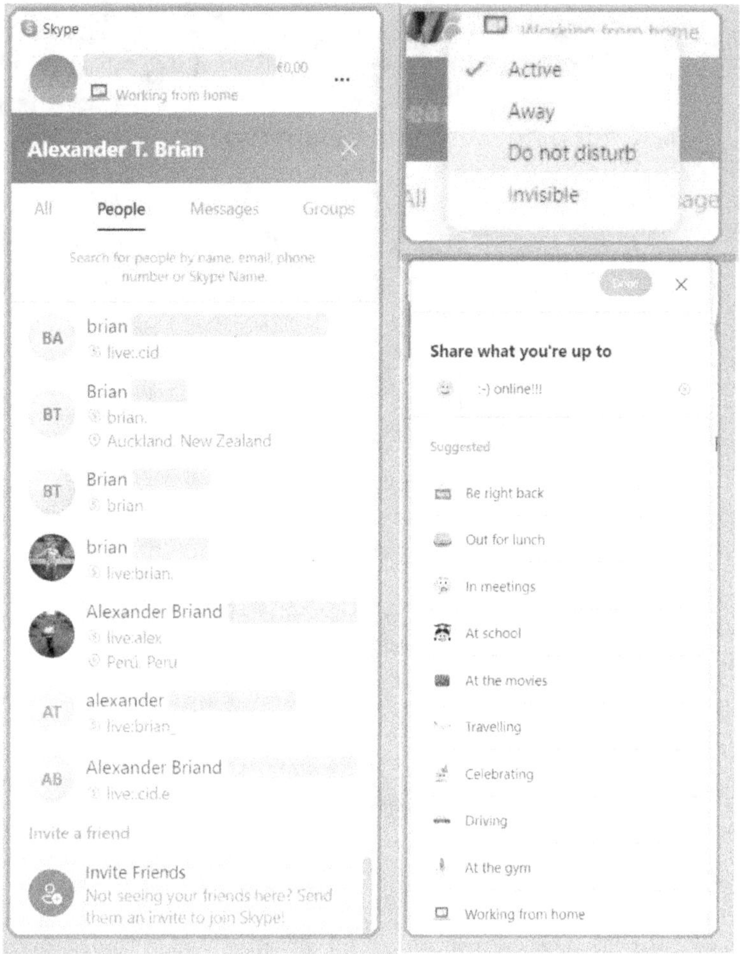

Starting Conversations in Skype

Skype supports multiple ways to communicate, from text and voice to video calls, supporting both individual and group interactions. Here's a detailed guide:

1. **Beginning a Text Chat**

   - Search your contacts and select the person you want to message
   - Click their name, which opens up a conversation window
   - Find the message box at the bottom where it says "Type a message" and start writing

Productivity Tip: *Use keyboard shortcuts to speed up your messaging - press Alt + 1 to jump to recent chats, Alt + 2 for contacts list, and Ctrl + N to start a new conversation instantly.*

2. **Enhanced Communication Tools** - Skype enriches your conversations with several features:

   - Share contact details with others through the chat
   - Create and send voice recordings
   - Let others know your current position through location sharing
   - Record and share quick video messages
   - Set up future calls with scheduling tools
   - Create interactive polls within conversations

Productivity Tip: You can drag and drop files directly into the chat window instead of using the attachment button. This works for multiple files at once and maintains their original folder structure.

3. **Changing Communication Types** - At the top of your chat window, you'll find two blue buttons:

    - A camera symbol for starting video calls
    - A phone icon for beginning voice calls These buttons allow you to smoothly switch from text messaging to either video or audio communication.

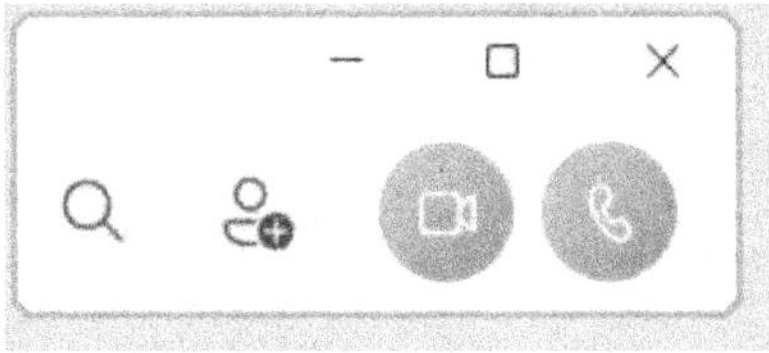

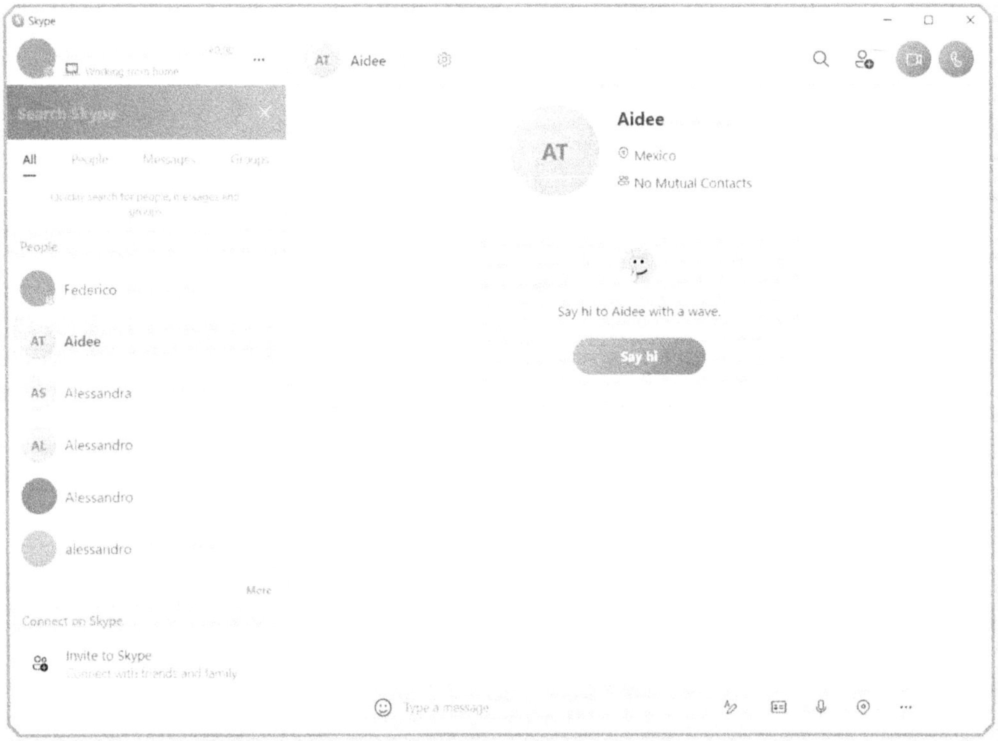

Productivity Tip: Before switching to a video call, quickly press Win + P (on Windows) or Command + F3 (on Mac) to check your display settings if you're using multiple monitors. This ensures your video appears on the intended screen.

This comprehensive messaging system gives you flexibility in how you connect with others, letting you choose the most appropriate form of communication for each situation.

Working with Your Skype Contacts

Skype provides comprehensive tools for contact management:

1. **Quick Contact Actions** - Find and click the icon beside any contact's name to reveal options:

    - Launch a video chat
    - Start a voice call
    - Transfer files
    - Pass along contact details
    - Access additional features

2. **Updating Contact Details** - Look for the pencil symbol next to contacts. Clicking it enables you to:

  - Modify how their name displays in your list
  - Update or add phone numbers
  - Delete them from your contacts
  - Restrict their access to you

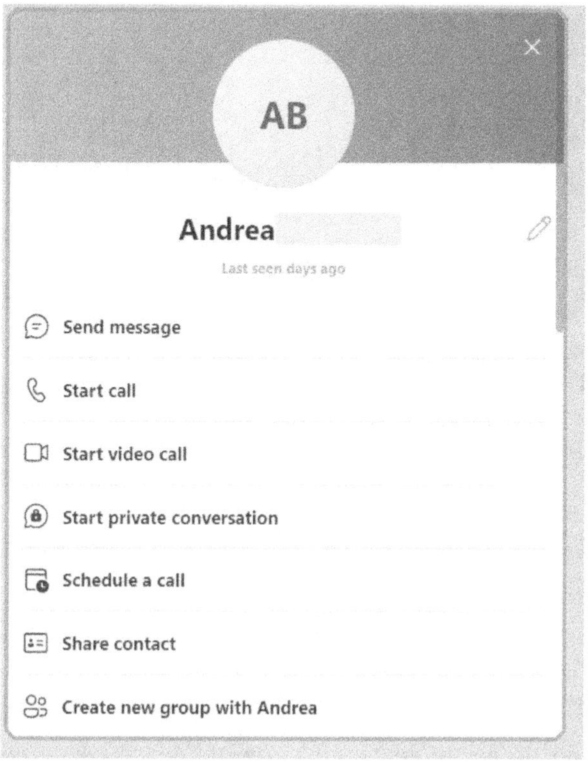

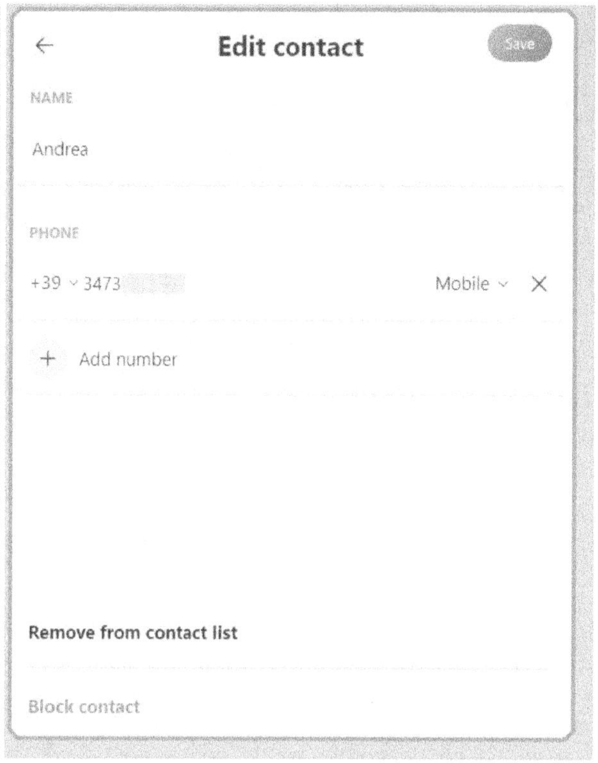

Productivity Tip: *When you frequently communicate with certain contacts, right-click their name and select "Add to Favorites" to keep them at the top of your contact list for quick access.*

Managing Blocked Users

How to Block Contacts in Skype

1. Find the contact you want to block in your contact list
2. Right-click their name or click the three dots (...) next to it
3. Select "Block contact" from the dropdown menu
4. Confirm your choice in the popup window
5. The contact will be removed from your visible list

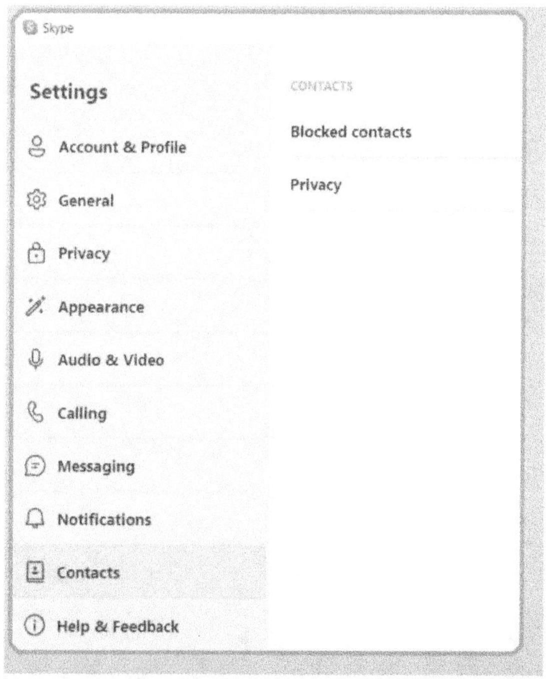

How to Unblock Contacts in Skype

1. Click your profile picture at the top
2. Select "Settings" from the dropdown menu
3. Choose "Contacts" from the left sidebar
4. Click "Blocked contacts"
5. Find the contact you want to unblock
6. Click the "Unblock" button next to their name
7. Confirm your decision when prompted

***Productivity Tip**: Before blocking someone in a professional context, consider using the "Do Not Disturb" status first. This less permanent solution allows you to control when you receive notifications while maintaining the ability to communicate when necessary.*

***Note**: When you unblock someone, they won't automatically return to your contact list. You'll need to add them again if you want to restore the connection.*

Setting Up Group Conversations in Skype

Skype provides two distinct approaches to create group chats, helping you better manage team collaboration and social connections.

1. **Expanding From a Current Chat**

    - Open an existing one-on-one conversation
    - Look for the "Add Participant" symbol (shown as a person with a plus sign)
    - Click it to include more people in your current discussion This method works especially well when you need to bring others into an ongoing conversation quickly.

2. **Creating a Fresh Group Chat**

    - Select the "Chats" option in your contacts area
    - Click "New Chat"
    - From the menu that appears, select "New Group Chat"
    - Add the people you want from your contacts
    - Give your group a name to find it easily later

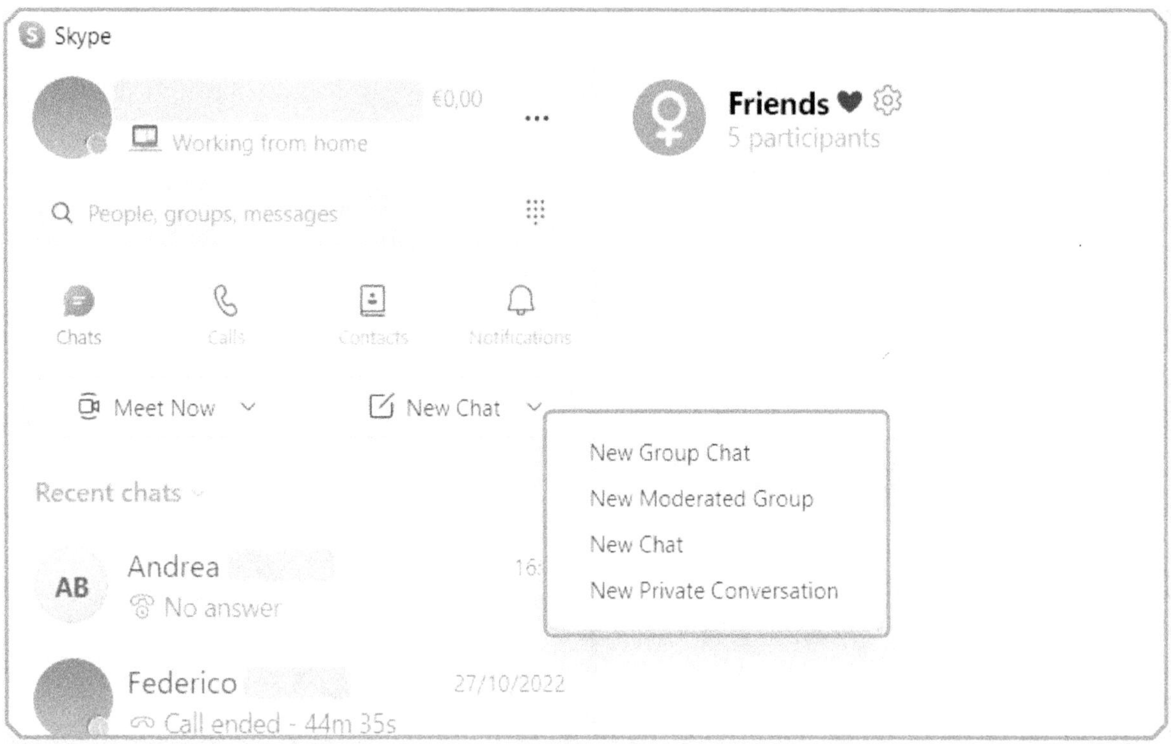

Group Chat Features

After establishing your group chat, you'll have access to several tools:

- Share documents and files
- Start group video conversations
- Begin voice calls with multiple participants
- Create interactive polls

The person who creates the group typically becomes the administrator, with power to:

- Add new members
- Remove existing participants
- Manage group settings

Productivity Tip: *Fine-tune your notification preferences for each group chat individually. Use the bell icon within the chat to choose between options like "All Messages," "Mentions Only," or "Nothing" - perfect for staying in touch without constant interruptions.*

Text Formatting in Skype Messages

Basic Formatting Tools

1. **Bold**: For emphasizing important text
2. ***Italics***: For subtle emphasis or titles
3. **~~Strikethrough~~**: To show corrected or outdated text
4. **Link insertion:** For embedding clickable web addresses
5. **Code snippets:** Shows text in monospace font, perfect for code sharing

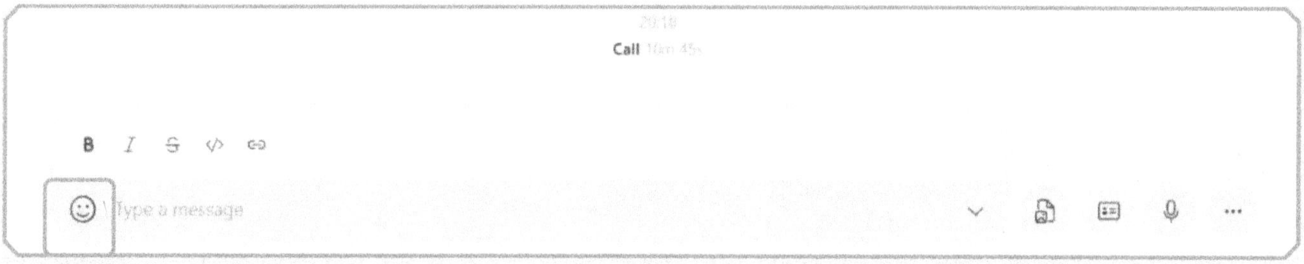

Accessing Format Options

- Find the "A" symbol with a pen beside your message box
- Select it to show the formatting toolbar
- Choose your format before writing or highlight text to format it

- Formats can be combined (like using bold with italics)
- Code format preserves spacing for technical discussions
- Links often display previews automatically

Working with Emojis

- Click the smiley face icon by the message area
- Explore different emoji categories (faces, animals, food, etc.)
- Use shortcuts with parentheses for quick emoji insertion: Type (happy) for a smiling face. Try (cat), (pizza), or (heart)
- Consider cultural differences when using emojis
- Use appropriately in professional conversations

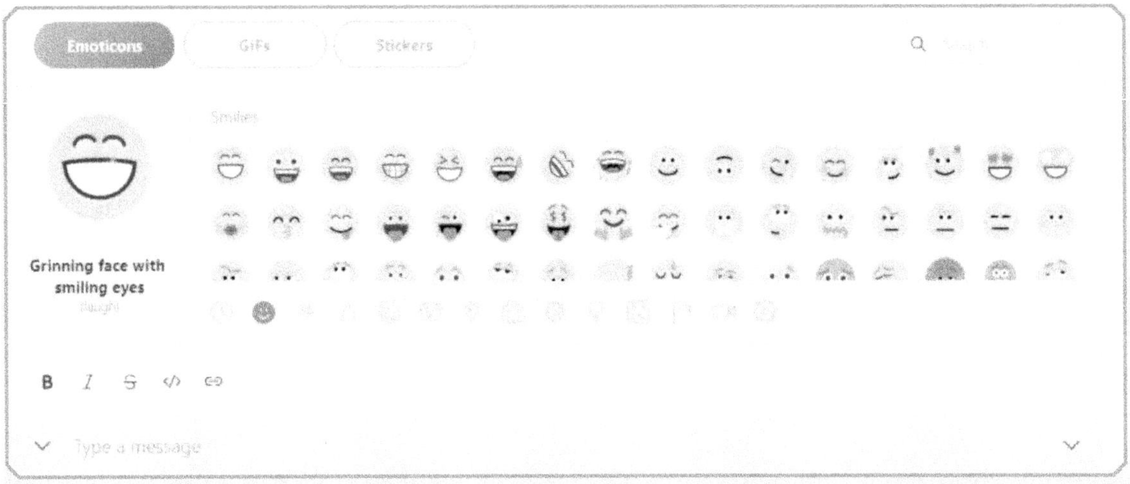

Creating Line Breaks

- By default, Enter/Return sends your message
- For line breaks within messages:

    1. Hold down the Shift key
    2. Press Enter (PC) or Return (Mac) while holding Shift
    3. This creates a new line in the same message

Productivity Tip - *Use line breaks to: Create organized lists, separate text into paragraphs, Improve message readability*

Extra Messaging Features

- Drop files directly into chats
- Record voice messages when typing isn't ideal
- React to messages with emoji responses
- Preview links before sending
- Format code snippets for technical discussions

Productivity Tip: *Create message templates with your most-used formatting combinations. Copy these templates to a note file for quick access during frequent conversations, saving time while maintaining consistent formatting.*

Keyboard Shortcuts on *Skype*

Function	PC Shortcut	Mac Shortcut
View keyboard shortcuts	*Ctrl + /*	*Command + /*
Open settings	*Ctrl + ,*	*Command + ,*
Open themes	*Ctrl + T*	*Command + T*
Open or close dark mode	*Ctrl + Shift + T*	*Command + Shift + T*
Search contacts	*Ctrl + Shift + S*	*Command + Shift + S*
Next conversation	*Ctrl + Tab*	*Command + Tab*
Previous conversation	*Ctrl + Shift + Tab*	*Command + Shift + Tab*
Zoom in	*Ctrl + Shift + +*	*Command + Shift + +*
Zoom out	*Ctrl + -*	*Command + -*
Quit Skype	*Ctrl + Q*	*Command + Q*
Start new conversation	*Ctrl + N*	*Command + N*
Open contacts	*Alt + 2*	*Not available*
Add people to conversation	*Ctrl + Shift + A*	*Command + Shift + A*
Send a file	*Ctrl + Shift + F*	*Command + Shift + F*
Mark as unread	*Ctrl + Shift + U*	*Command + Shift + U*
Search within conversation	*Ctrl + F*	*Command + F*
Start video call	*Ctrl + Shift + K*	*Command + Shift + K*
Mute or unmute conversation	*Ctrl + M*	*Command + M*

7. Teams:

Streamlining Workplace Collaboration

Microsoft Teams stands out as the preferred choice for boosting **digital teamwork** and **communication** in organizations. While it shares some capabilities with **Skype**, Teams goes further by offering **real-time file collaboration**, **meeting recording** capabilities, and dedicated **team workspace** creation.

The platform includes integration with the **Microsoft Suite**, though a **free version** remains available for basic use. Users can access Teams across both **computers** and **mobile devices**, ensuring flexibility in how they connect and work.

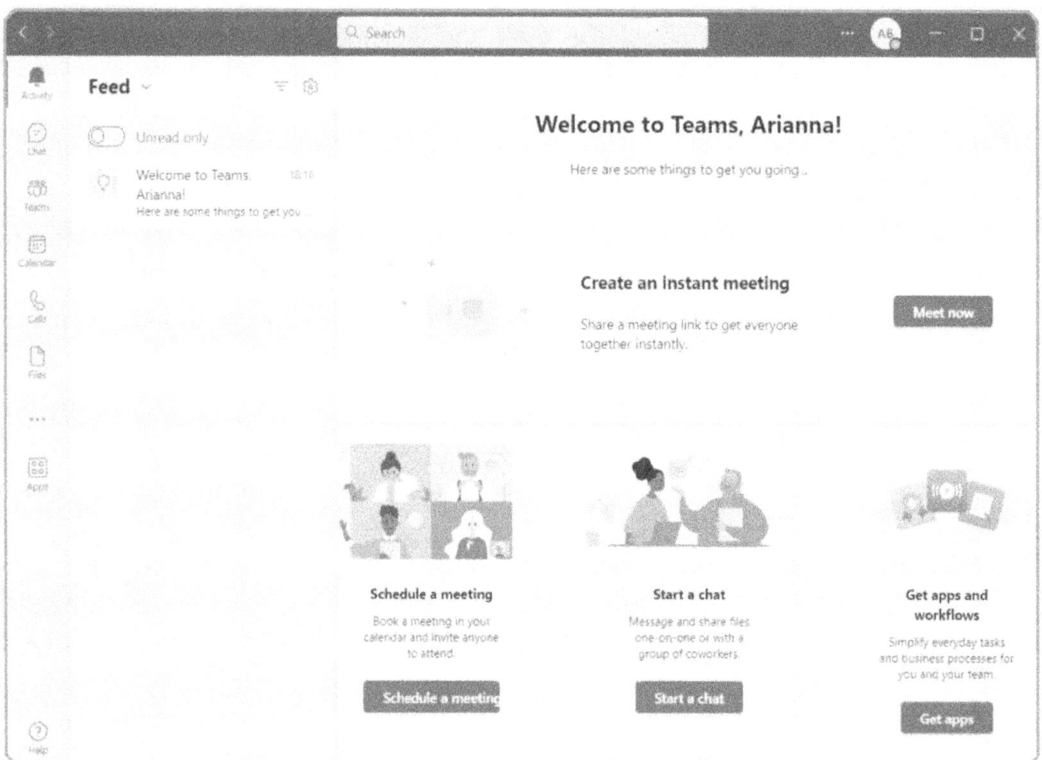

Upon **signing in**, users are greeted with a **chat interface** designed for team communication. The main navigation bar features six essential buttons:

- **Activity**
- **Chat**
- **Teams**
- **Calendar**
- **Calls**
- **Files**.

These core navigation elements provide quick access to the platform's main features and seamlessly connect with other tools and applications.

***Productivity Tip**: Pin your most frequently accessed teams and channels to the top of your list by right-clicking them and selecting "**Pin**." This creates a personalized **quick-access section**, making it easier to reach your important workspaces without scrolling through long lists of channels.*

Create a Team

The fundamental process begins with understanding how to establish a **team** - which is essentially a **collaborative group** focused on a common subject or organizational division. Here's how to start:

Initial Steps:

1. Select the **Teams** button on your left sidebar
2. Locate the **"Join or create team"** icon at the bottom
3. Select this icon

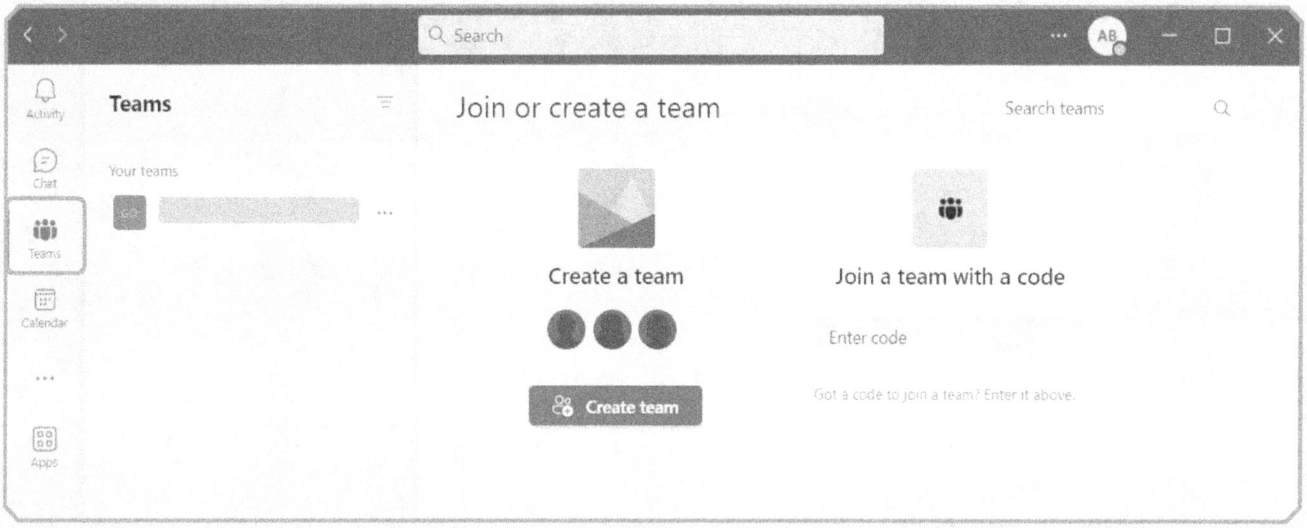

Available Options -You'll be presented with two primary choices:

- **Create** a completely new team
- **Join** an already existing team

For **joining with a code**, enter it when prompted. For **creating a new team**, you can choose from these approaches:

1. Begin with a blank slate
2. Build from an existing group structure
3. Utilize a pre-made template designed for:
    - Project management scenarios
    - New employee integration
    - Event coordination

Setup Process:

1. Determine team visibility (public/private)
2. Assign a team name
3. Write a descriptive summary
4. Choose appropriate data classification
5. Begin member recruitment

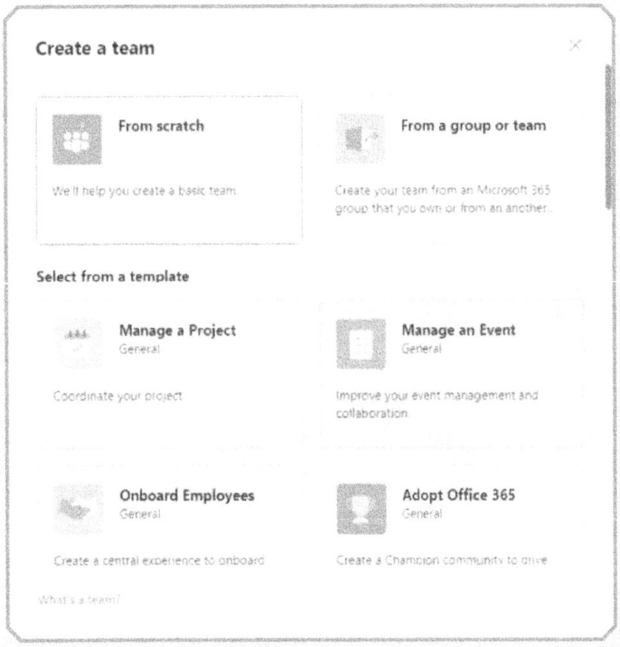

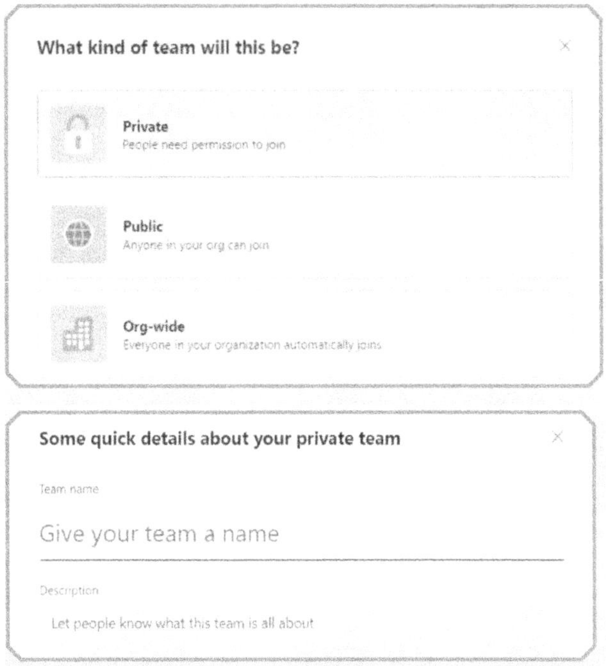

Member Addition Methods:

- Use the ellipsis menu beside names to add members
- Send email invitations to external contacts
- Distribute a team-specific link generated through the team settings

Important Management Note:
*The platform enables the designation of **team owners** with enhanced privileges. Teams can have multiple owners who possess authority to: manage membership, incorporate guests, and adjust team configurations. Additional roles include standard members and guests, whose access levels are determined by the owners.*

Building Communication Channels

Channels are vital elements within Microsoft Teams that function as **dedicated spaces** for specific topics within a team. They enhance collaboration by organizing team communications more efficiently.

Channel Applications for Education - Teachers can establish channels for:

- Dedicated homework assistance ("Homework Help")
- Subject-specific questions ("Physics Q&A")
- General classroom communication ("General Classroom Chat")

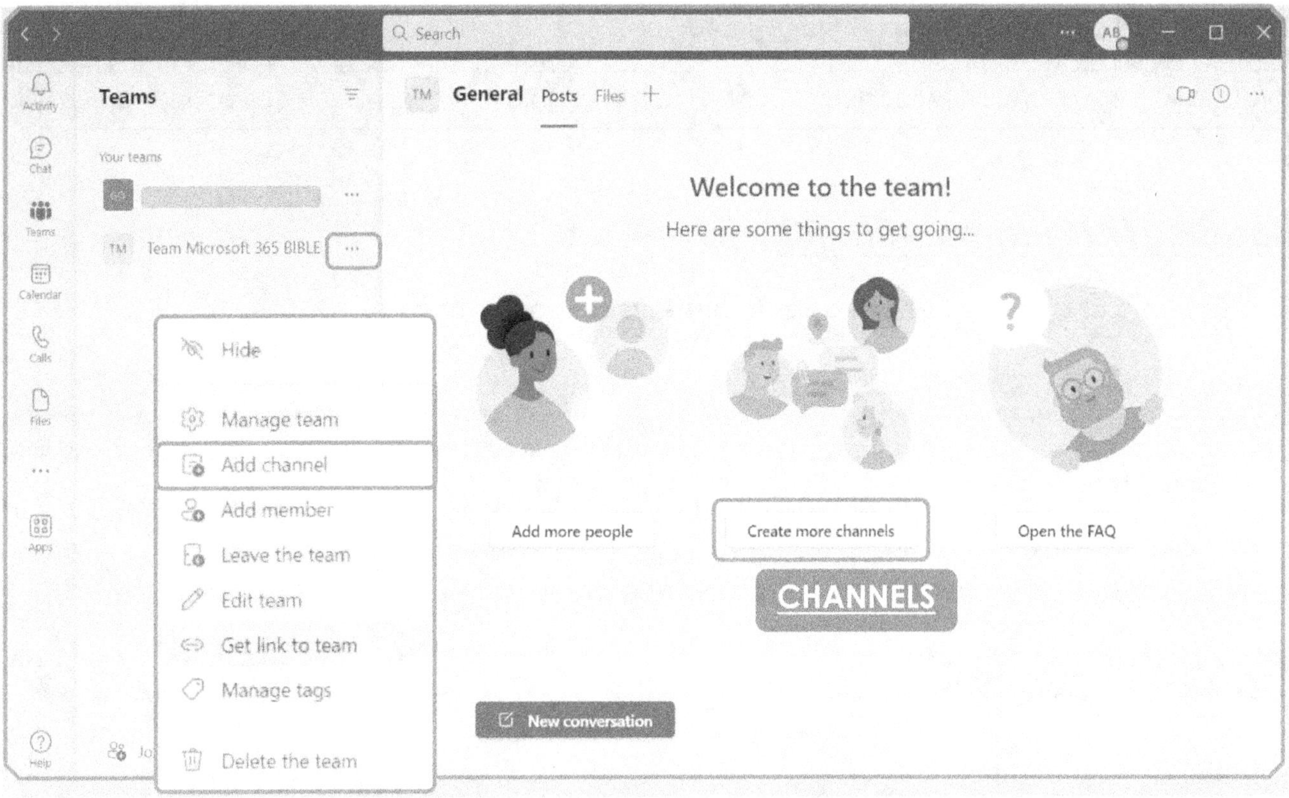

Channel Applications for Professional Settings - Business teams can create channels for:

- Project status updates ("Project Alpha Progress")
- Team-wide communications ("Team Announcements")
- Informal discussions ("Water Cooler Chat")

Essential Channel Characteristics - Universal access for team members (unless privately configured)

- Enhanced topic organization that reduces main chat congestion
- Secure file sharing with version tracking
- Topic-specific chat functionality
- Seamless integration with Microsoft 365 applications

Channel Framework - The standard structure includes:

- A **Posts** section for threaded discussions
- A **Files** area for document management
- A **Wiki** space for collaborative note-taking
- Capability to add custom tabs for additional tools

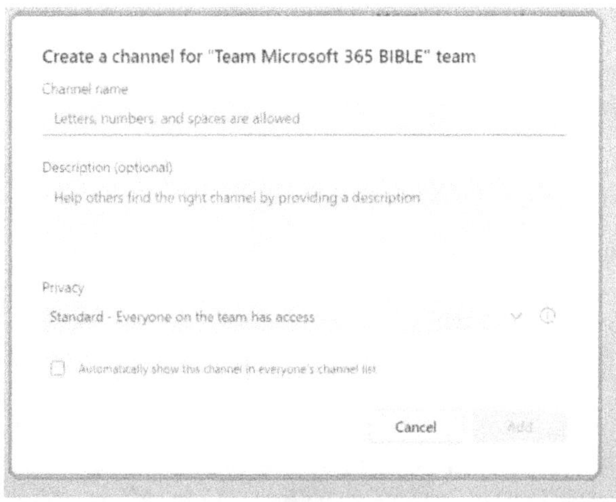

Channel Creation Process- Select your target team

1. Click the ellipsis beside the team name
2. Choose "Add channel"
3. Input channel name and description
4. Set privacy preferences
5. Confirm creation

Productivity Tip: *The* ***Activity indicator*** *on your left panel signals new channel developments. This feature provides a comprehensive view of updates across all channels, with highlighted relevant information. You can review past notifications to maintain awareness of all team communications.*

Uploading/Attach Documents

After creating a channel, you can **share documents** with other users.

Primary Methods for File Upload

1. Add documents through your active chat window, which automatically stores them in the Files section

2. Navigate directly to the **Files tab** and upload documents through the dedicated interface. This method provides more control over file organization.

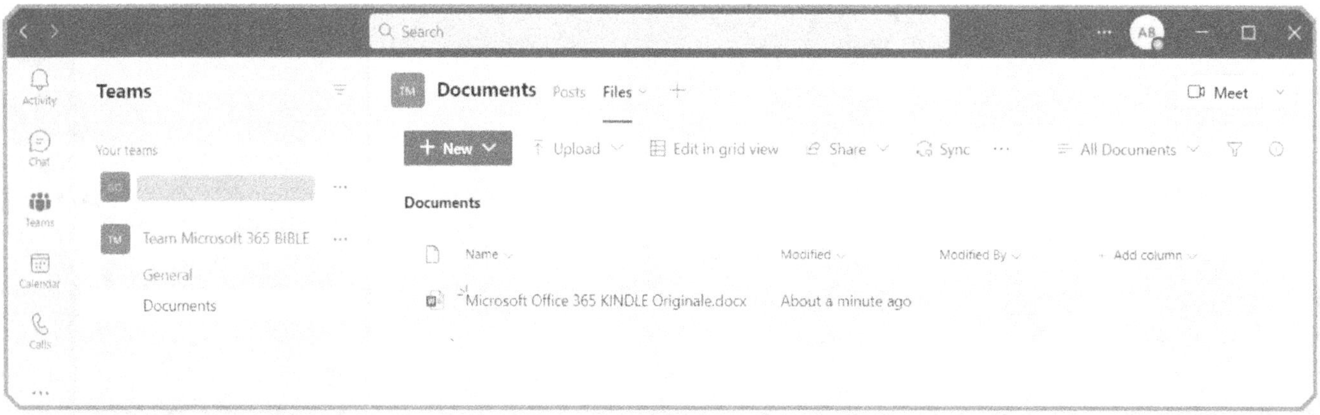

Files Tab Advanced Features and Capabilities

- **Document Creation**: Initiate new documents for real-time team collaboration, including Word, Excel, PowerPoint, and OneNote files

- **Synchronization Management**: Keep all file versions synchronized across team members, with automatic version tracking and history

- **Local Device Access**: Download documents to your personal devices for offline work or local editing

- **Link Generation and Sharing**: Create and distribute shareable links with customizable permissions and expiration dates

The seamless integration between communication tools and file storage systems within Microsoft Teams creates an efficient collaborative workspace. This integration allows team members to discuss documents while viewing and editing them simultaneously.

Troubleshooting and Maintenance

If files aren't displaying consistently for all team members, the sync function serves as a quick solution to resolve version conflicts and access issues, ensuring every team member has the most current information at their disposal.

Chats and Calls and Communication Tools

While Microsoft Teams excels as a collaborative platform, it also provides sophisticated **private communication capabilities.** Users can seamlessly switch between team-wide discussions and confidential conversations within the same interface.

Adding Participants to Private Conversations

1. Locate the **person-plus icon** positioned in the top right corner of your chat window
2. Click to access your comprehensive contact directory
3. Search for and select desired participants using name, email, or department filters
4. Optionally add a message to introduce the new participant to the ongoing conversation

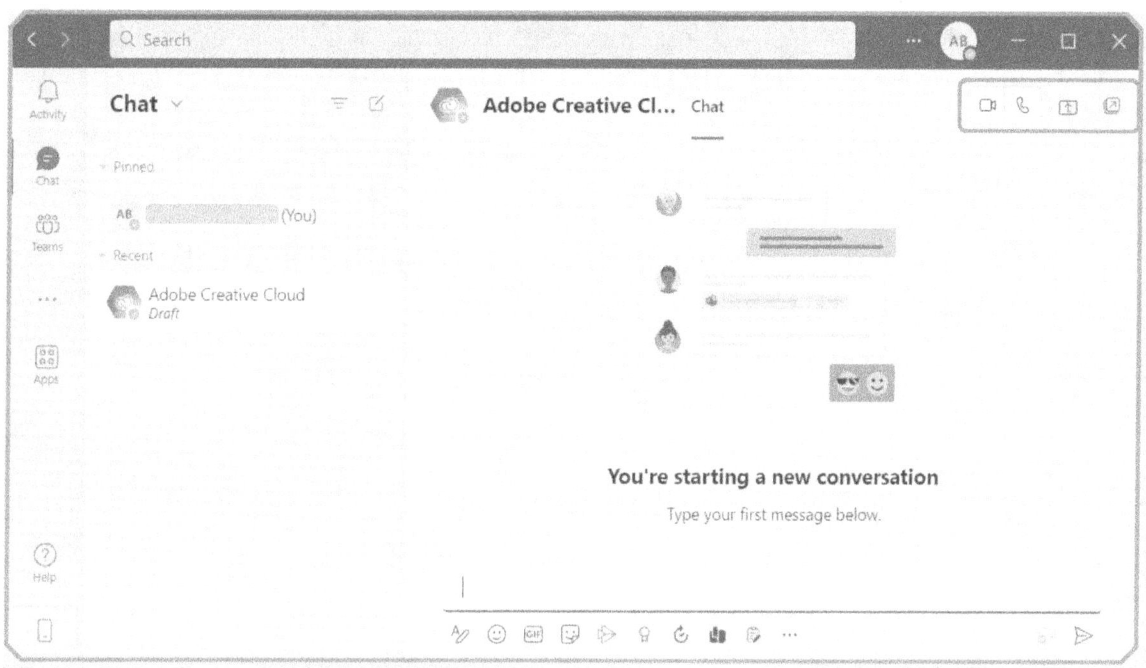

Enhanced Communication Features

- **Video Conferencing**: Enable face-to-face virtual meetings with high-definition video and background customization options
- **Voice Calls**: Conduct audio-only communications with crystal-clear sound quality and noise suppression
- **Screen Sharing**: Facilitate visual collaboration through comprehensive screen sharing options, including:
  - Full screen sharing

- Specific window sharing
- Program-specific sharing
- PowerPoint presentation mode
- Whiteboard collaboration

Advanced Multitasking Capabilities - The pop-out chat feature enhances productivity by allowing users to:

- Monitor and participate in multiple conversations simultaneously
- Maintain visibility of important chats while working in other applications
- Reference information across different conversations without switching windows
- Organize chats by importance or project relevance
- Customize chat window sizes and positions for optimal workspace organization

Message Composition and Advanced Features

Microsoft Teams provides sophisticated text formatting options that exceed standard messaging platforms. While composing messages, users can access:

- **Text Enhancement Tools**: Apply bold, italics, and underline formatting to emphasize key points
- **Visual Customization**: Modify font colors and styles to highlight critical information
- **Structure Elements**: Create organized bullet points and numbered lists for clear instructions or sequential steps

These comprehensive formatting tools ensure precise communication tone and emphasis within digital conversations.

Message Priority Management

- Utilize the **exclamation mark icon** to designate message importance
- Perfect for urgent communications
- Essential for time-critical announcements
- Helps recipients prioritize their responses

Draft Management: The formatting toolbar includes a **trash can icon** for efficient draft message removal, streamlining the composition process.

Advanced Message Features

@ Mentions System

- Directly tag specific users to capture their attention

- Ensure critical messages receive proper notice in active channels
- Target questions or assignments to specific team members
- Generate immediate notifications for mentioned users

Threaded Conversations -The Reply function creates organized discussion threads that:

- Group related messages cohesively
- Facilitate topic tracking within busy channels
- Minimize main channel congestion
- Enable focused discussions on specific subjects

Enhanced File Sharing - Drag-and-drop functionality provides seamless file integration:

1. Drag files directly from your local system into the message area
2. Files appear instantly in the conversation thread
3. Automatic storage in the channel's Files section occurs simultaneously
4. File previews generate automatically for supported formats

This comprehensive storage approach ensures:

- Immediate file accessibility
- Proper document organization
- Efficient long-term file management
- Simplified file retrieval

Channel Wide Notification System - To notify all channel members simultaneously:

- Use '@' followed by the channel name
- Generates alerts for all channel members
- Ideal for broad announcements
- Perfect for time-sensitive communications
- Requires thoughtful usage to prevent notification overload

These integrated features create a robust communication ecosystem within Microsoft Teams, enabling precise information delivery to appropriate team members at optimal times.

Teams Meeting Features

Microsoft Teams provides one of the most sophisticated virtual meeting platforms available, offering:

- **Participant Management**: Send invitations, add attendees during meetings, manage roles
- **Screen Sharing**: Share your entire screen, specific windows, or applications
- **Background Customization**: Use blur effects or custom backgrounds for professionalism
- **Session Recording**: Capture meetings for future reference or absent team members
- **Interactive Tools**: Raise hands, react with emojis, participate in polls
- **File Sharing**: Share documents during meetings for real-time collaboration
- **Meeting Notes**: Create and share notes visible to all participants
- **Live Captions**: Enable real-time captioning for accessibility
- **Breakout Rooms**: Create smaller discussion groups within meetings
- **Live Reactions**: Express feedback without interrupting speakers

Meeting Scheduling and Integration

Teams and Outlook operate in perfect synchronization, providing automatic calendar updates across both platforms, real-time availability checking, meeting reminder synchronization, integrated notification management, and cross-platform meeting modifications.

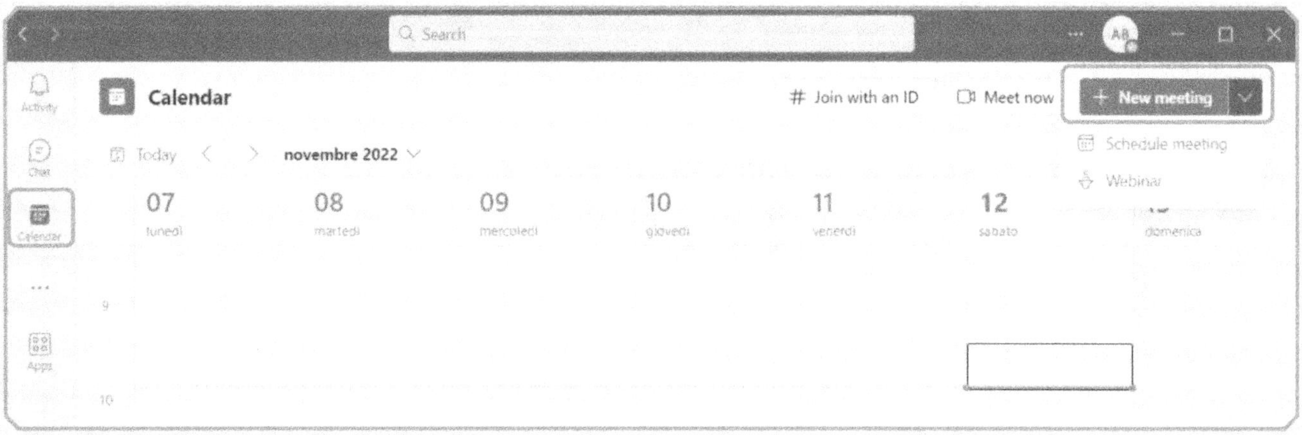

Creating a Meeting in Teams

1. Find and click the **calendar icon** on the left sidebar
2. Review your calendar for availability
3. Click the **"+ new meeting"** button at the top
4. Complete the required meeting details:

   - **Meeting Title**: Clear, descriptive name
   - **Participant List**: Required and optional attendees
   - **Date and Time**: Specific meeting schedule
   - **Channel Selection**: If applicable to a specific team
   - **Custom Message**: Optional additional information
   - **Duration**: Meeting length
   - **Recurrence**: Set up recurring meetings if needed
   - **Meeting Options**: Configure advanced settings

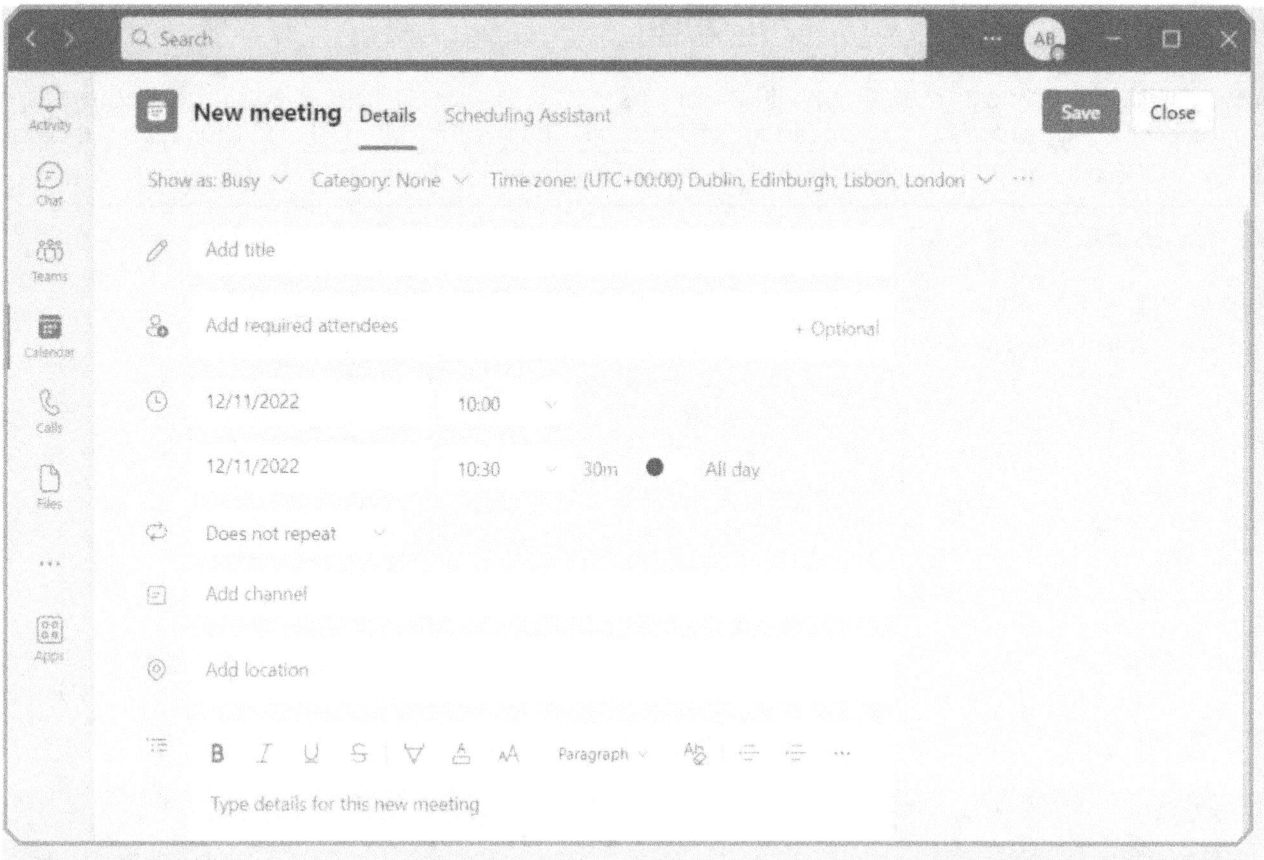

Advanced Meeting Settings - The top menu provides extensive control over:

- **Time Zone Management**: Set multiple time zones for global teams, with automatic time conversion for attendees and daylight savings time adjustments.

- **Response Options**: Configure accept/decline settings, tentative response allowance, delegate attendance permissions, and response tracking.

- **Meeting Security**: Manage lobby settings, participant permissions, recording permissions, and chat settings.

- **Resource Management**: Control virtual meeting rooms, physical room booking, equipment reservation, and bandwidth requirements.

Additional Features:

- **Recording Management**: Configure auto-recording options, storage settings, and sharing permissions.
- **Transcription Services**: Enable live captions, full meeting transcripts, and multi-language support.
- **Presentation Tools**: Access PowerPoint live, whiteboard integration, and screen annotation tools.
- **Attendance Tracking**: Generate participant reports, monitor join/leave timestamps, and track engagement metrics.

These comprehensive features establish Teams as a powerful platform for virtual collaboration, supporting everything from small team discussions to large-scale presentations and global meetings.

Joining Meetings and Customization

Teams provides automatic meeting notifications as start time approaches. Organizers have responsibility for lobby management and participant admission. Upon joining, you'll configure initial audio/video settings, which remain adjustable throughout the meeting session.

Background Customization

1. Select the background filters button beneath your video preview
2. Choose from multiple options:
    - Background blur effect
    - Standard Teams templates
    - Custom corporate backgrounds
    - Personal image uploads
3. Click "join now" after finalizing your selection

Productivity Tip: *Adding corporate branding to backgrounds enhances professionalism. Access this by selecting "add new" at the top of the background options panel. You can upload company logos, office environments, or branded templates.*

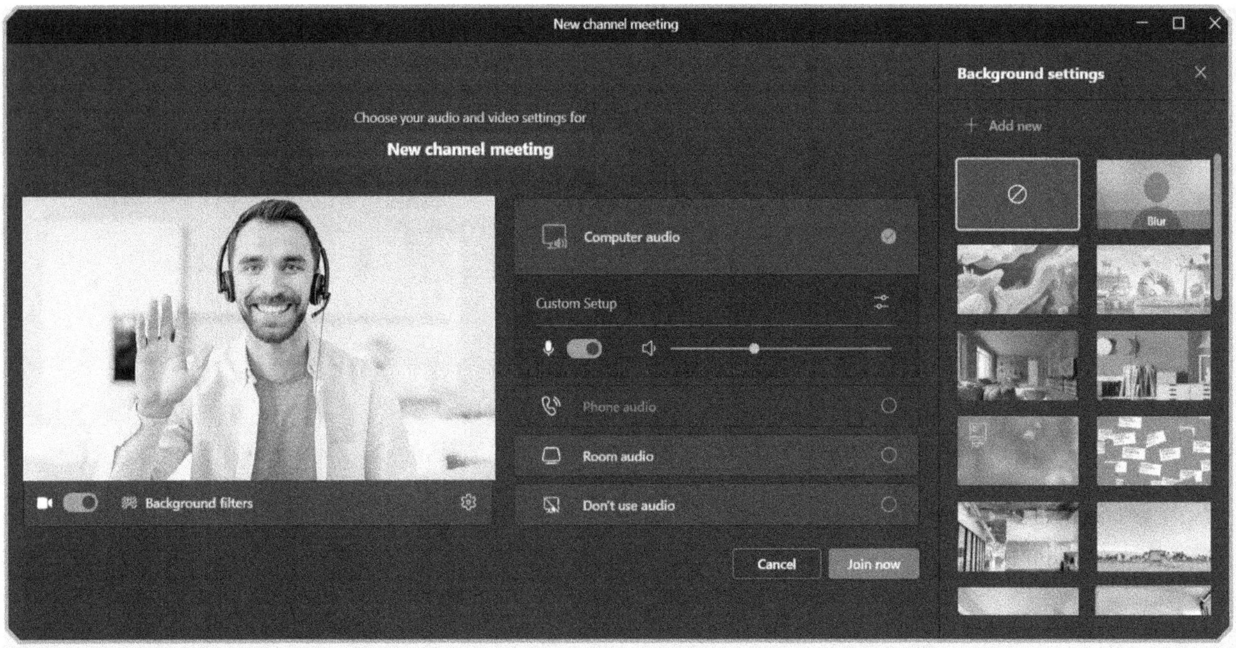

Meeting Configuration Controls

1. **Core Parameters:**
    - Meeting duration settings
    - Role assignment capabilities
    - Screen sharing permissions
    - File sharing controls
    - Participant management
    - Recording functions

2. **Role Management** - Define specific participant roles including:

    - Meeting organizer
    - Co-organizer status
    - Presenter privileges
    - Attendee limitations

Configuration Process:

1. Navigate to Teams calendar
2. Select target meeting
3. Access meeting options button
4. Configure desired parameters including attendance tracking, lobby settings, recording preferences, chat permissions, file sharing rights, and screen sharing controls.

> ***Productivity Tip:*** *When scheduling recurring meetings, create a backup organizer by assigning co-organizer permissions to another team member. This ensures meeting continuity if you experience technical issues or cannot attend unexpectedly. The co-organizer can start the meeting in your absence, manage participant access, control recording settings, adjust meeting permissions, and share presentations and files.*

During Team Interactions

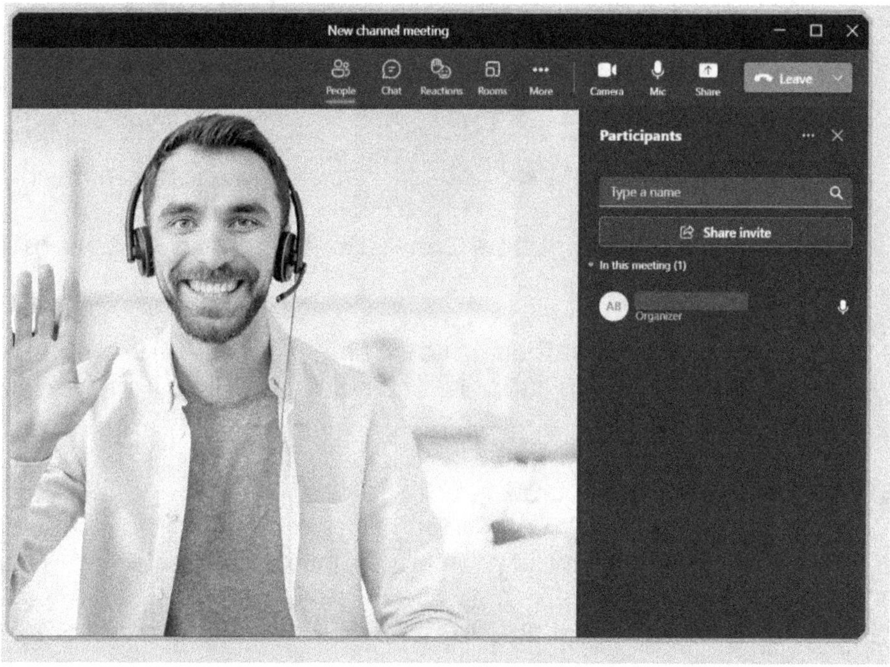

In a Teams meeting environment, participants can utilize multiple interactive elements. Let's examine these capabilities thoroughly:

Navigation Elements at Top

The upper section of your meeting interface contains several **essential control icons**:

- The **participant roster** enables you to monitor all meeting attendees, which proves invaluable in managing large-scale meetings or keeping track of who's present.

- The **messaging interface** reveals a lateral communication panel, ideal for distributing web links or posing questions without disrupting the current speaker.

- The **hand-raising functionality** provides a method to alert the meeting facilitator about your desire to contribute, helping maintain structured discussion.

- The **window separation feature** enables independent positioning of the meeting window, beneficial for multitasking scenarios or setups with multiple displays.

Advanced Options Menu (...):

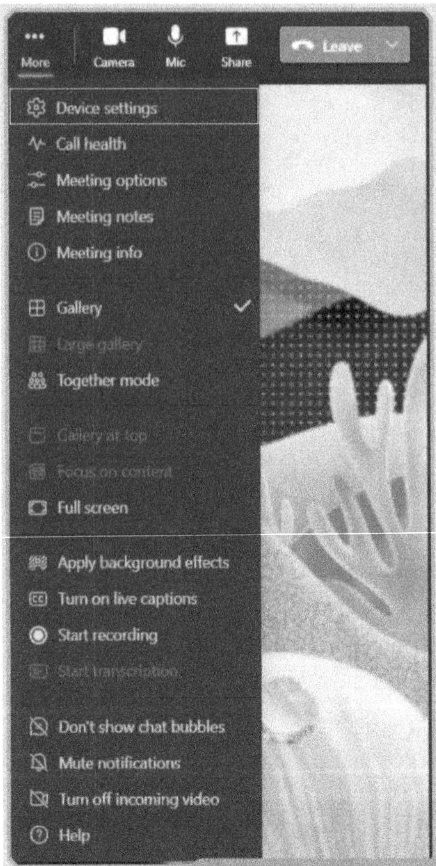

OPTIONS MENU

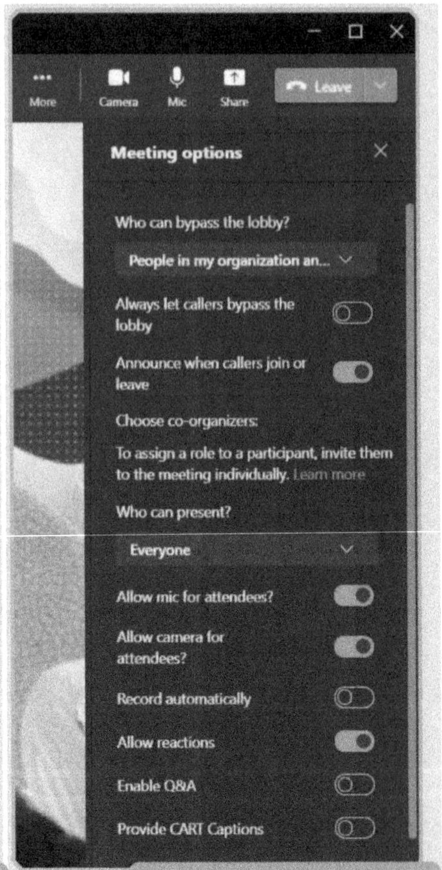

MEETING OPTIONS

This menu, particularly **crucial for meeting administrators**, provides sophisticated capabilities:

- **Meeting Documentation**: Preserves both visual and audio components of the entire session.
    - **Important Note**: Always notify attendees when initiating recording for privacy considerations.
    - Recorded content becomes accessible through Teams chat storage or OneDrive sharing options.
- **Live Text Display**: Converts spoken content into written text in real-time.
    - Improves accessibility for those with hearing limitations or in sound-challenged environments.
    - Assists non-native language speakers in better following the discussion.
- **Simultaneous Language Conversion**: Transforms captions into various languages as the meeting progresses.
    - Eliminates communication barriers during international collaborations.
    - Currently offers support for a select group of languages, with ongoing expansion planned.

Dynamic Control Features

The meeting environment provides real-time management tools for flexible administration:

- The **role modification system** through "meeting options" enables instantaneous adjustments to participant permissions
    - Particularly valuable when temporarily elevating attendees to presenter status for their designated segments
- The **collaborative documentation feature** facilitates shared note creation during and after sessions
    - Effectively captures **important decisions**, follow-up tasks, and significant discussion points
    - Implements automatic saving and distribution to all meeting participants

Content Distribution Tools

The sharing functionality reveals multiple presentation alternatives:

- **Application-specific sharing** enables focused window presentation
- Maintains confidentiality by limiting visibility to selected application windows
- **Enhanced PowerPoint Integration** provides advanced slide presentation capabilities
- Enables independent slide navigation for audience members, supporting individual review pacing
- Maintains presenter control over the primary presentation display
- **Interactive Digital Canvas(Microsoft Whiteboard)** provides a shared space for real-time group work
- Perfectly suited for creative ideation sessions and visual demonstrations
- Supports simultaneous input from all participants

Productivity Tip: *Direct PowerPoint presentation through Teams delivers superior performance with improved transition smoothness and reduced network bandwidth consumption compared to traditional screen sharing methods while running PowerPoint separately.*

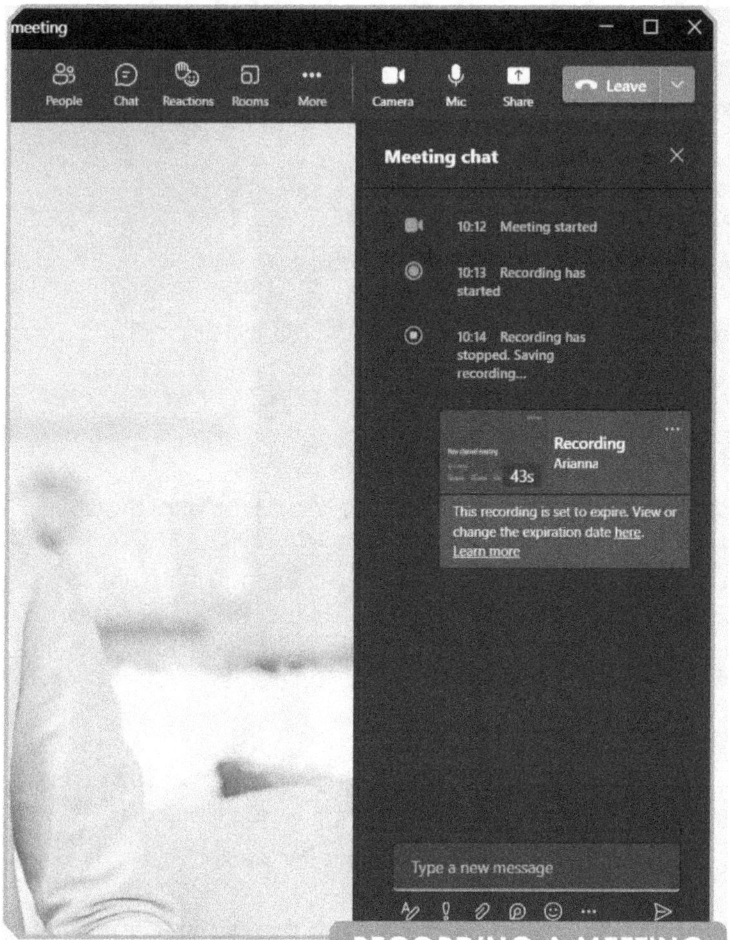

RECORDING A MEETING

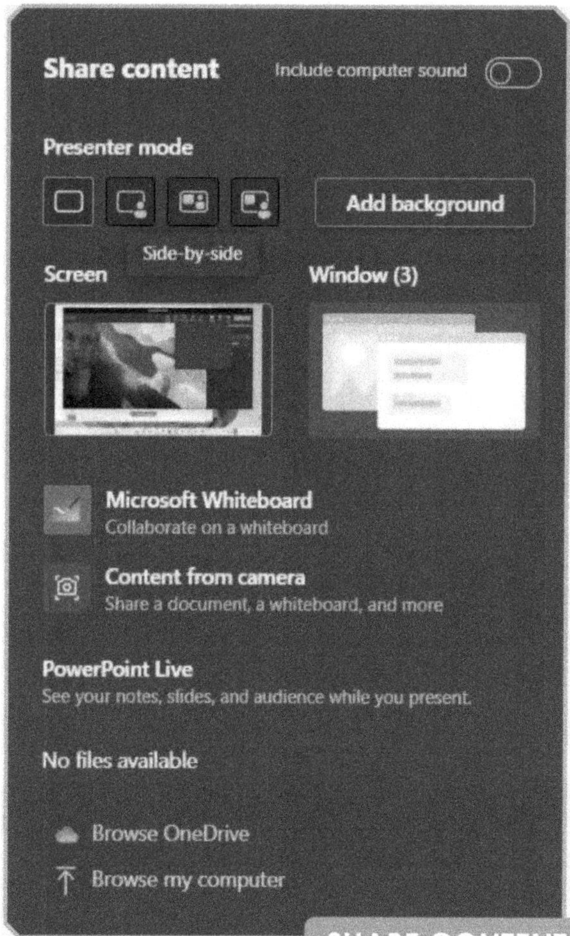

SHARE CONTENT

Meeting Conclusion Phase

When your Teams session approaches its end, the platform provides critical functionalities for proper meeting closure:

Participant Documentation

The system enables extraction of **attendance records** with these key aspects:

- Meeting hosts can obtain a comprehensive list of all meeting attendees
- This function creates an official record of session participation
- **Critical Timing Note**: This information must be retrieved before meeting termination, as it becomes inaccessible afterward

Session Exit Alternatives

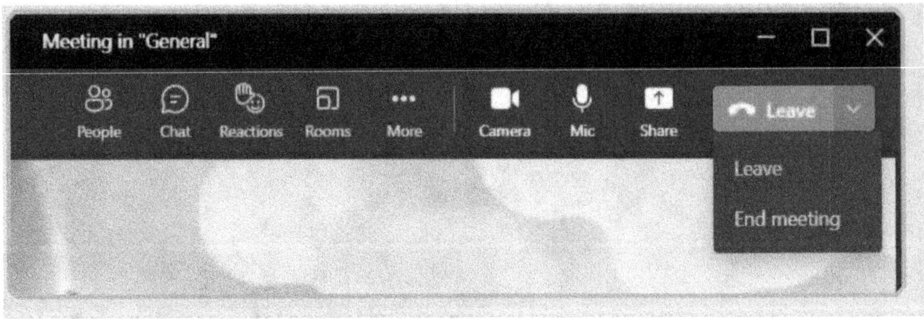

Teams provides two distinct **meeting conclusion methods**:

1. **Complete Meeting Termination:**
    - This action initiates a **comprehensive session closure** affecting all participants
    - Typically executed by meeting organizers to signal definitive conclusion
    - Automatically terminates all ongoing screen sharing and discussions
    - Recommended for ensuring clear meeting conclusion and preventing extended lingering

2. **Individual Departure Option:**
    - Enables personal exit while maintaining active session status for others
    - Perfect for scenarios where ongoing discussion continues beyond your participation
    - Maintains meeting functionality for remaining attendees
    - Particularly valuable in situations such as:
    - Meeting facilitators who establish the session but aren't required for the entire duration
    - Participants managing overlapping schedule commitments

Post Meeting Material Access

The meeting platform provides comprehensive **resource management** after session completion:

Recording Accessibility:

- Meeting recordings undergo **automatic processing and storage** within chat file sections
    - Provides convenient access for subsequent review sessions
    - Enables asynchronous participation for team members who couldn't attend the live meeting

File Sharing Options

Two primary **sharing pathways** exist:

Internal Distribution:

- Facilitate direct sharing through the Teams platform
- Maintains seamless integration within the organizational ecosystem

External Sharing Process:

- Requires download and subsequent OneDrive upload
- Ensures secure content distribution to external stakeholders
- Maintains controlled access through established security protocols

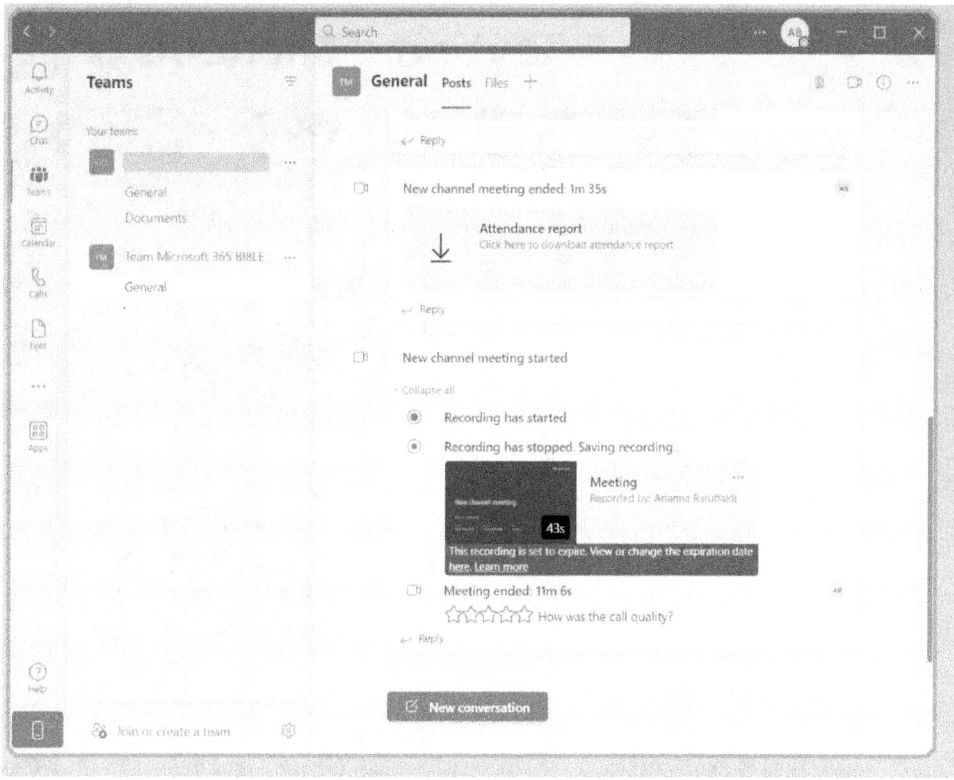

Keyboard Shortcuts on *Teams*

Function	PC Shortcut	Mac Shortcut
Search or access command bar	*Ctrl + E*	*Command + E*
Start a new chat	*Ctrl + N*	*Command + N*
Open settings	*Ctrl + ,*	*Command + ,*
Toggle mute	*Ctrl + Shift + M*	*Command + Shift + M*
Toggle video	*Ctrl + Shift + O*	*Command + Shift + O*
Start a call	*Ctrl + Shift + K*	*Command + Shift + K*
Show keyboard shortcuts	*Ctrl + Shift + H*	*Command + Shift + H*
Show commands	*Ctrl + .*	*Command + .*
Navigate to Activity	*Ctrl + 1*	*Command + 1*
Navigate to Chat	*Ctrl + 2*	*Command + 2*

Keyboard Shortcuts on *Teams*

Function	PC Shortcut	Mac Shortcut
Navigate to Teams	*Ctrl + 3*	*Command + 3*
Navigate to Calendar	*Ctrl + 4*	*Command + 4*
Navigate to Calls	*Ctrl + 5*	*Command + 5*
Navigate to Files	*Ctrl + 6*	*Command + 6*
Go to	*Ctrl + G*	*Command + G*
Raise or lower hand	*Ctrl + Shift + E*	*Command + Shift + E*
Decline call	*Ctrl + Shift + D*	*Command + Shift + D*
Accept call	*Ctrl + Shift + A*	*Command + Shift + A*
Take a screenshot	*Ctrl + Shift + S*	*Command + Shift + S*
Toggle share tray	*Ctrl + Shift + Space*	*Command + Shift + Space*
Toggle fullscreen	*Ctrl + Shift + F*	*Command + Shift + F*
Expand compose box	*Ctrl + Shift + X*	*Command + Shift + X*
Start a new line	*Shift + Enter*	*Shift + Return*
Mention someone	@	@
Increase font size	*Ctrl + Shift + >*	*Command + Shift + >*
Decrease font size	*Ctrl + Shift + <*	*Command + Shift + <*

8. OneDrive:

Empowering Your Digital Storage Experience

OneDrive, Microsoft's **cloud storage platform**, delivers comprehensive digital content management capabilities. It accommodates various file types - from **documents** to **multimedia content** - while providing universal access through cloud-connected devices. Microsoft Suite subscribers receive a **substantial 1TB storage allocation**.

Distinctive Features: A distinctive capability of OneDrive lies in its computer settings synchronization, enabling automatic cloud backup without manual local storage intervention. While comparable to alternative cloud solutions, OneDrive distinguishes itself through enhanced features and native Microsoft Office integration.

Cloud-Based Advantages: The cloud-centric architecture of OneDrive delivers multiple advantages, including cross-platform accessibility, generous storage capacity, and automated saving functionality. This combination, alongside its deep Microsoft ecosystem integration, establishes OneDrive as a powerful productivity tool ensuring continuous file availability.

Accessing OneDrive-In

To begin using OneDrive:

- Navigate through your preferred web browser to the OneDrive portal
- Select the appropriate access link for login
- Enter your registration email address
- Input your corresponding password

Important: These credentials must match your other Microsoft application credentials for proper system synchronization and document access

Authentication Process - The login system offers multiple security layers:

- **For Returning Users**:
- Password credentials may be automatically saved
- Single-click access becomes available
- Previous authentication details remain stored securely
- **Enhanced Security Options**:
- Two-factor authentication available for additional protection

- Mobile device verification codes sent during login attempts
- Real-time security confirmation through unique codes
- Highly recommended for sensitive file protection

Dashboard Interface

The OneDrive initial screen presents a comprehensive **control center** for managing your files through these distinct sections:

1. **Primary Display Zone:**

    - Exhibits your main folder structure and recent file access history
    - Delivers clear visualization of cloud storage organization
    - Features rapid access to commonly used content items
    - Enables intuitive navigation through stored content

2. **Navigation Panel** - The left sidebar contains essential navigation elements:

    - **Files Section**: Complete repository of stored documents and folders
    - **Recent Activity**: Swift access to newly modified or uploaded content
    - **Photo Gallery**: Specialized area for image file management with preview functionality
    - **Shared Content**: Centralized access point for collaborative files
    - **Recovery Zone**: Access to deleted items with restoration or permanent removal options

3. **Integration Bar** - The upper blue section provides:

    - Seamless connectivity with Microsoft's online application suite
    - Quick transitions between OneDrive and other productivity tools:
    - Word document processing
    - Excel spreadsheet management
    - PowerPoint presentation creation

4. **Function Controls** - Located beneath the integration bar, this toolbar offers:

    - Direct access to essential OneDrive operations
    - Primary functions including:
    - File upload capabilities
    - Synchronization controls
    - Content sharing tools
    - File management utilities

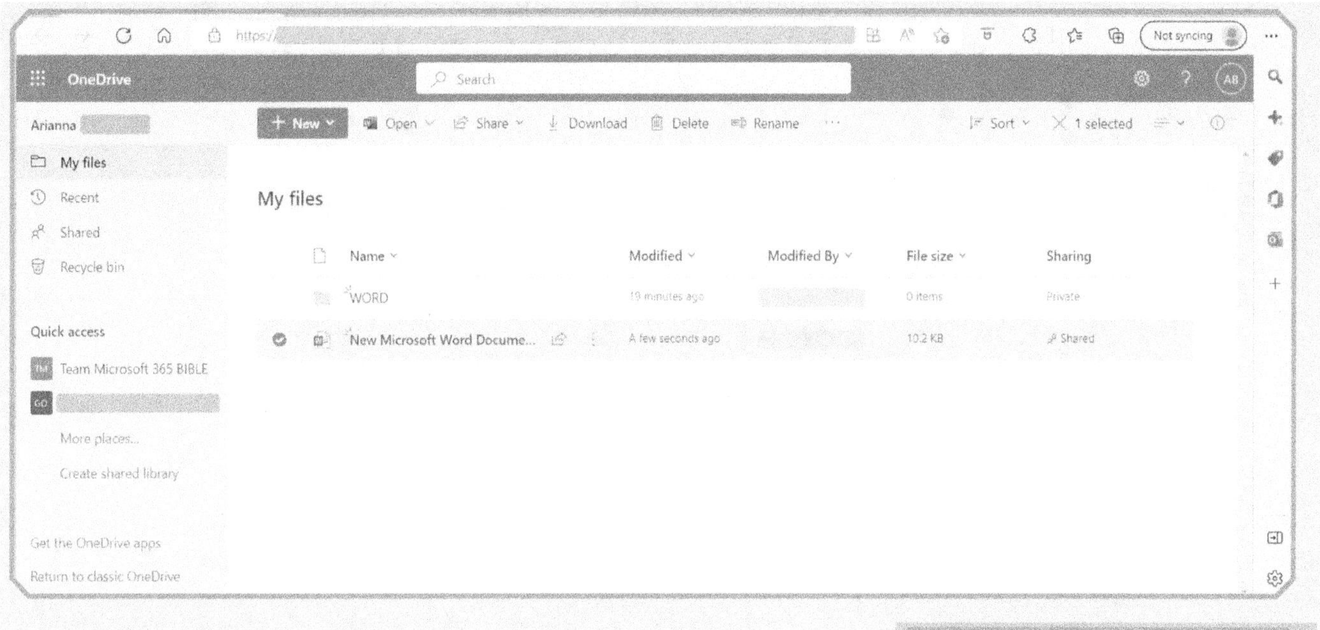

Cloud-Based File Creation and Modification

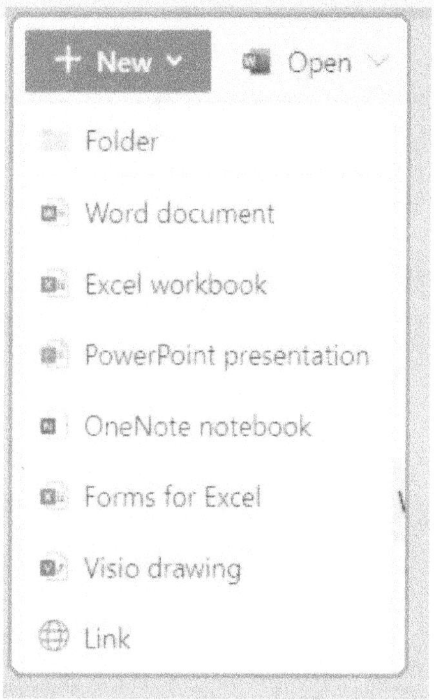

The **"+ New" function** serves as your entry point for generating content within OneDrive:

1. **Available Document Types:**

    - **Word:** For crafting professional documents, detailed reports, and formal correspondence
    - **Excel:** For generating analytical spreadsheets, performing calculations, and managing data
    - **PowerPoint:** For designing visual presentations, meeting materials, and business proposals
    - **OneNote:** For maintaining digital records, organizing thoughts, and collecting information
    - **Forms:** For developing questionnaires, feedback collection, and survey distribution
    - **Plain Text:** For creating basic documents without formatting requirements
    - **Folders:** For establishing structured content organization systems

2. **Web-Based Editing Capabilities:**

    - Each selection launches a browser-based version of the corresponding application
    - Online versions maintain strong similarity to desktop software, preserving core functionalities
    - Continuous cloud synchronization ensures automatic preservation of all modifications

3. **Storage Configuration:**

    - Document creation flexibility allows placement in either root directory or specific folders
    - Organizational structure can be implemented immediately during file creation

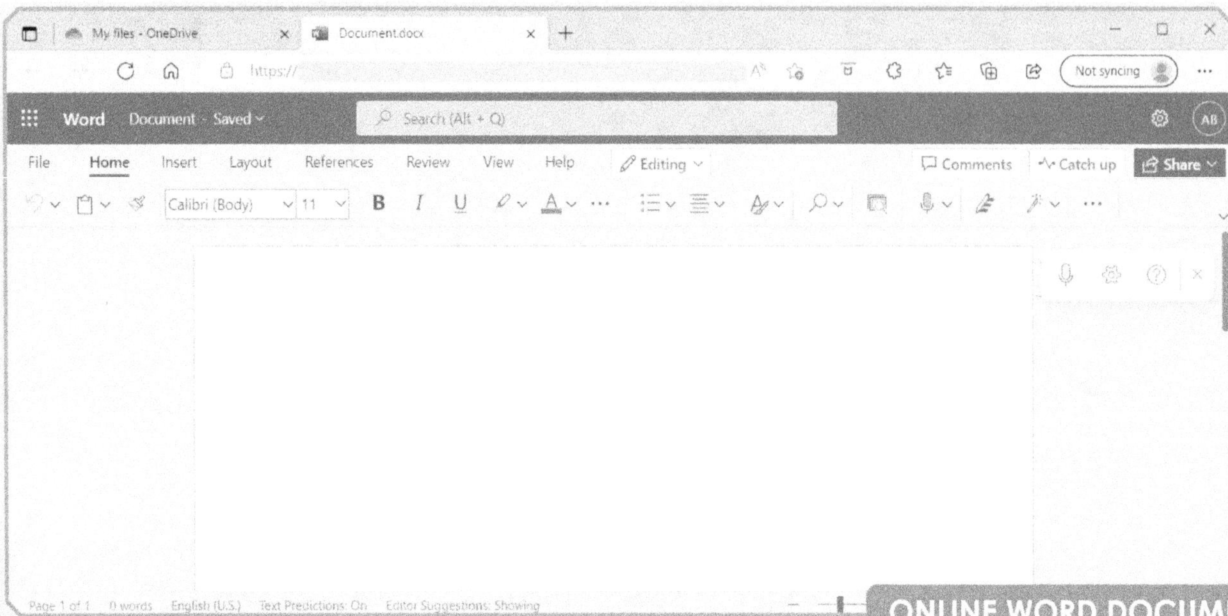

ONLINE WORD DOCUMENT

Advanced File Operations

Right-clicking on any file or folder name reveals extensive management capabilities:

1. **Essential Controls:**

    - **Preview/Open:** Quick content examination without complete file launch
    - **Download:** Creation of device-based local copies
    - **Delete:** File transfer to Recycle Bin storage
    - **Move/Copy:** Internal content reorganization within OneDrive system
    - **Rename:** Direct cloud-based filename modification

2. **Shared Access Tools:**

    - **Share:** Access distribution to colleagues with customized permission levels
    - **Version History:** Historical document version access and restoration capabilities

3. **Content Insights:**

    - **Details:** Access to comprehensive file metadata documentation
    - **Modification History:** Chronological tracking of content alterations

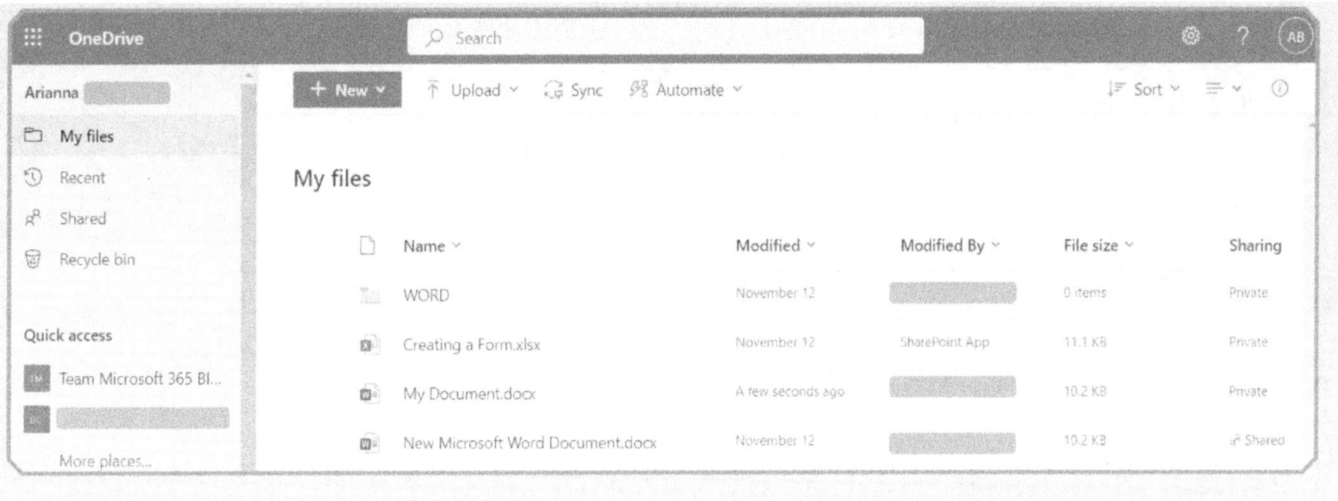

Uploading and Downloading Documents

To incorporate files into your OneDrive environment, you'll discover an efficient upload functionality positioned adjacent to the **"+ New" control** within the main interface. This versatile feature accommodates both single-file transfers and comprehensive folder uploads. Here are the principal upload methodologies:

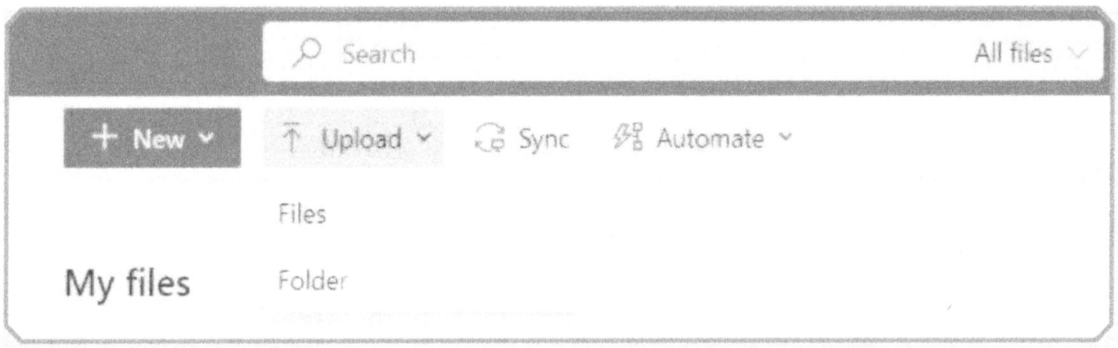

1. **Interface Button Method**: Positioned beside the **"+ New"** control on the primary screen. Presents dual options:

   - Single file upload
   - Complete folder upload

   Sequential Steps:

   - Activate the upload control
   - Select desired transfer type
   - Browse local system directory
   - Identify target content
   - Execute transfer confirmation

2. **Direct Manipulation Approach**: An enhanced, streamlined methodology

   Implementation Process:

   - Launch OneDrive in separate window
   - Access source content location
   - Engage desired content via mouse press
   - Transfer to OneDrive environment
   - Position content at intended destination

Progress Tracking:

- Status indicator displays transfer progress
- Real-time upload speed monitoring
- File size and remaining time display
- Transfer completion confirmation

Productivity Tip: *OneDrive's drag and drop capability functions across all areas of the platform. You can utilize this universal feature to transfer fresh content to the cloud, relocate files across different directories, establish new organizational structures, manage multiple files simultaneously, and create folder hierarchies efficiently. This seamless functionality makes file organization intuitive and time-efficient.*

Productivity Tip 2: *Maximize your upload efficiency by using keyboard shortcuts:*

- *Ctrl + click to select multiple specific files*
- *Shift + click to select a range of files*
- *Ctrl + A to select all items in a folder*
- *Esc to cancel ongoing uploads*
- *F5 to refresh your view after transfers*

Local File Retrieval from OneDrive - To transfer files from OneDrive storage to your device:

1. **File Selection:**

- Activate the selection circle adjacent to target filename
- Observe toolbar modification reflecting available actions

2. **Download:**

- Select "Download" option from updated toolbar menu
- Alternative method: access context menu via right-click and choose "Download"

3. **Download Location:**

- Respond to system dialog prompt
- Direct system to preferred storage location
- Validate destination selection

4. **Progress:**

- Observe progress through browser's download interface
- Access file in local storage upon completion

Additional Download Options:

- Batch download multiple files simultaneously
- Download entire folders as compressed archives
- Resume interrupted downloads automatically
- Schedule downloads for large files
- Configure default download locations for efficiency

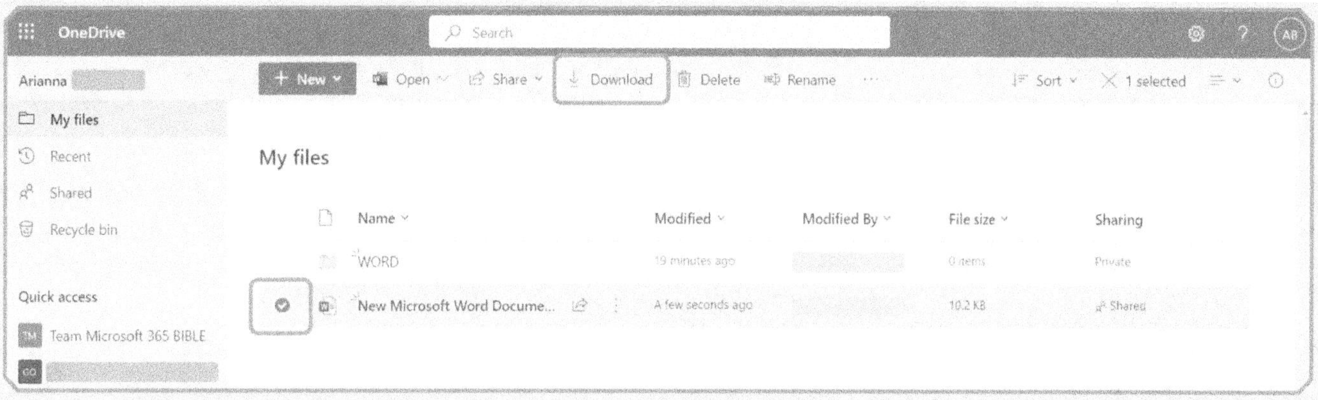

***Security Note**: Always verify your local device has sufficient storage space and appropriate permissions before initiating downloads. Consider scanning downloaded files with security software before opening, especially when retrieving shared content.*

Enhanced Sharing Capabilities

When selecting content within OneDrive, the upper command bar expands to display supplementary functions. The **"Share" function** represents a crucial element. Activating this control reveals a configuration window enabling you to:

- Input recipient email addresses
- Create custom accompanying messages
- Create shareable access links

File status indicators transition from **"private"** to **"shared"** post-distribution, signifying expanded access permissions.

Access Control Management

Users maintain comprehensive control over shared content permissions. During the sharing process:

- Access the permission settings via the pen icon beside recipient details
- Toggle between **"can edit"** and **"can view"** authorization levels
- Modify access privileges at any subsequent time as required

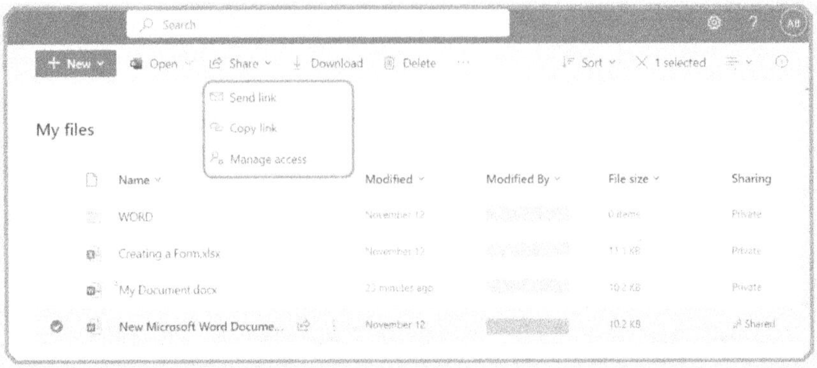

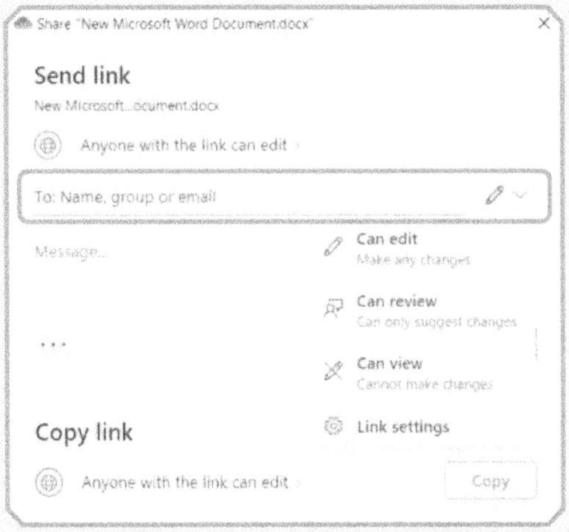

***Productivity Tip 1**: OneDrive supports simultaneous selection of multiple content items. Available toolbar actions adapt dynamically based on your selection combination (files with files, files with folders, or folders with folders).*

***Productivity Tip 2**: For enhanced security when sharing sensitive documents:*

- *Set link expiration dates*
- *Protect files with passwords*
- *Restrict downloading capabilities*
- *Monitor access through sharing analytics*
- *Revoke access instantly when needed*

***Note**: Remember to periodically review your shared items to ensure appropriate access levels are maintained and remove unnecessary sharing permissions.*

Web Integration Options

OneDrive provides advanced embedding functionality for web presence enhancement. Upon content selection, the **"</> Embed"** control generates HTML implementation code through a lateral panel, facilitating direct OneDrive content display within web environments.

Security Considerations: A critical aspect to understand: embedded content becomes publicly accessible without authentication requirements. Exercise appropriate discretion - limit embedding to content suitable for unrestricted public viewing.

***Productivity Tip**: Before embedding sensitive materials, create a separate folder specifically for public-facing content. This organizational approach helps prevent accidental exposure of private information through embedding.*

File Synchronization

Microsoft OneDrive's connection with the Microsoft Suite delivers **powerful automatic file syncing** capabilities for your digital work process. The OneDrive sync function usually comes **pre-configured** when Microsoft Suite is installed on your computer, allowing for immediate file synchronization.

When properly configured, this **seamless integration** ensures that every **new document**, saved file, or change made on your computer is instantly **mirrored** in your OneDrive cloud storage. This **two-way synchronization** also works with **online modifications**: changes made through OneDrive's website will appear when you access the file on your computer.

This **bi-directional synchronization** provides exceptional **flexibility** in your work approach. It enables you to achieve the following **key benefits**:

- **Remote access**: View and edit your most current files from any internet-connected device
- **Location independence**: Continue working on documents without needing your main computer
- **Real-time collaboration**: Work simultaneously with team members, with changes visible immediately to everyone

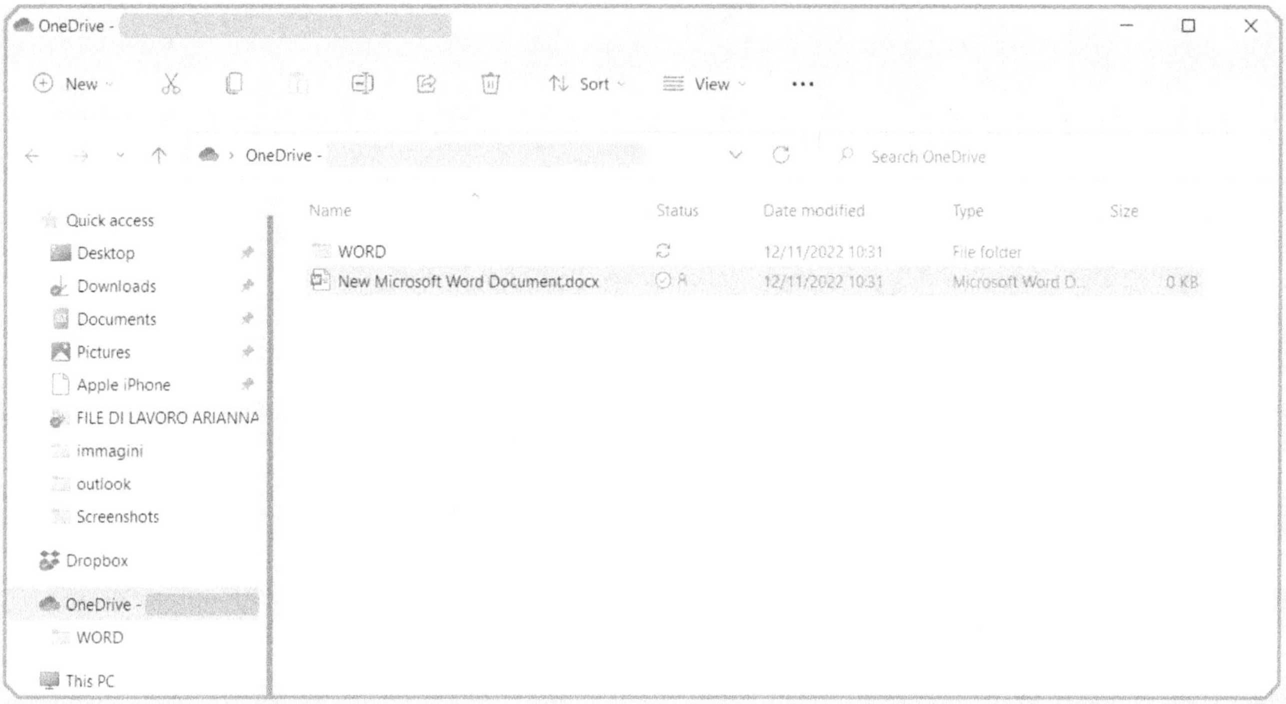

***Productivity Tip**: OneDrive implements a **subtle visual indicator** to notify you of recent changes. You'll observe **three blue dashes** appearing beside a file's name in the directory when it has been recently added or modified in OneDrive. This **visual cue** helps you quickly identify recently updated or new files in your cloud storage.*

Cloud Storage and Backup

OneDrive functions as both a **cloud storage service** and an **automated backup system**. The files you keep in OneDrive are inherently **backed up**, making separate backup methods unnecessary. This **protective feature** provides value even when you don't frequently use cloud-based file access.

A **key advantage** of OneDrive is its **robust file preservation**. When you permanently remove a file from your computer using Shift + Delete, a **backup copy** remains available in OneDrive's cloud-based recycle bin. This creates a **safety mechanism** to protect against unintended file deletions.

The process for **file recovery** involves these **essential steps**:

- Navigate to OneDrive's web platform
- Select the **"Recycle Bin"** feature from the sidebar menu
- Search for your deleted file
- Choose and restore the file, which will sync back to both cloud storage and your local computer

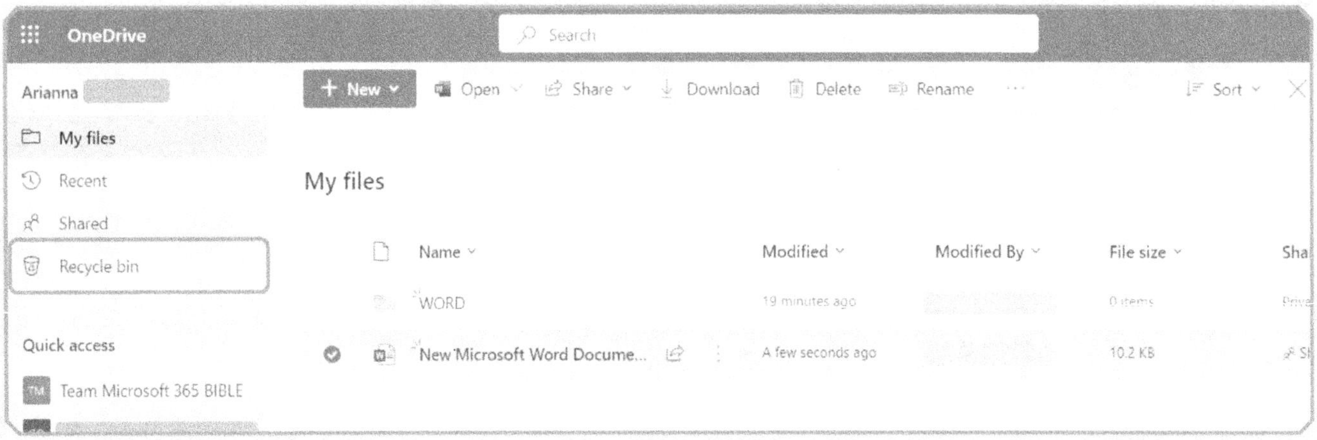

Storage Management

OneDrive provides new users with a **generous 1 TB storage allocation**. You can **monitor your usage** through a blue progress bar displayed at the bottom of the left task pane. This **visual indicator** shows your storage consumption both graphically and numerically, providing a clear understanding of your available space.

Storage Expansion: When you need more space, OneDrive offers **storage upgrade options.** The process involves:

- Opening the "Options" menu
- Choosing your desired storage increase
- Setting up automatic monthly billing to your linked credit card

For **detailed storage analysis**, you can access the "Manage Storage" feature within the Options menu, which provides comprehensive insights into your cloud storage utilization.

Account Configuration

To access your OneDrive account settings, follow these **primary steps**:

1. Locate your initials within a circle in the top-right corner
2. Click on this circular icon
3. Select "my Microsoft account" from the menu

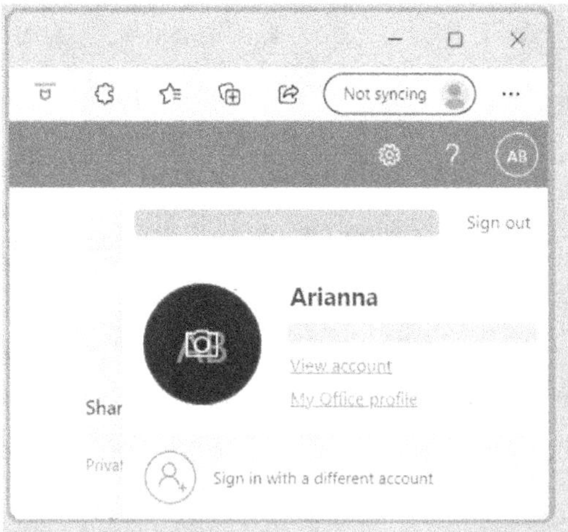

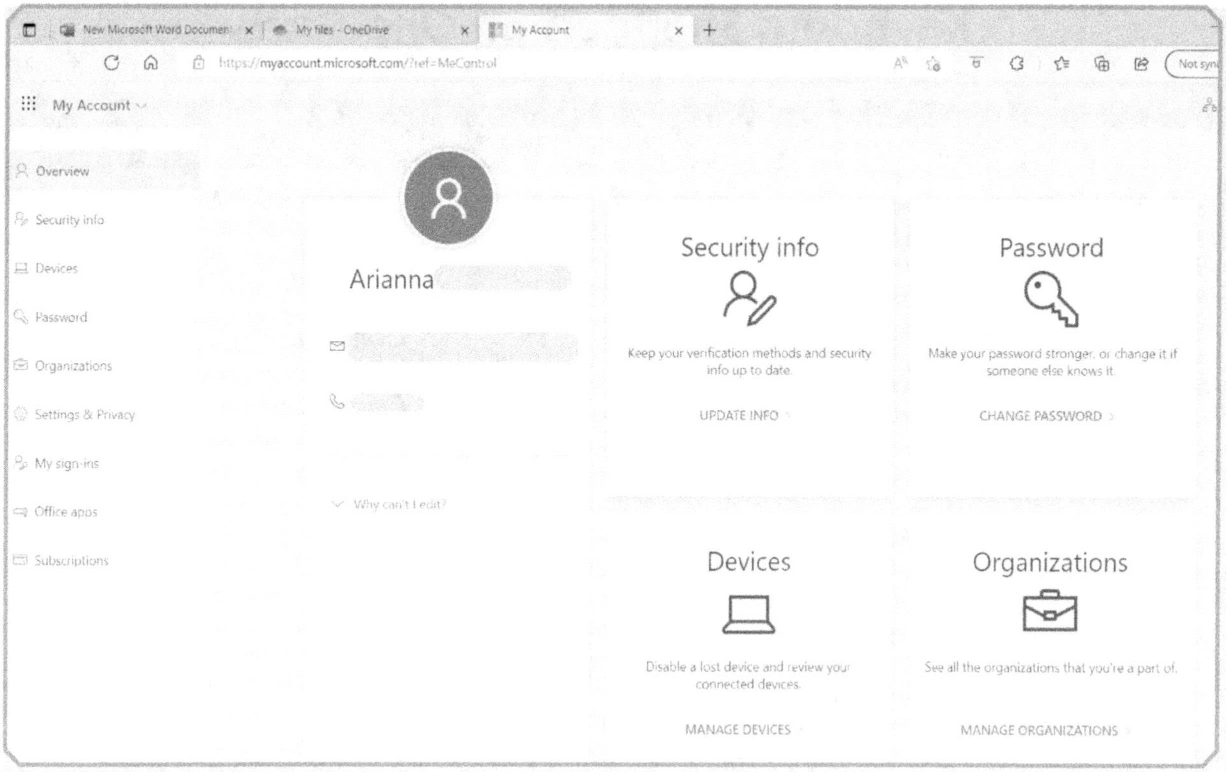

The account section allows you to manage these **key areas**:

1. **Security and Privacy Management:**
    - Update your password settings
    - Control privacy preferences
    - Configure security features including two-factor authentication, security questions, and device trust settings
2. **Device and Product Administration:**
    - Review devices running Microsoft Suite
    - Check your Microsoft product inventory
    - Maintain payment information for future purchases
3. **Enhanced Features:**
    - Include family members in your Microsoft subscription
    - Access Outlook through any web browser
    - Connect with additional Microsoft services including Xbox Live, Microsoft 365 applications, and Skype communication tools

Keyboard Shortcuts on One Drive

Function	PC Shortcut	Mac Shortcut
Select all items	*Ctrl + A*	*Command + A*
Copy selected items	*Ctrl + C*	*Command + C*
Cut selected items	*Ctrl + X*	*Command + X*
Paste items	*Ctrl + V*	*Command + V*
Delete selected item	*Delete*	*Delete*
Rename selected item	*F2*	*Enter*
Refresh the page	*F5*	*Command + R*
Create a new folder	*Ctrl + Shift + N*	*Command + Shift + N*
Open selected item	*Enter*	*Command + O*
Select multiple items	*Ctrl + Click*	*Command + Click*
Select a range of items	*Shift + Click*	*Shift + Click*
Move up one level	*Backspace*	*Command + Up Arrow*
Search	*Ctrl + E*	*Command + E*
Toggle item preview pane	*Alt + P*	*Option + P*
Toggle details pane	*Alt + Shift + P*	*Option + Shift + P*
Open context menu	*Shift + F10*	*Control + Click*
Close OneDrive	*Alt + F4*	*Command + Q*
Open OneDrive settings	*Ctrl + ,*	*Command + ,*
Undo last action	*Ctrl + Z*	*Command + Z*
Redo last action	*Ctrl + Y*	*Command + Shift + Z*
Move selected items	*Ctrl + Shift + V*	*Command + Option + V*

9. Forms:

An Essential Online Survey Tool

When browsing through OneDrive to create a new file, you might have spotted an unexplored program: **Microsoft Forms**. This application deserves attention as it represents a crucial component of the Microsoft suite.

Microsoft Forms functions as the company's dedicated platform for developing **online surveys** and **quizzes**. This adaptable tool enables users to design custom questionnaires and share them with their audience, making it perfectly suited for conducting research or collecting feedback. A significant benefit is the automatic storage of all responses in your **OneDrive**, providing convenient access to your data whenever needed.

A distinctive characteristic of **Microsoft Forms** is its **real-time capabilities**. The platform immediately updates as participants submit their responses, delivering instant access to current data. For those who prefer more control over their surveys or quizzes, the system also provides the option to establish specific **start** and **end dates**.

This smooth integration with **OneDrive** establishes **Microsoft Forms** as an effective solution for developing, distributing, and examining various types of questionnaires.

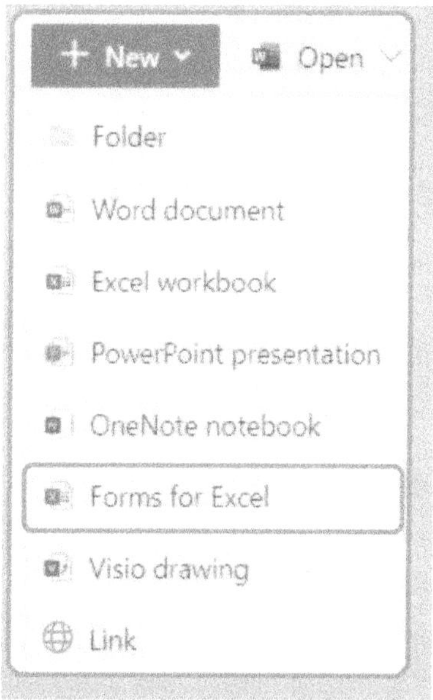

Creating a Form

Here's how to create a basic form and add questions in Microsoft Forms:

Initial Form Setup:

1. **Starting your Form:**
   - Navigate to OneDrive and click the **"+ New" button**
   - Choose **"Forms"** from the **dropdown options**
   - This launches the Forms start page in a new window
2. **Basic Form Configuration:**
   - Enter your form's title at the top
   - You can include a description below (optional) to provide context or instructions
   - Both elements are editable by clicking directly on them

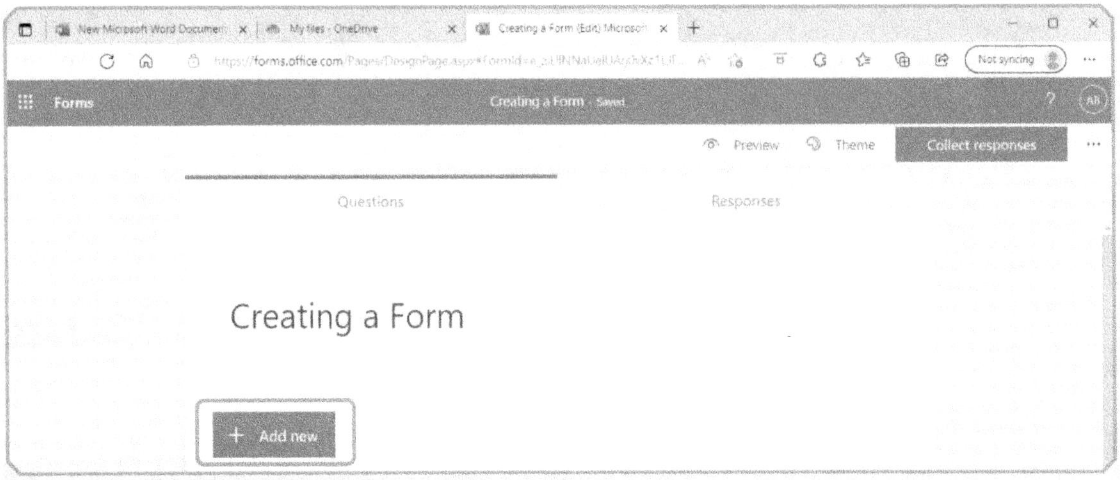

Creating Questions:

1. **Adding New Questions:**

    - Locate and click the **"Add new"** button
    - Select from these question types:
    - Choice questions (multiple choice or checkboxes)
    - Text responses (short or long format)
    - Rating scales (stars or numbers)
    - Date selections (using a calendar)

2. **Working with Choice Questions:**

    - Type your question text
    - Fill in the possible answer choices
    - Use **"+ Add option"** for more choices
    - Enable the **"Other"** option if you want to allow custom answers

3. **Question Options:**

    - Check **"Multiple answers"** to let people select several options
    - Toggle **"Required"** to make the question mandatory

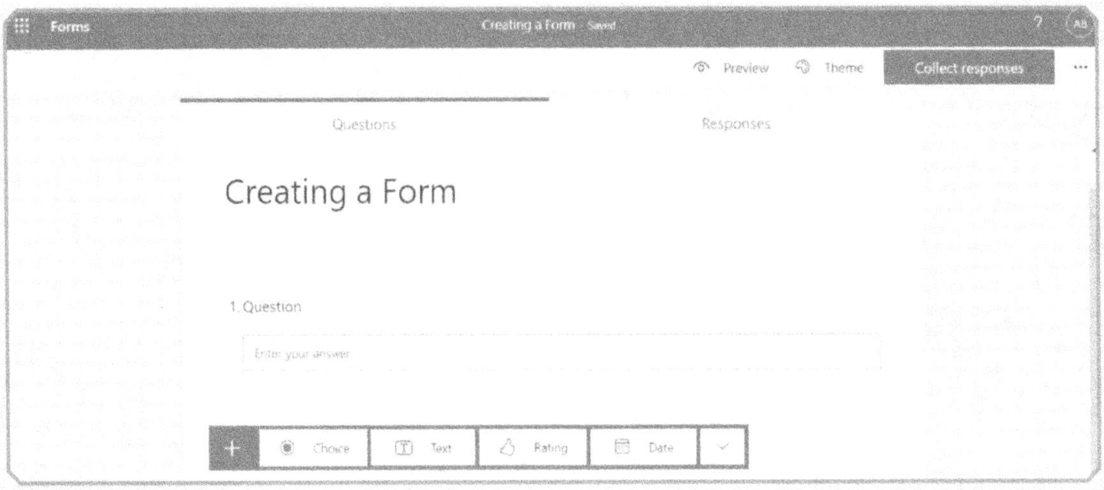

Advanced Features and Finalization Steps

1. **Branching Logic Implementation**
    - Access "Add branching" to create conditional pathways
    - Set up question sequences that adapt based on respondents' previous answers

2. **Question Management**
    - Rearrange questions using up/down arrows or drag-and-drop functionality
    - Access additional options (duplicate, delete, etc.) through the ellipsis (...) menu

3. **Section Organization**
    - Insert section breaks to create logical question groups
    - Improve navigation in longer forms by breaking content into manageable segments

Finalizing Your Form and Distribution Options

1. **Testing Your Form**
    - Use the Preview function to experience the form as respondents will
    - Run through all questions and branching logic to verify functionality

2. **Visual Customization**
    - Access Theme settings to modify your form's appearance
    - Select from available color schemes or personalize with a custom background image

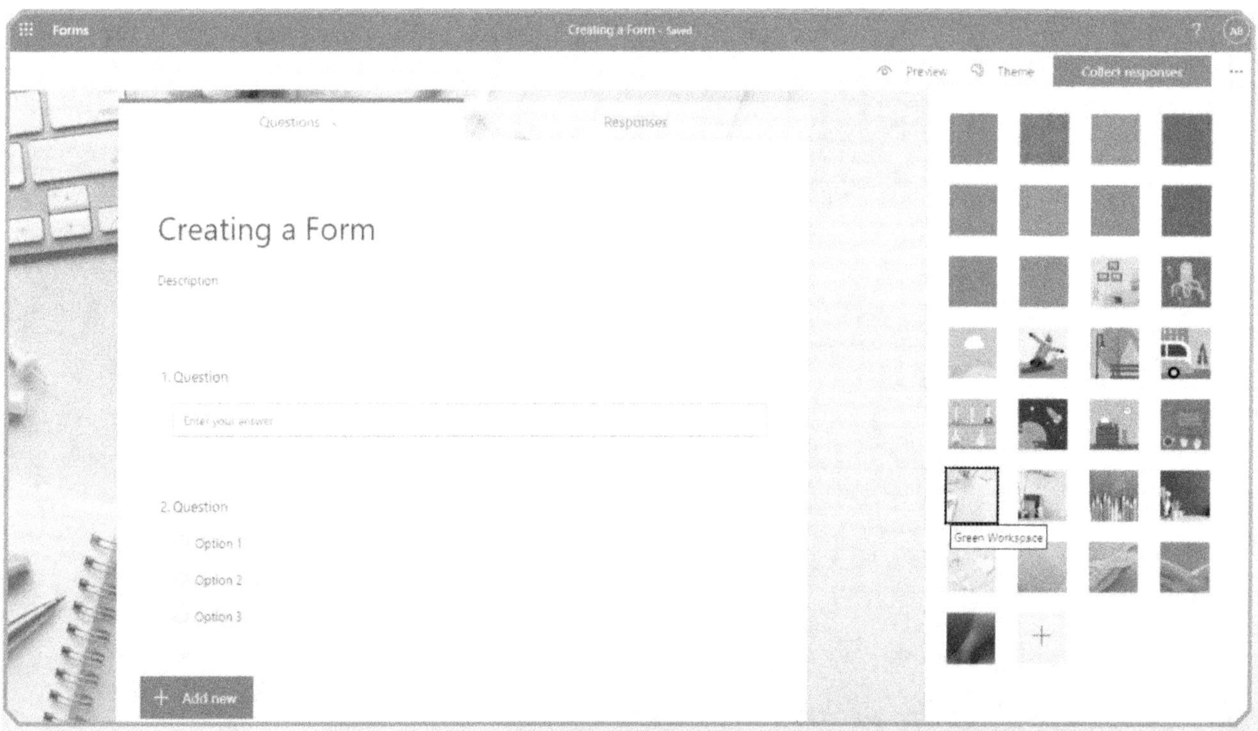

3. **Distribution Options**

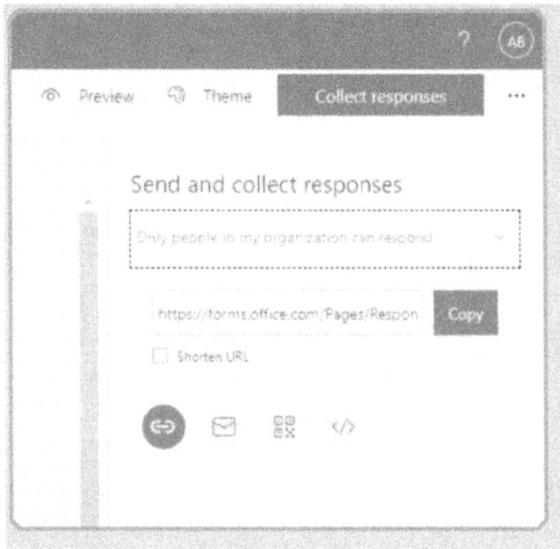

- Utilize the Send button to access sharing methods:
- Generate a direct link
- Create a QR code
- Get embed code for websites
- Send via email

4. **Managing Responses**

- Monitor submissions through the Responses tab
- View automated graphical summaries of response data
- Export data to Excel for in-depth analysis

Pro Tips:

- ***Keyboard Shortcuts:*** *Use shortcuts like Ctrl+D to duplicate questions and Ctrl+Z to undo changes, significantly speeding up form creation*
- ***Dynamic Scoring****: For quizzes, implement automatic scoring with custom point values for each question, and set passing thresholds for instant feedback*
- ***Scheduled Release****: Schedule your form's availability by setting specific start and end dates, perfect for timed assessments or limited-time surveys*
- ***Theme Consistency****: Save your custom themes with specific colors and backgrounds to maintain brand identity across multiple forms*
- ***Response Export****: Set up automatic export of responses to Excel at regular intervals to maintain up-to-date backups of your data*

Remember*: Your form settings and responses are automatically synced across devices, allowing seamless access and management anywhere.*

10. OneNote:

The Digital Notebook That Adapts to Your Thinking

OneNote represents Microsoft's comprehensive note-taking solution within their Suite, offering seamless integration with Outlook. This versatile platform enables users to compile various types of information into organized notebooks, from cooking recipes to professional and academic materials. A standout capability of OneNote is its drawing functionality, which effectively turns your device into a digital canvas for sketching and design work. Let's explore the fundamental aspects of notebook creation and organization:

Starting Your Digital Journey

Upon launching OneNote, you'll encounter options to either create a new notebook or access an existing one. For new users starting fresh, the first step involves naming your notebook. After naming, you'll see a clean page with a hidden ribbon interface. To enhance navigation, select the home tab, expand the ribbon, and secure it at the top by clicking the thumbnail located on the task pane's far right edge.

Familiar Interface Design

The interface mirrors other Microsoft Suite applications, providing a comfortable user experience. You'll find standard tools including font customization, copy-paste functionality, and list creation options. The review section includes helpful features like translation and spelling verification.

Section and Page Organization

Your new notebook displays a colored tab representing your first section. To personalize this section, simply double-click its name and enter an appropriate title. For example, if you're creating a culinary notebook, you might name the section "recipes."

The top line of each page serves as your title space. Using our previous example, this could be your recipe name. To expand your section, use the "add page" button located in the right pane to create additional pages as needed.

Productivity Tip*: Don't stress about page naming - OneNote automatically generates names based on your page title entries.*

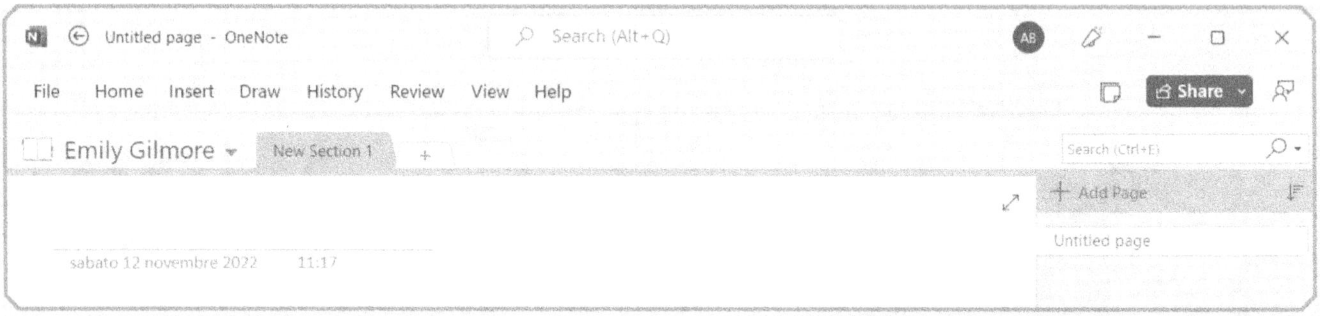

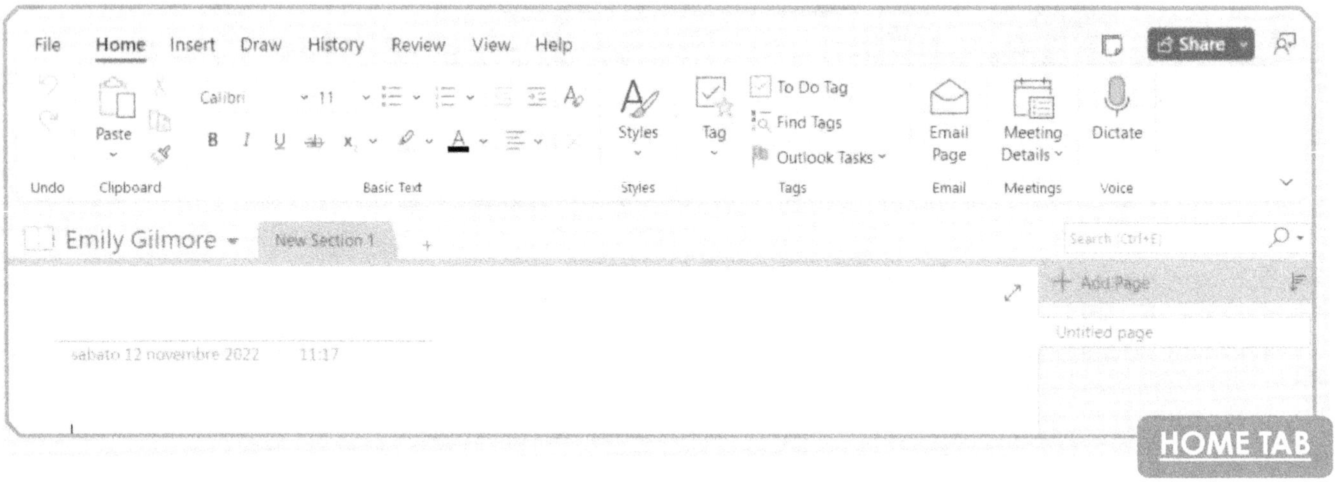

Expanding Your OneNote Organization

Let's explore how to enhance your notebook structure beyond basic sections by creating a robust **organizational system**:

1. **Adding New Sections:**
   - Locate the **+ symbol** adjacent to the first **colored tab**
   - Click to generate a **new section** with a default color scheme
   - Quick Tip: You can create **unlimited sections** to match your organizational needs

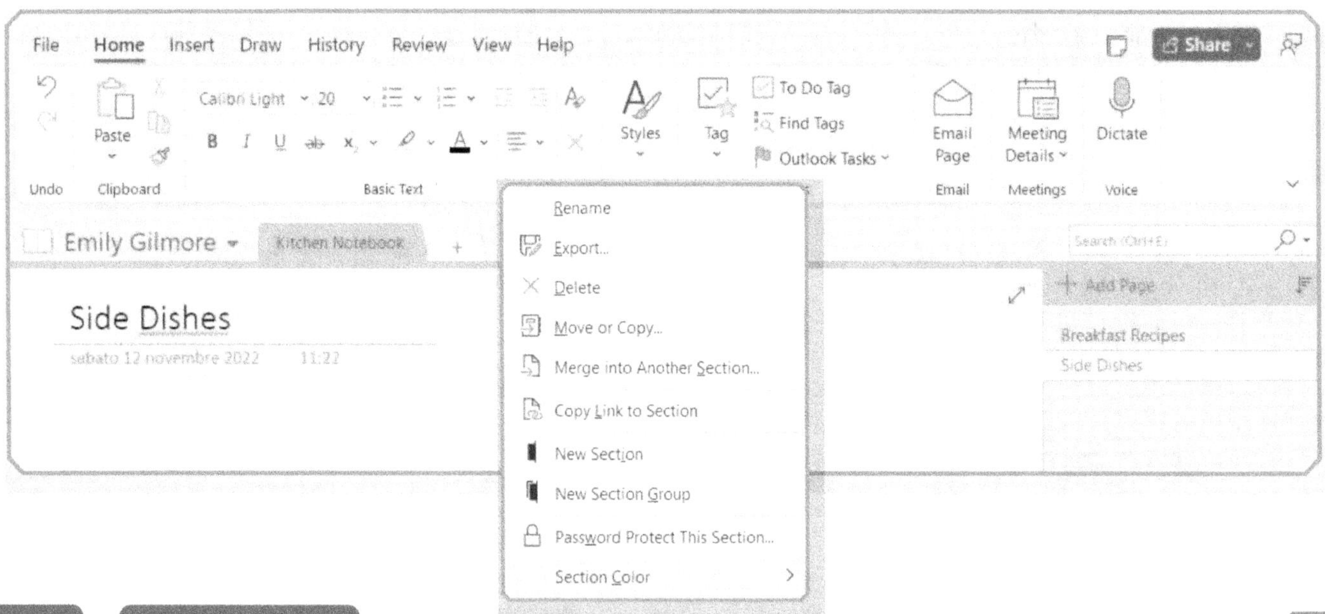

2. **Section Color Management:**

   - Right-click the tab to access customization options
   - Select from various color options to create visual organization
   - Use colors strategically to group related content visually

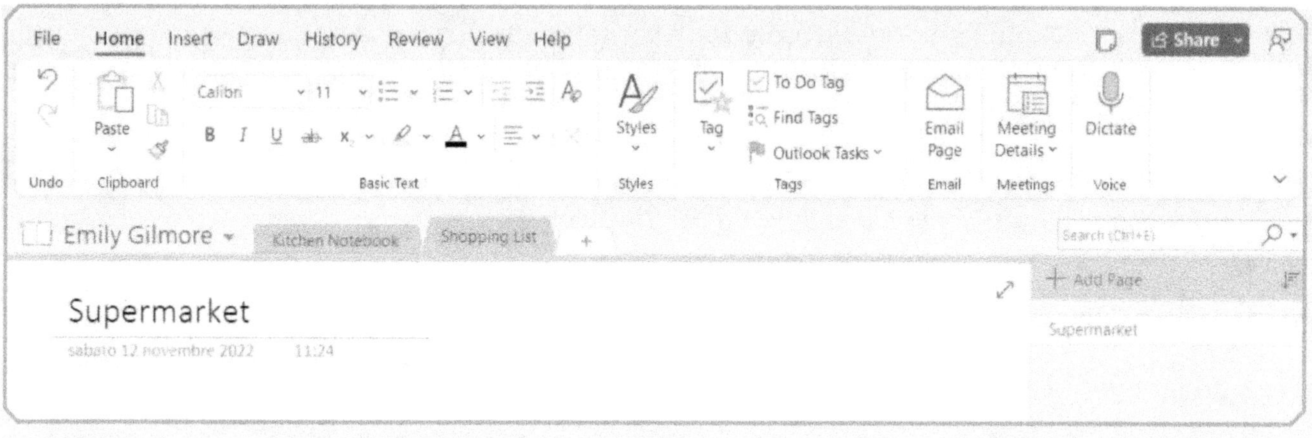

3. **Advanced Section Controls** - When right-clicking a section tab, you can:

   - Remove unwanted sections
   - **Export** section content
   - Generate **section groups** for better organization
   - **Move sections** between notebooks

4. **Understanding Section Groups** - For comprehensive organization, like managing home-related information:

   - Right-click and select "**Create new section group**"
   - A new **organizational level** appears above your workspace
   - Customize the **group name** through right-click options

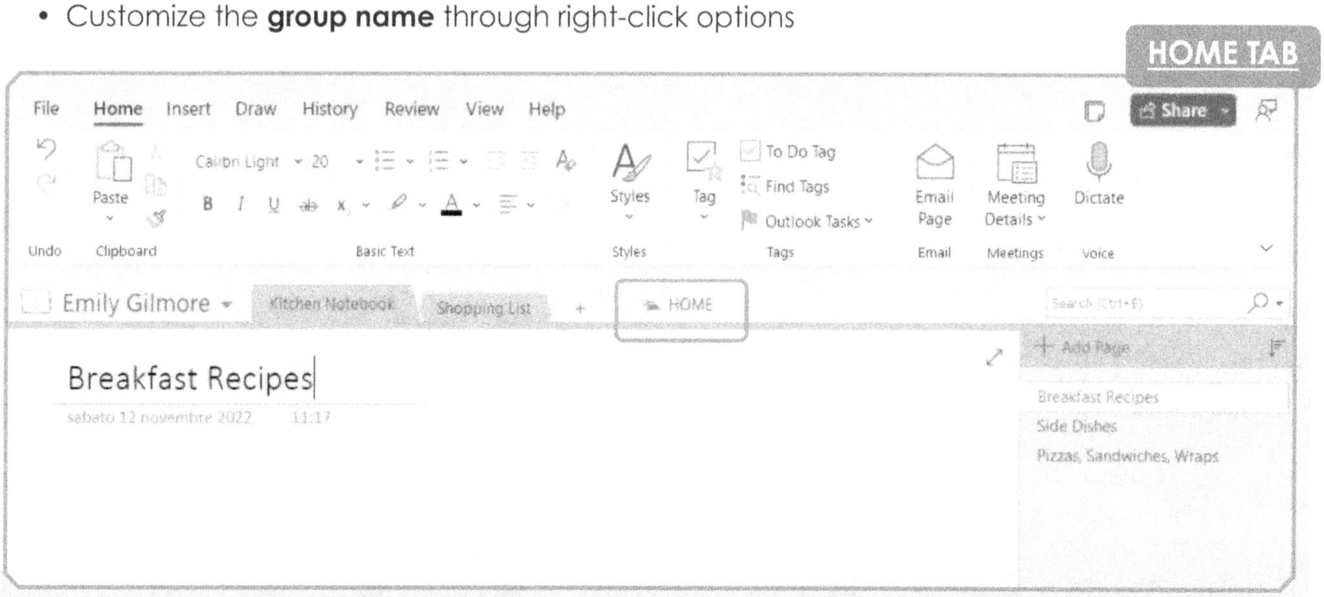

*Productivity Tip: Think of section groups as **digital filing cabinets** for related content*

5. **Hierarchical Organization:**

   - Create themed **groups** (like "Home Management")
   - Arrange relevant sections within each group
   - Example Structure:

     - **Kitchen Group**: Recipes, Inventories, Maintenance
     - **Documents Group**: Warranties, Manuals, Contracts
     - **Projects Group**: Renovations, To-Do Lists, Budget

Productivity Tip: *This **structured approach** becomes increasingly valuable as your notebook content grows, making **navigation** and **information retrieval** more efficient.*

Enhancing OneNote Content with Templates and Media

Let's discover how to enrich your notes using OneNote's diverse formatting options:

1. **Pre-Built Templates:**

   - Access the **insert tab** in the ribbon
   - Select **page templates** from the pages section
   - Browse through template categories including:

     - **To-do lists** for task management
     - **Lecture notes** for academic purposes
     - **Index cards** for study materials
     - Your page automatically transforms to match your chosen template

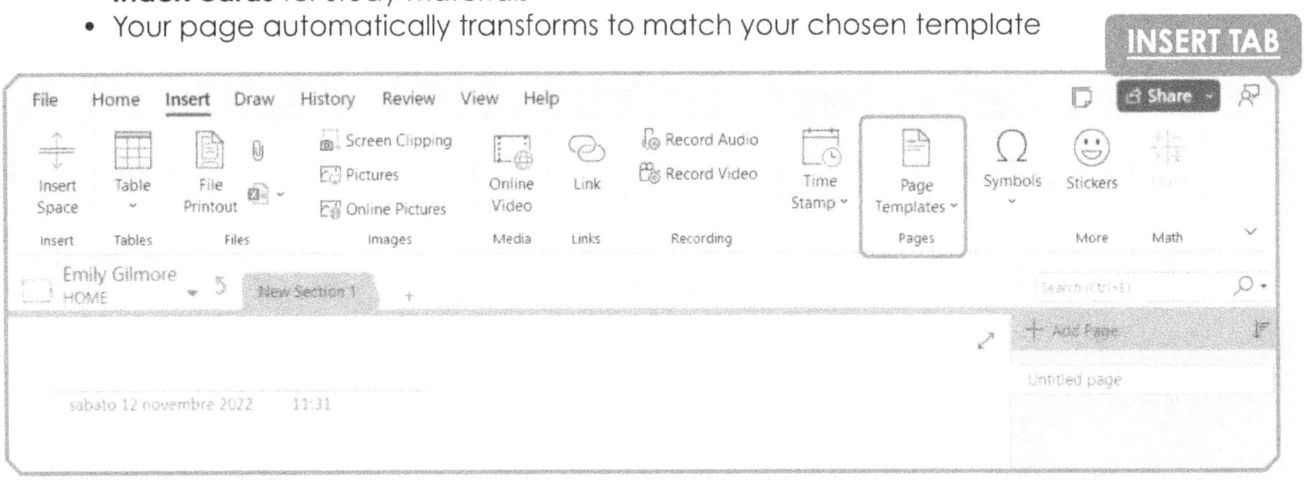

2. **Advanced Formatting Tools** - For personalized page layouts, OneNote provides various **multimedia elements**:

   - Insert **spreadsheets** for data manipulation (mini Excel functionality)
   - Add **images** for visual documentation
   - Embed **video content** for comprehensive learning materials
   - Create structured **tables** for organized information
   - Include **mathematical equations** for technical notes
   - Insert special **symbols** and **stickers** for enhanced visual appeal

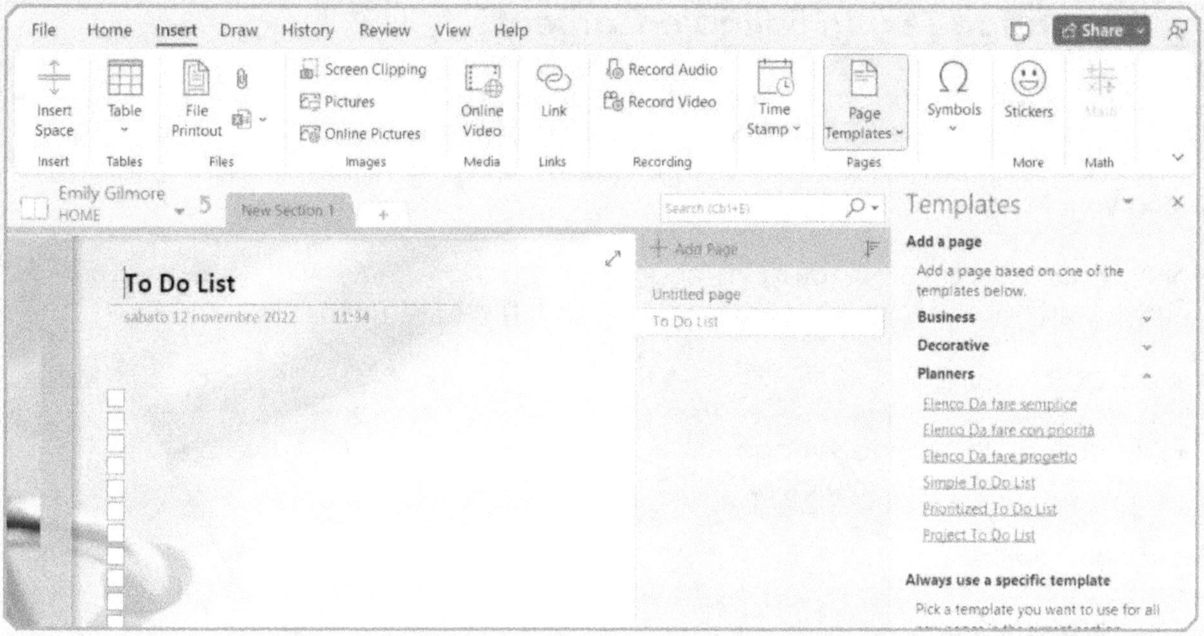

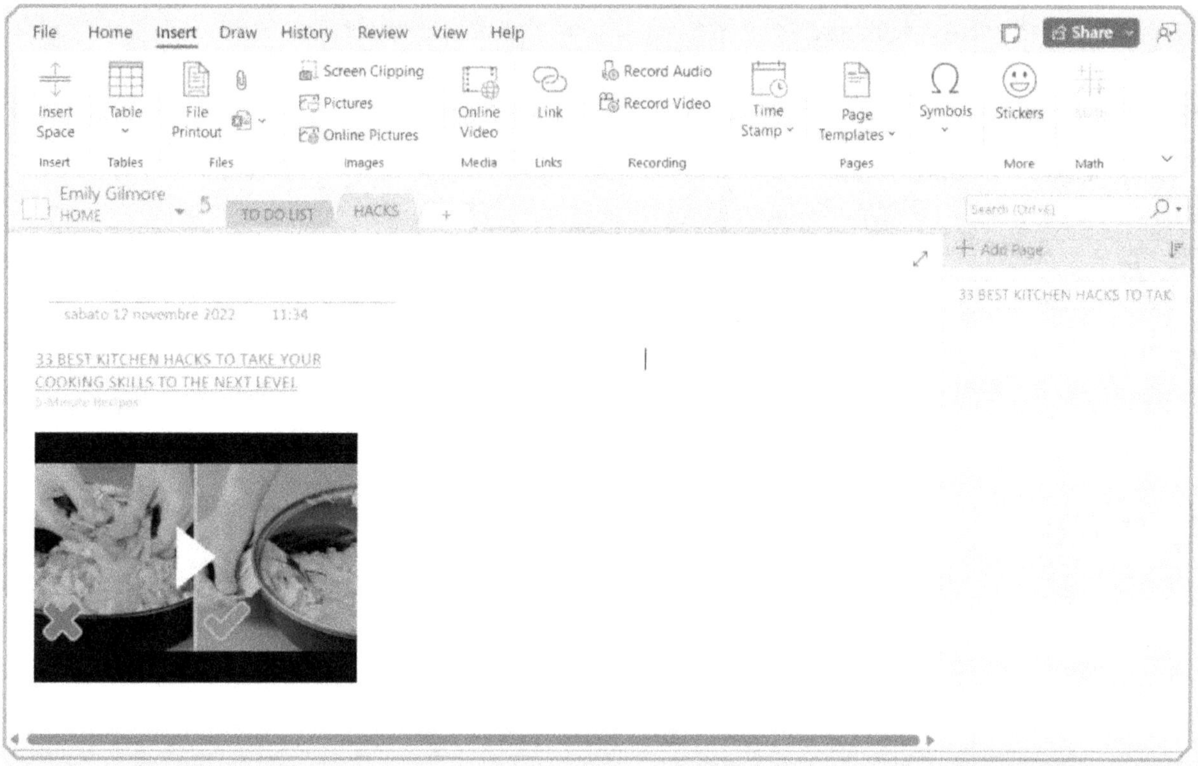

3. **Element Interaction -**

- **Interactive components:**
  - Spreadsheets remain fully functional
  - Tables can be modified and updated
  - Equations can be edited as needed

- **Static elements:**
  - Decorative stickers become fixed once placed
  - Embedded media maintains original formatting

***Productivity Tip:** Combine multiple elements on a single page to create rich, interactive documentation that suits your specific needs.*

Converting Image Text to Editable Content

OneNote's **OCR** (Optical Character Recognition) capability is a powerful yet often overlooked feature. Here's how to transform text within images into editable content:

1. **Import your image:**
   - Simply copy and paste or drag the image into OneNote
   - The image can be from any source (screenshot, photo, document scan)
2. **Access OCR feature:**
   - Right-click on the inserted image
   - Look for "**Copy text from picture**" option
3. **Extract and edit:**
   - Click anywhere on your page
   - Paste the extracted text (Ctrl+V)
   - The text is now fully editable

Productivity Tips:

- *Works best with clear, high-resolution images*
- *Can handle both printed and typed text*
- *Particularly useful for digitizing printed documents*
- *Great for converting screenshots into editable notes*

Remember: *Always review the extracted text for accuracy, as the OCR process isn't always perfect.*

Page Configuration Options

OneNote provides multiple ways to personalize your page settings. Let's examine these capabilities :

1. **Basic Page Modifications** (accessible through the view tab's page setup) :
   - Modify your page background with different color schemes
   - Include ruled lines with various style selections
   - Remove the page title from view
   - Enable dark mode through the background switch function
2. **Print Configuration** - You can modify the paper specifications to ensure optimal printing results. Access these options by selecting the paper size control, which reveals a side window containing:
   - Paper dimensions
   - Page positioning (choose between landscape or portrait)
   - Edge spacing adjustments

3. **Template Creation -** Within the advanced configuration menu at the bottom of paper size settings, users can:

    - Enable template preservation by selecting the appropriate checkbox
    - Assign a unique name to your template configuration
    - Select whether to implement these settings across all pages within the section

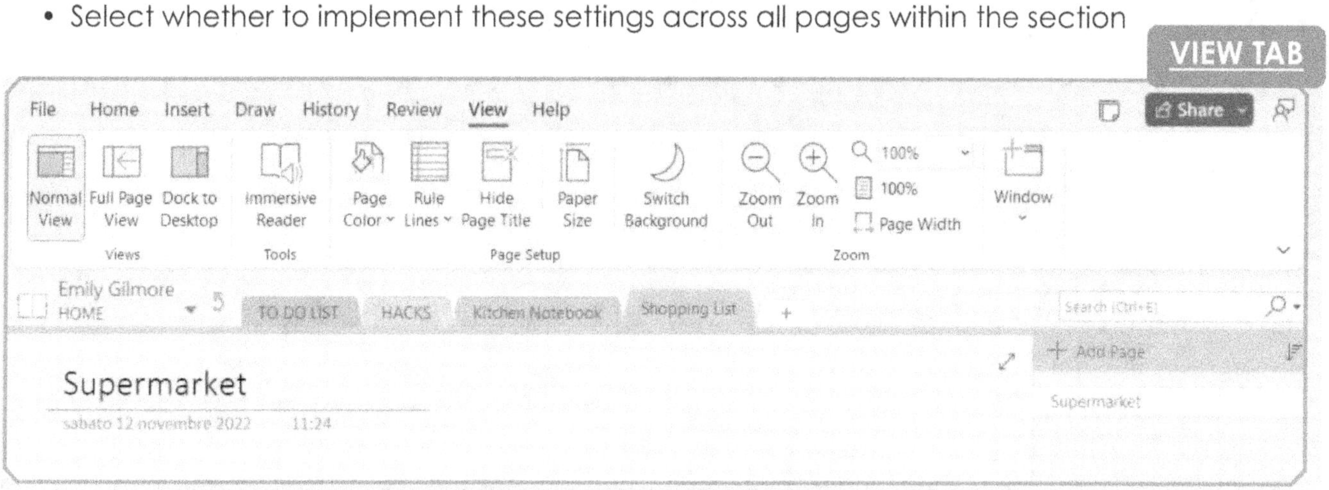

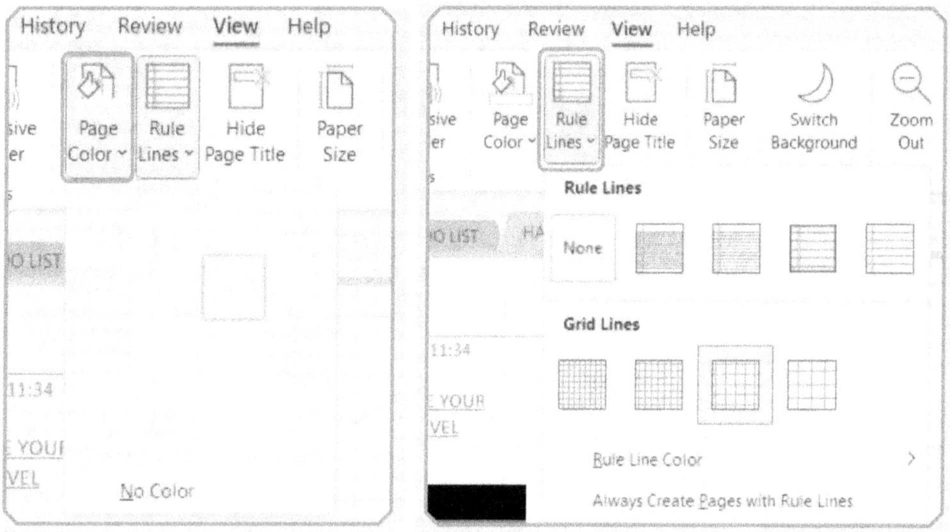

Detailed Instructions for Custom Page Formatting

1. Access the view tab in the ribbon interface
2. Find the page setup area
3. Select paper size options
4. Within the side panel, determine your preferences for:

    - Paper dimensions
    - Page orientation
    - Margin specifications

5. For template creation:

    - Enable the template option checkbox
    - Input your desired template name

6. Choose whether to extend these settings to all section pages
7. Complete the process by selecting either "Save" or "Apply" based on your selections

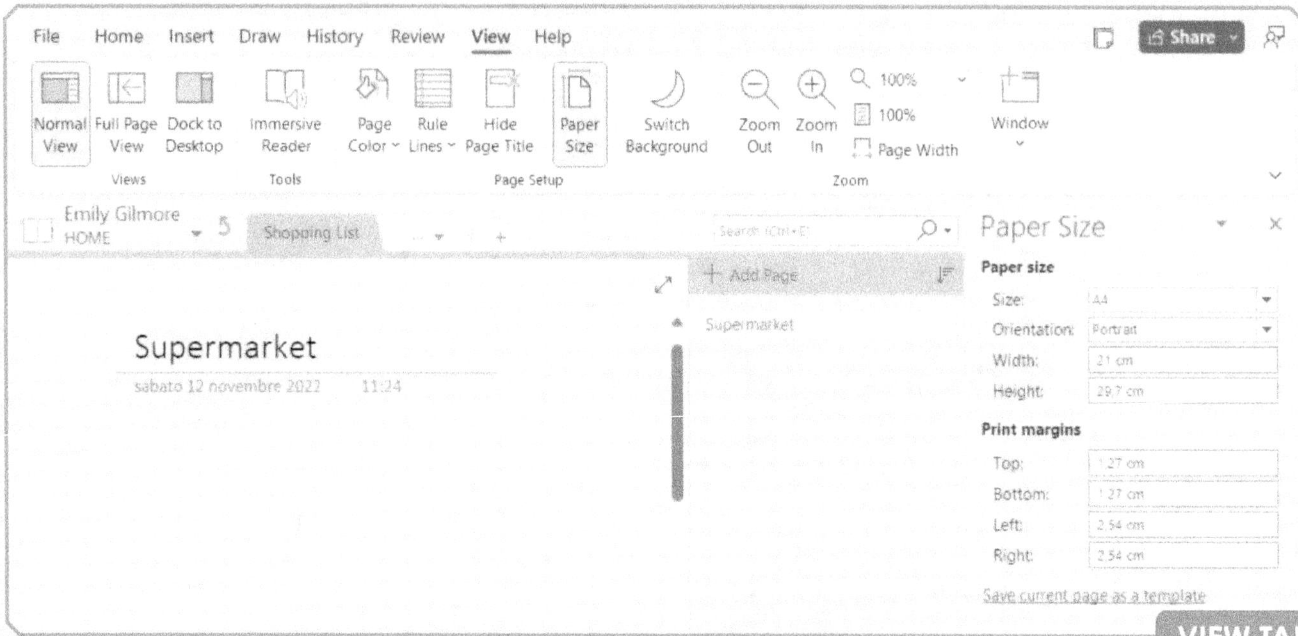

VIEW TAB

Note Creation and Formatting Features

The **note-taking process** begins after you've established your **page title**. While basic text is sufficient, **OneNote** enhances document organization through specialized **tags** located in the ribbon's **home tab**, complete with corresponding **keyboard shortcuts**. Available tags encompass **task checkboxes**, specialized **icons** for sensitive information (like passwords, contact details), and **text emphasis** tools.

Tags automatically position themselves at your cursor's location on the document. Thanks to OneNote's flexible **canvas design**, you can reposition these elements through simple **drag-and-drop** actions, allowing for intuitive organization based on your preferences.

HOME TAB

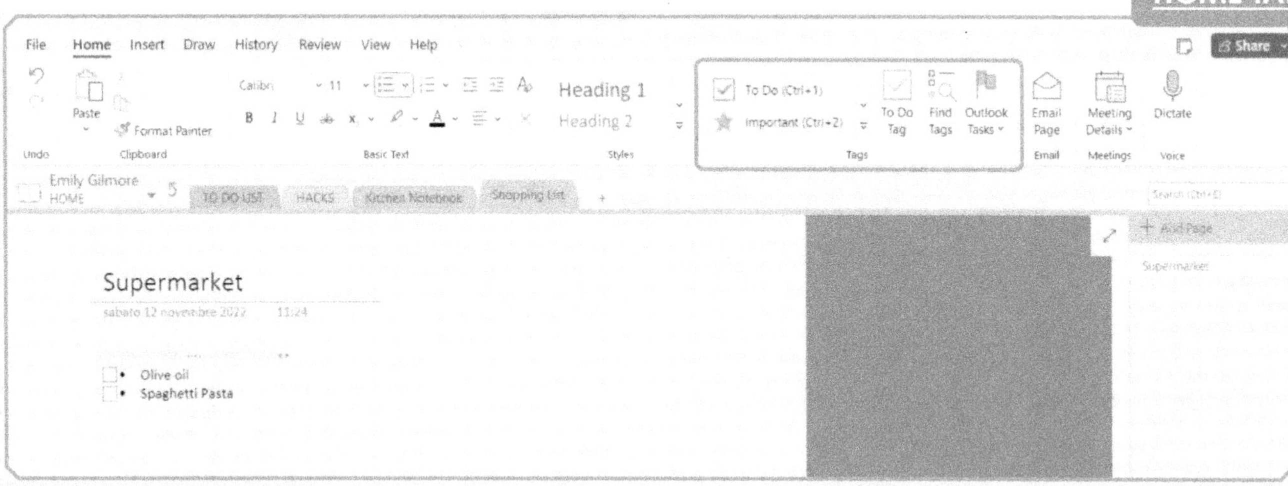

Tag Management and Customization

When you interact with a tag, a **boundary box** appears around it. The **ellipsis menu** at the top provides quick access to **formatting options** and modifications. The **adjustment arrow** enables resizing of the dialogue container. For **tag removal**, you have two methods available: either use the **delete key** while the tag is selected, or click the **X icon** found in the home tab's basic text area.

Customizing Tags

1. Navigate to the **home pane**
2. Select the **find tags** button
3. Click **customize tags** at the bottom of the pane

HOME TAB

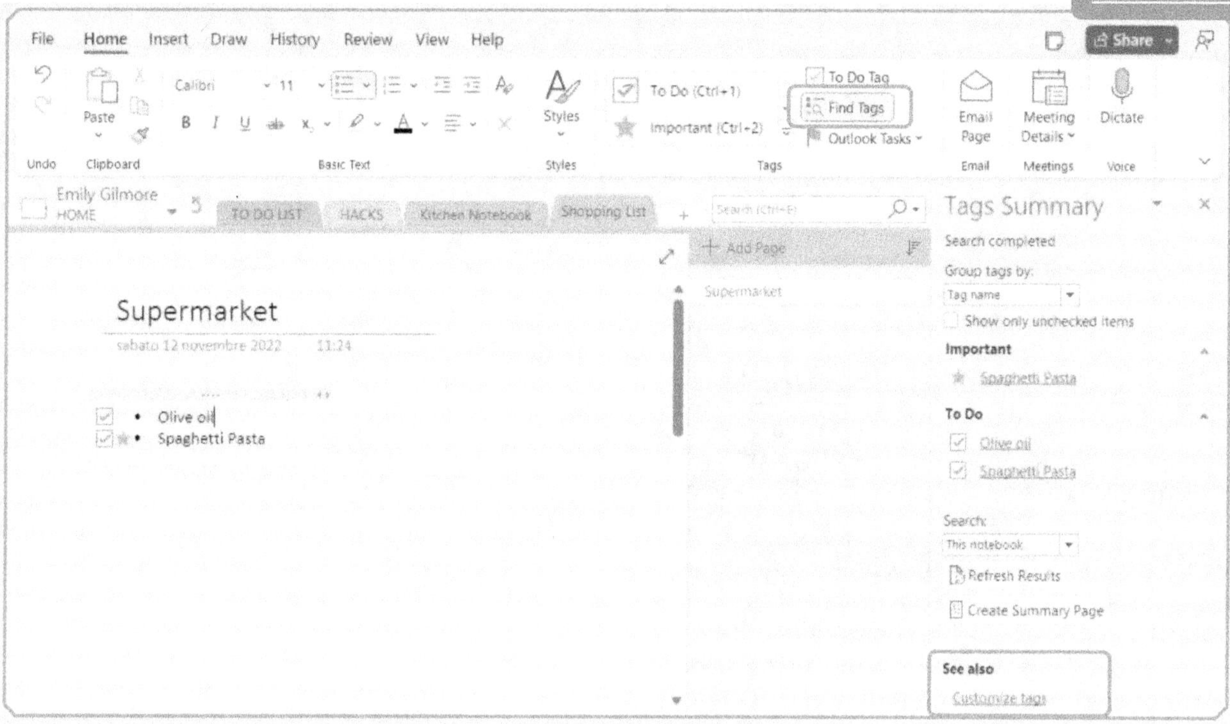

Configuration Options -When the **dialogue box** appears, you can:

- Create a **new tag** from scratch
- Modify an **existing tag** configuration

New Tag Creation Process:

1. Click the **"New Tag"** button
2. Configure these essential elements:
    - Assign a **name**
    - Select a **symbol** from the available collection
    - Choose your preferred **font color**
    - Enable or disable **highlight** feature

A **preview window** displays your tag's appearance in real-time. Finalize creation by clicking the **ok** button.

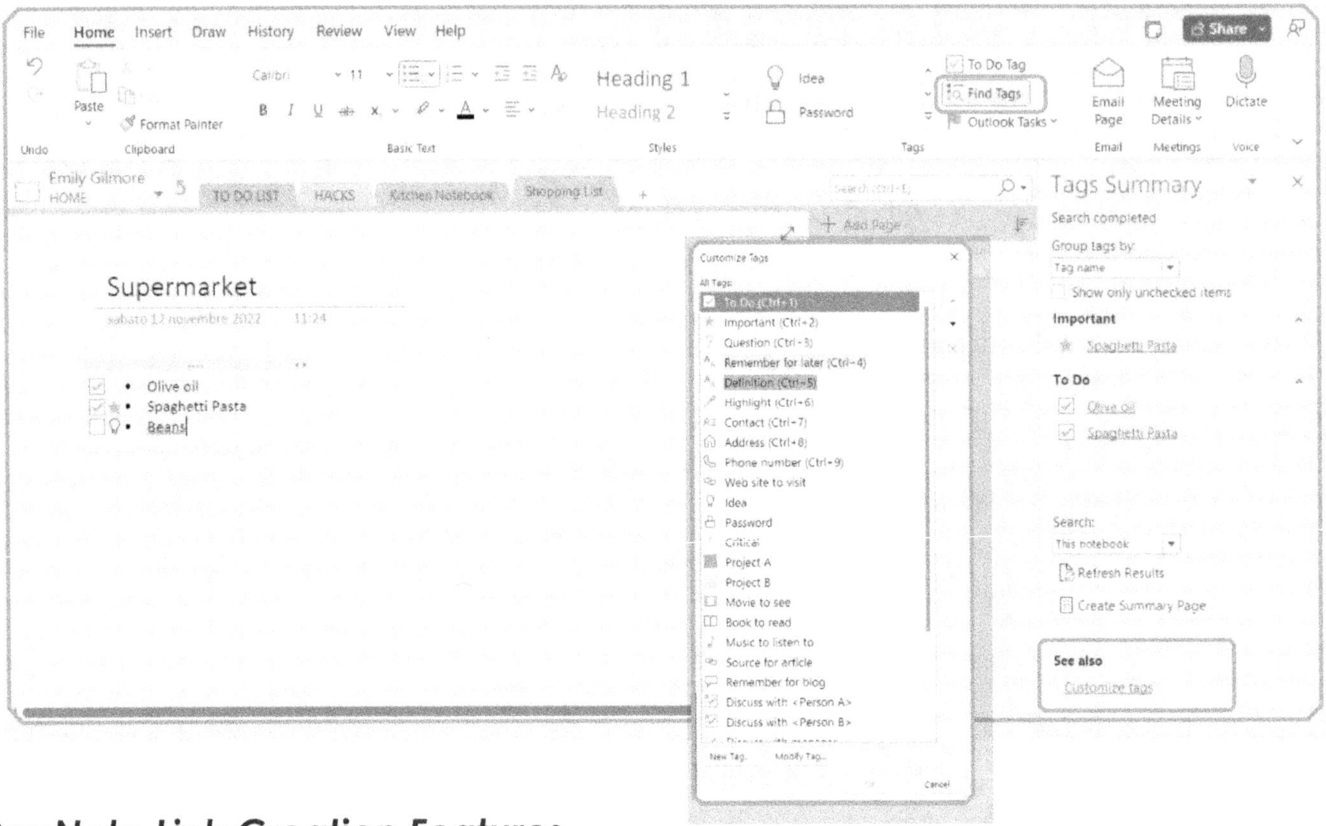

OneNote Link Creation Features

Basic Link Creation: OneNote's **linking capability** stands out as a key feature. The process begins throu-gh the **right-click menu**, which provides access to the **create links** function.

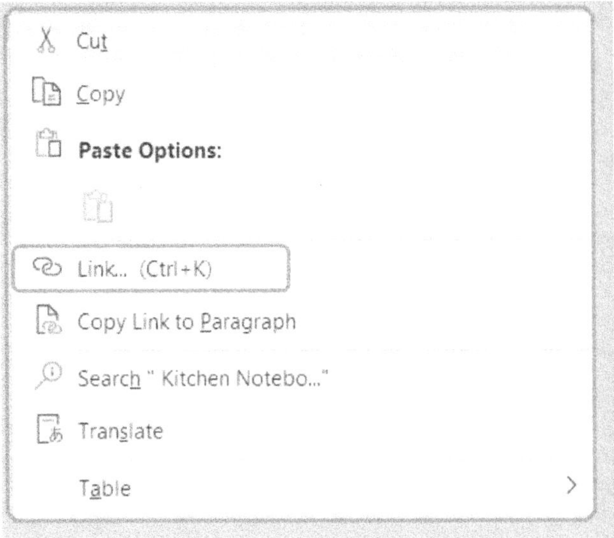

Step-by-Step Link Creation Process:

1. Select your desired **link location** on the canvas
2. Activate the **right-click menu** and select **link**
3. Enter your preferred **display text** in the dialogue win-dow

Available Link Types:

1. **External Links:**

   - Link to **local documents** from your device
   - Insert **web URLs**

2. **Internal OneNote Links:**
3. Navigate through your **notebooks** and **sections**
4. Choose the target **page** or **section**
5. Confirm by clicking **ok**

Productivity Tip: *Utilize* **drag-and-drop** *functionality to adjust your link's position as needed on the page*

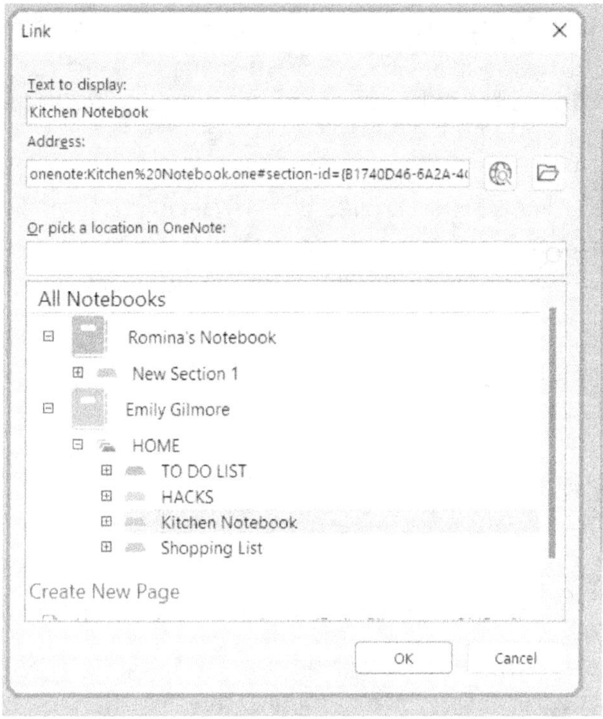

Digital Drawing and Sketching

OneNote provides comprehensive **drawing capabilities** through the **draw tab**, making it particularly valuable for **tablet users** who want to create digital notes with the feel of pen and paper. The interface offers various **pen tools** that enable direct canvas interaction - ideal for **stylus input** when precise control is needed. Users can explore different **pen styles**, from ballpoint pens that provide a smooth writing experience to felt tip options that create bold, expressive strokes.

When it comes to creating shapes, OneNote offers flexibility through both **pre-made shapes** and **freehand drawing** capabilities. Users can either select standard shapes from the dedicated shapes section and place them with a simple click-and-drag motion, or draw shapes manually using freehand tools when more organic forms are desired.

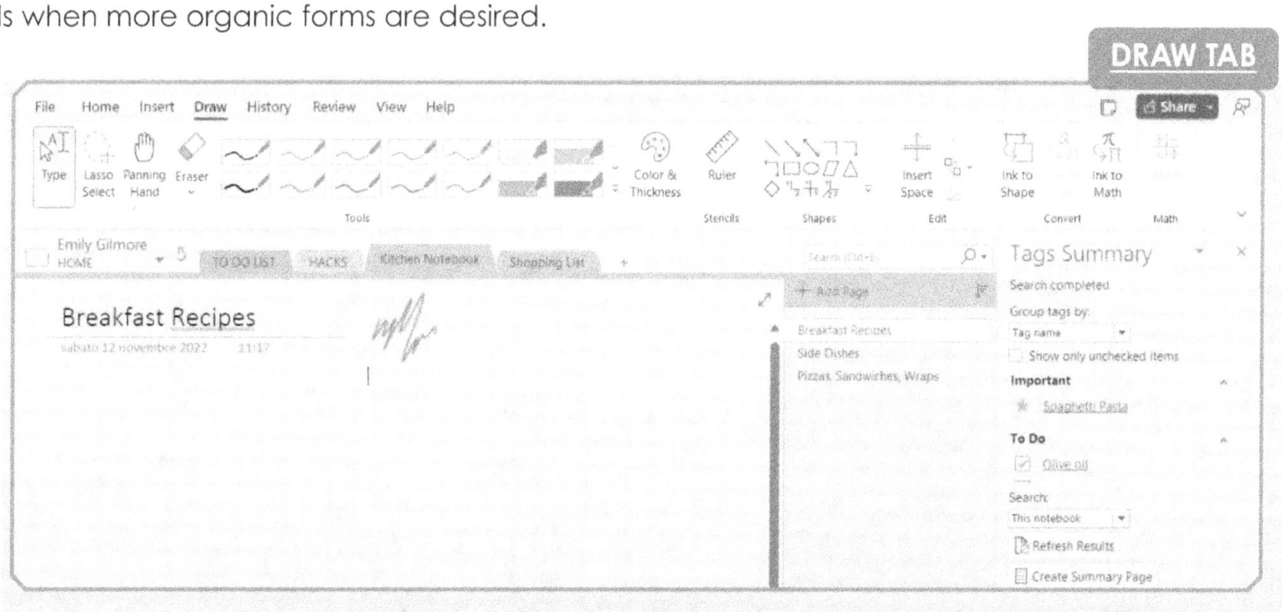

The **drawing tools** feature extensive personalization options that let you create exactly the look you want. You can fine-tune the **line thickness** for different emphasis levels, choose from a spectrum of **color selections** for visual organization, and add **highlighting effects** to emphasize key points. Creating **custom color palettes** helps maintain consistent styling across all your notes and documents.

For correcting mistakes, the **eraser tool** provides precise editing capabilities that rival physical erasers. With its **adjustable size** settings, you can handle both broad corrections and detailed touch-ups. The click-and-drag functionality makes erasing as intuitive as using a real eraser, while enabling more **detailed correction** than would be possible on paper.

OneNote's sophisticated **conversion tools** transform your handwritten content into digital formats:

1. **"Ink to Shape"** converts rough sketches into crisp, professional geometric forms - perfect for creating clean diagrams and flowcharts in presentations or technical documents.

2. **"Ink to Text"** transforms your handwriting into clear, typed text, making it ideal for digitizing meeting notes or brainstorming sessions while maintaining the spontaneity of handwriting.

3. **"Ink to Math"** specializes in converting handwritten mathematical equations into properly formatted digital expressions, essential for students and professionals working with mathematical content.

The **conversion process** is straightforward: begin by creating your content using your preferred drawing tools, then select the appropriate conversion option from the Draw tab.

Recording Features

The ability to create **audio and video recordings** directly within OneNote enhances its versatility as a note-taking platform. Here's how the recording system works:

Basic Recording Access

1. Navigate to the **Insert tab** in the ribbon
2. Locate the **Recording option**
3. Select either **audio** or **video** recording mode

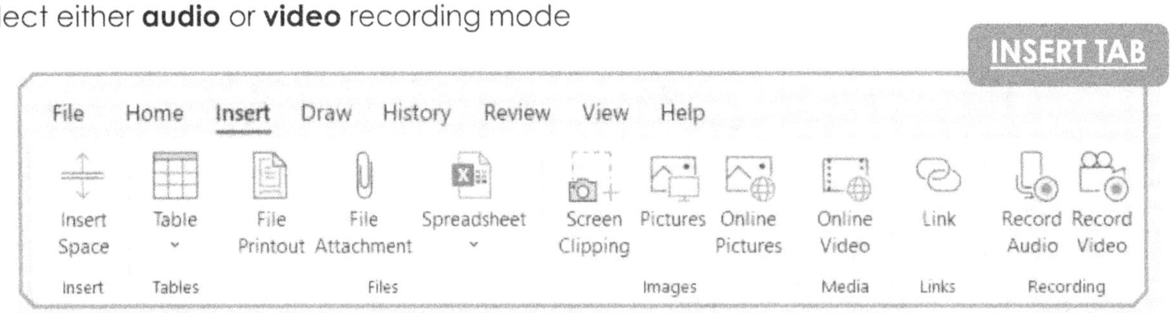

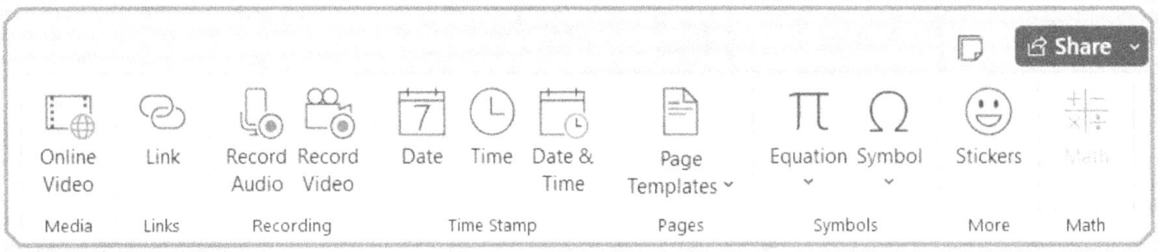

Recording Process Features

When initiating an **audio recording**, OneNote displays a unique behavior - a **thumbnail** labeled "Audio Recording" appears immediately on your canvas. This thumbnail indicates that recording has begun, though it's not yet complete. The **recording continues** until you manually activate the pause or stop control in the ribbon. This differs from most applications where icons typically appear after completion.

Playback Management

After creating your **media file**, OneNote introduces a dedicated **Playback tab** above the status bar. This specialized taskbar offers :

- Media playback controls
- Forward/rewind capabilities
- Volume adjustment options
- Advanced settings access

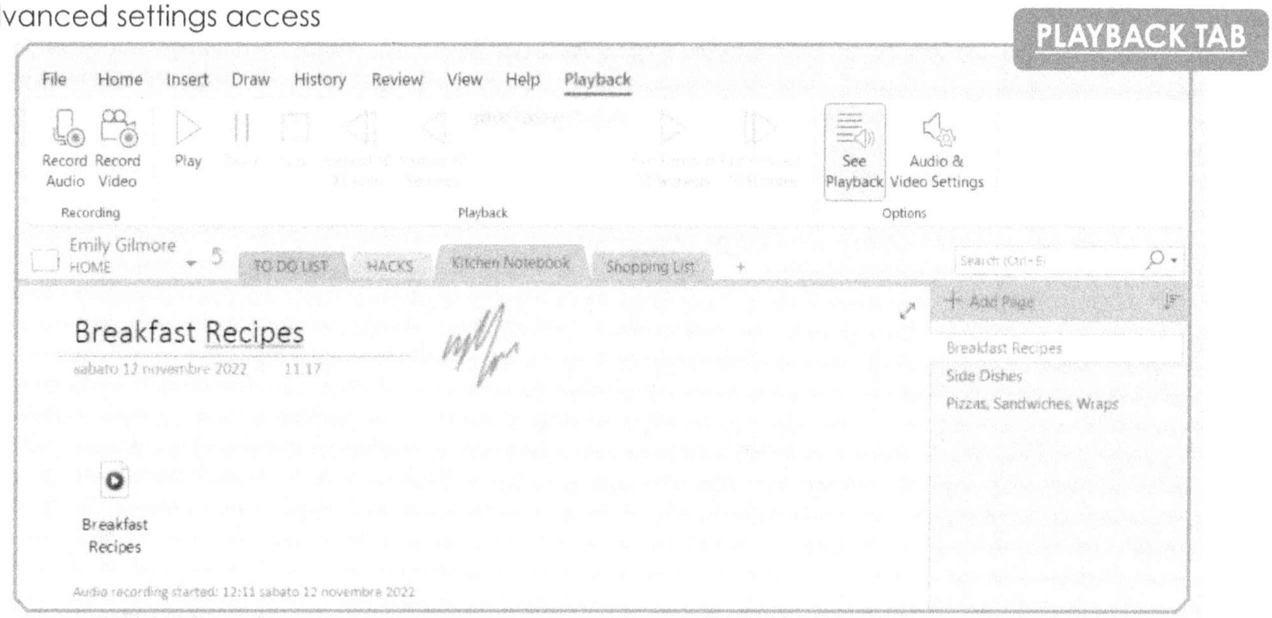

Settings Configuration

The **settings menu** mirrors the options available in the main File tab's Options menu, but provides direct access to your device's **audio and video settings**. For optimal recording quality, verify that your **microphone** and **camera** are properly enabled and configured.

Productivity Tip: *To quickly* ***save time while recording****, use the keyboard shortcut* ***Windows + Alt + R*** *to start and stop audio recording without navigating through the ribbon menus. This enables seamless recording during meetings or lectures when you need to focus on taking notes simultaneously.*

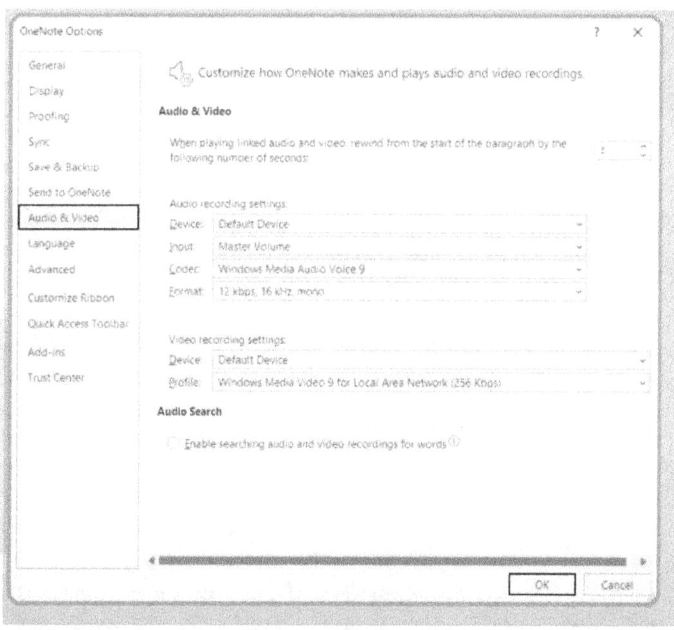

OneNote Integration with Microsoft Suite

OneNote can communicate with other programs in the Microsoft Suite, particularly Outlook, which is the last thing you need to know about it.

Core Integration Features

Task Synchronization with Outlook

1. Access via the **Outlook Tasks** button in Tags section
2. Set completion deadlines (with available keyboard shortcuts)
3. Create task descriptions directly on canvas
4. Tasks automatically appear in Outlook with OneNote page links

Bi-directional sync: Create tasks in Outlook using OneNote button for seamless integration

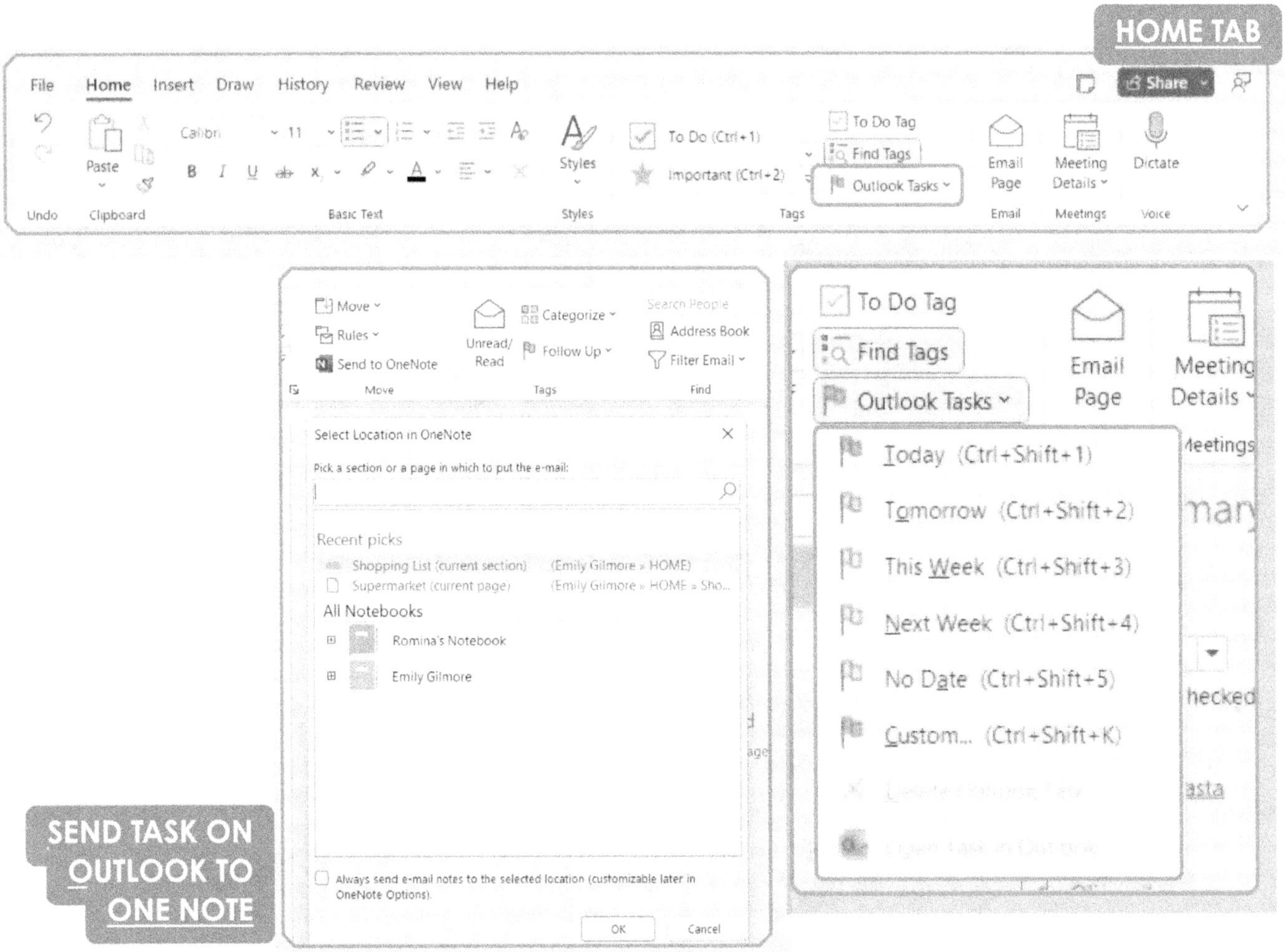

Email Sharing Capabilities

1. Share specific pages without exposing entire notebook
2. Access through **Email Page** button in Home tab
3. Pages automatically format into email body
4. Full access to standard Outlook email features

Security Features

1. Enable **password protection** via Review tab
2. Access yellow Password padlock
3. Configure protection settings in dedicated pane
4. Note: Protected sections require unlocking for search functionality

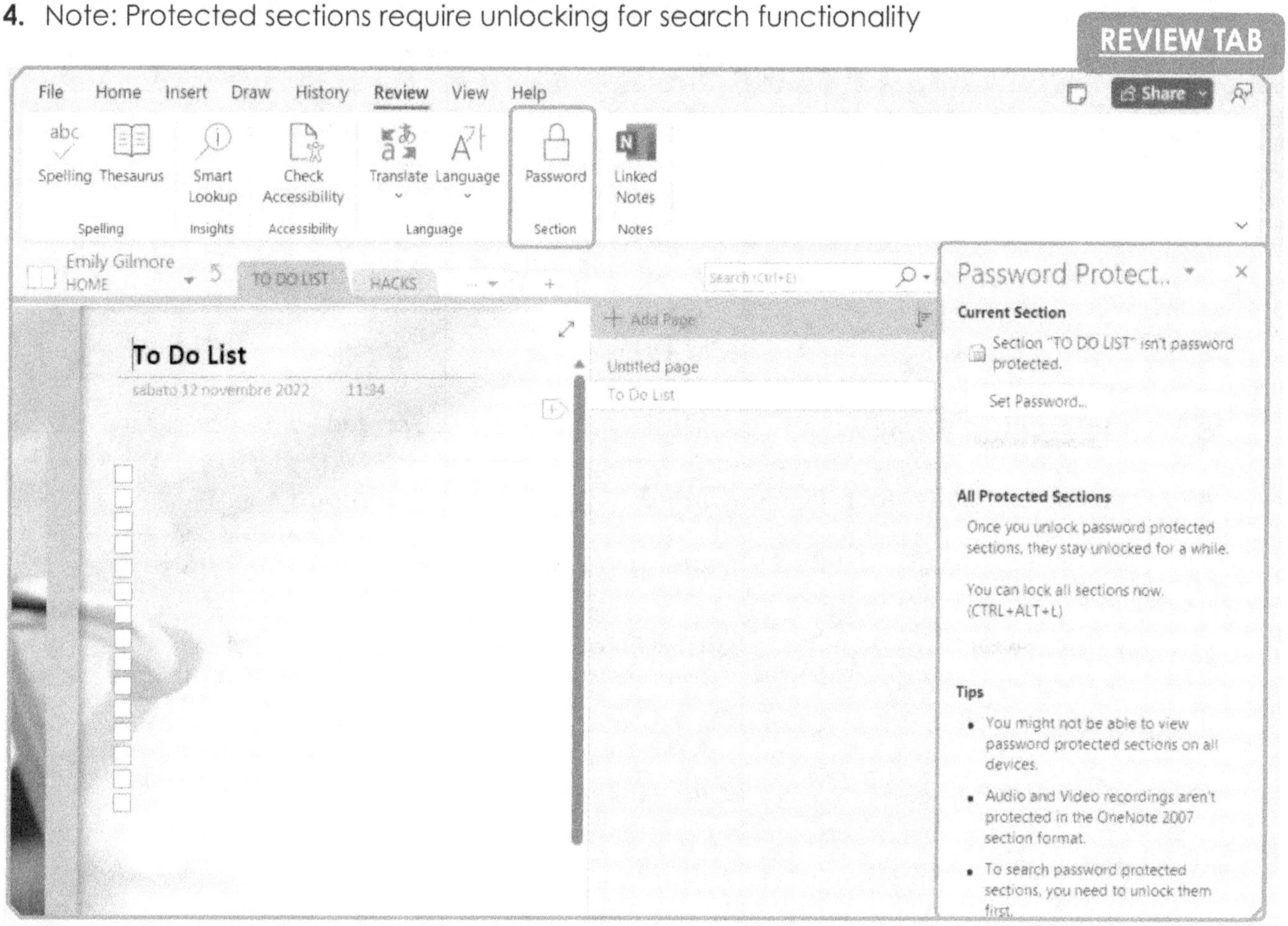

Meeting Integration

1. Automatic sync with **Outlook calendar**
2. Access via **Meeting Details** in Home tab
3. View current or future meetings
4. Create dedicated note pages for each meeting
5. Easily distribute notes to all meeting participants

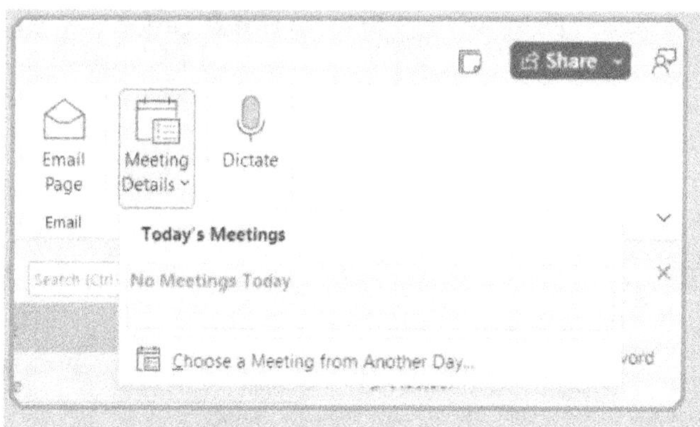

The **Meeting Details** feature streamlines meeting documentation by providing instant access to scheduled meetings and creating dedicated note-taking spaces. This integration enables efficient note distribution to all participants while maintaining organization within OneNote's structure.

Productivity Tip: *Save time during meetings by using the* ***"Share with Meeting"*** *button - it automatically shares your notes with all attendees as soon as the meeting ends, eliminating the need for manual distribution.*

Keyboard Shortcuts on OneNote

Function	Shortcut on PC	Shortcut on Mac
Create a link	*Ctrl + K*	*Command + K*
Search all notebooks	*Ctrl + E*	*Command + E*
Search the current page	*Ctrl + F*	*Command + F*
Type a math equation	*Alt + +*	*Not available*
Create a new page	*Ctrl + N*	*Command + N*
Align paragraph to the left	*Ctrl + L*	*Command + L*
Align paragraph to the right	*Ctrl + R*	*Command + R*
Show or hide line rules	*Ctrl + Shift + R*	*Command + Shift + R*
Insert a line break	*Shift + Enter*	*Option + Return*
Start a math equation	*Alt + =*	*Control + =*
Close current notebook	*Ctrl + Shift + W*	*Command + Shift + W*
Synchronize all notebooks	*Ctrl + S*	*Command + Shift + S*
Enter full screen mode	*F11*	*Command + Control + F*
Review list of open notebooks	*Not available*	*Control + G*
Open other notebooks	*Ctrl + O*	*Command + O*
Switch between sections	*Ctrl + Tab*	*Command + Shift + { or }*
Insert emoji	*Alt + N, S*	*Command + Control + Space*
Insert current date	*Alt + Shift + D*	*Command + D*

11. Publisher:

Layout and Design Excellence

While Microsoft Word is **proficient** in creating documents and editing text, Publisher addresses a vital need by providing **advanced layout features**. Publisher was **designed** to assist users in creating **precise layouts** for items like invitations, business letters, and cards. It functions as a **cost-efficient substitute** for more expensive design software.

With Publisher, users can create **magazine-style layouts** and **format documents** to match their creative vision. This **tool** enables users to **configure pages** with exact precision, extending beyond Word's standard capabilities. This chapter explores how to utilize Publisher's **features** to achieve your desired document designs. We will examine the process of creating **professionally formatted documents** using this adaptable software.

Setting Up Your Document

When initiating a new document, you'll notice **blue margin indicators** that establish your working space. Unlike Word, Publisher requires using the **Margins button** in the Page Design tab for margin adjustments. This tab also provides options to modify **page orientation** and **paper dimensions**.

To improve your layout process, Publisher includes **grid lines** and **guides**. These **tools** are particularly valuable when designing items such as flyers or magazine-style layouts. The **Guides button** located in the Layout section of the Page Design tab presents various options for establishing your page structure. These **guidelines** and **margin lines** are only visible during the design phase and won't show up in your final printed document.

Basic Page Layout Setup

1. Open a new document in Publisher
2. Navigate to the Page Design tab in the ribbon
3. Use the Margins button to adjust page margins:

    - Choose from preset margins
    - Set custom margins by entering specific measurements
    - Apply margins to selected pages or the entire document

4. Set Orientation:

   - Portrait (vertical)
   - Landscape (horizontal)

5. Choose the appropriate Paper Size:

   - Standard sizes (Letter, Legal, A4)
   - Custom dimensions for special projects
   - Consider printer capabilities

HOMETAB

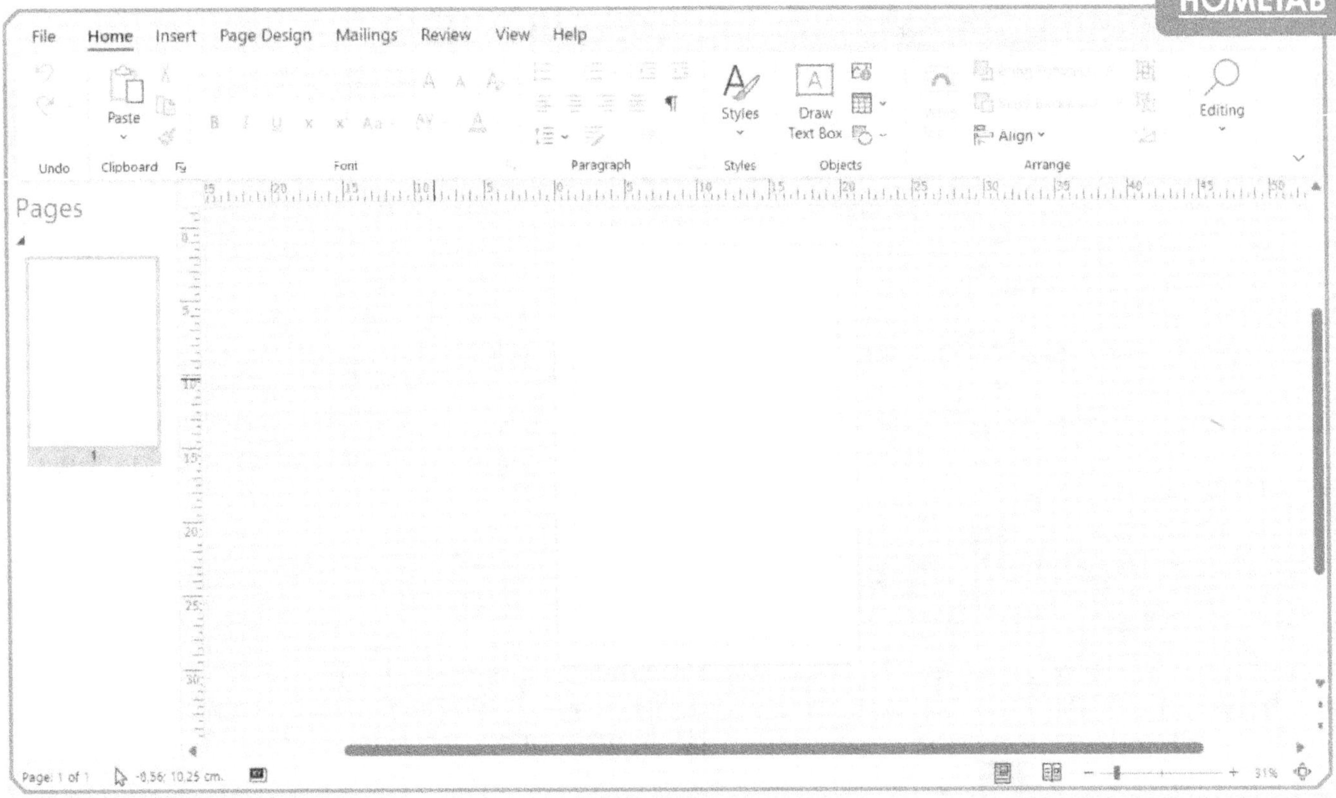

Working with Grid Lines and Guides

1. In the Page Design tab, locate the Layout section
2. Click on the Guides button
3. Select guide types:

   - Ruler guides
   - Margin guides
   - Grid guides
   - Baseline guides

4. Adjust guides to fit layout needs:

   - Set spacing between grid lines
   - Align with key design elements
   - Create columns and rows

PAGE DESIGN TAB

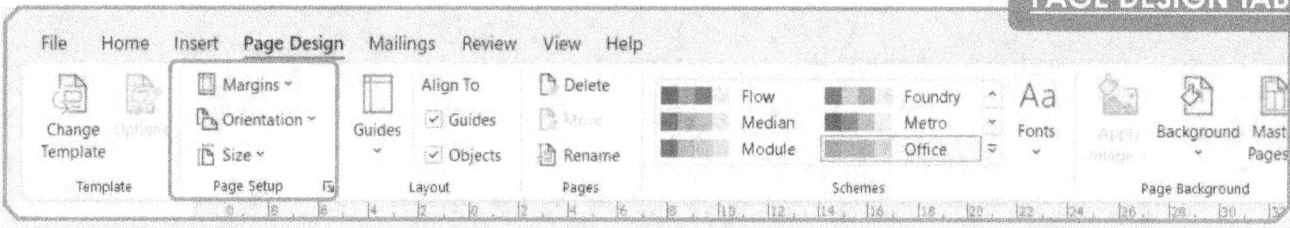

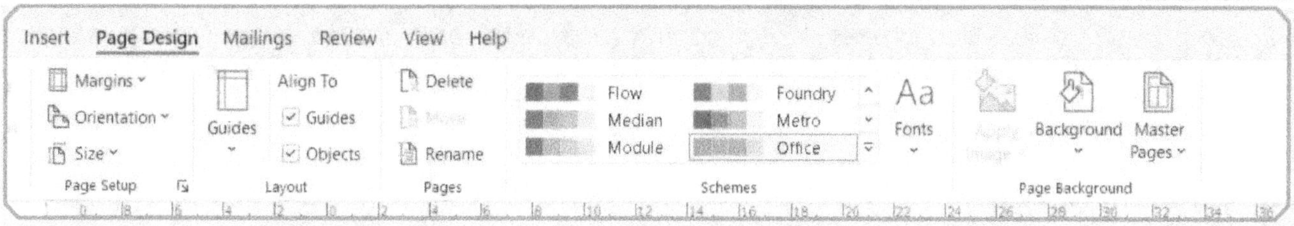

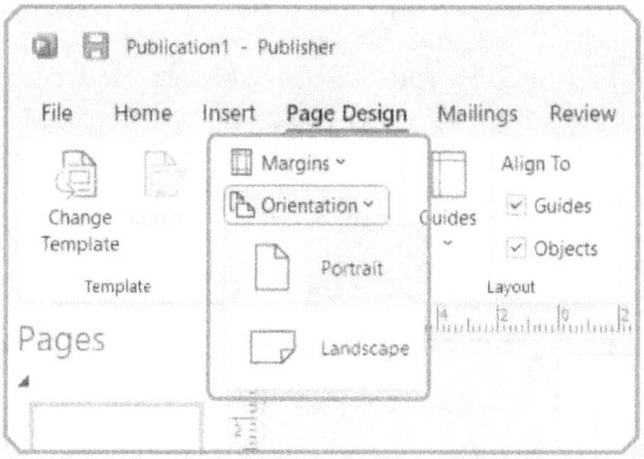

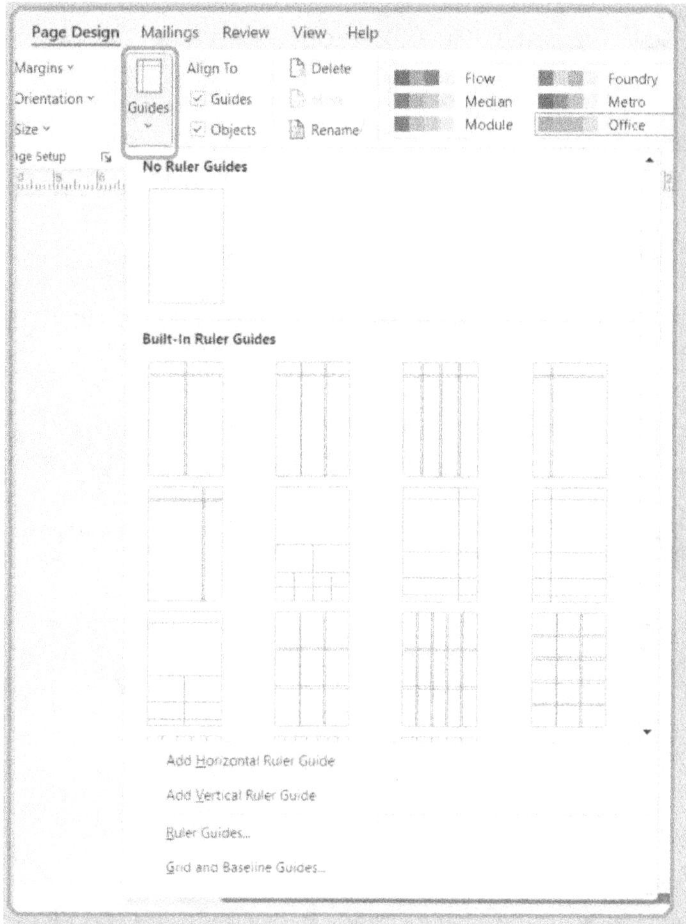

Managing Grid Lines

1. **Adding Grid Lines:**
   - Click and drag from rulers to create new guides
   - Use precise measurements for exact placement
   - Add both horizontal and vertical guides
2. **Adjusting Grid Lines:**
   - Click and drag existing lines to reposition
   - Hold Shift while dragging for straight alignment
   - Use arrow keys for fine-tuning positions
3. **Removing Grid Lines:**
   - Drag unwanted lines off the page
   - Right-click to delete individual guides
   - Use the Clear All Guides option for complete reset

Productivity Tips:

- *Use the Snap to Grid feature for precise alignment*
- *Toggle guide visibility using View options*
- *Save layouts as templates for future use*
- *Create master guides for multi-page documents*
- *Use different colored guides to organize different elements*

Remember: *Grid lines and guides are formatting tools that won't appear in your final printed document or digital publication.*

Inserting Elements

Creating content in Publisher begins with proper text placement. The foundation of any document starts with the Draw Text Box button, located conveniently in the Home tab of the ribbon. When you select this tool, you gain the ability to precisely define where your text will appear on the page. As you draw your text box, keep in mind that it should align within your established grid and margin lines - this ensures your final document will print and display exactly as intended.

Setp by Step Guide:

1. Locate the **Draw Text Box button** in the Home tab
2. Click and drag to create your text box:

    - Size can be adjusted by dragging corners
    - Position must be within margins and grid lines

3. Release mouse button to finalize the text box
4. Begin typing or paste your content

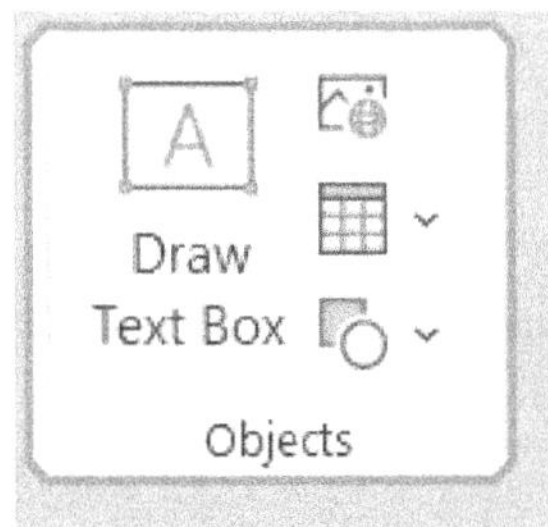

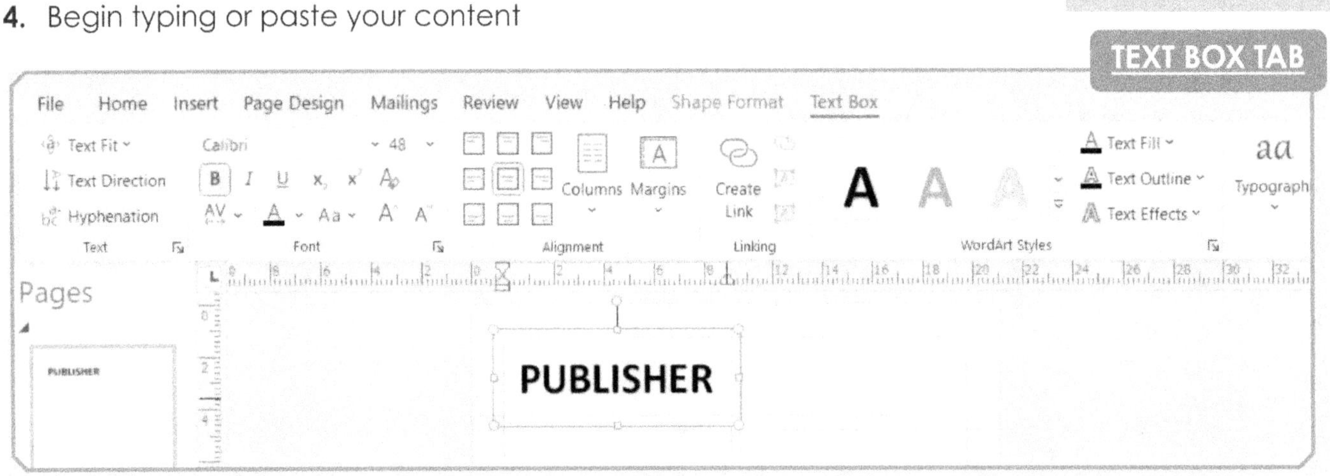

Working with the Insert Tab

The Insert tab houses a comprehensive suite of tools that enhance your document's functionality and visual appeal. Understanding these features is crucial for creating professional publications.

Tab Features:

- **Calendars**: Create customizable date displays
- **Bookmarks**: Add navigation points in your document
- **Headers and Footers**: Include consistent page information
- **Page Borders**: Enhance page appearance
- **Picture Elements**: Add visual content

INSERT TAB

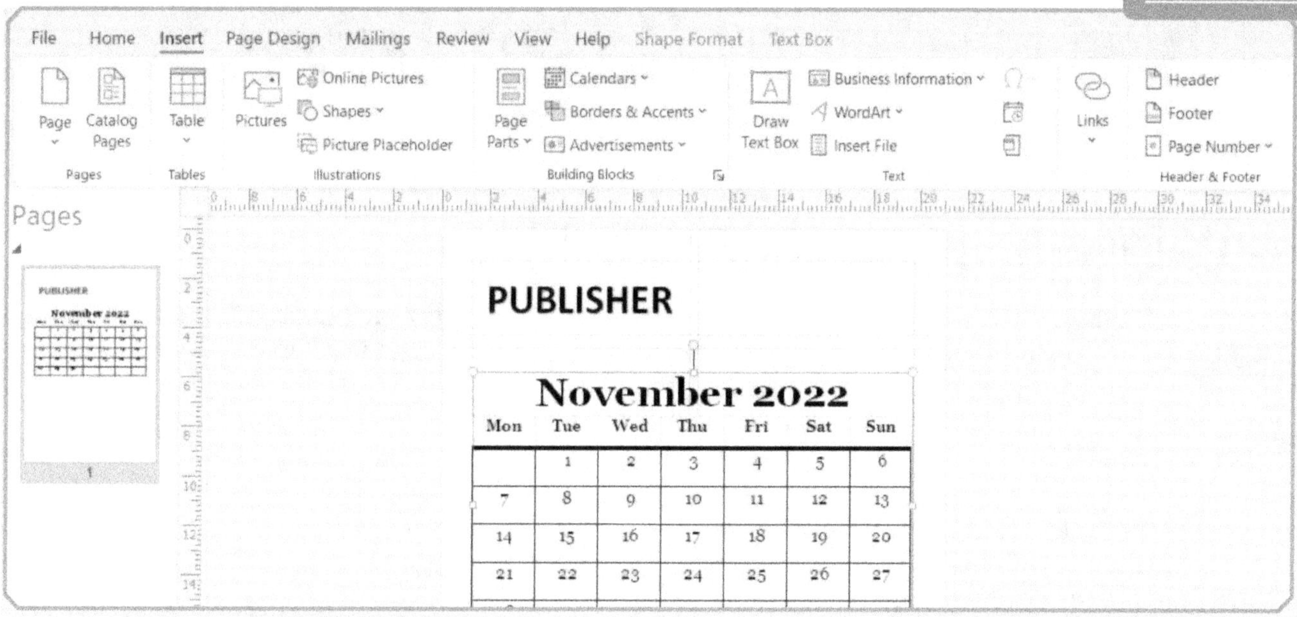

Working with Images and Placeholders

Publisher offers remarkable flexibility when it comes to handling images in your documents. You can seamlessly integrate pictures from both online sources and your local computer storage. One particularly useful feature is the picture placeholder system. This tool allows you to maintain your creative flow even when you haven't finalized your image selections. Simply insert a placeholder, continue with your design work, and replace it with your actual image when ready - the layout and formatting will remain intact.

Image Insertion Methods:

- Import from online sources
- Upload from local storage
- Use picture placeholders for layout planning
- Replace placeholders with final images

Customization and Professional Touches

What sets Publisher apart is its robust customization capabilities. Nearly every element you add to your document can be modified to match your specific needs. Whether you're aligning with corporate branding or creating a unique style for your school project, you can adjust colors, sizes, and formatting with ease. To access these customization options, simply right-click on any element to reveal a wealth of formatting choices.

Customization Options:

- Modify colors to match branding guidelines
- Adjust element sizes and positions
- Apply special effects and styles
- Format text to maintain consistency
- Create custom borders and backgrounds

Productivity Tip: *The key to professional-looking documents is finding the right balance between text, images, and other design elements while maintaining consistent formatting throughout your publication.*

Understanding Common Microsoft Office Interface

Publisher builds upon the familiar Microsoft Office interface, making it accessible for users of other Office programs. The text formatting capabilities mirror those in Word, creating an intuitive experience for users already comfortable with Microsoft's ecosystem.

Key Familiar Features

- Text formatting tools in Home tab
- Font selection and sizing
- Paragraph alignment options
- Bullet points and numbering
- Basic styling tools

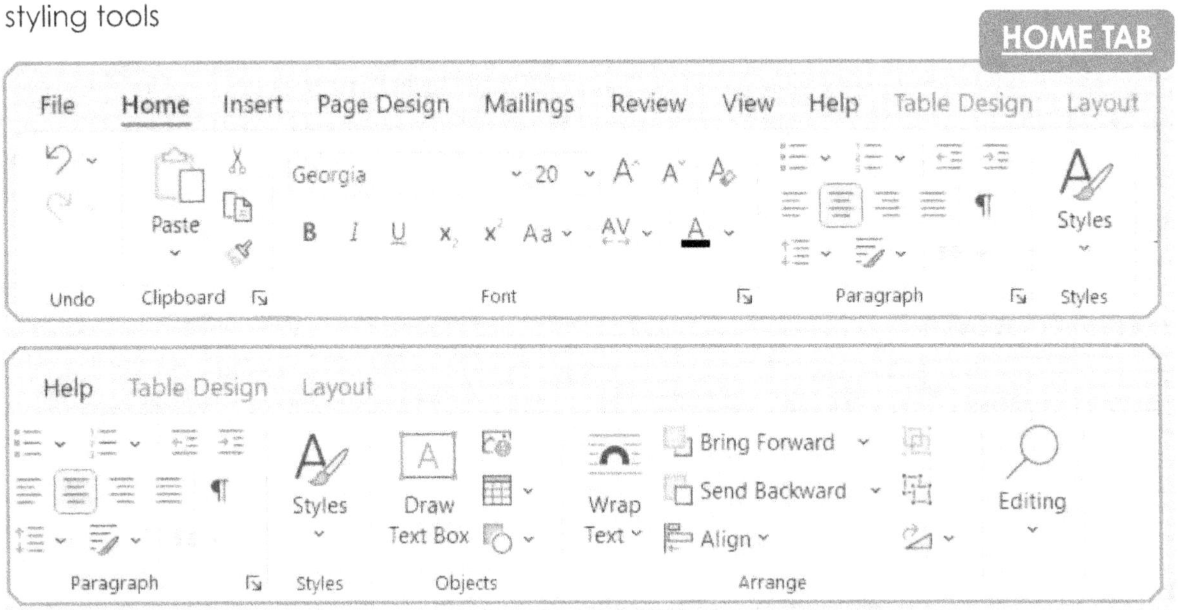

Document Overview and Navigation

The interface utilizes a thumbnail view system similar to PowerPoint, offering a comprehensive overview of your publication. This visual approach makes document navigation and organization notably efficient.

Page Management Methods - There are several ways to add new pages to your publication:

1. **Through the thumbnail pane:**
    - Right-click on existing thumbnail
    - Select "Add Page" option
    - Choose page position
2. **Via the Insert tab:**
    - Navigate to the Pages section
    - Click the Page button
    - Select desired page layout

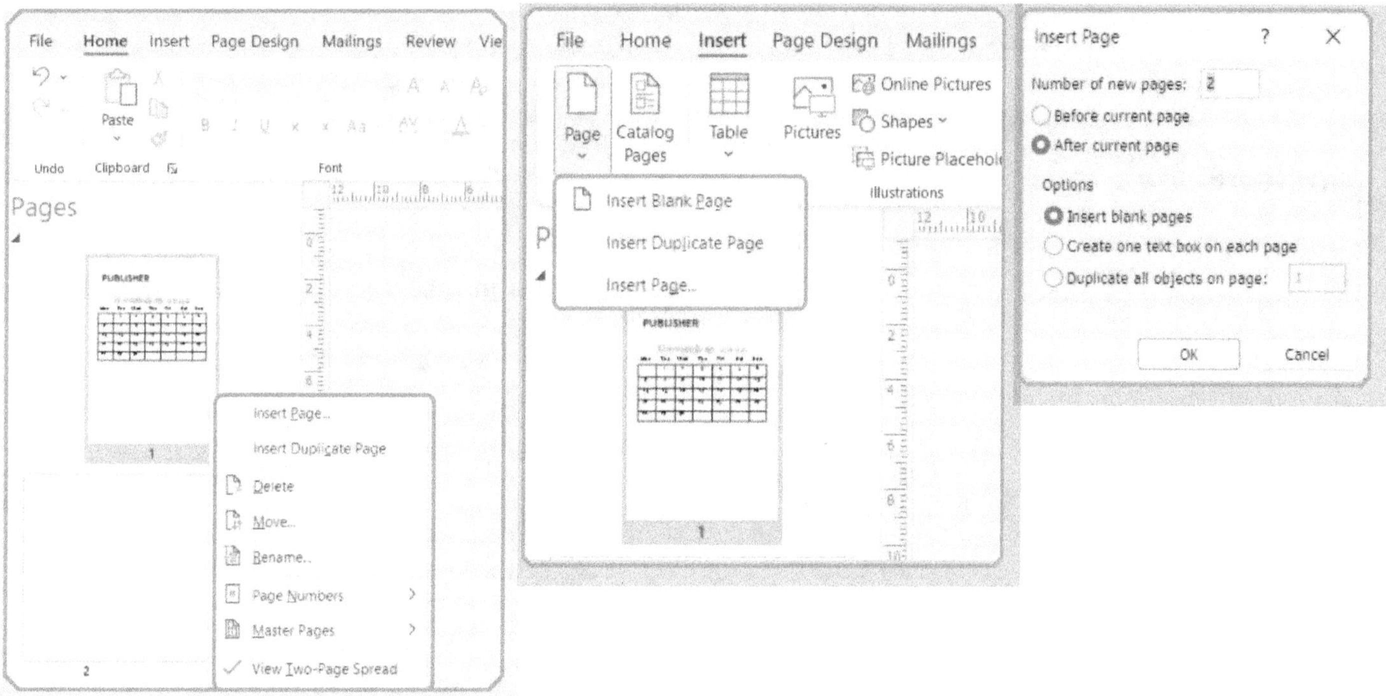

Advanced Page Features - Publisher enhances the basic page management system with several sophisticated options:

- **Page Arrangement Tools:**
    - Drag and drop thumbnails for reordering
    - Use Move button in Page Design tab
    - Rename pages for better organization
    - Delete unnecessary pages

Important Considerations:

- *Margins automatically carry over to new pages*
- *Guides must be manually added to new pages*
- *Page numbers can be automatically updated*
- *Master pages maintain consistency*

View Tab: Display Options

The View tab offers flexible display options:

1. Single page view for detailed work
2. Two-page spread for layout planning
3. Thumbnail view for overall organization
4. Custom zoom levels for precise editing

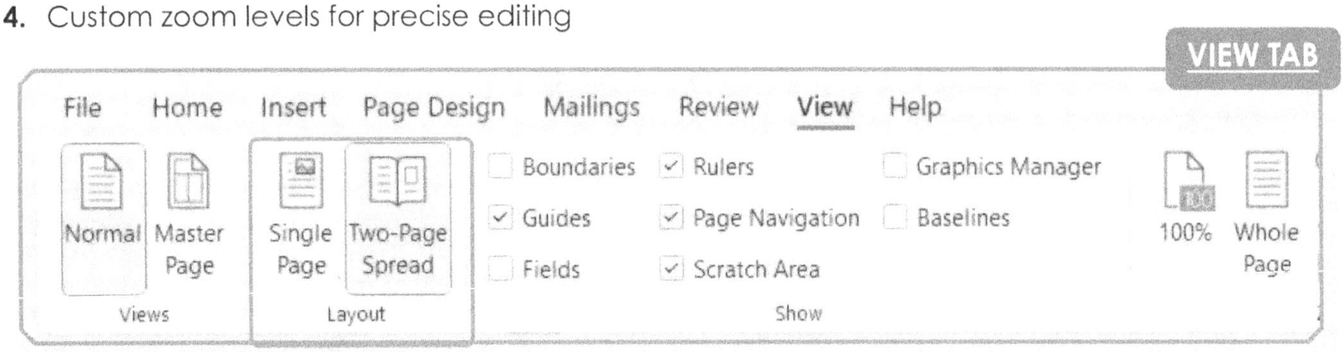

Master Pages

Master pages function as the architectural foundation of your document, ensuring every page maintains a professional and cohesive look. Through the **Page Design tab**, you can effortlessly establish a template that propagates across your entire publication.

Key Master Page Elements

- **Design Foundation**: Set backgrounds and color schemes that reflect your brand identity
- **Structural Elements**: Define margins and guides for precise layout control
- **Recurring Content**: Place headers, footers, and logos that appear on every page
- **Layout Guidelines**: Establish consistent spacing and alignment rules

Advanced Master Page Techniques

Consider your publication's unique needs when setting up master pages. A magazine might require different left and right master pages, while a business report might need distinct chapter introduction pages. Publisher allows you to:

1. Create multiple master pages for different sections
2. Apply master pages selectively to specific pages
3. Override master page elements when needed
4. Update master pages globally with a single edit

Pro Tips for Master Page Efficiency:

- *Save frequently used master pages as templates*
- *Create a master page checklist for consistency*
- *Test master pages with different content types*
- *Review master page elements in both screen and print views*

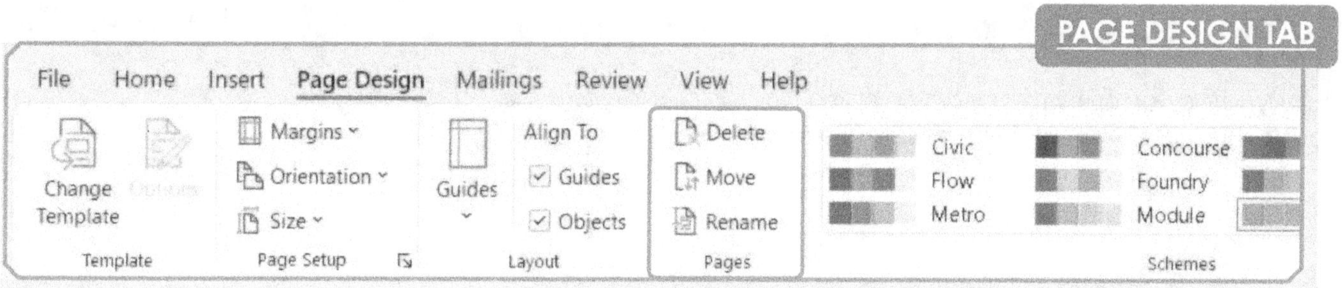

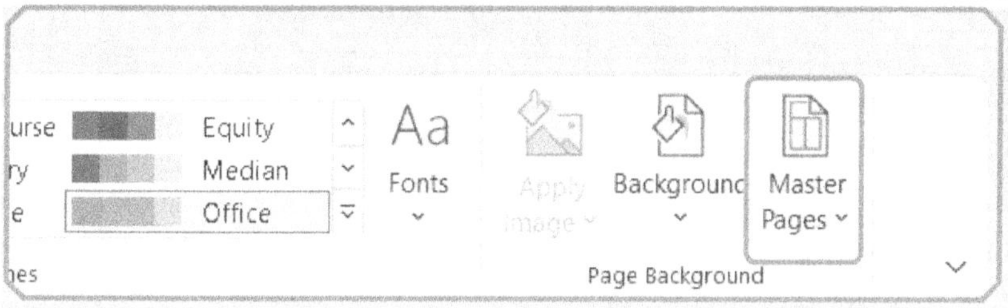

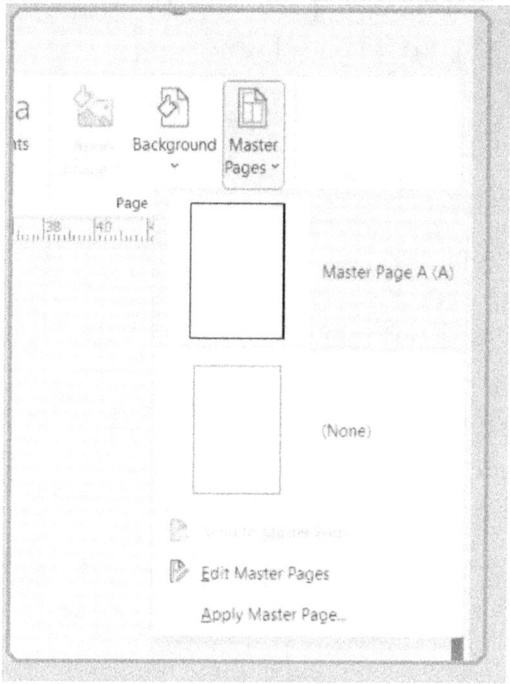

Creating Professional Product Catalogs

Publisher elevates catalog creation through its dedicated toolset, making it easier than ever to showcase products in an engaging and professional format. When you're ready to start, head to the Insert tab and locate the Catalog Pages button. Upon clicking, you'll notice Publisher automatically adds a Catalog Format tab to your ribbon - this specialized tab contains all the tools you'll need for catalog design.

Getting Started with Catalog Creation

1. **Access Catalog Features:**
    - Open the Insert tab in the ribbon
    - Click Catalog Pages button
    - Notice the new Catalog Format tab appears
    - Select your preferred layout template
2. **Layout Configuration:**
    - Adjust product box dimensions
    - Set spacing between items
    - Configure columns and rows
    - Define margin specifications

Catalog Structure and Layout

The catalog format provides a flexible structure for organizing your products. Think of it as creating a visual grid where each product gets its own space to shine.

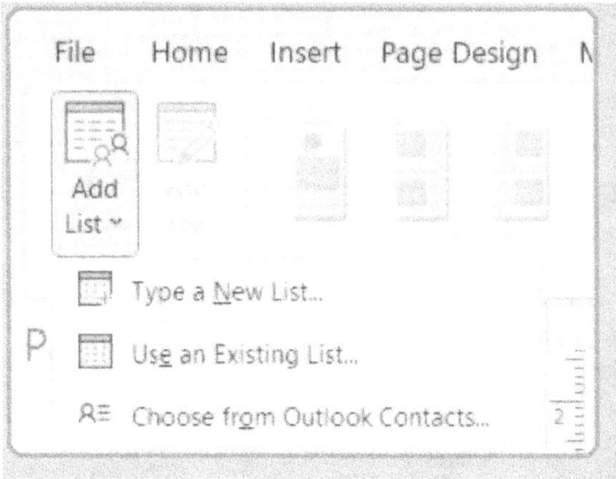

Creating Product Lists

- Click Add List in Catalog Format tab
- Enter product details:
    - Name and description
    - ID numbers and pricing
    - Product images
    - Custom fields as needed
- Save lists for future use
- Update existing entries

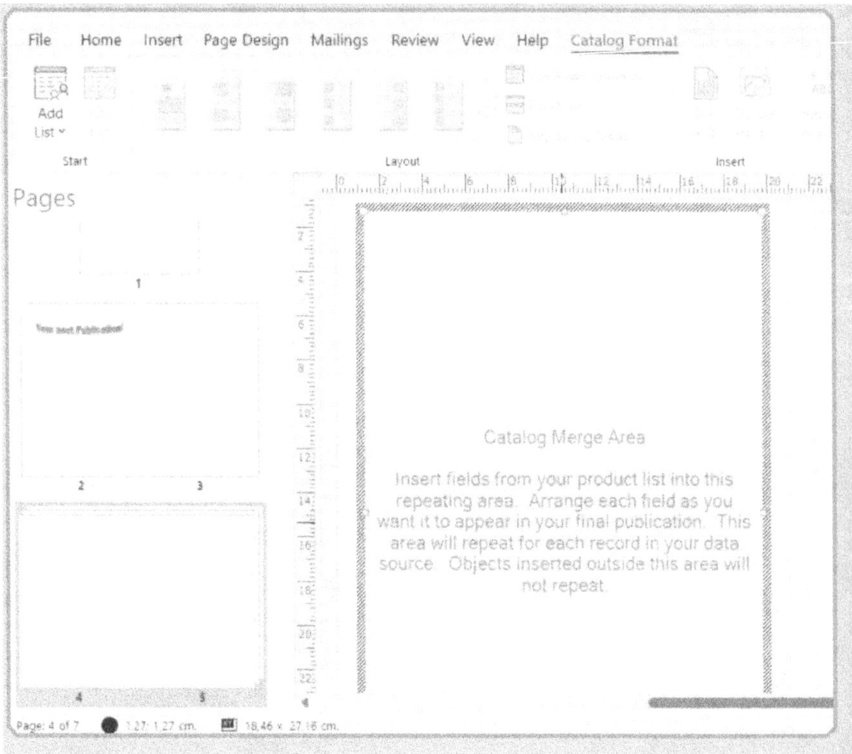

Customization Features

1. **Layout Options:**
    - Adjust box sizes for products
    - Modify spacing between items
    - Create custom grid patterns
    - Set consistent image sizes
2. **Product Information Display:**
    - Format price presentations
    - Style product descriptions
    - Arrange product details
    - Add custom fields

Enhanced Sales Features

Publisher includes built-in tools to highlight special offers and promotions. **Sale Stickers:**

- Access via **Insert tab**
- Choose from pre-designed options under **Advertisement button**
- Customize colors and styles
- Modify text and fonts

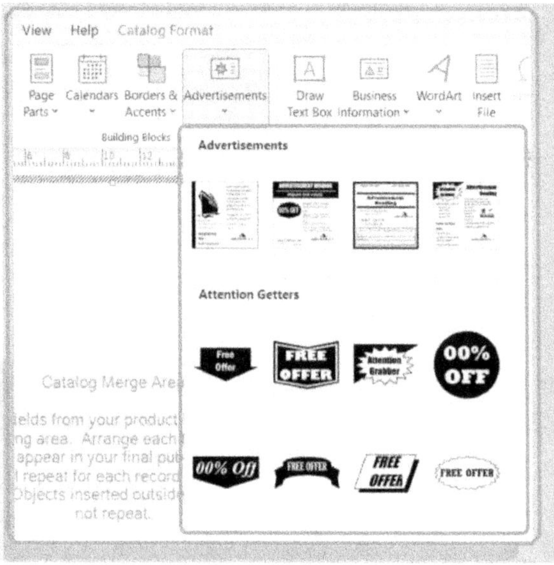

Productivity Tips:

- *Save product lists for future catalogs*
- *Use consistent formatting for pricing*
- *Maintain organized product databases*

Mastering Mail Merge

Publisher's advanced mailing system transforms how businesses communicate with their audience. Through its sophisticated mail merge capabilities, you can create personalized documents that speak directly to each recipient, enhancing the professional impact of your communications.

Setting Up Your Data Source - Publisher offers remarkable flexibility in managing contact information. You can import data from:

- Excel spreadsheets for large-scale mailings
- Access databases for complex data management
- Outlook contacts for seamless integration
- Custom-created lists for specific campaigns

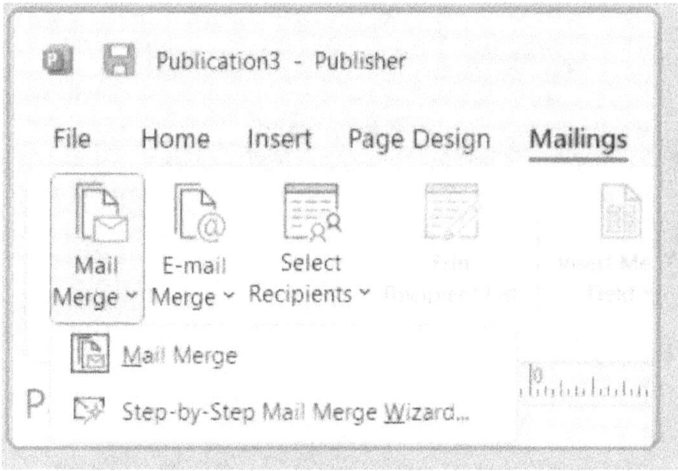

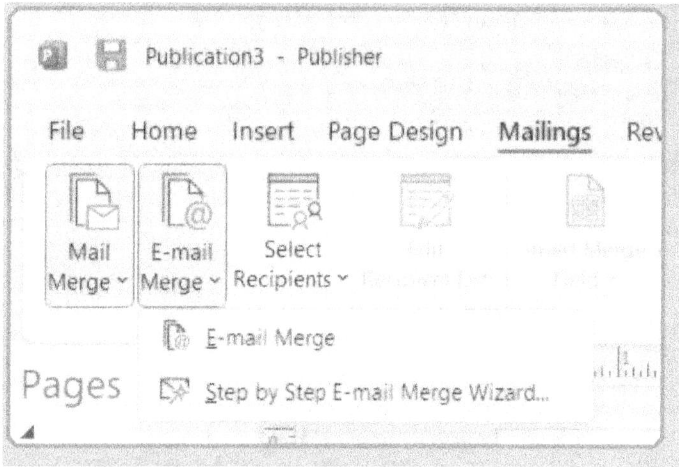

First, prepare your publication and establish your data source:

1. **Begin Mail Merge:**

   - Open your Publisher document
   - Navigate to the Mailings tab
   - Click **"Start Mail Merge"**
   - Choose your merge type (letters, emails, labels)

2. **Select Your Data Source:**

   - Click **"Select Recipients"**
   - Choose from these options:

     - Use existing Excel spreadsheet
     - Import Access database
     - Select from Outlook contacts
     - Type a new list
     - Choose from previous lists

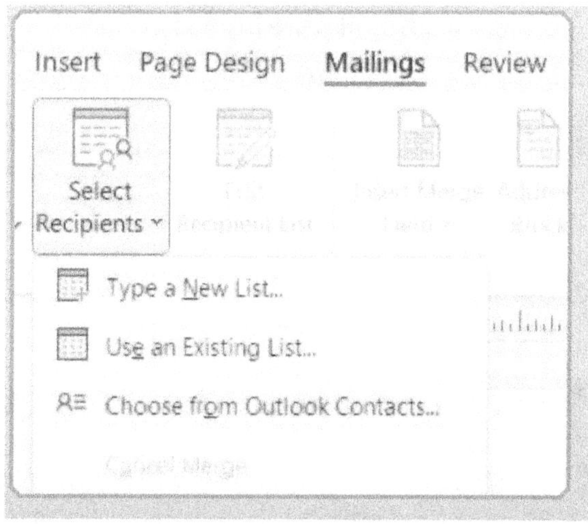

Personalizing Your Publications

The magic of mail merge lies in its ability to customize content for each recipient. Whether you're creating newsletters, invitations, or marketing materials, you can automatically insert personalized details exactly where you want them. The system intelligently places names, addresses, and custom fields while maintaining your document's professional formatting.

Digital Communication Options

Beyond traditional mailings, Publisher streamlines email communications through its email merge feature. This tool integrates seamlessly with Outlook, allowing you to:

- Create personalized email content
- Manage distribution lists efficiently
- Track delivery and responses
- Schedule automated sends

Creating New Contact Lists

For those starting fresh, Publisher provides intuitive tools for building recipient lists. Through the Mailings tab, you can create, edit, and manage contact information with ease. The system allows for detailed record-keeping, including:

- Multiple contact fields
- Custom categorization
- Easy updates and modifications
- Export capabilities for future use

If you're starting fresh:

- Click "Type New List" under Select Recipients
- In the dialog box, enter:
    - Names and addresses
    - Email contacts
    - Custom fields as needed
- Save your list for future use
- Click OK to confirm

Adding Merge Fields - Now customize your document with personalized information:

1. Position your cursor where you want personalized content
2. Click "Insert Merge Field" from the Mailings tab
3. Select desired fields from your data source
4. Repeat for each personalization point

Preview and Completion - Before finalizing your merge:

1. Use "Preview Results" to check formatting
2. Navigate through records using preview arrows

3. Make any necessary adjustments
4. Select "Finish & Merge"
5. Choose your output option:

- Print documents
- Send emails
- Edit individual documents

Productivity Tip: *A successful mail merge requires clean data and careful planning. Take time to review your recipient list and document formatting before completing the final merge.*

Managing Business Information: A Time-Saving Strategy

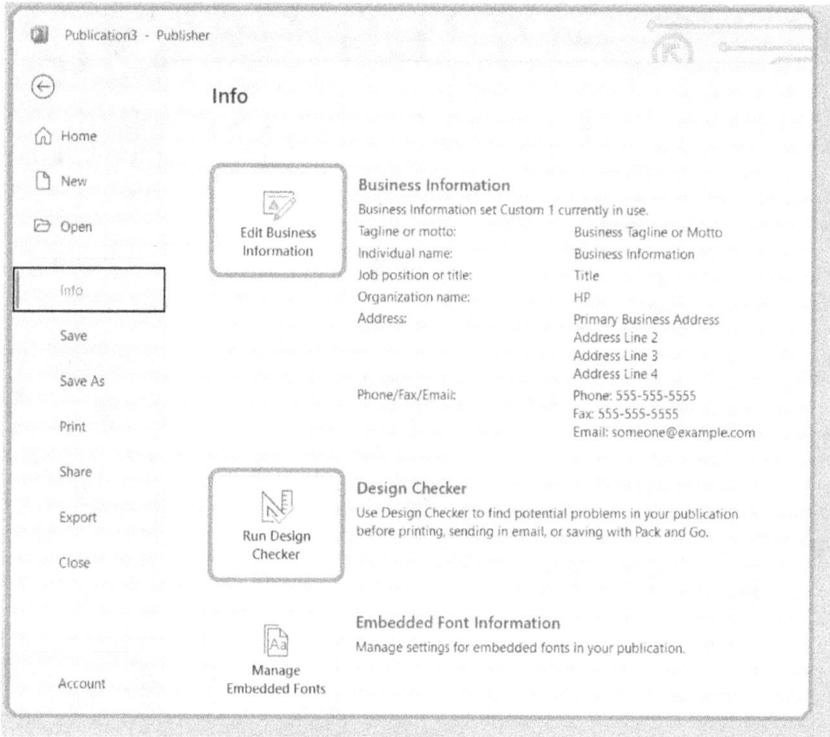

Publisher's business information management system serves as a centralized hub for your company's key details, streamlining document creation and ensuring consistency across all publications.

This powerful feature eliminates repetitive data entry and maintains professional standards throughout your business communications.

Setting Up Your Business Profile

The initial setup process establishes your business identity within Publisher:

- **Access Point:**
  - Open **File tab**
  - Select **Info** button
  - Choose "**Edit Business Information**"

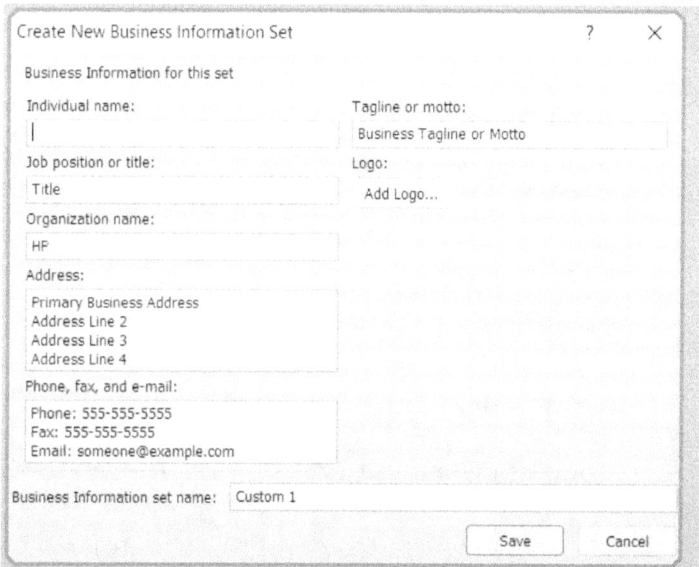

- **Key Information Fields:**
  - Company name and contact details
  - Physical and digital addresses
  - Registration numbers
  - Professional credentials
  - Company logo and branding elements
  - Social media profiles

Implementing Business Details

Once your information is stored, Publisher makes it incredibly easy to incorporate these details into any document. The process is straightforward:

1. Navigate to the Insert tab
2. Locate the Business Information button
3. Select specific details from the dropdown menu
4. Watch as Publisher automatically formats and places your information

> **Productivity Tip:** *Maintaining current business information ensures all your publications reflect the most up-to-date details, preserving your professional image and saving valuable time in document creation.*

Design Checker: Your Quality Assurance Tool

Publisher's Design Checker acts as your personal quality control system, scanning documents for potential design issues before they reach your audience. This powerful feature helps maintain professional standards across all your publications.

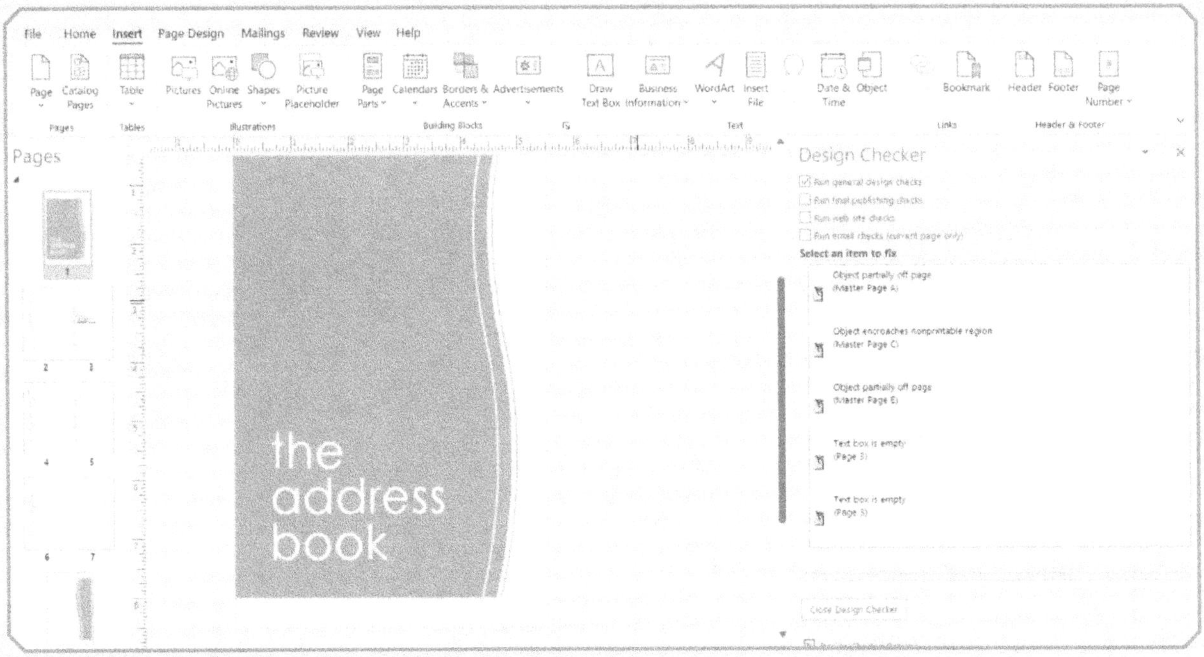

Accessing Design Checker - The tool resides in a convenient location:

- Open the File tab
- Select Info section
- Click Design Check button

Comprehensive Check Options - The Design Checker offers multiple inspection categories:

- **Document Analysis Types:**
  - General design evaluation

- Publishing-specific checks
- Website compatibility
- Email format verification
- Custom check combinations

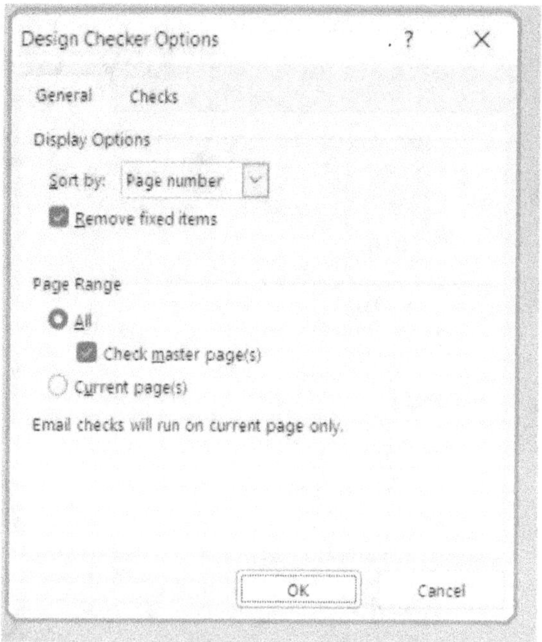

Common Issues Detected - The system identifies various potential problems:

- Elements extending beyond page margins
- Inconsistent white space distribution
- Text box overflow issues
- Missing or broken links
- Resolution problems with images
- Color consistency errors

Customization and Control - Fine-tune your checking process through Design Checker Options:

1. **Sort Preferences:**
   - By error type
   - By page location
   - By severity level
2. **Scope Settings:**
   - Select specific pages
   - Choose error categories
   - Set priority levels

Productivity Tips:

- *Run checks regularly during design*
- *Address critical errors first*
- *Save preferred settings for future use*
- *Create custom checking profiles for different projects*

Remember: *The Design Checker serves as your last line of defense against design flaws. Using it consistently helps ensure your publications maintain professional quality standards.*

Keyboard Shortcuts on *Publisher*

Function	Shortcut on PC	Shortcut on Mac
New Publication	*Ctrl + N*	*Command + N*
Open Publication	*Ctrl + O*	*Command + O*
Save	*Ctrl + S*	*Command + S*
Print	*Ctrl + P*	*Command + P*
Undo	*Ctrl + Z*	*Command + Z*
Redo	*Ctrl + Y*	*Command + Y*

Keyboard Shortcuts on *Publisher*

Function	Shortcut on PC	Shortcut on Mac
Cut	*Ctrl + X*	*Command + X*
Copy	*Ctrl + C*	*Command + C*
Paste	*Ctrl + V*	*Command + V*
Select All	*Ctrl + A*	*Command + A*
Find	*Ctrl + F*	*Command + F*
Replace	*Ctrl + H*	*Command + H*
Bold	*Ctrl + B*	*Command + B*
Italic	*Ctrl + I*	*Command + I*
Underline	*Ctrl + U*	*Command + U*
Align Left	*Ctrl + L*	*Command + L*
Align Center	*Ctrl + E*	*Command + E*
Align Right	*Ctrl + R*	*Command + R*
Justify	*Ctrl + J*	*Command + J*
Increase Font Size	*Ctrl + Shift + >*	*Command + Shift + >*
Decrease Font Size	*Ctrl + Shift + <*	*Command + Shift + <*
Zoom In	*Ctrl + +*	*Command + +*
Zoom Out	*Ctrl + -*	*Command + -*
Insert Page	*Ctrl + Shift + N*	*Command + Shift + N*
Show/Hide Rulers	*Alt + Shift + R*	*Option + Shift + R*
Group Objects	*Ctrl + G*	*Command + G*
Ungroup Objects	*Ctrl + Shift + G*	*Command + Shift + G*
Bring to Front	*Ctrl + Shift + F*	*Command + Shift + F*
Send to Back	*Ctrl + Shift + B*	*Command + Shift + B*

Note: *Some of these shortcuts may vary depending on the version of Microsoft Publisher you're using. Also, Publisher for Mac might not have all the features available in the Windows version, so some shortcuts may not be applicable.*

Microsoft Office Mastery: A Journey Completed

This comprehensive guide has taken you through the vast landscape of **Microsoft Office applications**, equipping you with **essential skills** for both **professional** and personal success. At its core, the tutorial has covered the fundamental quartet of Office applications: **Word** for document creation, **Excel** for data management, **PowerPoint** for impactful presentations, and **Outlook** for email communication. These applications form the backbone of modern office **productivity**, particularly in corporate environments.

The journey extended beyond these foundational tools, venturing into the broader **Microsoft ecosystem**. You've explored **database management** through **Access**, embraced modern communication platforms like **Skype** and **Teams**, and discovered cloud storage solutions with **OneDrive**. The tutorial also introduced you to specialized tools such as **Forms** for survey creation, **OneNote** for digital note-taking, and **Publisher** for professional layout design.

One of the most valuable aspects of the Microsoft Office suite is its consistent **design philosophy**. The familiar **ribbon interface**, shared across applications, creates an intuitive experience that accelerates learning and enhances productivity. This consistency extends to **keyboard shortcuts**, with commands like copy and paste remaining uniform throughout the suite, streamlining your workflow and saving precious time.

This guide stands as your comprehensive **reference**, ready to clarify concepts and refresh your memory whenever needed. Despite potential **software updates**, the core principles and techniques covered should remain relevant and applicable. The **knowledge** you've gained positions you well for both current and future technological challenges in your professional journey.

Your **mastery** of these tools represents more than just technical proficiency – it opens doors to enhanced **productivity** and professional growth. As you apply these skills in real-world scenarios, remember that effective **program management** can significantly impact your daily efficiency and success.

We value your experience with this guide and encourage you to share your thoughts through **reviews** and **comments**. Your **feedback** not only helps improve future content but also guides others on their learning journey. As you move forward, may your newfound knowledge serve as a foundation for continued growth and achievement in all your endeavors.

> ***Remember:*** *This isn't just about learning software – it's about* ***empowering*** *yourself with tools that can transform your* ***professional capabilities*** *and personal productivity.* ***Congratulations*** *on completing this comprehensive journey through the Microsoft Office suite!*

GET YOUR FREE BOOK BONUSES NOW!

(DOWNLOAD FOR FREE WITH THE BELOW INSTRUCTION!)

DO YOU WANT TO UNLOCK THE FULL KNOWLEDGE ABOUT MICROSOFT OFFICE SUITE?

1) BONUS 1: 300+ Excel Templates: Business | Personal | Project | Tracker | Chart | Invoice | List | Calendar | Analysis | Schedule | Budget
2) BONUS 2: Guide on How to Manage your Time
3) BONUS 3: Guide on How to Manage your Productivity
4) BONUS 4: Guide on How to Prepare Yourself For a Job Interview
5) BONUS 5: How to Improve Fast your Office 365 Skills

SCAN THE QR CODE BELOW AND UNLOCK THE FULL POTENTIAL OF OFFICE 365 SUITE!!

SCAN ME

Index

A

E

F

K

O

P

S

T

W

www.ingramcontent.com/pod-product-compliance
Lightning Source LLC
LaVergne TN
LVHW080048210926
848481LV00011B/3299